# THE ILLUSTRATED HISTORY OF
# WWII

# THE ILLUSTRATED HISTORY OF
# WWII

John Ray

WEIDENFELD & NICOLSON

Weidenfeld & Nicolson

The Orion Publishing Group Ltd
Orion House
5 Upper Saint Martin's Lane
London WC2H 9EA

British Library Cataloguing-in-Publication Data
A catalogue record for this book is available from the British Library

ISBN 0-297-84663-9

Cartography by Malcolm Swanston, Arcadia Editions Ltd
Designed by Rod Teasdale

Printed and bound in Italy by L.E.G.O. Vicenza

# Picture Credits

The Publishers would like to thank the following organisations and individuals for their assistance in providing photographs.

8: US National Archives. 10: US Army. 11: US National Archives. 12: R Tomasi. 13: LGS/IWM. 14: US National Archives. 15: IWM. 16: LGS. 18: US National Archives/LGS. 19: IWM/R Tomasi. 20: William Martin. 21: LGS/IWM. 22: William Martin. 23: R Tomasi/LGS. 24: US National Archives/LGS. 25: LGS/IWM. 26: LGS/William Martin. 27: R Tomasi. 28: US Army Signal Corps. 29: US Navy. 30: IWM. 32: R Tomasi/LGS. 34: LGS/William Martin. 35: US National Archives. 36: R Tomasi. 38: R Tomasi. 39: IWM. 40: LGS. 41: IWM/LGS. 42: R Tomasi/LGS/LGS. 44: US National Archives/US Navy. 45: IWM. 46: LGS/William Martin. 48: US National Archives. 49: IWM/LGS. 51: LGS. 52: LGS. 53: US National Archives/LGS. 54: US National Archives. 55: LGS. 56: LGS. 57: LGS. 58: LGS. 59: LGS. 60: LGS/IWM/LGS. 61: US Army Signal Corps. 63: IWM. 64: Library of Congress/LGS. 65: LGS. 68: API. 69: API. 70: API. 71: API. 72: LGS/Library of Congress. 73: IWM. 74: LGS/IWM. 75: LGS. 76: IWM. 77: LGS/William Martin. 78: Library of Congress/US Navy. 79: IWM. 80: IWM/US Naval Historical Center. 81: IWM. 83: R Tomasi. 84: LGS/R Tomasi. 86: LGS. 87: IWM/LGS. 88: R Tomasi. 89: LGS. 90: LGS. 92: LGS. 93: LGS. 94: LGS/R Tomasi. 95: LGS/US National Archives. 96: LGS/US National Archives. 97: LGS. 98: LGS. 100: R Tomasi. 101: LGS. 102: LGS. 103: LGS. 104: US Naval Historical Center. 106: LGS/IWM. 107: US Navy. 108: LGS. 110: US National Archives. 111: US Navy. 112: LGS/US Navy. 113: LGS/IWM. 114: LGS/IWM. 115: LGS. 116: US Air Force. 118: US National Archives. 120: US Naval Historical Center/LGS. 121: LGS. 122: IWM. 124: US Navy. 125: LGS/US Navy. 126: US Navy. 128: US Navy. 130: IWM.

131: IWM. 132: LGS/US National Archives. 134: US National Archives. 135: R Tomasi. 136: IWM/R Tomasi/LGS. 137: US National Archives/US Army Signal Corps. 138: IWM. 139: R Tomasi. 140: R Tomasi. 142: US Army Signal Corps/R Tomasi. 143: US National Archives. 144: LGS/IWM. 145: IWM/R Tomasi/R Tomasi. 147: IWM. 148: IWM. 149: IWM. 150: IWM. 151: IWM. 153: LGS/IWM. 154: LGS. 155: LGS. 156: LGS. 157: US National Archives. 158: LGS. 159: IWM/LGS. 160: LGS/R Tomasi. 162: US Army. 164: IWM. 165: US Navy/LGS. 166: William Martin. 167: US Navy. 168: LGS/IWM. 169: LGS/US Air Force. 170: R Tomasi/LGS. 172: US National Archives. 174: R Tomasi/IWM. 175: LGS. 176: IWM. 178: IWM. 179: US Army. 180: US Army. 182: IWM. 183: US National Archives. 184: IWM. 185: LGS. US Air Force 187: LGS. 188: LGS. 190: IWM. 191: IWM. 193: US National Archives/IWM. 194: LGS. 195: US Navy/US Navy. 196: IWM/US Navy. 198: IWM/US Navy. 200: US National Archives. 201: US National Archives. 202: US Army. 203: US Army. 204: LGS. 205: US Army. 206: IWM. 208: R Tomasi. 209: R Tomasi. 210: LGS. 212: US National Archives. 213: US National Archives. 214: R Tomasi. 215: IWM. 216: LGS. 217: IWM. 218: IWM. 219: US Air Force/IWM. 220: US Air Force. 221: Naval Historical Center/US Air Force. 222: R Tomasi. 223: R Tomasi. 224: R Tomasi. 225: IWM. 226: US Navy. 227: US Navy. 228: Library of Congress/Library of Congress/Library of Congress. 229: Library of Congress. 230: IWM. 232: US Navy/US Navy. 233: US Air Force. 234: US Navy/US Navy. 236: US Navy/US Navy. 239: US Navy/US Navy. 240: US Navy. 241: US Navy. 242: IWM. 243: Library of Congress/US Air Force. 244: US Navy/US Navy/IWM. 245: US Navy. 246: US Navy/US Navy. 247: US Navy. 248: US Navy/US Navy. 249: LGS. 249: US Navy. 250: US Navy. 251: US Navy.

# Contents

Key to Maps                                                    6

List of Maps                                                   7

Introduction                                                   8

Chapter 1:    Why the Nations Went to War                      12

Chapter 2:    German Success                                   36

Chapter 3:    Britain Alone                                    62

Chapter 4:    The Russian Campaign, 1941–42                    82

Chapter 5:    The Far East, 1941–42                            104

Chapter 6:    Africa and the Mediterranean, 1940–43            130

Chapter 7:    War on Three Fronts, 1943–44                     154

Chapter 8:    Bombs and Torpedoes                              182

Chapter 9:    The End in Europe                                200

Chapter 10:   The End in the Far East                          226

Appendices                                                    252

Index                                                         253

# Key to Maps

## Military units–types

⊠ infantry

◨ armoured

▱ motorized infantry

◠ airborne

⊕ parachute

⊡ artillery

## Military units–size

XXXXX
▭ army group

XXXX
▭ army

XXX
▭ corps

XX
▭ division

X
▭ brigade

III
▭ regiment

II
▭ battalion

## Military unit colours

▮ Allied

▮ German

▮ British

▮ Japanese

▮ French

▮ Russian

▮ Polish

▮ Finnish

▮ other territory

## General military symbols

—XXXXX— army group boundary

—XXXX— army boundary

⌣ front line

⌁ defensive line

⊓⊔ defensive line (3D maps)

⌄ field work

◯ pocket or position

⊥ field gun

⊕ paratroop drop

⚓ sunken ship

⊕ airfield

⚔ battle

## Geographical symbols

▰ urban area

—— road

▬ railway

—— river

- - - seasonal river

⊦⊦⊦ canal

—— border

⊃⊂ bridge or pass

▢ marsh

▦ rocks

## Military movements

➤ attack

⇢ retreat

➤ air attack

# List of Maps

Europe in 1920   9

Hitler's Annexations 1936–39   17

The expansion of Japan 1920–41   31

'Plan Yellow', September 1939 – April 1940   33

Campaign in Poland, 1–28 September 1939   37

Russo–Finnish War 1940   43

Denmark and Norway, April–June 1940   47

Invasion of the West, May–June 1940   50

Panzer strike through the Ardennes, 12–14 May 1940   51

Battle of Britain, July–October 1940   66

The Balkans, 6–30 April 1941   85

Crete, 20 May – 1 June 1941   87

Invasion of Russia, June–December 1941   90

The Caucasus, June–November 1942   99

The Battle for Stalingrad, January–February 1943   101

Pacific situation, December 1941 – July 1942   105

Pearl Harbor, second wave attack, 7 December 1941   108

Invasion of Malaya, 8 December 1941 – 31 January 1942   117

Attack on the Philippines, 8 December 1941 – May 1942   119

Japanese invasion of Burma, January–May 1942   123

Battle of the Java Sea, 27 February 1942   126

Battle of the Coral Sea, 28 April – 11 May 1942   126

Attack in the Coral Sea, 1 January – 11 May 1942   127

Admiral Yamamoto's plans to seize Midway, May–June 1942   128

Battle of Midway 2, 4 June 4.00 am – 10.30 am   128

Battle of Midway 3, 4 June 10.30 am – 6 June 12.00 am   129

Campaign in East Africa, June 1940 – November 1941   133

Operation Crusader, 18–24 November 1941   138

Operation Crusader, 24–28 November 1941   139

Rommel's Pursuit, January–June 1942   140

Battle of Gazala, 26 May – 14 June 1942   141

The Mediterranean, late 1942   146

Operation Torch, 8 November 1942   148

Convoy – Operation Pedestal, 11–13 August 1942   152

Battle of Kursk, 5–13 July 1943   156

Operation Bagration, June–August 1944   161

Italy, 1944–45   171

D-Day, 6 June 1944   176

Operation Market Garden, September 1944   179

Battle of the Bulge, 16–24 December 1944   181

Dambusters Raid, 16–17 1943   185

A cold night over Germany, 22–23 October 1943   187

Allied Bombing, 1944–45   189

Battle of the Atlantic, 1942–45   192

Commercial losses to U-boats, January–May 1942   197

The Bay Offensive, 1 June – 2 August 1943   199

Battle of Berlin, 16 April – 6 May 1945   211

Allied recapture of Burma, December 1944 – 5 May 1945   231

Pacific, general situation up to Operation Cartwheel, End 1942 – November 1943   233

Guadalcanal, August 1942 – February 1943   234

Allied offensive in the South Pacific, February 1943 – April 1944   236

Iwo Jima, February 1945   238

US invasion of Okinawa, 26 March – 30 June 1945   241

# Introduction

The term 'Second World War' refers to several conflicts, some linked, others separate, fought by nation states over a period of six years from 1939, although preliminary engagements had occurred as early as 1931. Basically, the land and air war occurred in two main theatres. One was Europe, a conflict which overflowed into African campaigns. The other was Asia and the Pacific. As fighting spread, the sea war took place on and under every ocean.

In a century of unparalleled bloodletting and destructive war, the six years after 1939 were unequalled in

**ABOVE:** German soldiers in Italy during March 1944. Their opponents there included British, Brazilians, Indians, Africans and soldiers from all over Europe in addition to the US 5th Army. There was a large Polish contingent, fighting with dour determination despite the occupation of their homeland for over four years. Professionally excellent though it was, the German army would eventually be overwhelmed by the coalition of forces united to crush the Nazi regime.

ferocity. By the close, approximately fifty million men, women and children world-wide had been killed, with millions of others scarred physically or emotionally. No other war has proved so extensive or costly or has had such widespread repercussions not only for the combatants but also on those who remained neutral. The legacy can be traced, at the end of the twentieth century, through the mutual attitudes and antipathies of various nations. Wounds of memory, dislike and mistrust heal slowly, if at all. For a number, in Lenin's words, peace has been only a continuation of war by other means.

People born after 1945, who never lived through the war, are sometimes puzzled and repulsed by the actions of an older generation. They look at their parents and grandparents, now usually placid with age, and can hardly

believe that once they fought murderously. Did granddad really run his bayonet into a fellow human being before finishing him off with a bullet? And can it be true that grandma helped to build the plane that dropped the bomb that hit the house that collapsed on ten little children and killed the lot? Surely not, grandma!

Today, there are people of all nations who believe that such a scale of devastation can never occur again. The threat of atomic bombs has, in their opinion, outlawed war. The influence of television, radio and the Press is now so great that widespread images of impending Armageddon would bring whole populations rapidly to their senses. Everywhere, they claim, the sights and sounds of devastation would prompt people to defy any government attempting to promote conflict. They would refuse to take part as cannon-fodder. World war died in 1945.

Did it? Such optimists should reflect on the history of the human condition. Firstly there has been no year since 1945 when a war, large or small, has not been fought somewhere in the world. The unhappy and geographically diverse catalogue includes Afghanistan, the Gulf, Vietnam, Israel, the Falklands, Indonesia and Kosovo. The post-war years seem to confirm Fisher's view of history as being 'one damn thing after another'. Dreadful experiences of the Second World War have certainly not deterred some later

generations from a desire to fight. For them, as Clausewitz argued, war is nothing but the continuation of politics with the admixture of other means. Nor has the awesome power of nuclear weapons been outlawed by nations. In 1945 one country possessed atomic bombs; at the close of the twentieth century the number having the ability to produce them has approached double figures.

Secondly, during the 1920s and 1930s, following the slaughter of the First World War, in which at least eight million fighting men died, many young people of various nations swore that they would not join another conflict. Heartfelt cries resounded of 'Never again'. They were greatly affected by anti-war images portrayed particularly in films and literature. And yet when the call to arms came, especially in 1939, most stepped forward to serve. Consequently, just twenty years after the signing of a peace treaty concluding 'the war to end all wars', four European nations again took up arms. Each was convinced of the justice of its own cause.

Unravelling the threads of war is no easy task, but two other factors merit consideration. First, was this conflict inevitable? Some historians think not. For them it was what Churchill called 'the unnecessary war' and could have been avoided had statesmen followed a different course, especially in 1936 and 1938. Hitler, they suggest, was allowed to get away with too much. Others, nonetheless, see the conflict as a continuation of the First World War. In their view, the conferences, treaties and settlements after 1918 were so unsatisfactory that further trouble was unavoidable. 'This is not peace,' claimed Marshal Foch of the Versailles Treaty, 'it is an armistice for twenty years.' His prediction was uncannily accurate. 'The first war explains the second,' wrote A. J. P. Taylor, 'and in fact caused it, in so far as one event causes another.'

Secondly, was this a just war? The two words may appear incompatible, or at least sit together uneasily. To the victors of 1945, nevertheless, there was little doubt that Nazi Germany and Imperial Japan in particular, and Fascist Italy to a lesser extent, represented evil forces which had been overcome by the armed strength of

**EUROPE IN 1920**

The peace treaties that ended the First World War carved up the territories of the losers: the German, Austro-Hungarian, and Ottoman Empires. But the re-drawing of national boundaries was to create as many problems as it solved. Three new 'countries' were established: Yugoslavia, Czechoslovakia and Iraq. Only one has survived into the 21st century. The most controversial element was the creation of a 'corridor' of Polish territory between East Prussia and the rest of Germany.

**Europe in 1920**
(post peace treaties)

Arctic Circle

Iceland
(Danish)

(Danish)

N O R W A Y

S W E D E N

F I N L A N D

Helsinki

Oslo

Stockholm

Leningrad

Tallinn

ESTONIA

Riga

LATVIA

LITHUANIA

Kaunas

Glasgow

Edinburgh

DENMARK

Copenhagen

Danzig
(free city under
League of Nations)

Königsberg

East
Prussia

USSR

UNITED KINGDOM

Dublin

Liverpool

Hamburg

Berlin

Warsaw

Brest Litovsk

IRELAND

Amsterdam

NETHER-

P O L A N D

Bristol

Birmingham

G E R M A N Y

London

Brussels

Cracow

Lvov

Calais

BELGIUM

LUX.

Frankfurt

Prague

C Z E C H O S L O V A K I A

SAAR
(autonomous under
League of Nations)

Paris

Vienna

Orléans

Budapest

R O M A N I A

Bern

AUSTRIA

HUNGARY

F R A N C E

SWITZ.

Lyon

Milan

Trieste

Bucharest

Bordeaux

Venice

Belgrade

Genoa

Y U G O S L A V I A

BULGARIA

Marseille

Sofia

ANDORRA

I T A L Y

Rome

ALBANIA

TURKEY

P O R T U G A L

Madrid

Barcelona

Naples

GREECE

Smyrna

S P A I N

Athens

Alicante

(Italian
occupied)

Cádiz

Gibraltar
(British)

Almeria

Tangier
(international zone)

Morocco
(French)

A l g e r i a
(French)

T u n i s i a
(French)

L i b y a
(Italian)

democratic nations employed in a righteous cause. Few people among the Allies questioned that the war was both necessary and just. What would have happened if they had lost? The world had been saved from the powers of darkness.

On the other side of the fence millions of citizens of the Axis powers viewed events in a different light. They believed that their rightful aims, for which they had fought and sacrificed so much, had been thwarted by defeat. This did not destroy their cherished hopes and ambitions, but curtailed the means of achieving them. Since then, both the Germans and the Japanese have made prodigious efforts in the field of economic development and expansion, and have become two of the world's most successful industrial states.

The Second World War ended in two stages in 1945. In early May, shortly after the death of Adolf Hitler, the Germans surrendered in Europe. Then, on 14 August, Emperor Hirohito of Japan announced his

nation's capitulation in the Far East. The concluding act was played out on 2 September when, aboard the American battleship USS *Missouri* anchored in Tokyo Bay, Japanese officers signed 'an instrument of surrender'. The last Axis power had acknowledged defeat by the Allies. Peace had finally broken out.

Another date is less easily located. When did the war start? The answer depended on where people lived. In Asia, an unresolved conflict had continued since 1931, with breaks, when Japanese troops attacked Chinese forces in Manchuria. In Africa the Italians defied the League of Nations by launching a colonial war against Abyssinia (Ethiopia) from late 1935. The Spanish Civil War, which drew in forces from Germany, Italy and Russia, as well as an International Brigade, opened in the following year. Germany, Poland, Britain and France began fighting in Europe at the start of September 1939. The USSR was invaded by the Germans in June 1941 and that marked the opening of 'The Great Patriotic War' for the Russians (who, however, overlooked the fact that their own forces had earlier marched against Poland, the Baltic States and Finland). To the Americans, war began in December 1941 with the Japanese raid on Pearl Harbor – although the United States, while officially neutral, had been openly hostile to the Axis powers for a year before then.

The generally accepted date for the start of the Second World War is 1 September 1939. At 4.45 that morning

German troops, closely supported by aircraft, struck at Poland. The two nations shared borders 1,750 miles long and the assault was launched from three main directions. Frontier barriers were pushed aside as thousands of soldiers with lorries, tanks and guns, all under the umbrella of the *Luftwaffe*, poured across. Polish troops attempted to halt the tide and the first shots were exchanged in the European war. German forces made rapid progress, with many opposing units quickly overwhelmed or compelled to retreat before a barrage of ground and air attacks.

Under such intense pressure, the Polish Government at once looked for help to its two major allies. Britain and France had given undertakings that they would come to the aid of Poland in the event of aggression from another national state; both had Germany in mind as the potential belligerent. Treaties offer security to nations, in the fashion of a group of mountaineers roped together for safety. If one climber falls, however the others risk being catapulted unwillingly into space. One slip can spell disaster for all.

At first inspection, both nations honoured their commitments speedily by issuing ultimatums to the German government: either cease fire then retire to your own frontiers, they stipulated, or we shall intervene. Their warnings were ignored and Hitler refused to stop. Therefore both declared war on Germany. Britain took up arms at 11 a.m. on 3 September, while France followed suit at 5 p.m. on the same day. Within a period of about sixty hours almost two hundred million Europeans were launched into war.

These happenings appeared to result from definite steps taken by strong governments, each having a clear policy and powerful resolve. There seemed to be no break in the sequence of events, each move leading swiftly and inexorably to the next. The reality was more opaque. Greater anxiety, confusion and irresolution affected all government circles more than the public either suspected or were allowed to discover. In many respects the war of 1939 was unexpected and unwelcome, and caught the nations involved unprepared.

**LEFT:** Hitler's motorcade makes a typically stylish progression through Vienna. One of the first politicians to campaign for office by whistle-stop airplane tour, Hitler swore to avenge Germany's defeat of 1918. His success in extracting concessions from the British and French boosted his power and undermined the remaining internal opposition. The German armed forces were expanded at a ferocious pace during the 1930s, but the army, navy and air force were all planning on a conflict that would begin in the mid-1940s. The crisis of 1939 came too early for all of them.

# CHAPTER 1: Why the Nations Went to War

## Germany

Nations do not go to war lightly. Whether they are dictatorships, with one man or a single party wielding overwhelming power, or democracies in which several groups have the opportunity of influencing policy, whole nations have to be led into conflict. At least a general consensus is required for the course being followed. From the start of September 1939 four nations decided to fight in Europe, another joined in some two weeks later, while a further three, though subsequently embroiled in war, stayed neutral. At that stage, what were the reasons for their decisions?

Why did Nazi Germany invade Poland on 1 September 1939? A widespread impression still exists that Adolf Hitler, at once messianic and omnipotent, led a mesmerised nation into conflict. A number of writers refer to 'Hitler's War' as if he were a supreme evil puppet-master – the Pied Piper of Nazism. One spoke of 'the insatiable appetite of Adolf Hitler'. His friend Rudolf Hess claimed that

'Hitler is Germany and Germany is Hitler'. Nonetheless, as other historians have remarked, he could not have succeeded without a general acceptance and cooperative agreement from many individuals and national groups. Some estimated that they could control him. The Sorcerer's Apprentice once believed that about a broom.

Basically, by moving against Poland, Hitler intended to win back by force of arms territory which the German people believed was rightly theirs. This was land which, in their estimation, was unfairly taken from them at the end of the First World War. The Treaty of Versailles had created an independent Poland from parts of the old empires of Austria, Russia and Germany. In a move to afford the new nation access to maritime trade, the port of Danzig, on the Baltic coast, was given the status of an independent 'Free City'. However, Danzig was German, having been part of Prussia since the eighteenth century. So that the Poles could reach the port,

a corridor of land was taken from West Prussia and awarded to them, a move which automatically separated East Prussia from the rest of Germany. Consequently German inhabitants of the Corridor came under the control of a foreign power, a situation unsatisfactory to both sides. Not surprisingly, Germans there wanted to be reunited with their homeland, and Poland encountered an uncooperative population of Germans sitting across her trade route to the Baltic coast.

Ironically, it was the British Prime Minister Lloyd George who suggested that Danzig should be a 'Free City', with the League of Nations installing a High Commissioner. This move, made for Germany's benefit, substantially led to war twenty years later. Subsequently the new Poland was a buffer-state, with powerful neighbours on each side and with restless internal minorities. Statesmen had tried to create a nation from people who had previously lived in provinces on the boundaries of three empires.

At the start of his book *Mein Kampf*, Adolf Hitler stated that 'kindred blood should belong to a common empire'. In September 1939 he was attempting to achieve that object. He claimed to have tried peaceful, diplomatic negotiations so that Danzig and the Corridor would be returned to German control. These efforts had failed. Only then, in Hitler's reckoning, had he been compelled to use force. However, the question of who owned a city and nearby parcel of land was the selected occasion of war. The real causes ran deeper, into the roots of German history.

To German eyes, the Treaty of Versailles was a *Diktat* or 'slave treaty', and the worst example of victors' justice. The Germans believed that Britain, France and the United States had not only humiliated them but had also severely damaged their economy. Consequently the German people had suffered two decades of hardship and deprivation after 1919.

A particularly grating point was that, at Versailles, Germany and her allies had been blamed for starting the First World War. The War Guilt Clause (Clause 231) laid at their door 'all the loss and damage to which the Allied and Associated Governments and their nationals have been subjected'. The entire conflict had come from 'the aggression of Germany and her allies'. To the innocent victims of, for example, Belgium, who had endured devastation from the uninvited German entry of 1914, the Clause was fair retribution. However, to those Germans who believed that they had been compelled to take up arms, such justice appeared one-eyed.

Through being forced to accept that clause, Germany had had to pay reparations. These were to be compensation for 'all the damage done to the civilian populations of the Allied and Associated powers and to their property'. By 1921, when the suffering nations had submitted their claims, the figure stood at 132,000 million gold marks, or about £6.6 billion – an astronomical sum. Before long a number of Germans were taking the view, 'Can't pay, won't pay'.

The Germans believed that other stipulations of the peace treaties were excessively punitive. Allied forces

occupied a demilitarised Rhineland. Overall, about 12 per cent of German territory was taken and awarded to the newly formed nations of Poland and Czechoslovakia or to France, Belgium and Denmark. The Saar Basin, a hub of German industrial production, was placed under international control. The nation's overseas colonies were removed into the authority of the newly formed League of Nations, then passed as mandated territories to France, Japan and Britain.

Germany's armed services were speedily dismembered. A force of 100,000 men could be retained, but the remainder of the army, together with its famously competent General Staff, was disbanded. No aircraft, tanks or submarines were permitted, and most of the German Fleet surrendered, finishing its days at Scapa Flow. The many Germans who believed that their armed forces had never been truly defeated in battle, but rather had been betrayed by certain groups at home, found the price hard to pay. They spoke of being 'stabbed in the back' by minor revolutionaries, or by those who had signed an ignominious treaty.

Nevertheless, neither Versailles nor subsequent treaties made with Germany's allies solved what might be termed 'The German Question'. After

**ABOVE:** The body of a German soldier killed in the First World War. Many casualties were buried where they fell and were disinterred by subsequent shelling or the excavation of trenches. German attitudes to the war were very different from those in France: having suffered so much only to be defeated, many German veterans were fully prepared to fight again. By the mid-1930s Germans attending the commemorations at Verdun were arriving with swastika flags.

**LEFT:** Some of the thousands of German soldiers captured by the British at Bapaume in September 1918. The German high command secured an armistice in November which stopped the victorious Allies marching into Germany itself. This later helped the Nazis re-write history, claiming the army was never defeated, but 'stabbed in the back' by Jews and Communists within Germany.

the proclamation of the Second Reich in 1871, Germany had grown into the strongest state in central Europe, with the largest population, expanding industries and a highly successful army. The German people, vigorous, proud and self-confident, wanted to exercise a powerful influence over their neighbours. Around them lay Czarist Russia, the Austro-Hungarian Empire and, to the south-east, the old Ottoman Empire. On the further side of the continent was France, which possessed an overseas empire, while offshore lay Britain, the greatest imperial power ever known. German attempts to equal or exceed these other Great Powers with an expansion of territory, influence and prestige contributed deeply to the outbreak of the First World War. Possibly by 1970 Europe had still not recovered from the unification of Germany a century before.

A prime aim of the Treaty of Versailles was to prevent Germany from again taking up a dominant and aggressive role. However, together with the other post-war treaties, it failed particularly by leaving a series of vacuums in central and southern Europe. Nature, we are told, abhors a vacuum; human nature certainly does. To the east, the Romanov Empire collapsed with the Bolshevik Revolution, leading to the fading of Russian influence in European affairs. First Lenin, then Stalin buried themselves deeply in their nation's internal changes, burying thousands of their own people in the process. The Bolsheviks were regarded as pariahs and feared by most other states. The great Austro-Hungarian Empire was fragmented into a collection of smaller states and the Hapsburgs no longer exercised authority over large areas in central and south-eastern regions of the continent. In the Near East the old Ottoman Empire, which had tottered for so long, finally disintegrated.

Germany alone after 1919 remained as a single, powerful nation. The government had been allowed to sign an armistice, but the country had been neither invaded nor completely occupied by Allied forces. The destruction of war which had devastated areas of northern France and Belgium was not experienced in German towns and villages. No French cavalry rode through the streets of Berlin, British shells did not fall on the Ruhr, and American infantry did not dig trenches in Westphalia. The Fatherland was left at seven-eighths of its pre-war size and retained sovereignty. After the Kaiser's abdication in 1918 the Weimar Republic was established but German identity was mainly unaffected by changes.

Over the following decade, as a republic with a national assembly at Weimar, Germany slipped into deep trouble. Economic disasters accompanied political crises. The costs of war reparations and rebuilding could not be met and by 1923 the country was swamped by massive inflation. Recovery followed, but not before thousands of people had lost their savings and investments. The dormant, yet

**BELOW:** Hitler's rise to power: the future German dictator stands above the crowd (in raincoat) as a detachment of SA 'stormtroops' parade past. The bald man facing the camera in front of Hitler is the rabidly anti-Semitic publisher of the stormtroopers' propaganda magazine *Der Sturmer*, Julius Streicher. He was one of the Nazi leaders executed after the war crimes trials at Nuremberg.

potentially strong, nationalist movement blamed not only the Allies for this predicament, but also their own Weimar government. Their ambition to shine in Europe had never gone away. Weimar, they claimed, had crippled the nation. Democracy did not work.

A turning point arrived in 1929 when the Great Slump affected countries world-wide and was accompanied by extensive unemployment. Germany was hit worse than any other European state. In that year two million were without work, a total which trebled by 1932. Large sums of foreign capital, especially from the United States, were rapidly withdrawn by investors who were in trouble in their own countries. At that stage millions of Germans looked away from democracy to find salvation. Extreme circumstances called for radical solutions. One was at hand.

Fear of communism, combined with a weakened economy and the spectre of social disorder, led many Germans towards the Nazi Party. More than any other political party of the time, the National Socialists pledged to lead the German people out of domestic troubles. Also offered were promises to restore the nation as a proud and important international power. The appeal was seductively attractive: here was an offer few could afford to refuse. Landowners, industrialists, church leaders and the old Army commanders wanted Germany reinstated to its position in 1914. The middle classes and many workers felt betrayed by the Weimar government. Hitler's promises to revive industry and trade while restoring the greatness of the past had a twofold allure. Consequently, the Nazi Party's support grew dramatically from twelve seats in government in 1928 to 230 in July 1932. By that time they constituted the largest single party, and on 30 January 1933 Hitler became Chancellor. The rise to power was meteoric.

During the next six years the German Reich's economy certainly appeared to flourish, but at a heavy cost. Renewal was tied particularly to enormous spending by the armed forces. Between 1936 and 1940, through a Four-Year Plan, over half the national investment was guided into production for war. Other prices

also had to be paid by the German people, millstones which hung around their necks until the end of the Second World War. One was the dictatorship established by Hitler and his party, particularly through the Enabling Act of 1933, whereby political opposition and trade unions were abolished and a police state was enforced. The second was the propagation of a policy of Aryan racial supremacy – the theory of the 'Master Race'. This led to a fervent hatred of Slavs and Jews, a cardinal part of Nazi belief and teaching. One of the Twenty-Five Points issued by them in 1920 stated that 'none but those of German blood, whatever their creed, may be members of the nation. No Jew, therefore, may be a member of the nation.' Put into everyday practice, the nation was poisoned by a rabid, evil racism which treated Jews as sub-humans (*Untermenschen*). 'There is no making pacts with Jews,' wrote Hitler in *Mein Kampf*, 'there can only be the hard "either-or".'

Were the German people at the time unwilling victims of the Nazis? Were they duped into giving up democracy and forced to hate Jews? The point is debatable. Some, certainly, were shocked by the regime which had been

unleashed on them. Most, however, lived at ease in a traditionally autocratic society where dormant feelings of anti-Semitism had existed for decades. Most were pragmatic. The Nazis reduced unemployment, raised production and brought security. Such success was its own recommendation.

But it was the second plank of Hitler's political platform which led directly to war. Ever since the end of the First World War, in which he served as a soldier, he detested the terms imposed at Versailles. He and the Nazi Party pledged to repudiate them in short time. Through starting on this task, Germany began her restoration into the league of Great Powers, giving Germans a sense of national pride that had been severely dented in 1919.

As early as October 1933 Germany withdrew from the League of Nations, an organisation despised by Hitler. In January 1935 the inhabitants of the Saar chose by plebiscite to re-join Germany. Two months later Hitler announced the rejection of the military limits laid down at Versailles and restored conscription. Plans were made to establish the German Army at over half a million men in peacetime.

**ABOVE:** A detachment of German 'stormtroops' pose for the camera after a successful raid on Allied lines, summer 1918. Many of these elite troops refused to accept Germany's defeat in 1918 and fought on against the Communists in Germany. Others joined the *Freikorps,* mercenary armies fighting in the Baltic states. They provided a good proportion of recruits to the right-wing parties from which the NSDAP emerged.

At the same time, the *Luftwaffe*, forbidden after 1919, was re-formed. The German Navy also began to rebuild.

These moves brought wide support for the Nazis, especially from the young, who felt a new strength of purpose in their nation. Through organisations such as the Hitler Youth, the Nazis aimed particularly to appeal to young people. Speaking of his opponents, Hitler announced, 'You will pass on. Your descendants, however, now stand in the new camp. In a short time they will know nothing else but this new community.' All were regarded as servants of the State, their public life injected with the excitement of rallies and parades, dominated by propaganda and

ABOVE: Nazi rallies were brilliant political theatre, expertly staged and filmed. Hitler discovered his talent for public speaking in 1919 when hired by the German army to keep up the morale of soldiers as they were discharged. His political career was founded on this talent, his histrionic performances attracting ever larger crowds.

uniforms. 'In Germany in one day,' wrote a British visitor in 1936, 'you see more uniforms than in England in a whole year!' By then Hitler was gaining supreme control of Germany. At home his position was secure, with political opponents removed or imprisoned.

He was treated as a demigod. 'I swear to you, Adolf Hitler, as *Führer* and Reich Chancellor, loyalty and bravery,' ran the oath sworn by all members of his élite troops, the Waffen SS. 'I vow to you, and to those you have named to command me, obedience unto death, so help me God.' They meant it. No dictator could have greater command over the souls, as well as the bodies, of his followers.

He was now ready to embark on an active foreign policy, one which would lead three years later to the outbreak of war. Unknown to the German nation these were steps to the scaffold. Historians differ over judging his policy. Some believe that it was carefully

premeditated and then ruthlessly followed to expand Germany's frontiers. His plan, they estimate, was followed like a railway timetable. Others call him an opportunist. Chances arrived and he took them. When successful he waited for the next prize to appear, then seized it. In aviation terms, they judge that he flew 'by the seat of his pants'. The truth probably lies in a combination of both factors. Certainly he planned from his early days to restore German unity and the Fatherland's international standing, especially in eastern Europe. Then, as he began to implement his policy, openings appeared which he quickly turned to his advantage. To the Germans, the *Führer* seemed to possess a golden touch.

A searching test arrived in 1936. The Rhineland, demilitarised at Versailles, was an area Hitler was intent on restoring to Germany. At the back of his mind, nonetheless, rested doubts over the reactions of the British and, more particularly, the French. Would they intervene if his troops marched in? He noted with satisfaction that in the previous October, when the Italians attacked Abyssinia, neither Britain nor France had moved to stop them. Their response had been half-hearted and Mussolini's campaign had continued unabated. Hitler therefore decided to chance his arm. On 7 March 1936 about 60,000 German soldiers and armed police entered the Rhineland and Hitler waited for the reaction. There was little. Many British politicians by then believed that the Germans were merely recovering their own territory. The French, who vastly overestimated the strength of the German force, did nothing. Hitler's *coup* was entirely successful, with no blood being shed.

Another step in Germany's active foreign policy was taken in July 1936 when support was offered to General Franco, the Nationalist leader in the Spanish Civil War. One reason for this was Hitler's desire to prevent a left-wing government from taking power in Spain. Germany's main contribution was through the Condor Legion, consisting of units from the budding *Luftwaffe*, as well as a small ground force. The particular benefit for the Germans was the experience gained by

airmen, both in strategy and tactics, which was to be invaluable in the early stages of the Second World War.

Before the outbreak of war the German leader took three other major steps in international affairs. These brought him fame and glory with his own people, who believed that the *Führer* was restoring their former greatness. To most other European nations they were unwelcome signs of a resurgent Germany which was prepared to achieve her aims by force. Shades of 1914 returned.

The first of these steps was less controversial than the other two. A new Austria, separated from Germany, had been created by Versailles and other treaties. Over the following years pressure grew from the Austrian Nazi Party for an *Anschluss*, or union with the Fatherland. It was apparent that many Austrians wanted this, and by 1938 Hitler believed that the time was ripe for incorporating his homeland into the emerging *Grossdeutschland* (Greater Germany). Early on 12 March 1938 German troops entered Austria and the deed was done. Once again the *Führer* had been successful.

Hitler, a child of the Austro-Hungarian Empire, had disliked Czechoslovakia ever since that country was formed from a mixture of nationalities after 1918. About one-fifth of the population were Germans, living mainly close to the frontiers with Austria and Germany. During the 1930s many supported the expanding Nazi Party and then sought self-government in their own area, the Sudetenland. As their demands intensified, the German government offered support and encouragement. Through the early months of 1938 a crisis developed. Hitler was set on having a showdown with the Czechs over the rights of Germans in the country, and by the summer war appeared to be likely.

The formation of Czechoslovakia had been guaranteed at Versailles, and the Czech government, with good frontier defences and a not inconsiderable army, looked for support. The French, nevertheless, would not act alone, although they had signed alliances with the Czechs in 1924 and 1935.

The mantle of decision fell on an unwilling British government. The often-told story of the Munich Crisis of

## HITLER'S POLITICAL ANNEXATIONS

September 1938, usually offered as an example of craven appeasement, does not always explain the difficulties faced by the prime minister, Neville Chamberlain. Britain's innate reticence to become involved in the affairs of eastern Europe, combined with the effects of the Great Slump on her economy, were not least among the reasons why Chamberlain sought a negotiated settlement. The prime minister's three visits to Germany averted war, although at the end of the month, when Hitler increased his demands, both Britain and France mobilised their forces. For several days Europe was balanced on the edge of conflict.

Nonetheless, Hitler held the whip hand. His army stood on the borders of Czechoslovakia, and although he did not want to fight in 1939 the presence of his troops and aircraft was a strong bargaining factor. At the final confer-ence, with representatives of Germany, Italy, Britain and France present (but none from the Czech government), Hitler obtained what he wanted. Poland and Hungary also demanded a share of the spoils, the former reclaim-ing land round Teschen while the latter took territory near its border. The Czechs appeared to be expendable pawns in a territorial game. 1938 was certainly Germany's year.

With the Czechs safely under his belt, Hitler's domination of central and eastern Europe – *Mitteleuropa* – was well advanced. Germany was again the most powerful nation, with possibilities of controlling or influenc-ing states to the south-east, turning them into political or economic satel-lites. To the south, Italy, under a fellow and acquiescent dictator, Mussolini, became an ally in May 1939, signing a 'Pact of Steel'.

### HITLER'S POLITICAL ANNEXATIONS

In March 1936 Hitler took a great gamble and ordered his army to re-occupy the Rhineland in defiance of the British and French. He did not know, but may have suspected, that some of his own generals were preparing to remove him from power if the British and French reacted. They did not. Like a predator sensing weakness, Hitler pressed on with his mission of overturning the Versailles settlement. By bullying and bluster, he achieved union with Austria and then progressively swallowed up the Czechoslovak state. The British and French betrayal of the Czechs led him to believe they would accept anything rather than risk another conflict. Hitler was genuinely surprised when his invasion of Poland triggered declarations of war from Britain and France.

**Hitler's Annexations** 1936–9

- Germany after 1919
- troops into demilitarized Rhineland March 1936
- Anschluss (union with Austria), March 1938
- occupation of Sudetenland October 1938
- original Czechoslovakian border
- formerly Czechoslovakia occupied March 1939
- Moravian territory to Poland October 1938
- Memel territory to Germany March 1939
- Protectorate of Slovakia territory to Hungary Nov. 1938
- Czechoslovakian territory to Hungary March 1939
- conquest of western Poland September 1939

# Poland

**ABOVE:** A German 105 mm field gun battery on the move, winter 1939–40. This would remain the German army's standard medium artillery piece throughout the war, although supplemented from 1942 by increasing numbers of self-propelled versions.

**RIGHT:** Giant concrete obstacles form part of the 'Siegfried Line' border defences, the German equivalent of the French Maginot Line. From the beginning of the war, the British sang about 'hanging out the washing on the Siegfried Line' but it took six years before they were able to do so.

Germany and Poland had experienced a mixed relationship since 1919. At first, feelings had been mutually unfriendly, with only a slow improvement. However, in 1934 the two nations signed a non-aggression pact. Yet the question of Danzig was never far from Hitler's mind. 'All our agreements with Poland have a purely temporary significance,' he announced privately at the time. He had no intention of fostering a lasting friendship.

Pressure on the Poles was applied from late 1938 and intensified during the following spring. By then Hitler's generals were drawing up plans for an attack while the veneer of diplomatic talks continued. The Poles, however, were no wilting flowers, stubbornly refusing to give up either Danzig or the Corridor. They felt vulnerable, wedged between the two giants, Germany and the USSR, yet believed that their position as a buffer nation could assure their survival: perhaps they could play off one country against the other. They shared Hitler's mistrust and dislike of Russia. 'With the Germans, we risk losing our liberty,' remarked one of their leaders. 'With the Russians we shall lose our soul.'

By the summer of 1939, however, the Poles had gained allies. The British and French governments, widely accused of flaccid appeasement, through which both had been outmanoeuvred at Munich, had a change of heart. The catalyst for their particular anxiety started in March when Czechoslovakia disintegrated and the Germans marched into Prague. Supported by growing public concern at home, they were now convinced that Hitler had designs on every remaining European nation.

Poland was the obvious next victim. Therefore, on 31 March 1939, Chamberlain gave a guarantee to support the Polish government if its independence were threatened. The French offered a similar promise. Both hoped that their warnings would be sufficient to deter the Nazis. The reality, however, was to bring the two allies face to face with Germany in an approaching showdown. Some swift calculations were forced on Hitler. Within Germany he was lauded as a hero who was reclaiming stolen national territory. His methods were not repulsive to a people steeped in a military tradition dating back to the old successes gained by the Prussian Army. Hitler reasoned that as Britain and France lay on the opposite side of Europe from Poland, they could not intervene effectively. At the last moment, he reckoned, they would suffer a severe attack of appeasement and give way, and another 'Munich' would follow. In May Ribbentrop, the German Foreign Minister, claimed that 'within a few months not one Frenchman nor a single Englishman will go to war for Poland.'

The only nation with the potential strength to block Hitler's plans was the USSR, but, although talks were held by French, Russian and British representatives, there was no agreement. Too much mutual distrust existed. The Germans then held talks with the Russians. The *Führer* realised that by gaining Stalin's support he would isolate Poland. To the world's surprise, on 19 August a Soviet-German economic agreement was signed, followed four days later by a non-aggression pact, dashing Poland's hopes. Those who knew of Hitler's and Stalin's mutual antipathy were amazed. What had brought the two rivals together?

The explanation was simple, although generally unknown at the time. The pact had a secret protocol. Under the terms, the Germans and Russians agreed to divide Poland between themselves, together with the Baltic states of Latvia, Estonia and Lithuania which had been established at Versailles. Hitler's attack on Poland, planned for 26 August, was now ready to roll. At the last moment he was flustered when Britain signed a treaty of alliance with the Poles, so he postponed the invasion for a few days. Nevertheless, all was set. Any further delay could cause the campaign to finish during the bad weather of the forthcoming winter.

Hitler certainly anticipated a European war involving Germany fighting against France and Britain. However, he was planning for the action to start about 1942, by which time his armed forces would have grown to overwhelming strength. The German people generally believed that tackling Poland was a just cause, restoring territory and people to the Fatherland. This would consolidate their position as Europe's greatest power. The *Führer* cherished wider ambitions. He was set on erasing both Poland and its people from the map, opening up lands in the east for German settlement and living-space – *Lebensraum*.

The final order for the assault was issued by Hitler at 6.30 a.m. on 31 August. His troops crossed the Polish border at 4.45 a.m. the next day and he still estimated that Britain and France neither could nor would intervene effectively. When he received the British ultimatum he was stunned. His interpreter wrote that after 'an interval which seemed an age' he turned to Ribbentrop, who had remained standing at the window. This was the man, formerly ambassador to London, on whose diagnosis of British attitudes the *Führer* had relied so strongly. Unfortunately he was also the man whose gaffes and misjudgements of the British had brought him the nickname of 'Herr Brickendrop'. 'What now?' Hitler savagely demanded.

The answer was six years of unmatched destruction.

**ABOVE:** French motorcyclists pass a column of British lorries in France, October 1939. By remaining passive behind their defences, the Allies allowed the German army to crush Poland without difficulty.

**LEFT:** Belgian heavy artillery on exercise, February 1940. Three months later, the Belgian army would disintegrate on contact with the German invaders.

# Great Britain

The effects of the First World War were branded deeply into the memory of the British people. Altogether Britain and the Empire lost about one million men dead, whose names can still be read on war memorials countrywide. Tens of thousands had fallen on the fields of northern France and Belgium and were regarded as martyrs of a great continental struggle into which Britain had been drawn unwillingly.

The United Kingdom's allegiances lay mainly elsewhere. Geographically, although Britain is part of Europe, it is separated from the mainland and its interests have generally looked away to the west and the south for maritime trade. The nation's prime involvement after the First World War lay in the Empire and Dominions built up over the previous three centuries. These territories, lying in other continents, required great resources for maintenance, and the British government was more concerned with providing them than with dabbling in the affairs and squabbles of central Europe. The pro-

tection of ocean trade was essential, across routes to the colonies and Dominions, and therefore Britain was determined to prevent threats from other nations. In some respects Italy and Japan, each with a considerable navy, were seen as greater potential dangers than land-locked Germany, until the later 1930s.

For a period in the 1930s there was in Britain some sympathy for the Germans. They appeared to be trying hard to restore their economy after the Slump, and Hitler was certainly a dynamic leader. A few British politicians, including Lloyd George, Lord Londonderry and Lord Halifax, visited Germany. Undoubtedly the *Führer* would have liked Britain to combine with him in a struggle against Communism.

Growing Nazi power, the reoccupation of the Rhineland and subsequent events compelled the British government to act. Rearmament began tentatively with a Four-Year Plan for building up the armed services, particularly the RAF and the Royal Navy. At the same time the government hoped, through a policy of appeasement, to placate Hitler and to resolve problems by peaceful means. The formal, careful methods of diplomacy, evolved particularly in

**LEFT:** A German bomb aimer's view of London, taken during one of the daylight attacks of 1917–18. There was widespread belief that the Second World War would begin with poison gas attacks from the air and the British led the world in air defence by 1939, a wise precaution as events would soon demonstrate.

**BELOW:** Hoisting in a 16-in shell aboard one of the Royal Navy's 'Nelson' class battleships. Most of the Royal Navy's capital ships dated back to the First World War, some modernized, some not. The 'Nelsons' were post-war ships, heavily armed but much slower than US, Japanese or German battleships entering service during the 1930s.

the nineteenth century, would iron out difficulties without recourse to war. The politicians were accustomed to international affairs following a course of what has been called 'civilised Machiavellianism'.

How wrong they were. 'If ever that silly old man comes interfering here again with his umbrella,' Hitler said of Chamberlain after Munich, 'I'll kick him downstairs.' Nevertheless, the efforts of the appeasers were supported by most British people. When Chamberlain agreed to Hitler's demands during the Munich Crisis he was widely regarded as a saviour who had rescued Europe from disaster. Yet at heart he, together with an increasing number of the British, knew that the reprieve was no more than temporary. Therefore rearmament was speeded up, together with civil defence, in which, late in 1938, more than 1.4 million civilians were serving. This force was twice as large as all the armed services added together – an augury of the nature of the war to come.

Preparations for war increased early in 1939. Unwillingly, yet inevitably, the nation appreciated that a war was coming. The die was cast in March, with the pledge to support Poland against Nazi aggression. As the events of that summer brought contest closer in eastern Europe, Britain and France were drawn together in a common resolve to stand against German expansion. Appeasement had run its course. By August 1939 the British people accepted that war was at hand. Their mood

was fatalistic: 'It's bound to happen, so let's make a start.' Preparations were well advanced. Gas masks had been issued, air raid shelters dug and evacuation arranged. But there was none of the heady triumphalism of 1914. Sombre people looked again at the names on local war memorials.

Until the last moment, the apostles of appeasement, especially Chamberlain and Halifax, hoped that a peaceful solution could be reached over Danzig and the Polish Corridor. Even after the German invasion of Poland had started and a British warning despatched to Berlin, there was delay while the declaration of war was coordinated with the French. At length the ultimatum was sent. It failed. Therefore, at 11 a.m. on Sunday 3 September, Chamberlain broadcast to the nation: 'Everything I have worked for, everything I have believed in during my public life has crashed into ruins,' he announced.

# France

Across the Channel, France's experiences after 1918 were different from Britain's. In the first place, her losses were relatively heavier than those of any other nation involved in the First World War, over 1.3 million men having been killed. This human devastation was felt strongly by the French during the inter-war years, leading to strong movements towards only yards away across a land frontier, while both Britain and the United States were protected by sea boundaries. The French went on to insist that Germany honour the terms agreed at the conference table. When reparation repayments were slow, French troops occupied the Ruhr in 1923.

A fear of Germany never left the French between the wars. From the and economically. Communist and Fascist groups grew in influence, and frequent demonstrations threatened social order. Uncertainty at home brought a number of changes of government, and these in turn affected foreign policy at a time when stability was needed to counter the growing menace from Germany. For example, the re-occupation of the Rhineland in

ABOVE: Graves of some of the 1.3 million Frenchmen killed during the First World War. French politics became viciously polarized in the 1920s and 1930s between left- and right-wing parties. The French army was virtually reduced to a militia, manned by short-term conscripts interested only in getting back to civilian life.

disarmament and pacifism. A widespread belief grew that the Republic could never afford another contest on that scale.

France finished the war as a strong European power, maintaining armed services at a high level while other nations were disbanding theirs. The policy was understandable. Twice in the lifetimes of older people German armies had invaded from the east. In 1870–71 the Prussian Army had been triumphant and the French had been compelled to sign a humiliating armistice. Then in 1914 the Germans had attacked again through neutral Belgium. The war had been a close-run contest, with France saved by her allies. In 1919 French leaders were determined to prevent Germany from ever repeating these invasions.

Consequently, at Versailles the French appeared revengeful, bringing some condemnation from their former allies. In France, naturally, a different view was held. The Germans were end of 1929, therefore, they began to build a powerful defence line along the eastern frontier. Named after the Minister of War responsible for its construction, the Maginot Line was a triple layer of positions, with barbed wire, pillboxes, concrete gun emplacements and underground railways. Based on the static defence of the First World War, the Line was intended to hold back any future German invasion. The weaknesses of the Line, however, are made obvious by studying a map of the areas not covered. Nothing was built between the border of Luxembourg and the Channel coast, leaving the whole northern sector open to any attack entering France through Belgium. The French appeared to have forgotten 1914. In that region the defence of France would depend heavily on how well the Belgians would perform in the event of a German assault.

During the 1930s the French nation was often deeply divided politically 1936 brought no definite response from the French, who wanted peace yet feared that the British would not intervene with support.

As with Britain, France followed a policy of appeasement in 1938. The armed services were not trained and were unready to engage the Germans. The widespread feeling against war had prevailed since 1918. Consequently Daladier, the prime minister, went to Munich and took part in the handing over of Czechoslovakia to Hitler. Afterwards, the general mood in France appreciated that war with Germany was bound to come, so wider preparations were made. The French and British governments drew closer in planning for joint action.

For France, Poland was the deciding case. Although no help could be sent to eastern Europe for the Poles, the French sat on Germany's western border as a potential threat. At heart they knew that Poland would not be able to withstand a Nazi onslaught for more than a few months, but it was imperative for France not to give in again.

Time was taken for mobilisation to be ordered and an ultimatum despatched to Berlin. Hence the French declared war at 5 p.m. on 3 September, six hours later than the British. In an evening broadcast to the nation Daladier spoke of Germany's desire to overwhelm Poland 'so as to be able to dominate Europe and to enslave France'. He added that, 'In honouring our word, we fight to defend our soil, our homes, our liberties.' Like the British, the French were in combat not only to help the Poles but also for their own land.

Although it is easy from the stronghold of hindsight to blame Britain and France for apparent docility in not preventing German expansion before 1939, two often overlooked factors should be recognised. One is that both supported the League of Nations set up after Versailles as an arena where nations could settle differences without recourse to war. However, although the League enjoyed some minor successes, the organisation lacked the strength to enforce decisions. There was no international army or police force to send against countries which refused to accept decisions. The Americans never joined.

LEFT: A French howitzer on exercise during the winter of 1939–40, the so-called *drôle de guerre* or Phoney War. The solid wheels on this 105 mm weapon fold inwards to form part of the gunshield: an ingenious solution to a non-problem. When batteries like this came into action in May 1940, their main enemies were tanks and dive-bombers.

Later, the Germans and Japanese walked out and the Italians ignored the organisation's orders. Opponents regarded the League as little more than an idealistic, impotent talking shop. Consequently Britain and France, realising that aggressive expansion could be countered by force alone, had to rely on their own power. Debating collective security was hot air. That underscored the second factor.

Here, success would have been achieved only if the efforts of the two nations had been well coordinated. They needed common aims, to speak diplomatically with one voice and to standardise the disposition of their armed services. In fact, they needed a type of supreme generalissimo, as Foch had been in the First World War. In peacetime, with two nations of such dissimilar backgrounds and policies, this was no more than a pipe-dream. The beneficiary was Germany.

BELOW: French Char B heavy tanks on a pre-war exercise. With a 47 mm gun in the turret and a short barrelled 75 mm in the hull, these were the most powerful tanks in western Europe. Unusually among French tanks, they were also equipped with radios.

# Russia

**ABOVE:** Living conditions in rural Russia had gone from bad to worse under Communist rule, with even greater famines than those occasionally seen before the revolution. City-bred Party ideologues dictated agricultural policy with disastrous results. Many young people fled the countryside to work in the towns.

The armchair strategist many years on may well ask why in 1939 the three main European opponents of Hitler did not employ their collective strength to surround Germany with a new Triple Entente. A similar association had worked well in 1914, with the Germans having to fight simultaneously on two fronts, facing Russia in the east and Britain and France in the west. As Hitler's ambitions expanded, the resurrection of that alliance would have been an obvious, perhaps the only, way of stopping his advance. The thought of engaging the armed strengths of three opponents would have concentrated the *Führer*'s mind greatly.

However, one of the greatest surprises in modern diplomatic history occurred in August 1939 when Germany and Russia, two nations with a lasting and public mistrust of each other, signed a pact. How was it that Stalin, regarded by the Germans as the leader of evil Bolshevism, could come to an agreement with Hitler, who was believed by the Russians to personify the wickedness of Fascism? As with most causes of the Second World War, the origin can be traced back some twenty years.

After the Russian Revolution of 1917 many revolutionaries believed that similar uprisings would occur in every capitalist state. 'It will not be long,' Lenin claimed in 1919, 'and we shall see the victory of Communism in the entire world.' Not for the first time, he was wrong. No great Communist uprisings occurred in capitalist countries. Instead, in the nations of western Europe a great fear and mistrust of Russia, as the force fomenting discord, lasted for the next two decades.

In that time the Russians, first under Lenin and then under Stalin, turned away from world revolution and towards establishing the USSR as a powerful Communist state. In Stalin's phrase, this was to be 'Socialism in a single country first.' From the late 1920s until the outbreak of the Second World War he ruthlessly modernised Russia, forcing the pace of vast industrial expansion. Five-Year Plans changed the face of Soviet society. 'We are fifty or a hundred years behind the advanced countries,' he announced in 1931. 'We must make good the distance in ten years. Either we do it, or they crush us.' Stalin's methods were those of the complete autocrat. Opposition was crushed mercilessly, with hundreds of thou-

**RIGHT:** Cossack cavalry seen during the Russian civil war. Many of Stalin's henchmen came from the Red Cavalry Army with which he spent part of the war.

sands of people sent to labour camps or put to death. The USSR became a dictatorship to match, or exceed, that in Nazi Germany.

Russia had few friends abroad. In the 1920s there was some liaison with Germany with the common factor that both countries were at the time outcasts from the general community of nations. The USSR received greatly needed industrial equipment and, partly in return, the German armed services found covert bases in Russia where they could train secretly. However, after the advent of the Nazis in 1933, with their hatred of Bolshevism, the relationship cooled.

As Hitler's power increased, the Russians were worried by German ambitions in eastern Europe. They realised that only Britain and France were suitable allies to keep the balance of power, but neither side showed sufficient trust for a treaty to be made. Any hopes of an anti-Hitler coalition were blocked by mutual suspicion. For example, the Russians were not invited to the Munich Conference in 1938 to discuss the future of Czechoslovakia.

Therefore talks broke down and the old Triple Entente was never re-formed.

In 1939 the Germans started to make overtures to the Russians. They played particularly on the fact that both nations disliked Poland, which had been formed largely from their territory after 1918. When Stalin saw the chance of regaining lands and of subjugating the Poles, he was ready to reach an agreement with the Germans. That suited Hitler. With his eastern frontier safe from any Russian threat, the way was open to launch an invasion of Poland. He was convinced that it would be only a local campaign.

**ABOVE:** By the late 1930s, the Red Army had more tanks than the rest of the world put together. However, most of the competent tank commanders were executed on trumped up charges during Stalin's purge of the armed forces.

**LEFT:** Russia supplied aircraft, tanks and other weapons to the Republican forces in Spain during the civil war there. This T-26 tank was captured by Nationalist forces who paid their men a bounty for seizing such valuable equipment intact. Russian 'advisors' exercised ever greater political control within the doomed Republic and made away with most of Spain's gold reserves.

# Italy

ABOVE: Hitler was a political apprentice when Mussolini and his Fascists seized power in Italy. The Nazis borrowed a great deal from the Italian movement, but by 1939 roles were reversed and Mussolini depended on Hitler.

RIGHT: The Italian equivalent of the German stormtrooper in the First World War, complete with body armour and wire cutters that contrive to make him look like something from the Middle Ages. The Italian army suffered heavy losses in battle with the Austrians and Germans during 1915–18 yet the French blocked most Italian territorial claims after the war.

Dictatorship was widespread across Europe during the inter-war period and could be found in almost a dozen states. One of its earliest developments arrived in Italy from 1922, when Mussolini and the Fascist Party came to power. The regime there lasted for about twenty years.

The clue to why Fascism took root in Italy after 1918 can be traced directly to that nation's experiences in the First World War and at the subsequent peace talks. Italy had entered the war in 1915 on the side of the Triple Entente, having previously been an ally of Germany in the Triple Alliance. She had been promised various territories as bribes, to be awarded at victory – hence the smart about-turn. At the peace treaties, though, several of the promises were retracted. The Italians were bitterly disappointed. At the cost of 460,000 dead, they were angry at what was offered – or not offered – in return.

With that background and with a large national debt, together with heavy inflation, the strongly nationalist Fascist Party was able to take power in 1922. Under Mussolini's leadership the Fascists claimed to be a dynamic force which would invigorate the nation, bring international prestige and hold off the threat of Communism. Here was the kind of appeal that would be heard again in Germany ten years later. Certainly, over the next seven years improvements were made in agriculture, industry and transport. The often quoted quip was that Mussolini had the Pontine Marshes drained and made the trains run on time.

Progress, however, was bought at a cost. From 1926 the State controlled political parties, while opponents of the Fascists were imprisoned or forced into exile. Freedom was lost, particularly to the whims of Mussolini.

Italian society was at the mercy of a poseur, who deluded himself as much as his nation. Nonetheless, he was shrewd enough to retain power, not always a cap-and-bells man. 'A despot,' wrote Bagehot in 1867, 'must feel that he is the pivot of the State.' This is the position Mussolini strove hard to attain inside Italy.

By 1930 Mussolini had consolidated his position at home and turned increasingly towards making an impression abroad. He had two main aims. The first was to place Italy among the league of Great Powers, supported by a flourishing economy and strong armed forces. Stemming from that, the second was to build an empire to match those of France and Great Britain, an aim for which the Italians had striven with only limited success since the late nineteenth century. Mussolini wanted to recreate the ancient Roman Empire, with himself as a Caesar. The Mediterranean was to be 'Mare Nostrum', controlled by the Italian Navy – a policy hardly likely to endear him to the British or the French.

He looked to two areas for imperial success. One was Africa and the other Asia Minor. Before 1920 Italy had managed to gain colonies only in Eritrea and Libya. The nation had suffered humiliation in 1896 when Italian troops were defeated by local tribesmen while trying to add Abyssinia to their empire. The defeat was never forgiven nor forgotten by Mussolini, who vowed revenge.

The opportunity arose in 1935 when relations between Abyssinia and Italy were at a low ebb. The Italians, who had been planning a campaign for several years, used a minor border incident as a pretext for launching three army corps against the poorly equipped Abyssinian army. Mussolini's troops, with modern weapons, including aircraft dropping gas bombs, gained success, although fighting did not end until May 1936. France and Britain were disturbed by the invasion but took no active steps to prevent it. The League of Nations was hostile to the war, as both Italy and Abyssinia were members. Oil sanctions were imposed by the League in an effort to curtail vital supplies to Italy, but sufficient quantities still got through from other sources: there is always someone ready to profit from an embargo. The dictator had won a victory not only over Abyssinia but also over the League, Britain and France.

At home, *Il Duce* (The Leader) was extremely popular and his sense of self-importance expanded. He was a restless man. 'I advocate movement. I am a wanderer,' he told an interviewer. Later, as an addict to warfare, he claimed that 'the character of the Italian people must be moulded by fighting'. With such an outlook he fell victim to delusion. The Italian people generally did not want war and their armed services were neither as strong nor as competent as he believed. Claims that he could 'blot out the Sun with aircraft' or 'mobilise eight million bayonets' were costly fantasies.

His politics moved closer to those of Hitler. In October 1936 the Rome-Berlin Axis pact was signed, an alliance claimed by Mussolini to be a defence against Communism. He intervened to support the Nationalists in the Spanish Civil War. By 1937 more than 70,000 Italian troops had been despatched there, as well as air and naval units. When the Germans occupied Austria in March 1938, Italy did not intervene. 'Tell Mussolini that I will not forget this,' commented a grateful Hitler, 'never, never, never, whatever happens.' *Il Duce* was present at Munich, encouraging the democracies (which he despised) to give way to Germany. The role of mediator suited Mussolini's vain self-opinion.

Yet by early 1939 he felt himself overshadowed by Hitler's territorial successes. The *Führer* certainly never confided his own plans to Mussolini. Therefore, in April 1939 *Il Duce* announced that Albania, just across the Adriatic Sea, would be annexed into his 'empire'. The campaign was easy and short – hardly surprising when the strengths of the two sides are compared.

In May, Mussolini signed an agreement, grandiosely termed the 'Pact of Steel', by which he promised military aid to Germany in the event of war. He hoped and presumed that war would not arrive within the next three or four years, because his forces were quite unready. When the clouds of war approached in August, Mussolini's bluff was called and his promises were

quickly withdrawn. As Britain, France, Germany and Poland locked themselves in fighting, *Il Duce* still struggled not to lose face. Instead of admitting Italy's neutrality, he referred to the position as one of 'non-belligerency'. He decided to wait and see which way the war developed, planning to enter when conditions were suitable for Italy.

**LEFT:** An Italian army ration party. Primarily structured for mountain warfare, the Italian army nevertheless performed badly against the French and later the Greeks.

**BELOW:** Anti-aircraft gunners aboard an Italian warship. At the outbreak of war, Italy had the most powerful battle fleet in the Mediterranean and once France had been defeated, the British were heavily outnumbered.

# United States of America

**RIGHT:** American officers pose by the statue of King Alfred in Winchester, where US troops were stationed in 1918. US intervention in the First World War guaranteed Germany's defeat, but there was little appetite for another intervention in Europe twenty years later. When a second European war broke out in 1939 the overwhelming majority of Americans wished to remain neutral.

The Second World War is regarded mainly as a European struggle, and indeed most of the fighting certainly occurred in that continent. Nonetheless, it should not be forgotten that the war ended in Asia, with the conclusion of hostilities between the Allies, represented primarily by the United States, and Japan. In 1939 both of those countries were at peace with each other and neither became involved when Germany invaded Poland. So what were their reasons for staying neutral?

The origins of the reluctance of the United States to enter the European war can be traced back to 1918. American intervention, from the previous year, had been a deciding factor in the victory gained over Germany. Without the influx of American troops and equipment on the Western Front,

it is at least possible that Britain and France would have failed to win. Woodrow Wilson, the US president, went to Versailles in 1919 with an idealistic view of reforming international relationships. He mistrusted the old ways of diplomacy used by European states. The Fourteen Points for peace that he issued were a blueprint encouraging all countries to live in harmony, under the umbrella of the League of Nations. There would be no more war. To many European statesmen, the document sounded like a reissue of the Ten Commandments.

Sadly, no man is a prophet in his own country, and Wilson's ideas were welcomed by few Americans. Congress would not ratify the Treaty of Versailles and refused to join the League. Most people in the United States did not want to be entangled in

European affairs. The nation had been built largely by emigrants who had turned their backs on an old continent to start a life in the New World. For them, the United States offered freedom and opportunity unfettered by the past. In 1918, many felt that they had done their duty in ending the war and now wanted to shake off involvement in a distant part of the world. At that time, a sea crossing of the Atlantic Ocean could take a week. To the farmer in Nebraska or the shop assistant in Idaho, the empires of the Hapsburgs or the Romanovs were as far removed as another planet. Therefore isolationism grew strong, based on the sentiment that Europeans should manage their own affairs, without American involvement. One writer described isolationists as 'the true believers in the foreign policy of men who conquered and settled the American continental domain'.

During the 1920s, energies in the United States were turned mainly towards economic development and trade, both at home and abroad. Agriculture and industry expanded rapidly, together with building and transport. Standards of living rose generally for a nation intent on existing peacefully and wondering why everyone else could not do the same. There was a dislike of creating huge armed services, especially when no enemies were close at hand. Americans were not troubled by a mass of squabbling groups, separated by no more than ancient, disputed land frontiers. Their Civil War had ended in 1865.

A testing time arrived in 1929 with the Wall Street Crash, which expanded into the Great Depression in world trade. The American economy became a derailed locomotive, carrying the economies of many nations with it, like trucks leaving the track. The heaviest unemployment was found in the United States, where 13 million people were without work by 1933. Under the remarkable leadership of President Roosevelt, there was a slow recovery in trade and industry. His policy, the New Deal, was not popular with opponents, who believed that the plans smacked too strongly of state control, but gradually it succeeded. Unemployment fell while production and trade increased.

LEFT: USS *Wyoming* seen in the 1920s by which time the United States Navy had finally surpassed that of Great Britain to become the largest fleet in the world. The gap grew wider as the British could not afford to modernize their navy in the 1920s and agreed to a series of arms limitation treaties to regulate the size of the world's fleets. Japan signed some, cheated, then renounced them all.

At the same time the US government still favoured a policy of isolation from the affairs of Europe, and as the struggles between dictatorships and democracies developed from 1936, the Americans stayed aloof. Roosevelt suggested ideas for universal disarmament, but to European statesmen they appeared naive and totally impractical, idealistic theories in a tough environment. Dictators never turned the other cheek. America's main relationship with Europe came through trade, which continued with all nations, democracies and dictatorships alike.

In the early 1930s America's armed forces were small in number, with poor equipment, and were incapable of intervening to any great effect anywhere in the world. Having weak forces compelled the United States to employ policies of appeasement towards aggressive nations. This happened particularly in the Far East, an area of special interest to the Americans. The US West Coast was a frontier with the Pacific Ocean and, beyond, with China and Japan. When Japanese expansion began in the 1930s with war against China, the United States did not want to become involved, although her sympathies lay mainly with the Chinese. The American policy of non-intervention in Europe was therefore mirrored in Asia following the public desire to steer clear of war. Even when Japanese bombers sank an American gunboat in Chinese waters in 1937 the US did not retaliate. By 1939, nonetheless, the Americans were increasingly worried by Japanese militarism in the Far East, so they started to rebuild their armed services.

Although the United States still refused to become directly involved in European affairs, which were moving irrevocably towards war, American people generally started to form a dislike of the dictatorships, especially in the later 1930s. For example, German treatment of the Jews angered the powerful Jewish element in the population. Thus a widening sympathy was shown towards Britain and France from 1938 and an increasing flow of armaments was sold to the democracies. However, the Americans took no part in the Munich Conference – not our problem, they reckoned.

Roosevelt knew that his own armed forces were in no position to intervene, even if the American people had wanted them to. They did not. Even as the war opened in 1939, nine out of ten citizens believed in neutrality. Here was a case of 'America First'. At heart, the President realised that such a policy could not last. He then began the tremendous task of persuading the nation to rearm, foreseeing that at some future date the United States could be drawn into a conflict. Nevertheless, even as late as December 1941 the isolationist element in American society still pressed strongly for the nation to stay clear of involvement in the quarrels of others.

# Japan

At the opening of the European war in September 1939 the Japanese Army was already fighting in the Far East. A conflict with China had begun in Manchuria in 1931, developing into a grinding contest which was broken by a truce in 1933. By then, the separate Chinese Nationalist and Communist armies were scrapping with each other as fiercely as they were opposing the invader. War flared again four years later and the Chinese showed greater resistance than expected. When Nanking, the Nationalist capital, was captured the Japanese massacred over 200,000 prisoners and civilians. Other nations learned quickly how ruthless the Japanese Army could be, making them international outcasts.

not exactly similar, is inevitable. Bolstering this view of race, the Japanese nation shared an intense national spirit, resolved to succeed.

The second factor was economic. The islands of Japan had few natural resources and the drive to obtain these propelled the nation's policy after 1900, finally leading to the Second World War. By the early years of the century, the Japanese had already occupied territories in Chinese Manchuria and Korea, treating them as part of an expanding empire. Supplies of iron ore and coal were extracted to feed Japan's rapidly growing industries, which turned raw materials into manufactured goods.

To Westerners, used to dealing in

By 1919 the Japanese had helped the colonial powers to defeat the Chinese Boxer Rebellion (1900), signed a treaty of cooperation with Britain (1902), defeated both the Russian Army and Navy (1904–05) and joined the Entente powers in the First World War. They certainly made a rapid mark in world affairs. However, Japanese leaders gained far less than they expected from the Treaty of Versailles. It was their belief that the colonial powers connived to deny them the rightful fruits of victory. Therefore, they decided to follow their own course of expansion and do it their way. They intended to exercise the type of authority in eastern Asia that Germany was seeking to establish in eastern Europe. In fact, the Japanese received the sobriquet 'The Prussians of Asia'. At the same time, they needed an acceptance of equality from other Great Powers. To the Japanese it was imperative not to 'lose face'.

Throughout the 1930s the Japanese Army and Navy were powerful and their officers controlled or influenced much of the nation's policy. Once again, they were driven by economic needs. The Army looked mainly to the continental mainland, where Korea and Manchuria were the draw. For them, the USSR was the great potential enemy. As Japanese forces fought against China, the possibility of a future war with the Soviet Union was never far from their minds. Thus the eyes and preparations of the Army were turned westwards, planning for land battles. The Navy had a different vision. Their particular need was oil, so they looked eagerly southwards to the enormous supplies available in the Dutch East Indies. Such a tempting sight was too good to be missed.

In Japanese opinion, the main colonial powers – France, Holland, Britain and the United States – were self-seeking intruders with no legitimate right to possess empires in the Far East. Japan alone, they believed, was the Asian power destined to lead. A Japanese officer wrote that '450 million natives of the Far East live under the domination of less than 800,000 whites. If we exclude India, 100 million are oppressed by less than 300,000.' He claimed that 'imposing, splendid buildings look down from the

**ABOVE:** The heavy cruiser *Ashigara* sailed to Europe in 1937 visiting England (for the Spithead review) and Germany. She was torpedoed and sunk in 1945 by the British submarine *Trenchant*.

Why were the Japanese in Manchuria? They were there mainly because of a national urge for expansion, territory and prestige, prompted by two factors. First, the nation viewed itself traditionally as a pure, superior race with a 'divine mission' to govern and lead others. The emperor, Hirohito, treated more as a god than a human being, came from a line over twenty-five centuries old. The Japanese felt a destiny to become Asia's leading power, surrounded by less pure nations, who would be subservient. For example, they despised Koreans and Chinese as inferior people. A comparison with the racial views held in Nazi Germany, although

the Far East with local people as colonial subjects, the Japanese were an enigma. They were proud, independent and competent. In no way would they submit to being someone else's subjects: instead, they themselves wanted to be a colonial power. Japan had isolated herself from the rest of the world until 1853, when American expeditionary vessels arrived, uninvited, in Tokyo Bay. From then until the Treaty of Versailles, the Japanese people were catapulted spectacularly towards achieving the role of the modern state. The transition from medieval society to twentieth-century nation was made in under seventy years.

summits of hills on to the tiny thatched cottages of the natives'. Then he added that 'money squeezed from the blood of Asians' kept white minorities 'in their luxurious mode of life'. The Japanese were keen to imply that they, pure and altruistic, would arrive as saviours.

The British controlled large areas, including Malaya and Sarawak, India and Burma, while to the south lay the Dominions of Australia and New Zealand, as well as many Pacific islands. Hong Kong had been a British colony for a century. The French held Indo-China and various Polynesian islands. The Dutch had an empire in the East Indies, where they had traded since the seventeenth century. The Philippines, heading for independence, were a colony of the United States, which also had other island bases, including Pearl Harbor in Hawaii. A number of these territories provided economic resources, especially oil and rubber – and this was an even greater affront to the Japanese, who lacked them.

In 1933, after being criticised for their earlier invasion of Manchuria, the Japanese left the League of Nations, and, attempting to persuade other Asians to support their policies, they formed 'The Great Asia Association'. This aimed to include China, Siam and the Dutch East Indies as a trading group. The economic benefits to Japan were immense, as raw materials would be available for her industries. The Association later planned a 'Co-Prosperity Sphere' which claimed to bring benefits to all the peoples of East Asia. By late 1941 a branch of the Japanese Ministry of War produced an even more breath-taking vision: Australia and New Zealand would come under Japanese control, as would Alaska and Central America, including the West Indies, while, in the Far East, Ceylon, the East Indies, Burma, Malaya, Indo-China and Siam were also to come under

Japan's wing. Here was ambition to match, if not exceed, Hitler's in another part of the world.

By 1939 the Japanese had already reached agreements with Germany. The two nations signed an anti-Comintern pact in 1936, showing their mutual dislike and distrust of Communist Russia, whose forces stood at the Manchurian border. In that area, two years later, several frontier incidents occurred, with outbreaks of fighting. Consequently, the Japanese were surprised when Hitler signed a non-aggression treaty with the USSR, freeing his hands to attack Poland.

As the Second World War opened in Europe, Japan kept a watchful eye on events. How would they affect her position? Any change in the balance of power there could help her to gain or control the territories she coveted in the Far East. In the meantime, her armed forces would keep their powder dry.

**THE EXPANSION OF JAPAN**

Ruled by the politics of assassination during the 1930s, Japan left the League of Nations and embarked on a collision course with the United States and those European powers occupying colonies in the Far East. Short of resources for modern war, Japan planned a short war of aggression when the time was right. However, border clashes with Russia in 1939 left the Japanese army with a healthy respect for Russian capabilities and little enthusiasm to join Germany's war on Russia in the summer of 1941.

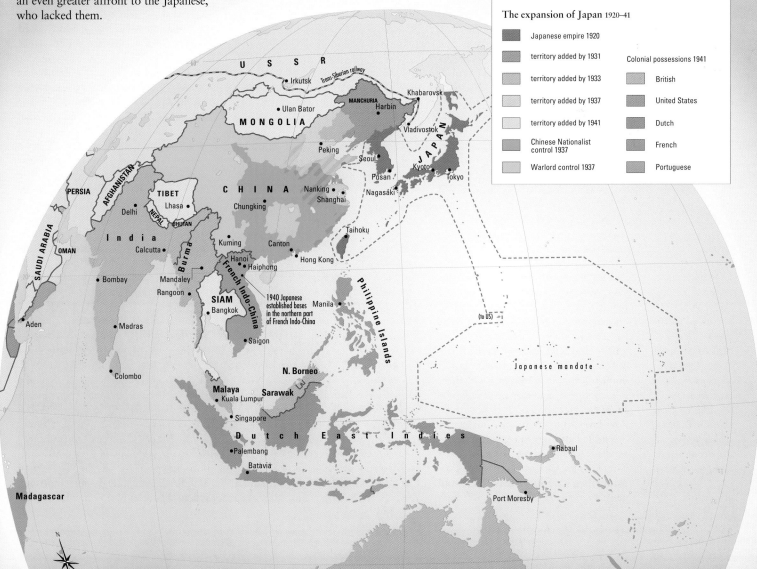

**The expansion of Japan** 1920–41

- Japanese empire 1920
- territory added by 1931
- territory added by 1933
- territory added by 1937
- territory added by 1941
- Chinese Nationalist control 1937
- Warlord control 1937

Colonial possessions 1941
- British
- United States
- Dutch
- French
- Portuguese

1940 Japanese established bases in the northern part of French Indo-China

# National Aims and Strengths

**ABOVE:** Looking little different from their fathers in the First World War, and lugging a machine gun dating from the 1914–18 war, German soldiers take up position on the western front, November 1939. Hitler ordered his forces back from Poland as quickly as possible, still fearing an Allied move in the west.

**RIGHT:** German gunners in action. The 1940 campaign went so quickly and so well that the German high command became understandably complacent. Having swept every opponent from the board, it seemed nothing could stand in the way of Hitler's army.

What were the strengths and weaknesses of the nations going to war in September 1939? Poland, with a population of 34.5 million, had a total armed strength of 370,000 men, with an extra 2.5 million trained reserves. The Polish Army could put 30 divisions into the field, with a further ten in reserve. There were also eleven cavalry brigades, a branch of which the army was very proud, although the First World War had demonstrated the impotence of massed horsemen on the battlefield. Ominously significant was the Polish weakness in mechanised vehicles. Only one cavalry brigade possessed tanks, and none of the infantry divisions was motorised. The army could muster just over 300 tanks, of which 90 were obsolete. In artillery, the Poles were also deficient, with a shortage of anti-tank and anti-aircraft guns.

Poland's particular weakness lay in the air. The Polish Air Force was composed mainly of obsolete bombers and fighters, although their aircrew lacked nothing in bravery. For example, the PZL P.11C fighter was a high-wing monoplane with fixed undercarriage, outclassed in speed, armament and numbers by its opponents. Poland's best bomber, the PZL P.37, was a small, fast machine of which there were only 40 to oppose the *Luftwaffe*.

The Polish hope was that, as soon as the war began, the French Army would invade western Germany. Hitler would then have to withdraw forces to meet the threat. On paper, France,

with a population of 41 million, had powerful land forces. The French pinned their hopes on the army. At the start of hostilities they could mobilise over 100 divisions, 65 of which were active formations. Although some were retained on the Italian frontier, or on colonial duties in North Africa, they were able, after mobilisation, to concentrate some 80 divisions in the area of north-eastern France facing the German border. Most of these consisted of infantry, supported by light armoured divisions and tank brigades. Altogether, the French had almost 2,700 tanks, contrary to the popular belief that the Germans had overwhelming superiority in their panzer armoured divisions. The French Char B series tank was the most powerful armoured vehicle on the Western Front. French forces were also well equipped with artillery, although, significantly, not with anti-aircraft guns.

France also possessed a formidable navy. There were five battleships, two battlecruisers, an aircraft carrier, 60 smaller vessels and 70 submarines. This force alone outweighed anything the Germans had produced. Together with the ships of the Royal Navy, there was the potential to strangle Germany's sea trade, as had been done in the First World War.

The weakness for France lay in air power. There were about 1,000 aircraft, of which half were fighters, but many were obsolete and no match for their opponents in the *Luftwaffe*. A rearmament programme for the *Armée*

*de l'Air* was under way, but it was not expected to be complete before 1942. Therefore the large French armies could be offered little aerial protection. The aircraft programme which was begun in the late 1930s was disastrous. The Morane-Saulnier MS.406 fighter was too slow, while other types suffered from a lack of spare parts, or from undertrained aircrew.

What of the British contribution? Unlike many European nations, Britain had no conscription for its 46 million people until the spring of 1939. At hand was a small, well-trained Regular Army, and Territorial detachments were preparing in order to supply enough soldiers to stand by the French on the Western Front. Consequently, in the autumn months of 1939 no more than four infantry divisions, together with 50 tanks, were sent from the United Kingdom to France. The aim was to achieve improvement in 1940. The conscription, equipping and training of soldiers was a slow business, especially for a nation which traditionally maintained only a small army.

In defence strength Britain relied far more on the Royal Navy, its bastion for centuries. For an imperial power, here was a force to match or exceed any other in the world. Ready for action in ascending order of size were 58 submarines, 184 destroyers and 64 cruisers. These supported seven aircraft carriers, three battlecruisers and twelve battleships. Among the many other warships then building or pro-

**'PLAN YELLOW'**

German war plans, like American ones, were code-named by colour. The original plan of operations for the invasion of the west was a conventional advance on a broad front. Hitler's generals expected they could conquer the Netherlands and much of Belgium, possibly entering north-west France by the time winter brought an end to active operations. Given the weaknesses of the French army exposed by the actual invasion, the result might have been the same, but this original plan would have given the Allies a lot longer to coordinate their efforts.

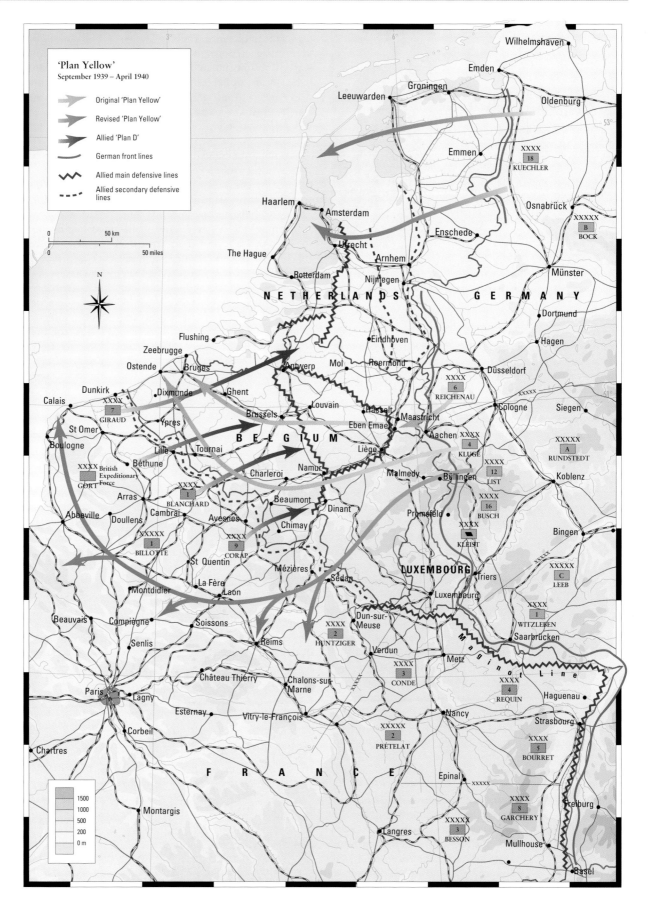

'Plan Yellow'
September 1939 – April 1940

Original 'Plan Yellow'
Revised 'Plan Yellow'
Allied 'Plan D'
German front lines
Allied main defensive lines
Allied secondary defensive lines

0    50 km
0    50 miles

N

1500
1000
500
200
0 m

ABOVE: German troops pass a pre-war concrete blockhouse during the invasion of France, May 1940. Hitler anticipated a showdown with Russia rather than a war in the west and expected the British and French to negotiate rather than fight. He was doubly surprised when the British fought on after France's collapse in 1940.

RIGHT: Hitler's naval Commander-in-Chief, Admiral Raeder, was taken aback by the outbreak of war. His plans assumed a war no earlier than the mid-1940s and his concentration on surface ships rather than submarines suggested a readiness for conflict with France or Russia, but not Great Britain.

jected were a further nine battleships and six carriers. This massive fleet could operate across all oceans and threaten Germany's sea trade – in the long run. However, in the short term it could render little help to Poland or affect Hitler's land campaigns on the continental mainland. Battleships could not sail up the Rhine.

From the mid-1930s Britain made increasingly urgent efforts to expand air power. The Royal Air Force grew rapidly to meet the growing threat from the *Luftwaffe*, whose numbers we now know were exaggerated. Bombers such as the Wellington, Whitley and Hampden were developed to launch daylight aerial raids on economic targets in Germany, while light bombers were sent to France after the outbreak of war to support ground forces. At the same time the development of large four-engine bombers was started from 1936, but these would not be ready for about five years. For home defence, Fighter Command was expanded. As fighter design and performance changed radically just before the war, Hurricanes and Spitfires were built, and at a stroke older biplanes were rendered obsolete. The trouble for Britain was that in September 1939 Bomber Command was in no position by itself to alter the course of a war, while there were insufficient modern fighters to defend both the homeland and the forces in France simultaneously.

The RAF then had about 2,500 aircraft, but of these only 26 squadrons comprised Hurricanes or Spitfires. Of 55 squadrons in Bomber Command less than half were at operational

strength. Although plans had been laid for bombing targets in Germany, some were 'recognised by their authors at the time as resting on future hopes rather than on present capability'. They were in no position to stop Hitler's drive to the east.

A great strength for the United Kingdom was the latent potential of the Commonwealth and Empire. As in 1914, those nations soon responded by entering the war against Britain's enemies. Thus huge resources of manpower, training areas and strategic bases round the world became available. However, in the short term the help offered, from territories as distant as New Zealand and Canada, the West Indies and South Africa and India and Australia, was limited. There could be no rapid flow of troops, tanks and aircraft to Europe. Germany, therefore, did not suffer the disadvantages that could only come from a long campaign. Hitler was seeking a quick knock-out.

'The German Army was not ready for war in 1939,' wrote Liddell Hart, 'a war which its chiefs did not expect,

relying on Hitler's assurance.' Certainly Nazi planners were not anticipating full-scale war for another three or four years. Nevertheless, of the combatants, the German armed forces were the best prepared and situated on 1 September 1939. Germany, unified with Austria in the previous year, had a population numbering about 75 million. Nearly 100 divisions could be raised, of which 52 were active divisions. Ten others would be fit for action when mobilised.

In many ways, most of the German Army's divisions were similar to those of their opponents, with large masses of slow-moving infantry. Much of the equipment was still horse-drawn. The difference, however, lay in its use of a small number of well-equipped divisions, quite unlike those of Britain, France or Poland. They consisted of four mechanised and four motorised divisions, together with six armoured divisions. These were the panzer formations which were about to revolutionise land warfare. For some observers, this small element was worth more than the whole remainder of the German Army. The highly mobile armoured force was stationed on the Polish borders, together with 27 infantry divisions, ready for a well-planned offensive.

To meet the risk on the French frontier, Army Group C was stationed to hold off any attack from French and British forces and, within a week, totalled about 40 divisions. These were positioned behind the Siegfried Line, a series of defences built in the 1930s to face the Maginot Line. From the start of hostilities the Allies did not invade western Germany to take the pressure off Poland. Critics usually overlook how unready the democracies were for war. Much time is needed to train armies. No British force took up position until early October. The French, especially after the costly failure of some of their offensives in the First World War, had changed strategy. They were now prepared to sit tight and fight a different campaign.

At sea the German Navy (*Kriegsmarine*) was considerably outweighed and outgunned by the Allied fleets. Admiral Raeder, the Commander-in-Chief, was another leader who believed that there would be no general war, especially as a rebuilding programme had been started which would not be completed for four years. 'Raeder considered Hitler's acceptance of the programme to be a guarantee that no war with Britain would be started soon.' Nonetheless, three pocket-battleships and two battlecruisers were already in service, together with six cruisers, seventeen destroyers and 56 submarines. Two very powerful battleships were being built. Of particular concern to the Allies was the U-boat fleet. In 1917–18 it had come close to eroding Britain's ability to stay in the First World War by sinking an enormous tonnage of merchant shipping. It was obvious that, once again, the Germans would attempt to strangle Britain's sea trade.

The greatest strength of the German armed forces in 1939 lay in the *Luftwaffe*. Here was the world's most powerful and best-trained air force, although its numbers had been overestimated by the British and French. A nucleus of aircrew had gained invaluable battle experience serving with the Condor Legion during the Spanish Civil War. At that time, the future role of the *Luftwaffe* had been decided. It developed particularly as a tactical air force used in close support of ground forces. Aircraft became a form of flying artillery, clearing the way for land attacks.

In total strength the *Luftwaffe* possessed just over 4,000 aircraft. Of these, 770 were Messerschmitt Bf 109s, fast, single-seat, low-wing monoplane fighters which were matched only by Hurricanes and Spitfires. A further 400 aircraft were Me 110 twin-engine fighters. The Germans could deploy nearly 1,200 medium bombers of which the biggest, the Heinkel He 111, carried some two and a half tons of bombs. The Junkers Ju 87 Stuka dive-bomber, of which there were 336, gave the whole German offensive a cutting edge.

A view held in a number of diplomatic circles was that although the Germans had the ability to fight a short, explosive conflict, they would not be able to maintain a long war. As the German armed forces grew after 1933, the nation needed new sources

of materials. Among other weaknesses, the Reich itself lacked, for example, tin, rubber, bauxite and cotton. There were only limited supplies of oil, iron ore, manganese and sulphur. With the seizure of Czechoslovakia in April 1939 the Germans gained armaments works and the equipment of the Czech Army, especially tanks. Nonetheless, economic troubles continued. 'In early 1939,' wrote a commentator, 'the regime had to reduce the *Wehrmacht*'s steel allocations by 30 per cent, copper by 20 per cent, aluminium by 47 per cent [and] rubber by 30 per cent.' As late as August, a report pointed out that aviation fuel would last only for four months of war. Coupled with

these shortages were the threats posed by an Allied naval blockade. Even after the early German successes, when Hitler was casting covetous eyes at Russian territory, he admitted, 'I need the Ukraine so that they cannot starve us out as they did in the last war.' Thus there were strong economic motives behind Hitler's drive for new conquests.

France and Britain lacked many of the materials needed for war but through their geographical positions were able to obtain them by sea. At

the time, both relied heavily on coal for motive power in industry and transport. Britain particularly had ample supplies. Territories of the Empire and Commonwealth were rich in such commodities as rubber, cotton, nickel and copper. France had a large agricultural production, whereas most of Britain's food had to be imported. Much meat came from Australia or New Zealand and wheat from North America. Oceans were highways for the Allies, enabling them to trade in a manner unavailable to the Germans. The threat, especially for Britain, would come from German naval campaigns against merchant shipping. Nations can be defeated in

the economic arena as readily as on the battlefield.

At the outbreak of fighting, pundits visualised two possible outcomes. In the first, the Germans would benefit from a short, sharp campaign, much as an aggressive boxer knocks out his opponent in the first round. In the second, if the Allies could stem the opening attacks and blunt the offensive, a long, grinding war would ensue. Economic weaknesses then would overtake Germany, leading to her defeat.

**ABOVE:** German war production declined in 1940 as Hitler assumed the war was as good as won. After the catastrophe in Russia, Hitler appointed Albert Speer to coordinate German industry and productivity soared. Seen here in February 1942, Speer announces his appointment as Reichsminister for weapons and munitions.

# CHAPTER 2: German Success

## The Polish Campaign

German armed forces opened the invasion of Poland with several advantages. The first was geographical. In front of them stretched the great Polish plain, providing excellent terrain for a swift advance, especially for armoured forces. Although few good roads existed, these were arteries leading to the heart of the country and were well used by the invaders.

Secondly, the weather was dry, so the countryside offered a firm, hard surface for armoured vehicles.

The campaign was mainly a three-fold thrust. Army Group North attacked from Pomerania and soon overran Polish forces attempting to defend the Corridor. They then pushed south-eastwards towards the interior. In support was an advance from East Prussia, where the German Third Army had been stationed. As well as helping to take Danzig and the Corridor, this drove southwards, aiming to cut off retreating Polish troops. Its progress took it towards Warsaw, the capital. The third, and main, push came from Army Group South, which entered from Slovakia and Silesia with a strong drive eastwards. By the time

that Britain and France joined the war on 3 September, German forces had already won crushing victories, making spectacular advances into Polish territory.

Panzer warfare was new, employed against an army composed largely of infantry. The Poles had little time to mobilise and lacked mobility. On 5 September Hitler visited the front line and saw the remains of a smashed Polish artillery regiment. He asked Guderian if dive-bombers had caused the damage. 'When I replied, "No, our panzers!" he was plainly astonished.' The Poles had no answer to the speed and ferocity of armoured assault. One corps advanced 140 miles in the first week.

None of this success could have been achieved without the close co-operation of the *Luftwaffe*. The Polish Campaign was a classic example of coordination between land and air forces in which bombers were employed as airborne artillery. Here was an innovation in the style of war – and lessons were subsequently learned by all other combatant nations. In the first stage, *Luftwaffe* raids destroyed

many Polish aircraft on the ground before passing on to bomb or strafe railways and road centres, together with enemy troops and strongpoints.

In general, the Poles were forced to retreat, but occasionally their counter-attacks had some success. For example, from 10 September, in the Battle of Bzura, German infantry were driven back. However, under General von Rundstedt, panzer divisions of the Tenth Army, closely supported by Stukas, turned the defenders' flank. On 19 September, 170,000 Poles were surrounded and forced to surrender. An obvious target for the invaders was Warsaw. German forces reached the city on 8 September but, faced with strong resistance, could not take it. By then, Polish armies, short of supplies, were disjointed in various parts of the country and were under unrelenting pressure.

Then came the fatal blow to Polish hopes. Before dawn on 17 September the Russian Army entered Poland from the east. Russian troops had been told that they were 'liberating the Polish workers from the yoke of the landowners' and their advance was

LEFT: Temporary friends: the crew of a Russian BA-20 armoured car talk to some of their German allies during the invasion of Poland. Stalin's alliance with Hitler stunned liberal opinion in Europe where many intellectuals accepted Communist propaganda at face value. It was not widely known that Russian military cooperation with Germany had begun in the 1920s and included the provision of training areas.

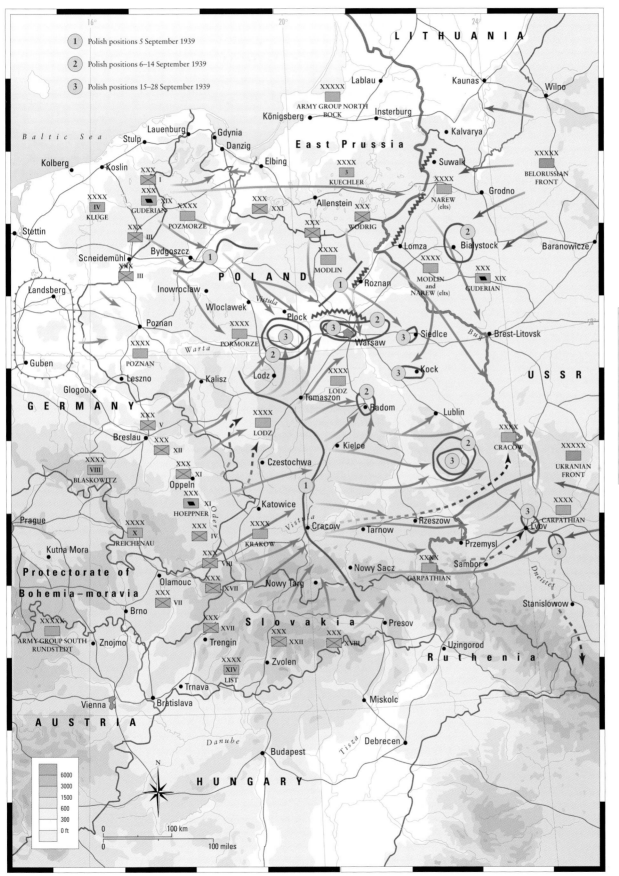

Polish positions 5 September 1939

Polish positions 6–14 September 1939

Polish positions 15–28 September 1939

## Campaign in Poland
### 1–28 September 1939

→ German advance

→ Russian advance

⇢ Polish retreat

ᐱᐱᐱ German field work

ᐱᐱᐱ Polish defensive lines

⌒ Polish positions

— German-Russian demarcation line

## CAMPAIGN IN POLAND

The Polish campaign lasted just under a month. Hopelessly outnumbered and technically outclassed, the Poles fought with great bravery but with the French and British forces remaining passive in the west, Germany was able to throw its full weight into the assault. The Russian invasion from the east was the final straw. Luckily for Britain, a good number of Polish pilots escaped the final collapse and would play a key role in the Battle of Britain.

**RIGHT:** Polish aircraft on the eve of war: the distinctive gull-winged PZL fighters in the background were highly manoeuvrable but under-gunned by comparison with the German Bf 109s. The Germans deployed over 1,500 aircraft against the 400 or so modern machines operated by the Poles. By 6 September, the Polish air force was effectively destroyed.

rapid. Most formations of the Polish Army had been moved to meet the German invasion and were, at that stage, in the death-throes of defeat. Some Poles at first believed the Russians to be liberators who had come to assist them against the Nazis. They soon discovered their error. A little fighting occurred before all Polish resistance was overcome and German and Russian soldiers came face to face on 20 September.

Various pockets of fighters remained to be eliminated by the invaders. After heavy bombardment from both land and air, the troops in Warsaw capitulated on 27 September. Other defending armies struggled on and fighting finally ended eight days later. By then over 100,000 Polish servicemen had managed to reach Rumania or Hungary. Later, after extraordinary journeys, some made their way to France and Britain, where they were able to continue the war. Yet the Germans took about 700,000 prisoners.

Hitler had told his generals earlier in the year that his intention was not merely to defeat Poland militarily; his additional aim was to obliterate the Polish nation, whom he regarded as racially inferior. This policy was soon put into practice as the Nazis quickly introduced their own form of government into western Poland. For the local inhabitants the consequences were disastrous. In the eastern sector, Communist rule was established. Shortly, all former Polish army officers there were sent to camps in Russia, especially Katyn. Their fate was sealed. Stalin, too, was prepared to allow Poland to be obliterated, as the two dictatorships worked together in agreement.

# All Quiet on the Western Front

Any Polish hopes that the French would come to their aid by invading Germany were soon dashed. How was it that two nations with the combined power of France and Great Britain sat back while on the other side of Europe the German and Russian assault was carving up their ally? Later, several German generals expressed surprise that the French did not immediately launch an invasion. 'We were surprised that France did not attack Germany during the Polish Campaign,' stated Keitel after the war. 'Any form of attack would have shaken our screen of 25 reserve divisions and could only have encountered feeble resistance.' In reality, the French had laid plans for an offensive but did not put them into practice: the policy followed by France's military leaders was to sit tight behind the strength of the Maginot Line.

The proposed advance into German territory was code-named Operation 'Saar', and details had been issued to the French Army in July 1939. The attack boiled down to little more than a reconnaissance carried out across a narrow section of the frontier in the area of Saarbrücken. By then the German defences stood at over 40, not 25, divisions. Starting on 7 September, troops of the French Third and Fourth Armies were able to occupy about seven miles of German territory before coming to a halt in front of the defences of the Siegfried Line. By 13 September the Commander-in-Chief of the French forces was warning his generals to be cautious. They already were. Their forces suffered fewer than 100 casualties and this action amounted to no more than a small dent in the German line. As French forces ground to a halt, the Germans hastened to reinforce the frontier. With the Polish Campaign rapidly finishing, Nazi troops were transferred across Europe. Helping the speed of transfer was an excellent lateral road and rail transport system.

Hitler was now forced to confront enemies who, he had been convinced, would not fight. He had to face the consequences of his misjudgement. What were his plans in late 1939? First, he recognised (as a number of Allied leaders believed) that a long war would work to Germany's disadvan-

tage. German superiority in anti-tank and anti-aircraft guns would not last long, so his relative strength in aircraft and panzer divisions could soon disappear. British industrial capacity was only just starting to expand and would grow steadily. Secondly, Germany needed naval and air bases along the Channel coast in order to protect vulnerable areas like the industrial Ruhr. To achieve these aims, Hitler decided that the Allied powers should be crushed as soon as possible. A number of his generals, however, harboured grave doubts, estimating that their armies lacked the strength to defeat the combined forces of Britain and France. Nevertheless, in spite of their misgivings, on 9 October they were ordered to draw up plans.

By the end of the month a scheme was in being. Based partly on the Schlieffen Plan, it proposed an attack on France by invading neutral Holland and Belgium. Over 100 divisions, fifteen of which were motorised or armoured, would drive towards the Channel coast. The Germans knew that as soon as they entered Belgium, the Allies would send in troops to help

the defenders. Consequently, they hoped to overwhelm French and British armies in that zone. It appeared that, once again, northern France and Belgium would be slaughter grounds. The attack was to open on 12 November.

On 7 November, however, meteorological reports predicted bad weather and the offensive was postponed. With the start of winter fog and frost, freezing winds and sleet, Hitler's plans over the next month were frustrated by the climate. To make matters worse for the Germans, one of their officers, carrying complete plans for the western attack, was in an aircraft which made a forced landing in Belgium on 10 January 1940. Before long these plans had been passed to the Allies. There were three particular results. First, the neutrals realised that, when the main battle started, their frontiers would not be respected. Secondly, British and French forces were spared from immediate assault. Nonetheless, the third result in the long run was to have a devastating effect: the Germans had to devise a different strategy of attack.

**ABOVE:** A field telephonist of a British artillery battery seen during the winter of 1939–40. British infantry divisions had excellent field artillery but lacked the plentiful mortars and light howitzers with which their German opposite numbers were equipped. The British had tremendous firepower but it was not employed with the same flexibility as the Germans managed to achieve.

# The Phoney War

The period from October 1939 to April 1940 is usually known as 'The Phoney War'. For the French this was the *drôle de guerre*; the Germans called it the *Sitzkrieg*, or sitting-down war. Churchill later referred to 'a prolonged and oppressive pause' in which, apparently, both sides were widespread across Europe, and all combatant nations went to great lengths to counter it by extensive service and civilian defences. However, the storm of bombs anticipated by the inhabitants of Paris, Berlin and London never arrived. In reality, at this stage none of the air forces sands of inhabitants to safer areas. Thousands left of their own accord to live with relatives or friends in the countryside. Sometimes a happy relationship grew between evacuees and their hosts; on other occasions there were misunderstandings when town met country, with little common

either unwilling or unable to embark on major campaigns.

One of the war's most remarkable features was what failed to happen at the start in the air. Throughout the previous twenty years, 'experts' from several nations had predicted that future conflicts would be settled in short time by the power of bombing; towns and cities would be devastated by an onslaught of gas, high-explosive and incendiary bombs which would rapidly break civilian morale. Within a few days panic-stricken civilians would force their governments to sue for peace.

The fear of aerial bombing was involved had either the policy or the strength to launch such massive raids. For the time being, the great European cities were spared.

One of the greatest effects on British civilians, in both town and countryside, came from evacuation. From London alone, between 1 and 3 September 1939, about 1¼ million people were moved under the official scheme. Many came from 'the poorest and most congested areas near river and dockside, railway yards and gasworks, where the threat of bombing was so obvious.' Other large and potentially vulnerable cities, such as Manchester and Birmingham, also despatched thou-

ground. By the end of the Phoney War many evacuees had returned to the cities. The feared aerial devastation had not arrived, and the danger appeared to have passed. There was no place like home – so back they went.

With the coming of war all governments assumed extra powers. In Germany, a dictatorship, this made little difference to people's lives. For the French and British, nevertheless, personal freedoms were curbed. In Britain people were prepared to put their previous democratic rights 'on ice' for the duration, although keeping a watchful eye on them. They accepted that, even in a democracy, a government would

ABOVE: German troops are landed in the Norwegian capital, Oslo, April 1940. Although the Allies planned to occupy Norway, the Germans struck first. Despite Allied naval superiority, the Germans gambled on speed and surprise and got away with it. Once the Norwegian air fields were in their hands, the Germans were able to drive off Allied warships and dominate local waters from the air.

need autocratic powers. This they agreed to voluntarily – but cautiously.

The first commodity to be restricted in Britain was petrol. It was rationed on 22 September but taken off three months later. Food rationing began in January 1940, with sugar, butter and bacon, followed in March by meat. In Germany, ration cards of different colours for various foods were issued – for example, blue for meat, pink for flour and bread and red for groceries. At that stage of war, however, there were few food shortages. The Allied blockade did little to prevent supplies from reaching Germany. Pre-war estimates that the Germans would suffer economic collapse showed more hope than judgement, and goods and raw materials continued to arrive in a steady stream from Russia, Italy and Sweden. On the British side, the import of materials was not yet affected by the U-boat campaign.

In accordance with plans laid before the war, the British Expeditionary Force was despatched to France, as the soldiers' fathers had been a quarter of a century earlier. The men were to take up positions supporting French troops. By the end of September, ships of the Royal Navy and Merchant Navy had transported over 160,000 servicemen and 24,000 vehicles. These troops were under the overall command of Lord Gort. They included 36 Regular battalions in the 1st and 2nd

Divisions of I Corps and in the 3rd and 4th Divisions of II Corps. By 12 October they had taken over a section of the front along the Belgian border with a French army positioned at each side.

Both Germany and the Allies showed a wary interest in the Low Countries. For their part the Allies made arrangements to send forces into Belgium in the event of a German invasion, giving support to the Belgian Army. On the other side, the Germans laid new plans. They intended to open their forthcoming attack in the West by invading Belgian territory but would make a main thrust through the wooded area of the Ardennes. From there they would swing round to cut off and annihilate Allied forces in Belgium. For the remainder of the Phoney War both sides watched and waited.

In Britain one politician above all others showed qualities of decisive leadership in war. Winston Churchill, from the start, encouraged a spirit of action, and soon Hitler recognised him as a powerful opponent. In his speech of 6 October suggesting peace at the end of the Polish Campaign, the *Führer* said, 'If, however, the opinions of Messrs Churchill and his followers should prevail, this statement will have been my last.' As First Sea Lord, Churchill was perturbed by the amount of Swedish iron ore that was

reaching Germany by sea, and to prevent this trade he suggested sowing mines in Norwegian territorial waters, through which the ships passed. On 9 April 1940 this was the region of Europe where the Phoney War ended.

**ABOVE:** British troops in France, occupying a trench system just like their fathers did in 1914–18. The positions occupied in the winter of 1939–40 were promptly abandoned in the spring when the Allies sent their best divisions into Belgium to forestall what they believed would be the main German assault.

**LEFT:** A stereoscopic range-finder at a French army observation post. The French were determined to fight from behind concrete fortifications in 1939 because these had proved so effective in the First World War. The famous Maginot Line was intended to inflict heavy losses on the German attackers but Belgian intransigence prevented its extension sufficiently far north.

# Finland

ABOVE: Some of the thousands of Russians taken prisoner by the Finns during the 'Winter War of 1939–40'. The Russian invasion of Finland was a shambles, exposing the damage done by Stalin's purge of the Red Army's commanders. It led Hitler to conclude that 'one kick and the whole rotten edifice will cave in'.

BELOW: Finnish troops with a captured Russian OT-64A flame-thrower tank. Stalin sent 26 divisions and 1,500 tanks against Finland's 10 divisions on 30 November 1939 but after a month of fighting, the Finnish defences held and they were even launching local counter-attacks.

While the opposing forces sat inactively on the Western Front, a short but brutal war broke out in northern Europe. From 30 November 1939 until 12 March 1940 the giant USSR was locked in conflict with Finland, a small country. For much of the nineteenth century Finland had been part of the Russian Empire but from 1917 was recognised as an independent state.

Yet Finland's geographical position brought trouble. From the time of the Munich Crisis of 1938 the Russians feared that the day might arrive when the Germans would attack them. The Nazi-Soviet pact of 1939 was a temporary agreement between two states concerned only with their own interests; it was no lasting pathway to sweetness and light. Therefore the Russians set out to improve their defences against any future German assault. One vulnerable Soviet city was Leningrad, which lay close to Finnish territory. The Russians asked for alter-

ations to be made to the frontier and for a Finnish port to be leased as a naval base, giving greater protection to Leningrad. In return, the Russians offered Finland larger stretches of territory along less vital areas of their mutual frontier.

Not surprisingly, the Finnish government declined. Talks between delegations came to nothing, and on 30 November 1939 the Red Army invaded, while Russian aircraft bombed the capital, Helsinki. Goliath had assaulted David, and popular sympathies lay with the underdog. The Russians, possessing over 3,000 tanks, were taking on an army which had none. To everyone's amazement, the Finns scored early successes, fighting cannily among marshes and forests. The Russians, with poor leaders and tactics, suffered ten times as many casualties as the Finns in early battles and lost over 1,500 tanks. By February 1940, nonetheless, Russian numbers were telling and the Finns were forced to sue for peace. They had to cede territory but had won a moral victory.

This small, distant campaign affected the Second World War. Britain and France prepared a force of 100,000 men to help the Finns, although they were never despatched. In France, this muddled policy led to the dismissal of the prime minister, Daladier. By intervention in Finland, Churchill saw the opportunity of cutting the supply route of iron ore between Sweden and Germany. On the German side, the poor showing of the Russian Army gave Hitler confidence over his intended attack on the USSR. Moreover, he knew that Finland would be an ally against the USSR in that forthcoming extension of the war.

The main immediate effect of the campaign, however, was to concentrate the *Führer*'s attention on Scandinavia. At all costs he had to ensure that supplies of iron ore were not stopped by the Allied blockade. If necessary he would send armed forces to Norway before the British intervened there. A military operation was quickly planned.

LEFT: A Russian T-28 tank lies abandoned in Finland. Extensive breakdowns caused by poor maintenance were one result of the execution or imprisonment of so many officers. Loyalty to the Communist Party was no substitute for technical knowledge once in battle in the Finnish forests.

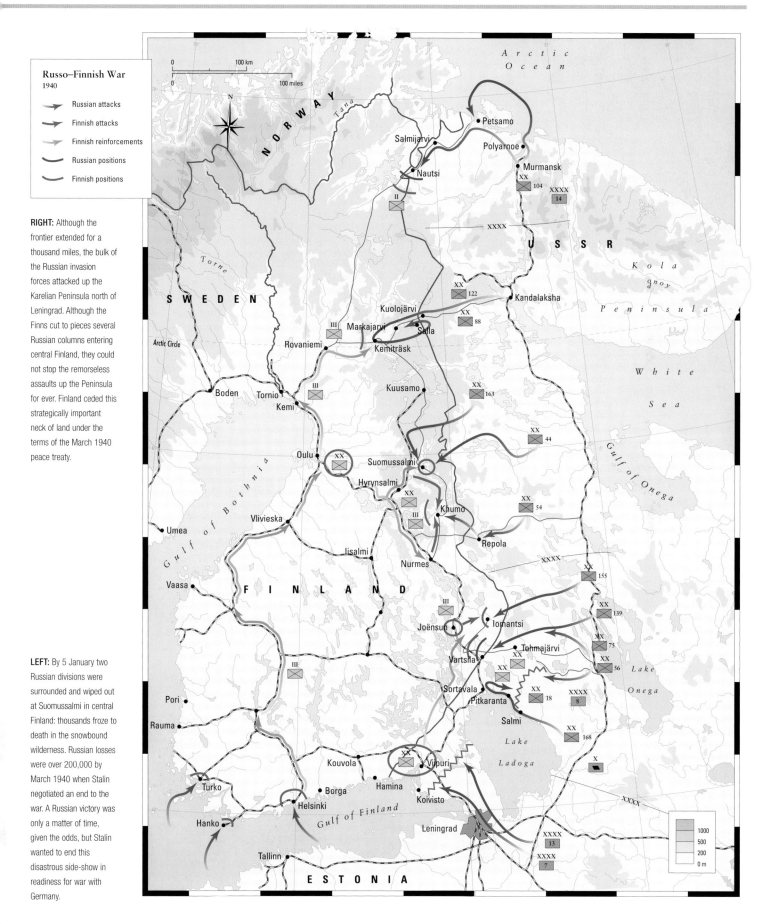

**Russo–Finnish War**
1940

→ Russian attacks

→ Finnish attacks

→ Finnish reinforcements

⌣ Russian positions

⌣ Finnish positions

**RIGHT:** Although the frontier extended for a thousand miles, the bulk of the Russian invasion forces attacked up the Karelian Peninsula north of Leningrad. Although the Finns cut to pieces several Russian columns entering central Finland, they could not stop the remorseless assaults up the Peninsula for ever. Finland ceded this strategically important neck of land under the terms of the March 1940 peace treaty.

**LEFT:** By 5 January two Russian divisions were surrounded and wiped out at Suomussalmi in central Finland: thousands froze to death in the snowbound wilderness. Russian losses were over 200,000 by March 1940 when Stalin negotiated an end to the war. A Russian victory was only a matter of time, given the odds, but Stalin wanted to end this disastrous side-show in readiness for war with Germany.

# The War at Sea, September 1939 – April 1940

ABOVE: This dramatic image was taken from the German heavy cruiser *Hipper* as the crippled British destroyer *Glowworm* steers in to ram during their battle off the Norwegian coast. Her CO, Lieutenant-Commander Broadmead Roope was awarded a posthumous Victoria Cross for this gallant attempt to cripple the *Hipper*.

RIGHT: The German heavy cruiser *Admiral Graf Spee*, one of the class dubbed 'pocket battleships' by the Allied press. Deployed to the Atlantic prior to the declaration of war, she preyed on British merchant ships in the South Atlantic and Indian Oceans until cornered off the River Plate in December 1939. Her ignominious scuttling after an indecisive action against British cruisers made headlines around the world.

At the start of the Second World War both sides recollected the importance of naval warfare a quarter of a century earlier. In 1917–18 the German U-boat campaign had brought about the sinking of so many ships that Britain was in danger of being forced out of the war. On the other side, by 1918 the Allied blockade of the Central Powers was a deciding factor in the overthrow of Germany. Consequently, in 1939 both appreciated the role played by operations at sea in ensuring victory. They laid careful plans to utilise naval power.

The German Navy relied heavily on submarines. From the start it employed about 25 ocean-going U-boats to attack trade routes. The combined British and French merchant fleets totalled 24 million tons, so there was no shortage of targets. Altogether during the Phoney War about 800,000 tons of British shipping was sunk. On the very first day of the war, the liner *Athenia* was torpedoed and sunk by *U-30* off the coast of Ireland, while sailing to Canada. A total of 112 passengers were lost. From that moment until the end of hostilities in 1945 the Battle of the Atlantic continued without intermission.

A brilliant submarine operation was carried out on 14 October by *U-47*, which secretly penetrated the Royal Navy's main base at Scapa Flow. Once inside, she torpedoed and sank the battleship *Royal Oak* before escaping. The *coup* was a blow to the prestige of the Royal Navy and proof of the value of submarine warfare.

Britain's greatest triumph in this period occurred in December 1939.

Lacking the power to match Allied naval strength in surface vessels, the Germans used two pocket-battleships as commerce raiders. One of these, *Admiral Graf Spee*, opened attacks on merchantmen from 30 September, operating in both the South Atlantic and Indian Oceans. By 13 December she had sunk nine vessels totalling 50,000 tons. But early that morning she encountered three Royal Navy cruisers near the River Plate, off the coast of South America. After a running battle, *Graf Spee* put into neutral Montevideo harbour, Uruguay, for repairs. Fearing that a large British naval force was gathering outside, the German captain scuttled his ship near the harbour on 17 December and later shot himself. His crew were interned.

The war at sea in this period offered one more happy surprise for the British. The German cargo ship *Altmark* had acted as a supply vessel to *Graf Spee* in the South Atlantic. When the pocket-battleship stopped and sank merchantmen, the captured crews were transferred to *Altmark*. On 16 February 1940 the latter was sailing back to Germany with some 300 prisoners aboard and had reached Jössingfjord in neutral southern Norway. A Royal Navy destroyer, ignoring Norwegian protests, sailed into territorial waters and an armed boarding party rescued the men. Furious argument followed over who had broken international law, the British or the Germans. The released prisoners had no doubts.

After this, Hitler realised that Britain would no longer respect Norwegian territorial waters. As his supplies of iron ore from Sweden passed through those waters, he would have to respond.

# The War in the Air, September 1939 – April 1940

Although pre-war estimates of the extent of aerial conflict were soon shown to be inaccurate, both sides sparred actively during the Phoney War, and lessons were learned which affected the strategy and tactics of both the *Luftwaffe* and the Royal Air Force at later stages.

Both were constrained by government regulations regarding attacks on civilians. 'It is against international law to bomb civilians as such,' Chamberlain announced in 1938, 'or to make deliberate attacks upon the civilian population.' As war started, the British government pledged that bombardments would be confined to 'strictly military

factories. However, Hitler's Directive No 1, issued on 31 August 1939, ordered the German Air Force to defend its own territory, especially the industrial Ruhr, and to dislocate Allied shipping, but to avoid raids on the British mainland. Over subsequent weeks attacks were made on Royal Navy ships in the North Sea and at Scottish naval bases. These worried the Admiralty so much that in mid-October British naval units were moved to the Clyde, on the west coast of Scotland. The *Luftwaffe* had scored a strategic success.

For the remainder of the Phoney War, German aircraft were widely employed in minelaying at night along

if assaulted with 3,000 sorties, at a cost of fewer than 200 aircraft. Such optimism would prove costly.

The hopes were moonshine. On 3 September 1939 Bomber Command had 920 aircraft in 55 squadrons but, because of the numbers which had to sent to France, only 352 were available for a strategic bombing offensive. Any success would have to wait for the arrival of the new generation of heavy bombers, planned from 1936–37. Furthermore, both service leaders and politicians were apprehensive that RAF attacks on Germany would lead to retaliation; the French also feared that Bomber Command raids from their

objectives'. Hitler also asserted that his air force would 'not make war against women and children'. Both governments then covered themselves by saying that the undertakings would apply only if their opponents followed suit. Obviously, if one broke the rules, retribution would follow.

The limitations affected what air forces were able to achieve. From pre-war days the *Luftwaffe* recognised the difficulty of devastating Britain by bombing, a fact unappreciated in the United Kingdom at the time. Unless the Germans were able to gain airfields in the Low Countries, aircraft would have to fly directly from Germany, with a limited range and a small bomb load.

In planning, the German High Command had selected two chief types of target. The first was shipping, which was to be hit with bombs, mines and torpedoes. The second was certain mainland areas containing docks and

Britain's east coast and in the Channel. Heinkel He 115 seaplanes were used, especially when magnetic mines were introduced. Thus the *Luftwaffe* played an important role in the early stages of the struggle at sea.

What of the RAF? During the first seven months of war, Bomber Command tried to put into practice some of the theories held for the previous twenty years. Sir Hugh Trenchard, 'The Father of the RAF', influenced the Air Staff with the opinion that the best form of aerial defence was to attack the enemy with bombers; in his view, they alone could bring victory by crippling an enemy's economy and breaking civilian morale. Estimates were made before the war, with a list of targets set out in 'The Western Air Plans'. These included German power stations, road, rail and waterway transport, and oil supplies. The Air Staff believed that Germany's war effort would collapse in a fortnight

territory would bring a German aerial assault in response. Consequently Bomber Command opened the war with two types of target. The first was warships in the North Sea area; the second was civilians, whose fate was to be deluged with thousands of propaganda leaflets, referred to by aircrew as 'confetti' or 'lavatory paper'.

In the early days of the war, Wellington and Blenheim bombers crossed the North Sea to strike at German warships, but with little effect. The turning point came in December. In a series of daylight raids, bombers were detected by German radar, then engaged by anti-aircraft guns and fighters. On 14 December half of the raiders were lost, while four days later the casualty rate rose to over 60%. Such losses could not be sustained. Policy changed, and Bomber Command turned to attacks by night.

**ABOVE:** Skua dive bombers of the Fleet Air Arm were the first aircraft to sink a warship in action. Flying from shore bases, they caught and sank the German cruiser *Konigsberg* on 10 April during the invasion of Norway.

# The Norwegian Campaign

BELOW: The British battleship *Royal Oak* was sunk inside the Royal Navy's fleet anchorage at Scapa Flow on the night of 13–14 October 1939 with the loss of 833 lives. The German U-boat *U-47* commanded by Gunther Prien penetrated the defences to hit her with two salvoes of torpedoes. Prien went on to become one of the U-boat 'aces' but was killed in March 1941 when *U-47* was sunk with all hands by the destroyer HMS *Wolverine*.

The shadow boxing and sparring of the first seven months had lulled many people in Western Europe into a semi-belief that the war might fizzle out. This attitude worried some Allied leaders. People, said Churchill, 'sometimes ask us, "What is it that Britain and France are fighting for?" To that I answer, "If we left off fighting you would soon find out."' On 9 April the question was answered starkly in an unexpected area. 'The peaceful countries of Norway and Denmark,' in the words of one observer, 'were struck by a flash of Hitlerian lightning.' At dawn, German ships, aircraft and troops moved against both countries, offering them 'protection' from Britain and France.

Both Britain and Germany had recognised the important position of Norway from the start of the war. For the Germans there was a double interest. First, essential supplies of iron ore, mined in Sweden, were transported to the northern Norwegian port of Narvik. Then they were carried by sea, legally within international law, through Norwegian waters, to German ports. Hitler was determined to allow no interference with this trade. Secondly, the *Kriegsmarine* had pressed him to gain bases along the coast of Norway. These would present the opportunity for German warships to break out into the Atlantic Ocean and threaten convoys – and the *Luftwaffe* would be able to operate against the Royal Navy in the North Sea.

The British were equally determined to interrupt the iron ore trade. Churchill, as First Lord of the Admiralty, wanted mines to be laid in Norwegian waters to stop the flow. Senior naval staff foresaw dangers resulting from German bases on the Norwegian coast. The Allies and the Germans both made tentative plans for sending expeditionary forces to Norway if required. For the British and French, the Russo-Finnish war offered an opportunity. Troops could be despatched, via Norway and Sweden, ostensibly to help the Finns but in reality to cut the iron ore route. This chance ended on 16 March when Finland surrendered. Each side wondered what the other would do next.

Hitler's mind was mainly resolved on 16 February by the *Altmark* incident. He now knew that the Royal Navy was prepared to enter Norwegian territorial waters and believed that before long troops also

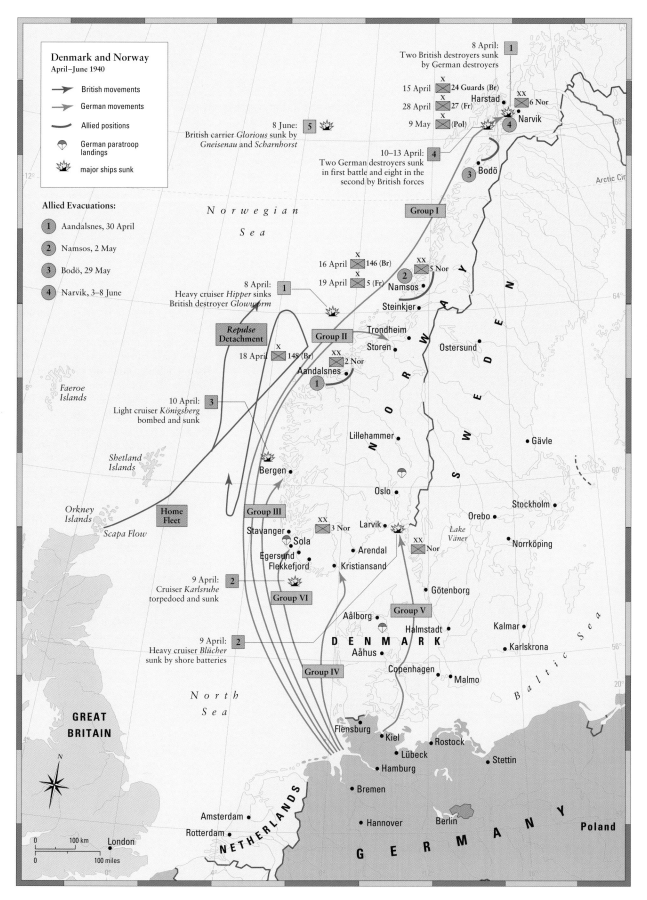

**Denmark and Norway**
April–June 1940

→ British movements

→ German movements

⌒ Allied positions

⬙ German paratroop landings

✸ major ships sunk

**Allied Evacuations:**

① Aandalsnes, 30 April

② Namsos, 2 May

③ Bodö, 29 May

④ Narvik, 3–8 June

8 April:
Two British destroyers sunk
by German destroyers | 1

15 April | X 24 Guards (Br)
28 April | X 27 (Fr) — Harstad
9 May | X (Pol) — XX 6 Nor
Narvik — 4

8 June: | 5
British carrier *Glorious* sunk by
*Gneisenau* and *Scharnhorst*

10–13 April: | 4
Two German destroyers sunk
in first battle and eight in the
second by British forces

③ Bodö

Arctic Cir

*Norwegian Sea*

Group I

16 April | X 146 (Br)
19 April | X 5 (Fr) — XX 5 Nor
② Namsos

8 April: | 1
Heavy cruiser *Hipper* sinks
British destroyer *Glowworm*

Steinkjer

*Repulse Detachment*

Group II

Trondheim

18 April | X 148 (Br)
XX 2 Nor
Aandalsnes — ①

Storen

Ostersund

10 April: | 3
Light cruiser *Königsberg*
bombed and sunk

*Faeroe Islands*

Lillehammer

Gävle

*Shetland Islands*

Bergen ✸

Oslo

60°

*Orkney Islands*

Home Fleet

*Scapa Flow*

Group III

Stavanger
Sola

XX 3 Nor

Larvik ✸

XX Nor

Stockholm

Orebo

*Lake Väner*

Norrköping

Egersund
Flekkefjord

Arendal

Kristiansand

9 April: | 2
Cruiser *Karlsruhe*
torpedoed and sunk

✸

Group VI

Göteborg

Group V

Aålborg

Kalmar

Halmstadt

*Baltic Sea*

9 April: | 2
Heavy cruiser *Blücher*
sunk by shore batteries

D E N M A R K
Aåhus

Karlskrona

56°

Copenhagen

Malmo

Group IV

*North Sea*

Flensburg
Kiel
Lübeck
Rostock
Stettin
Hamburg

**GREAT BRITAIN**

N

Bremen

Amsterdam

Berlin

Poland

Rotterdam
London

0   100 km
0   100 miles

N E T H E R L A N D S

G E R M A N Y

**DENMARK AND NORWAY**

Completely outnumbered by the Allied navies, the Germans relied on airpower to dominate Scandinavian waters while their various landing forces were dropped off along the Norwegian coast. Only at Narvik were the British able to counter-attack effectively.

RIGHT: German destroyers alongside at Narvik. The Germans lost two destroyers in an encounter with British light forces on 10 April. The British counter-attacked up the fjord, led by the battleship *Warspite* on 13 April and sunk another eight German destroyers, crippling the German destroyer fleet for the rest of the war.

BELOW: Some of the few survivors seen on the upturned hull of the *Glowworm* after she rammed the heavy cruiser *Hipper* on 8 April. Since all the survivors were made prisoner by the Germans, the truth about this remarkable incident did not become known until after the war.

would be put ashore. The difference between the two sides was now shown. The *Führer* decided on prompt action, fearing to be caught out. On 1 March his directive ordered plans to be drawn up speedily for occupying Denmark and Norway. 'This would anticipate English action against Scandinavia and the Baltic,' he wrote, 'would secure our supplies of iron ore from Sweden and would provide the Navy and Air Force with expanded bases for operations against England.' Within a month all was prepared.

At that stage the Allies, with plans and men ready, metaphorically hopped on one leg, waiting for a German move. In addition, British intelligence services reacted slowly, even when shown that German plans were well advanced. Senior naval staff doubted that the *Kriegsmarine* would risk sending vessels to Narvik when faced with British sea power; they estimated, wrongly, that the moves were an attempt to pass German warships out into the Atlantic. Consequently the Royal Navy lacked the 'Nelson touch' and failed to intercept the first landings, whereas decisive action brought the Germans strategic success.

On 9 April both the Danes and the Norwegians found Germans on their doorsteps. Danish resistance could not hold off overwhelming Nazi power and collapsed the same day. The Norwegians, though, fought back in spite of attacks by land, sea and air, but by the first evening all of Norway's main airfields, ports and cities had been taken. The speed of decisive German action, made with comparatively small forces, had surprised everyone.

A few naval actions occurred off the Norwegian coast, but no Allied troops went ashore until the 14th, by which time German positions had been consolidated. Further landings over subsequent days, at Namsos and Aandalsnes, were met by heavy *Luftwaffe* raids and made little progress. By early May most Allied soldiers had to be evacuated from central Norway, where local troops surrendered on the 3rd. The only Franco-British success was short-lived. On 28 May a combined force of French, British and Polish troops captured Narvik, but by then Nazi victories in France had undermined the whole campaign. Churchill ordered a withdrawal, which took place roughly simultaneously with the Dunkirk evacuation. Only then did Norwegian mountain troops in the north surrender.

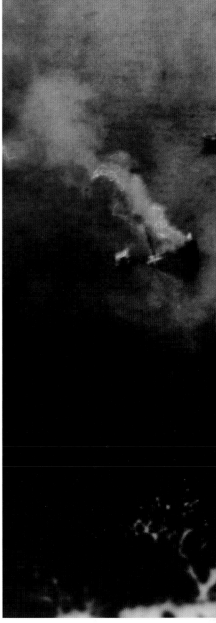

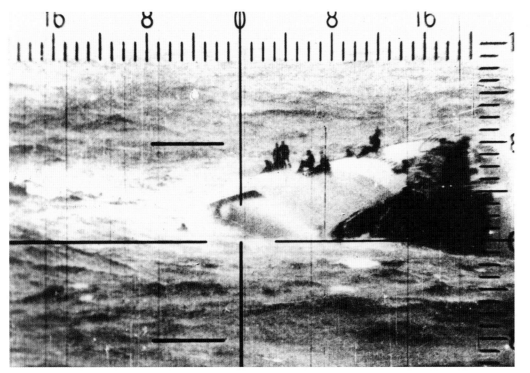

In the eyes of most people, the Norwegian Campaign was a disastrous muddle. Being slow to react, the Allies had been outmanoeuvred in an example of 'too little, too late'. The Royal Navy had failed to cut enemy supply routes, and the RAF had sent insufficient air support. Consequently, Allied ground troops had been outfought. The campaign had some important results for Britain. One was that Chamberlain, although a better politician and statesman than some have recognised, was seen to be no dynamic war leader. Parliament, that

arena of most severe judgement, turned against him and his administration. After two days of intense, stinging debate in the Commons Chamberlain offered his resignation to the King at Buckingham Palace on 10 May. Who would succeed him? The King asked Chamberlain's advice and was told that Churchill should be his successor. So, that same evening, Churchill took up the reins of office. He could not have done so at a more testing time. At dawn that morning the Germans had opened the long awaited offensive in the west.

**LEFT:** The new German heavy cruiser *Blucher* capsizes after taking two torpedo hits from a Norwegian coastal defence installation on 9 April. The *Blucher* was carrying hundreds of troops and their equipment which handicapped damage control efforts.

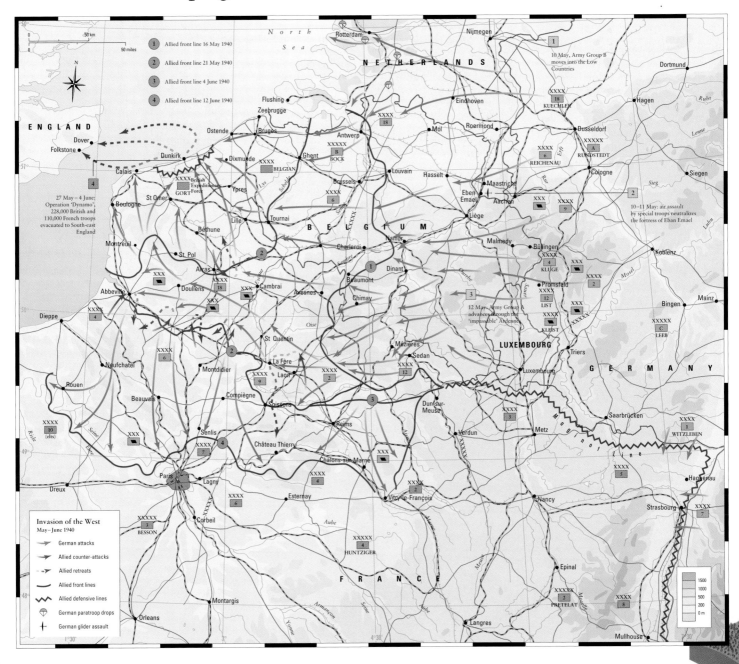

Invasion of the West
May – June 1940

→ German attacks

→ Allied counter-attacks

- → Allied retreats

— Allied front lines

∿ Allied defensive lines

⛉ German paratroop drops

✝ German glider assault

1 Allied front line 16 May 1940

2 Allied front line 21 May 1940

3 Allied front line 4 June 1940

4 Allied front line 12 June 1940

10 May, Army Group B moves into the Low Countries

27 May – 4 June: Operation 'Dynamo', 228,000 British and 110,000 French troops evacuated to South-east England

10–11 May: air assault by special troops neutralizes the fortress of Eban Emael

12 May, Army Group A advances through the 'impassable' Ardennes

To the authorities in France, Belgium, Holland, Britain and Germany it was apparent early on that the Low Countries would be involved in action as soon as a great offensive opened in the west at the end of the Phoney War. For most of the German General Staff, who had fought actively during the First World War, the obvious course was to move against Holland and Belgium. They knew that British forces would move in to help, and then a pounding match would follow, as there had been for four years after 1914. Even when the German

plans fell into Allied hands in January 1940, British and French generals were still convinced that the Nazi army would not change its route. The attack, whenever it came, would enter France through Belgium; therefore, their eyes were fixed in that direction.

On the German side a plan suggested by General von Manstein eventually found its way to Hitler's map-table, where it was well received, then modified. The plan, code-named 'Sichelschnitt' (Sweep of the Scythe), altered the balance of German forces facing the Low Countries and com-

## BLITZKRIEG IN THE WEST

The original German plan to invade France and the Low Countries followed the conventional strategy the British and French were prepared for. However, the radical plan advocated by General von Manstein caught Hitler's imagination: instead of attacking through Holland and central Belgium, the main blow would be delivered through the Ardennes forest. The massed German panzer divisions would cross the Meuse at Sedan and race north to cut off the Allied forces in Belgium.

pletely deceived the Allies. Hitler had at his disposal for the campaign 137 divisions, and in the early months of 1940 their strengths and objectives were rearranged. For the great offensive, 89 divisions were to be employed, with the remainder in reserve to follow up. There were three Army Groups. In the north, Army Group B was to launch an invasion from Germany against the Dutch, then move on to Belgium, tying down as many Allied forces as possible. Much further south, opposite the Maginot Line and running down to the Swiss frontier, Army Group C had seventeen divisions to occupy the French forces there. The conjurer's *coup de main*, however, was to come from Army Group A, which constituted the strongest force, with 44 divisions. Ten were panzer or motorised divisions, about three-quarters of the total armoured forces at Hitler's disposal. Their task was to move into Luxembourg, then pass through the wooded regions of the Belgian Ardennes. The Allies had considered the terrain there to be totally unsuitable for armour, so saw little need to defend it. They could have made no greater error. Army Group A, having broken through, was then to swing through southern Belgium into France, near Sedan, where they would cut off the Allied forces that would have moved forward to help the Belgians.

LEFT: The British army of 1939 was unusual in being fully motorised. All other European armies still depended on horse-drawn transport. Here, two Universal Carriers tow 2-pounder (40 mm) anti-tank guns through Belgium as the Allied armies advance to contact.

Sadly, such strategists were absent on the Allied side, or else were men of insufficient power to have their ideas adopted. This is tinged with irony because much of the new thinking on armoured warfare had originated in Britain between the wars. From March 1940, the French and British High Commands prepared to follow what was called the Dyle Plan. By this, about

35 of their best divisions would be sent into Belgium if the Germans invaded, taking up a position roughly from Namur to Antwerp. Their task was to meet the thrust of Army Group B. If the Belgian Army could defend stubbornly and hold up the Germans for five days, the Allies would have time to fortify their position. Then, in the reckoning of Allied commanders, the

**THE SEDAN CROSSINGS**
Like the Empire of Napoleon III, which it succeeded, the French Third Republic was destroyed in battle near the medieval fortress of Sedan. Across the same battlefield that had seen a French Emperor driven into captivity in 1870, General Guderian's panzer divisions tore a gap in the French frontline. Expecting this to be a quiet sector, the French had deployed their weakest units here. The crisis found their best units in Belgium and their high command had not bothered to retain any reserve: an elementary error from which they failed to recover.

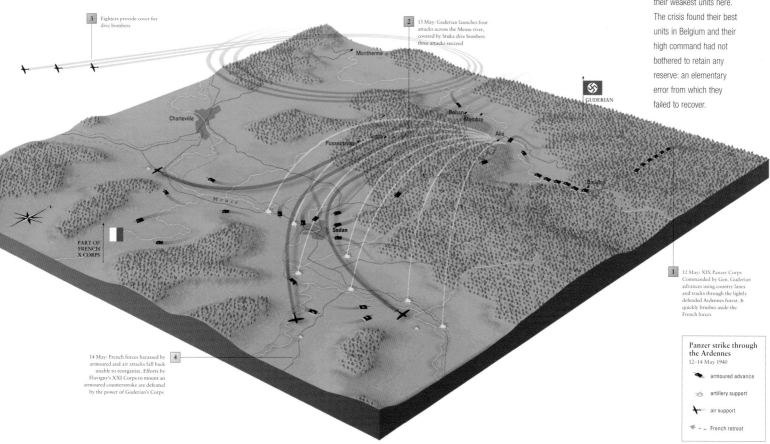

ABOVE: German gunners
haul a 37 mm anti-tank
gun away from the river.
The professionalism of the
German army's engineers
was never better
demonstrated than by the
speed with which they
bridged the Meuse in
1940.

war would become the type of slogging match experienced twenty-five years earlier, with the front line, on this occasion, lying much further to the east.

So much for theories. The practice started when the great German offensive opened at dawn on 10 May. Army Group B invaded Belgium and Holland as planned, making rapid progress. Glider and parachute troops

RIGHT: French heavy
artillery on exercise in the
winter of 1939–40. The
French army regarded its
guns as its primary
weapon just as they had
been in the First World
War. The idea that its
powerful batteries could be
rendered useless by air
attack had simply not been
accepted: few French units
were equipped with
modern anti-aircraft guns.

were landed in enterprising operations. The *Luftwaffe* raided incessantly, and within five days Dutch resistance was overwhelmed.

As planned, British and French forces moved hastily into Belgium to take up their agreed defensive positions. However, Allied troops discovered a lack of readiness. In many places positions were unprepared,

lacking trenches and barbed wire. Confusion reigned everywhere.

The news that the French and British armies had moved forward into Belgium pleased Hitler: they had entered his trap and he could have wept with joy. At the same time, the main German force, well equipped with panzer troops, was making steady, though unnoticed, progress through the supposedly impassable Ardennes. Its columns of vehicles and armour stretched for over 100 miles, going back 50 miles to the east of the Rhine. As the 44 Nazi divisions advanced, they were opposed only by a small French force, not containing the best troops. Crossing the French frontier near Sedan, they swept ahead at speed, with panzer divisions in the forefront of a relentless push from what one German general called 'the greatest traffic-jam in history'.

By 15 May the panzer units, led by able commanders like Guderian and Rommel, were smashing their way into northern France. The main brake on their progress appeared to be placed by senior officers of the German High

LEFT: A Panzer 38t seen during the invasion of France. Even with the addition of these Czech vehicles, the German army had fewer tanks than the British and French. But unlike the Allies, the Germans proved able to coordinate tanks, artillery, infantry and aircraft on the battlefield.

Command who could hardly believe in such success and were troubled that the Allies might have some masterly counter-stroke up their sleeves. They need not have worried: on the Allied side, disorganisation reigned supreme. On the 19th, Guderian's forces were across the old battlefields of the Somme and next day took Amiens, then Abbeville. That evening, the first German formation reached the Channel coast at Noyelles, having advanced more than 60 miles in a day.

Consequently the Allied forces were cut into two by the swift hitting power of Army Group A. Guderian then swung northwards along the coast to complete the envelopment of Allied armies trapped in that region; French resistance further south would be dealt with later. Initially the panzers were aiming directly at the port of Dunkirk, but first they had to take Boulogne and Calais, where a small British and French force defended ferociously. Calais was not captured until the afternoon of the 26th. Suddenly, much to the surprise of panzer commanders, they were told to halt, although many felt that Dunkirk, the last port open on the Channel coast, was there for the taking. The puzzling order had come from Hitler himself.

By then the main French resistance, fragmented and poorly coordinated, was being pushed back towards the coast. The British Army was in a quandary. Lord Gort, its commander, believed that the French were crumbling and he wanted to leave a way open to the sea. He was accused by the French of having an eye on the Channel ports instead of engaging the enemy to the south. During this period Churchill twice flew to France, attempting to discover what was going on. Mutual recrimination between Allied leaders then surfaced. The

French claimed that more British soldiers should have been sent earlier to the Western Front, and they wanted extra RAF aircraft to be despatched. The British, on the other hand, felt that French morale was cracking and that they might soon surrender, leaving the British Expeditionary Force stranded. Churchill was disturbed by the general air of chaos. 'In all the history of war, I have never known such mismanagement,' he said on 21 May. The British government, fearing a forthcoming invasion of the United Kingdom, decided to evacuate the BEF

BELOW: A British Fairey Battle light bomber on a French air field just prior to the German onslaught. These bombers suffered horrific losses in gallant but doomed attacks on the German bridgeheads. The German army reaped the benefit of its pre-war investment in mobile anti-aircraft guns.

ABOVE: Preparing for anti-tank action: the crew of a Pak 38 scramble to chamber the first round. While the British expected tanks to fight each other, the Germans realised that guns like this were very difficult to see from a moving vehicle. Anti-tank guns firing from hidden positions would take a dreadful toll of Allied armour throughout the war.

before it was lost entirely. Matters worsened. The Belgians, under great pressure, surrendered on the 28th, so the Germans had pinned, on the Channel coast, a combined Franco-British force of about 360,000 men. Their surrender was reckoned to be no more than a few days away.

Incredible as it may seem, bearing in mind the success of panzer divisions, the defeated French Army had more tanks than the Germans. In total, on 10 May the French and British forces together possessed some 3,500 tanks on the Western Front; the Germans had about a thousand fewer. In addition, many of the French tanks were very powerful, with thick armour and strong fire power. The Germans, nonetheless, made better use of their armoured strength, especially in the concentrated drive by Army Group A. Opposite them, the French High Command were constantly on the back foot, never having time amid the muddle of retreating divisions and hesitant commanders to synchronise large armoured attacks. They were too slow to see the arrival of the left hook sweeping from the direction of Sedan.

RIGHT: A tank battle in progress during the invasion of France. French tank designs failed to recognise that a vehicle commander cannot work effectively if he has to operate the turret armament as well.

ABOVE: A French tank explodes: it was extremely difficult to escape from Second World War tanks that caught fire. Hatches were awkward enough even for unwounded men to escape through and the use of petrol rather than diesel meant many vehicles detonated like a bomb with their crews still inside.

In the forefront were Guderian's tanks, scything forward to an amazing victory.

Closely tied, in effect, to the tank battle was the power of the *Luftwaffe*. If one aircraft had to be chosen to typify German success in the campaign, it would be the Junkers Ju 87 Stuka dive-bomber. These aeroplanes were used in conjunction with army ground units as a form of aerial artillery. When German troops were faced with stubbornly defended positions, Stukas were called in to clear the way. Allied forces, with poor anti-aircraft equipment, had no answer to the bombardment. The *Luftwaffe*, with larger numbers than both British and French air forces in France, acted as a safe aerial umbrella for most of the advance. German bombers raided transport columns, supply depots and railways, adding a third dimension to the nature of war.

The strength of air power, adding to the German Army's rapid success, underscored the importance of morale to both sides in 1940. By May, with the great offensive pending, the spirit of many French units was at a low ebb. The Phoney War, with long periods of inaction and little preparation, had bred lethargy. A number of Frenchmen thought themselves safe behind the Maginot Line, forgetting that the defences did not stretch to the Channel coast. They also reacted pessimistically to the spectacular successes gained so speedily by Hitler's troops in both the Polish and Norwegian Campaigns. The Germans appeared to carry an air of invincibility even before the main battle started.

LEFT: Panzer IIs accounted for a large proportion of the German tank arm in 1940. Only armed with a 20 mm gun and machine guns, in theory it stood little chance against Allied medium tanks with their 37 mm or even 47 mm main armament. However, there were few major tank versus tank engagements in the whole campaign.

# Dunkirk

The name Dunkirk still evokes different memories for many people in France and the United Kingdom. To some of the former, here was an example of the British Army retreating too hastily to the coast, then being evacuated, instead of trying to stem the German advance. To the latter, because of the French Army's collapse, unless evacuation had taken place, the whole of the BEF would have been forced to surrender. Britain then would have been rapidly invaded and defeated.

In the north, the BEF, under the command of Lord Gort, had nine infantry divisions and a tank brigade. With the German invasion of 10 May they moved forward into Belgium, but

ABOVE: The British failed to concentrate a single armoured division in France before they retreated to the beaches. Their 'cruiser' tanks like this example knocked out near Dunkirk were huge vehicles, almost as large as the armoured behemoths of 1944–45. They were fast, but lightly armed and scantily protected.

were soon retreating as Nazi forces began their inexorable advance. Shortly, they learned of the rapid progress of Guderian's panzers, which by the 20th had reached the Channel coast in their rear. At that stage, realising his responsibility not only to help the French and Belgians, but also to his own government to keep his forces intact, Gort contemplated falling back on Dunkirk. Around him, many units of the French Army were in disarray. They changed their commander-in-chief; communications were poor, with contradictory orders being issued. By 25 May, with the Germans at Boulogne and Calais and advancing on Dunkirk, he had to take a decision. Further hesitation would have been disastrous. Next day, the British Cabinet agreed to permit the retirement to Dunkirk. 'Only course open to you may be to fight your way back to west where all beaches and ports east of Gravelines will be used for

embarkation. Navy will provide fleet of ships and small boats.'

One of the war's greatest mysteries remains. Why did the Germans not take Dunkirk, as Guderian's forces could easily have done after capturing Boulogne and Calais? Why did Hitler order them to halt several miles short of the seaport? The real answer is unknown. The decision worried some German commanders. 'For two valuable days,' General Nehring commented later, 'our opponents were allowed to strengthen their defences and organise that miraculous evacuation of the mass of troops from Dunkirk.' It has been suggested that Hitler feared using and losing his armour in what was a marshy area. Others have made the unlikely claim that he wanted friendship with Britain and was offering an escape route for the BEF. Or did he give way to Göring, leader of the *Luftwaffe*, who claimed that his aircraft would annihilate the trapped troops without recourse to the German Army? Possibly there were disagreements among German commanders, with the result that Hitler, demonstrating his supreme power, overruled them all. The result of the hesitation was that a combined Franco-British force of about 380,000 men was able to form a salient in and around the sea port, surrounded by German divisions. There they were shelled on land and frequently attacked from the air.

As early as 19 May, the Admiralty in Britain, foreseeing what might happen in France, sent Vice-Admiral Ramsay to Dover to prepare ships for an evacuation. He worked from the dynamo room under Dover Castle – hence the venture was code-named Operation 'Dynamo'. Ramsay gathered hundreds of small ships from ports between Harwich and Weymouth. They included Dutch *schouts* and coasters, ferries and yachts, speedboats and tugs, even paddle-steamers and fire floats. These forces, together with units of the Royal Navy, especially destroyers, went into action from 26 May. The first estimate was that they might evacuate 45,000 troops before the enemy overran the defensive positions. On 27 May only 7,700 men were taken off, but a peak was reached on

31 May and 1 June, when over 132,000 were saved and brought to England. By then the bulk of the remaining BEF had been rescued. On the nights of 2 and 3 June, about 60,000 of the final French defenders were evacuated, leaving some 40,000 of their number to face captivity. At the final count, over 330,000 men had been brought to safety, of whom over 100,000 were French.

For the British people, the Dunkirk

evacuation was 'a miracle' that was, in some eyes, so great that it constituted a victory. It was not. 'We must be very careful not to assign to this deliverance the attributes of a victory,' Churchill told the House of Commons. 'Wars are not won by evacuations.' The BEF had suffered 68,000 casualties and had left behind most of its equipment, including 475 tanks, 90,000 rifles and 2,500 pieces of artillery. At sea, the Royal Navy had shown a mastery in carrying

out a brilliantly improvised plan, in which they were supported by merchant seamen and amateur sailors. The cost had been considerable, because nearly 250 vessels of various sizes had been sunk out of almost 1,000 employed. The precious fighters of the RAF, while inflicting on the *Luftwaffe* its first setback of the war, suffered heavy losses. All that now stood between the victorious German panzer divisions on the French coast and the

white cliffs of Dover was a water-ditch 22 miles across.

General Montgomery, then commanding a division of the BEF, later summarised the achievement of Gort, whose contribution is often overlooked. 'Gort saw clearly that he must, at the least, get the men of the BEF back to England with their personal weapons. For this I give him full marks and I hope history will do the same. He saved the men of the BEF.'

**ABOVE:** The most famous retreat of the war: the British Expeditionary Force on the beaches around Dunkirk where the 'little ships', civilian craft manned by volunteers, assisted in rescuing them. It was described as a miracle, and without it, Britain would have had difficulty resisting Hitler's peace overtures.

# The End of France

With the Low Countries and north-eastern France overrun by 5 June, Hitler had the choice either of launching an immediate attack on Britain or of dealing first with the remaining French territory. He chose the latter. The French, who would have needed at least ten days to reorganise troops and defensive positions to have any chance of resisting, were offered no respite. Although this time they generally fought with more spirit, they were still no match for the *Blitzkrieg* tactics of tanks and aircraft working in unison. By 8 June German forces were penetrating towards the heart of the country, while on the next day French troops were retreating towards Paris. The 10th was a day of ominous historic importance for the beleaguered nation. With the approaching enemy threat, the government left the capital, first for Tours, then Bordeaux – a sure sign of the pressure being exerted on national leaders as defeat loomed closer. Secondly, that very day Mussolini, the dictator of Italy, declared war on France, hoping to be part of the Axis action before the Germans tidied up the campaign by themselves. This was truly 'a stab in the back' for a stricken country. Paris was declared an open city to prevent its bombardment by the

Germans. French troops were ordered out of the city's centre and suburbs and Nazi forces made a triumphal entry on the 14th. Nothing, it appeared, could halt the German drive, which advanced southwards and westwards. Guderian's panzers swept down to the Swiss frontier, behind the Maginot Line, taking all forces there from the rear.

The French government was faced with two options. More belligerent ministers, like the young army officer Charles de Gaulle, wanted all the nation's remaining forces, army, navy and air force, to evacuate to North African colonies, from where they could continue the struggle. The majority opinion, led by Weygand and Pétain, were set on surrender. In spite of some heroic efforts, their army had been trounced. They had had enough.

As French resistance crumbled, the government sought an armistice on the 17th and the Germans presented their terms a few days later. Then, with a sense of theatre, Hitler ordered that the agreement be signed in the railway coach used in 1918 when the Germans had surrendered. The humiliating signature took place at Compiègne on 22 June and France was out of the war. Hitler then paid a short visit to Paris before relaxing. He anticipated that

the British would soon sue for peace and, as far as immediate and detailed planning for the next step of war was concerned, he 'went off the boil'. Consequently, the *Wehrmacht* lost both urgency and a sense of leadership when it was needed.

Looking round for help, both France and Britain believed that the only salvation for their dilemma could come from the United States, the most powerful of the democracies. By then the Americans, under President Roosevelt, showed far more favour to the Allied side than to the Axis cause. Pleas and messages crossed and recrossed the Atlantic, with the French hoping against hope for US military intervention, which their fathers had valued 23 years earlier. Churchill pointed out to Roosevelt the dangers that would follow for America if the Germans were totally victorious in Europe and gained possession of the British and French fleets. However, although Roosevelt offered words of support and ensured that supplies of war materials were increased and speeded up, he was in no position to commit his nation to war. The Axis powers had not attacked the United States directly and the isolationist lobby was still strong.

Thus France, on 22 June, entered a period of virtual captivity which would last for four years. Hitler, in an attempt to widen the gap between the British and the French, allowed the French government to retain power over about one-third of the country, an area mainly in the south known as the Unoccupied Zone. Its headquarters were at Vichy. German forces occupied Paris, as well as the whole of the northern and western coastline facing Britain and the Atlantic. In France, the parliament of the Third Republic was widely blamed for the defeat and subsequent humiliation. In the popular mind it had failed to see the approaching storm clouds of war and had neglected to prepare the armed forces. As the nation's new leader, Pétain on 11 July announced that he would 'assume the functions of head of the French State'. To gain what he believed would be the best deal for France, he was now ready to collaborate with the Nazis, using an authoritarian government.

## ORAN

Churchill had made clear throughout the débâcle in France that, come what might, Britain would not surrender. The pessimism and sense of impending doom which he discovered in French leaders during his meetings with them only strengthened his resolve. On 11 June he told the Supreme War Council that Britain 'would never give in'. Even if France were beaten, his nation 'would nevertheless carry on, if necessary for years'. She would fight in the air, and on the seas with the weapon of blockade. 'We will carry on the struggle, whatever the odds,' he wrote to Roosevelt on the 15th. There was no doubting the prime minister's resolve, however gloomy the prospect.

His spirit was transmitted to the British people generally. On 18 June he made one of his most memorable speeches to the House of Commons, then broadcast it four hours later. 'The Battle of France is over,' he announced. 'I expect that the Battle of Britain is about to begin.' Hitler, he added, 'will have to break us in this island or lose the war.' He warned of the dangers to the whole world which would follow a Nazi victory. 'Let us therefore brace ourselves to our duties and so bear ourselves that if the British Empire and its Commonwealth last for a thousand years men will still say, "This was their finest hour." These words touched the pulse of the nation, which then prepared itself for the ordeal to come.

The French collapse left one searching problem for Britain. What would happen to the French Fleet? By the terms of Article 8 of the armistice, the ships were to be sailed to ports where they would be disarmed and demobilised under Axis supervision; Hitler's worry was that otherwise the vessels might join the Royal Navy, tilting the balance of sea power further away from the Germans. The British War Cabinet had an opposite view: knowing the *Führer*'s record for breaking agreements and promises, they feared that the ships would be seized and transferred to the *Kriegsmarine*. Such a move posed a double threat. The vessels either could be used during an invasion of the United Kingdom, or could be employed alongside the Italian Navy in the Mediterranean,

altering the balance of sea power there. The War Cabinet first discussed the matter on 15 June, as France was collapsing, and concern grew over the next two weeks.

At the time, the French Fleet was based in several ports. Some ships were at Portsmouth and Plymouth in the United Kingdom, while others were based in Alexandria, Dakar, Casablanca and the French West Indies. Those of particular concern to the British – because they included two

powerful battlecruisers – were at Oran. Churchill and his ministers were on the horns of a dilemma, and faced with making a cruel choice. They knew that whatever they chose would bring praise from one direction but censure from the other. On the one hand, these were the forces of a former ally, who wanted them returned to home ports; on the other, if taken by the Axis powers, they would be a dire threat to the security of Britain which was fighting for its very life. How

**ABOVE:** Each panzer division operated hundreds of vehicles, stretching over vast distances as they uncoiled from the road net and plunged across country. By early June, leading tank commanders like General Rommel were describing French opposition as little more than a crowd control problem. Hundreds of men kept trying to surrender to his tiny headquarters as he sped toward the Channel, miles ahead of his own tanks.

**LEFT:** A Panzer 38t noses through standing crops. Painted grey overall, the German tanks carried national markings on the hull and often large regimental numbers on the turret side.

ABOVE: British soldiers are taken prisoner by the Germans near Calais. The forlorn vehicle minus its wheels is a French Panhard armoured car: an excellent vehicle of its type that the Germans were pleased to capture intact.

LEFT: The roads to Dunkirk were littered with abandoned vehicles after incessant German air attacks struck retreating Allied troops and civilian refugees without discrimination.

LEFT: One of a handful of Matilda II infantry tanks sent by the British to France. These British heavy tanks were so heavily armoured that German anti-tank shells simply bounced off them. Some Germans resorted to their 88 mm anti-aircraft guns to deal with Matildas and discovered just how versatile this fearsome gun could be. British tank crew would meet it again in the desert.

could such a problem be solved? The British government made a rapid decision and Operation 'Catapult' was prepared, coming into action on 3 July. At Alexandria and at British ports the French vessels were taken over with little trouble. At Oran, however, the French admiral refused to scuttle his ships, or sail them to neutral ports, or join with the Royal Navy. Consequently, British vessels opened fire, sinking or damaging several warships and killing hundreds of sailors.

The event had a stunning effect. Some blamed, and still blame, the British for turning violently on a former friend. Others appreciate that in war, where the security of a nation is at stake, desperate measures are sometimes required. To the French government the operation was treachery. To the Axis powers, and to neutrals, it was proof that Britain meant business. There was to be no dealing with Hitler, no falling at his feet to seek mercy.

Not all French people were pleased or relieved at their nation's surrender, which, to them, was an abject humiliation. As a result, a number made their way to Britain or British territories with the purpose of carrying on the fight. The most prominent of them was Charles de Gaulle, an army general who was also Under-Secretary for Defence in the French government. He believed that although the homeland of France had been overrun, his people could continue to oppose the Axis powers from lands of the French Empire, especially in Africa. 'Must we abandon all hope? Is our defeat final and irremediable?' he asked the nation in an appeal on 18 June. 'To those questions I answer – No!'

De Gaulle set up a Council of Liberation in London to organise and unite French resistance to Germany and this was soon recognised by the British government. However, the Pétain government in France were angry. The general was summoned to appear before a military tribunal in Toulouse to answer charges of disobedience and incitement. De Gaulle scornfully returned the summons, writing that, in his eyes, it 'has no interest whatever'. In Britain he started to create a force of Free French, which expanded and fought alongside the Allies for the rest of the war.

# Italy Joins In

In many disagreements or controversies there are people who first wait on the fringes to see who is going to win before entering the fray – on the victorious side. Mussolini, the dictator of Italy, had not joined Hitler at the start of the Second World War. Nevertheless, as the Germans gained victories, especially over France, he saw the opportunity of taking part. Several prizes, he believed, awaited Italy. First, he would be present at the conference table when peace terms were set. 'I need a few thousand dead,' he told one general, 'so as to be able to attend the peace conference as a belligerent.' He believed that both Britain and France would lose power in the Mediterranean region and that Italy would be bound to benefit. Thoughts of recreating the Roman Empire were never far from his mind, but in this his ambitions far outran his nation's capabilities.

On 10 June 1940 he stood theatrically at the Piazza Venezia in Rome and announced that Italy was 'entering the lists against the plutocratic and reactionary democracies' of Britain and France. A huge crowd chanted 'Duce, Duce', but, in truth, few Italians were either keen on, or ready for, war. The Germans, victorious on their own account, hardly needed or welcomed Italian help.

In battle, Mussolini's men hardly distinguished themselves. They launched an offensive across the French frontier with 32 divisions and were opposed by only five French divisions, which were part of an army facing defeat at German hands. However, the French forces comfortably held off the Italian attacks, inflicting heavy casualties. In the air, the Italian Air Force also enjoyed little success. The campaign did nothing for the reputation of the Italian armed services.

Italian forces were strong on paper. Altogether some 70 divisions could be raised, supported by an air force of 1,500 aircraft. The most powerful arm was the Italian Navy, with six battleships, eighteen cruisers and 60 destroyers, as well as more than 60 submarines, all of which posed a threat to British sea power in the Mediterranean. However, the Royal Navy started with one special advantage there. Apart from a few of its submarines, the Italian vessels were locked in the Mediterranean because of British naval bases at Gibraltar at one end and Suez at the other. Italy's entry into the war opened up the whole of the Mediterranean area, including North Africa, as a new fighting arena. Although the odds appeared to be stacked heavily against Britain in that zone, this war offered opportunities to strike at what became, in Churchill's words, 'the under-belly of the Axis'. Would Mussolini's intervention be a blessing or a burden to the victorious Germans? At least one German general claimed that the war would be won by whoever didn't have the Italians as allies. Investigations soon showed that fewer than twenty of the Italian Army's divisions were ready for action.

The first hints of disappointment for *Il Duce* came when the armistice with France was signed. The Italians had hoped to gain French overseas territories – Tunisia, French Somaliland, Corsica and Nice – but Hitler, wanting to appear generous in victory to the French, allocated only Nice and small areas of Savoy to Mussolini. 'The Germans are hard taskmasters,' the French ambassador in Rome had told the Italians on 10 June. 'You will learn this.' Here was their first lesson.

**BELOW:** A useful aerial shot of two of the tank types used by the Germans in 1940. Uppermost are two Panzer IVs, armed at this time with a short 75 mm gun and used for direct support of the infantry. The Panzer 38ts below would serve until the end of 1941 but the Panzer IV soldiered on until 1945, its armament and weight progressively increased, but still capable of taking on most late-war Allied tanks.

To bystanders, or the interested bookmaker, the odds were that, as soon as France collapsed, Britain would be forced to come to the conference table. The BEF, although rescued from Dunkirk, had suffered a heavy defeat and had left behind vast supplies of war material. The RAF had fought bravely but was faced by a *Luftwaffe* of stronger numbers which had played a vital role in the success of the German Army. The Royal Navy was still powerful, but might not be able to prevent an invasion force getting ashore somewhere on the British coast.

Although the cards seemed to be stacked against the United Kingdom, there were some advantages. Refusal to surrender was a positive choice. The onus of response was passed back to Hitler, who had not expected British resistance to continue and believed the war to be virtually over. On 22 June he ordered the demobilisation of thirty-five divisions and then, in Bullock's words, believed that his opponents 'must now surely accept the impossibility of preventing a German hegemony in Europe, and, like sensible people, come to terms'. Udet, the Head of *Luftwaffe* Supply and Procurement, was over-confident, reckoning that proposed expansion plans 'are not worth a damn. We don't need them any longer.' This air of victory, hardly surprising after the rapid demolition of France, served Germany badly. A mood of indecision appeared to affect the *Führer*, who was, even at that stage, already thinking about an attack on Soviet Russia.

When, on 21 May, Admiral Raeder showed Hitler a naval study of the possibilities of invading Britain, there was little response. By 17 June, Hitler had still not approved an invasion plan, while his directive of 2 July mentioned that 'the invasion is still only a plan'. Two weeks later Directive No 16 was also vague, announcing that an invasion was being prepared and that his forces should be ready 'if necessary to carry it out'. The directive even then asked only for proposals and plans to be submitted 'as soon as possible'.

On 19 July, Hitler addressed the *Reichstag* in Berlin, after the presentation of awards to his successful commanders in the Western Campaign. Britain, he said in a rambling yet part-ly conciliatory speech, could have peace or 'unending suffering and misery'. He claimed to speak as the victor, not the vanquished. What he wanted, basically, was for Britain to accept his widespread gains across Europe, and in return he was prepared to allow the British to carry on with their role as an imperial power overseas. Possibly he hoped that in the long run the United Kingdom would join him in the forthcoming crusade against the USSR. Churchill was unimpressed and refused to reply, 'not being on speaking terms with him'. It was left to Halifax, the Foreign Secretary, to respond. He rejected the offer. Only then were more urgent and detailed plans for an invasion drawn up.

Consequently, the period of almost seven weeks between the end of the Dunkirk evacuation and Hitler's speech were critical to the well-being of the British armed services. They allowed the government to organise for the forthcoming struggle, embracing all aspects of national life, from transport and food supplies to the formation of the Local Defence Volunteers (soon renamed the Home Guard). At every level plans were laid to deal with the anticipated invasion. For Britain's army, navy and air force this period was equally vital. The defeated army was re-formed and rearmed. The Royal Navy made final dispositions for meeting the invading forces at sea, confident that the Germans would suffer huge losses. The RAF also was given time to reorganise units, especially in Fighter Command, to deal with the massive *Luftwaffe* onslaught which would inevitably come. On 5 June, after he had flown over the Dunkirk beaches, Milch, the Inspector-General of the *Luftwaffe*, had recommended to Göring that air units should be brought to the Channel coast and that Britain should be invaded at once. He added, 'If we leave the British in peace for four weeks it will be too late.' Those were indeed prophetic words.

Sustaining Britain's determination not to surrender was the prime minister, Winston Churchill. People at the end of the twentieth century, who tend to hold statesmen and politicians in low esteem, will find it difficult to appreciate not only the strength of purpose and unyielding resolve which

Churchill contained within himself, but also the infectious confidence which he spread to others right across the nation. He epitomised the attitude of the British bulldog, even in darkest times. When Reynaud, the French prime minister, had asked him what he would do when 'all the great might of Germany will be concentrated upon invading England', Churchill replied that he 'would propose to drown as many as possible of them on the way over, and then to *"frapper sur la tête"* anyone who managed to crawl ashore'.

The crux was the sea. Churchill later wrote that 'whatever out shortcomings, we understood the sea affair very thoroughly'. To troops of the German Army

at Calais, viewing the white cliffs of Dover so clearly, it was incomprehensible that such a small water barrier should hinder their progress. Surely this was little more than a river crossing. Yet thousands of them had never seen the sea before, and few were aware of the powerful tides and currents that can make the short crossing perilous. The majority also did not appreciate that an army, once put ashore, would need regular supplies from maritime forces to sustain an invasion.

Although the German Army, in planning an invasion, Operation 'Sealion', wanted landings on a wide front, mainly from the North Foreland to Brighton, the German Navy could offer to protect only a narrow passage at the Strait of Dover. This, claimed more than one German general, would be like putting men through a sausage machine.

Each service tended to blame the other. The Army High Command believed that the Navy's heart was not in 'Sealion'. They were correct. The Navy naturally had a realistic sense of what was involved in a combined operation of that magnitude and knew its own limitations. Its commanders appreciated the potential carnage if, say, twenty British destroyers got among the slow-moving barges and landing craft in the Channel. One admiral later claimed that the *Wehrmacht* would never have crossed the Channel: 'The German soldier is sick if he crosses the Rhine!'

In spite of their differences, both services were confronted with a similar problem. First, before any operation could take place, the *Luftwaffe* would have to remove the power of the Royal Air Force over the battle zone. This was recognised by General Jodl on 30 June: 'A landing in England can be taken into view only if the command of the air has been gained by the German Air Force.' As a result, the spotlight fell on the *Luftwaffe*. The opening stage of the anticipated defeat of Britain therefore would take place in the skies over the Channel and over the British mainland, especially southern England.

# The Battle of Britain

ABOVE: A British convoy in mid-Atlantic. Although Germany had comparatively few submarines in 1940, a small number of expert captains started to run up huge 'scores', attacking on the surface at night. Despite the terrible losses they had suffered to U-boats in the First World War, the British regarded anti-submarine warfare as an unfashionable backwater before 1939.

In history, certain battles stand as landmarks for the nations involved. No American will ignore the importance of Yorktown, or the French forget Austerlitz. In British history, Hastings and Trafalgar were turning points in the nation's story. Some contests were settled within hours; others, like the defeat of the Spanish Armada, stretched over a week. One of the decisive battles of the Second World War lasted about three and a half months. This was the Battle of Britain, a struggle that the

British could not afford to lose and the Germans were unable to win.

For the Germans, the event was the first major setback of the war. They treated it as no more than an interruption to a string of victories across Europe, beginning with the Norwegian Campaign in April 1940 and closing with the defeat of Greece and the overrunning of Crete in May 1941. To them, at the time, the failure of the air campaign over Britain did not appear as a mortal wound, but the

long-term effect was deadlier than they imagined. In British eyes this was a separate battle: the daylight struggle which occurred between 10 July and 31 October 1940 stood in its own right. The dates are those given by Dowding, Commander-in-Chief of Fighter Command, in his despatch on the battle written in the following year. However, to gain a balanced view of what occurred, any study of the battle should take into account the subsequent Night Blitz, which was a sequel to the daylight attacks.

The daylight battle fell into four main phases over a period of weeks, as the Germans altered both strategy and tactics in a determined attempt to overwhelm Fighter Command. First came attacks on convoys, which continued to follow the customary sea trade off the eastern and southern coasts of England. These were tempting bait for the *Luftwaffe*. Particularly for a month after 10 July, they were raided by German bombers accompanied by fighters. In response, British fighters were despatched to protect the ships. Fierce air battles developed over the sea, and here the RAF suffered the disadvantage of having very short warning from radar of the German approach.

During the first half of August

RIGHT: While RAF Fighter Command struggled to beat back the German bombers over England, British bombers like this Bristol Blenheim attacked German shipping as it assembled for the invasion.

attacks were made more widely on coastal aerodromes in southern England, then came further raids inland on other airfields and aircraft factories. Göring hoped, with a great 'Eagle' offensive in the middle of the month, to crush Fighter Command. Although the Command suffered heavy losses, so many German bombers – obviously the main target for the defenders – were destroyed or damaged that the *Luftwaffe* was forced to change tactics.

Therefore, between 19 August and 7 September came a critical third phase of battle. The *Luftwaffe* concentrated its assault on fighter airfields, moving closer to London, attempting to engage and crush the RAF in a duel to the death. Göring insisted that his fighters should give close escort to the bombers, and Fighter Command came under the greatest pressure it had known. By the early days of September, Dowding was planning for his Command 'to go downhill', especially through a shortage of pilots. Then, on the 7th, came an intermission when the German plan altered again.

During the late afternoon of that day the *Luftwaffe* opened its offensive against London, despatching a force of almost a thousand bombers and fight-

ers to raid the capital, followed by a night-long onslaught. Great damage was caused and heavy casualties were suffered, but the crushing pressure was taken off Fighter Command's airfields and infrastructure. On the 15th, further daylight assaults on London were repulsed during what has been remembered ever since as 'Battle of Britain Day'. Although a few other daylight sorties were made over the capital, the main *Luftwaffe* offensive to destroy the RAF was coming to an unsuccess-

ful end. On the 17th, Hitler decided to postpone Operation 'Sealion', having suffered not only from the bravery and tenacity of Fighter Command pilots in the daylight battle, but also from the attentions of courageous Bomber Command aircrew against shipping in the invasion ports by night. The previously victorious *Luftwaffe* had met its match.

To understand the events of the air war, it must be appreciated that the battle fought was not the battle

ABOVE: Heinkel He 111 bombers flying in the tight formations they employed during the Battle of Britain. Mutually supporting defensive fire from their machine guns inflicted a steady stream of casualties on the British fighters and the bombers themselves were difficult to shoot down with the .303 machine guns carried by Spitfires and Hurricanes.

LEFT: The Battle of Britain was preceded by the *kanalkampf* or the 'battle of the Channel'. German bombers took a heavy toll of British shipping in operations also intended to draw the RAF fighters into action with superior numbers of Bf 109s.

anticipated. This had a bearing on the struggle. The campaign feared from pre-war days was that the *Luftwaffe* would despatch up to one thousand bombers a day, flying directly from Germany and unescorted because of the distance involved. These would cross the North Sea, making a landfall on the east coast, then would either raid the industrial Midlands and north or attack London and the south. Dowding disposed his forces to meet that anticipated battle. No 12 Group Fighter Command guarded the former areas and No 11 Group the latter, with the intention that the brunt of the assault would be shared by both Groups.

The reality of battle was quite different. Having overrun France and the Low Countries, the Germans found a series of airfields from which they were able to attack Britain from a mainly southerly or south-easterly direction. Being so close, these raids could be made with escorted bombers. The Air Ministry in London did not alter the balance of the defences to meet the battle as it was, rather than the battle they had predicted. In doing this they allowed the main burden to fall on No 11 Group, under its commander, Air Vice-Marshal Keith Park.

How strong were the two sides? There was at the time, and still is, a belief that a *Luftwaffe* of juggernaut size was faced by a mere handful of RAF fighters. Here were David and Goliath – and the origin of the term 'The Few'. This stemmed from the fact that fewer than 400 aircraft of No 11 Group were faced at close hand by the combined strengths of two German air fleets, *Luftflotten II* and *III*, which together comprised some 1,800 bombers and fighters. 'The Few' by the end of the battle were not so few. Pilots who served actively with Fighter Command between 10 July and 31 October 1940 were later awarded the Battle of Britain clasp to wear on their medal ribbon. They numbered 2,927.

Throughout the battle, RAF policy was to spread fighters across the United Kingdom so that, for example, on 8 July, of 50 operational squadrons in Fighter Command, only 22 were in No 11 Group to face the enemy's immediate onslaught. On that day, of nineteen squadrons of Spitfires, which

were the Command's fastest aircraft, no more than six were available in the south-east. Dowding's dilemma was clear. With bases stretching from the North Cape of Norway down to the Spanish frontier on the French western coast, the *Luftwaffe* might strike anywhere in Britain. His task was to keep Fighter Command in being as a composite force. Failure to do that would be a giant step towards a German victory.

The RAF started the battle with several advantages, and the *Luftwaffe* with some disadvantages, which at least partly redressed the imbalance in aircraft numbers. Fighter Command's main advantage lay in fighting the battle for which it had been created in 1936. This was the defence of the home base. The Command had been planned with no strategically offensive role, which was the main reason why Dowding was so adamant that as few of his fighters as possible should be sent to France. In 1940 Britain possessed the world's best aerial defence system. The scheme depended on the rapid transfer of information from radar (then known as radio direction-finding, or RDF). Messages were passed to Headquarters Fighter Command, then to Groups, then to Sectors, so that fighters could meet intruders at or beyond the coast. The British defensive system also included anti-aircraft guns and balloons, helping to protect vulnerable targets.

Another factor favouring the RAF was the slow start to the German campaign. Hitler's hesitation after the fall of France gave Fighter Command several weeks in which to reorganise its defences. The Germans' best opportunity of launching an invasion straight after Dunkirk was missed, much to British relief.

What were the German disadvantages? At root, the *Luftwaffe* alone was being asked to defeat Britain without help from the other two services: the German war engine was being required to operate on one cylinder out of three, a task beyond its capabilities. Göring, an ardent Nazi, confidant of Hitler and stranger to modesty, was pleased to offer the services of the *Luftwaffe*. However, there was no master plan for attacking the United Kingdom by air as part of an invasion.

THE BATTLE OF BRITAIN (RIGHT) was the essential prelude to a German invasion of England. The *Luftwaffe* had to win air superiority over southern England in order to safeguard the invasion fleet. However, the British were fighting for national survival and had developed a defensive system that worked well. By contrast, the German operations were almost amateur, poorly coordinated and often attacking inappropriate targets. German intelligence was poor and could not account for the apparently endless supply of Spitfires and Hurricanes; only after the war did they learn that British factories were producing 50 per cent more aircraft than their German rivals in 1940.

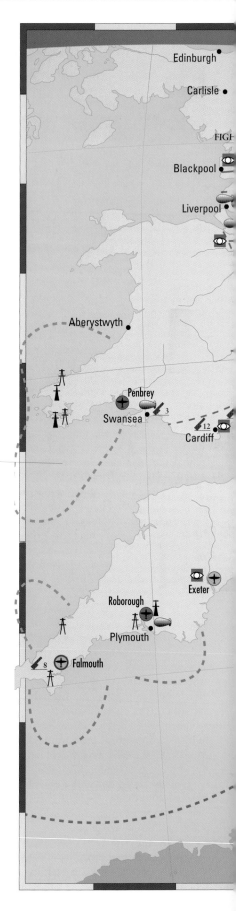

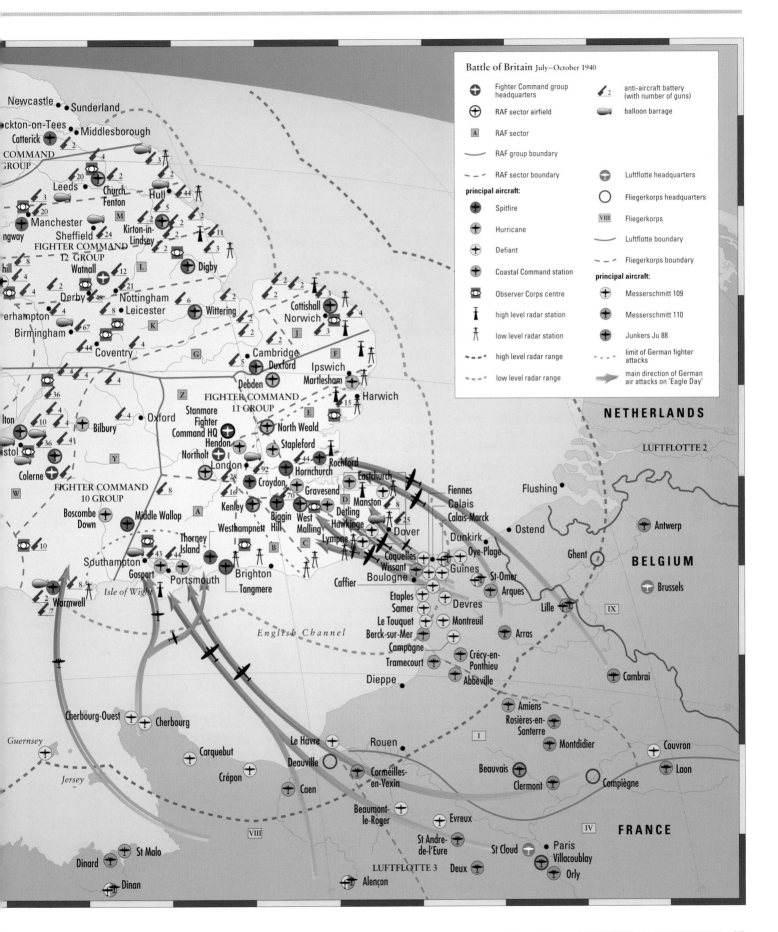

**ABOVE:** The Hawker Hurricane proved highly successful in combat over France in 1940. Although Spitfires soon dominated the headlines that summer, pilots in Hawker Hurricanes actually shot down more German aircraft than their comrades in Spitfires during the Battle of Britain.

**RIGHT:** A Hurricane undergoing maintenance. The wooden structure of the Hurricane made it easier and quicker to repair than the Spitfire. Some pilots thought the closer grouping of its guns made it easier to concentrate fire on the vulnerable areas of German bombers.

War with Britain had not been considered before 1938, and few plans had been drawn up until the following year. Then strategic attacks were suggested, particularly on British industry and seaborne supplies. The *Luftwaffe*, however, was a tactical, not a strategic air force. It had been so ever since the Spanish Civil War, when the development of cooperation with ground forces brought success which continued in land campaigns until the defeat of France. At the Channel coast, the system came to a halt.

Possibly the greatest constraint for the *Luftwaffe* was the narrow time scale offered to defeat Britain. Hitler's Directive No 17, finally ordering the destruction of the RAF, was not issued until 1 August, and the great 'Eagle' offensive, intended to achieve that end, did not come until the middle of the month. Bearing in mind the probable deterioration of the weather in the Channel from the end of September, the German Air Force was allocated a period of about seven weeks for success. Ambition certainly exceeded capability.

The Battle of Britain was essentially a contest between two sets of single-

seat monoplane fighters: on the German side the Bf 109, and for the RAF the Hurricane and Spitfire. These were the lords of the air and nothing could master them. The balance here is instructive. In the early stages of battle the *Luftwaffe* had about 760 Bf 109s; Fighter Command had some 710 Hurricanes and Spitfires. During the battle, British production and repair outstripped German, and overall in

1940 fighter production in the United Kingdom exceeded Germany's by a ratio of 3 to 2. Although wide credit for this has rightly been awarded to Lord Beaverbrook, the Minister of Aircraft Production, the pre-war work of Sir Wilfrid Freeman should not be overlooked.

What of the men, their machines and the tactics employed? Generally, the *Luftwaffe* pilots were more experi-

enced in war than their RAF counterparts. Many had gained experience in Spain, Poland and Norway, even before coming to the West. There is no substitute in war for learning from combat. German pilots believed strongly in what they were doing for their nation and had confidence bred from previous success. They were the élite of German youth.

RAF pilots appreciated how far Britain's fate depended on their efforts, although many modestly claimed that they were so busy trying to stay alive that there was little time to dwell on the future. They were of three main categories, the Regulars, the Auxiliaries and the Volunteer Reservists. A few had long flying hours to their credit, but the only battle experience had been gained in the French Campaign. Much was owed to flyers from overseas, who constituted about 15 per cent of the total. These men, from countries including Poland and Czechoslovakia, New Zealand and Canada – those from the former two organised in their own squadrons – made a vital difference, especially

during the later stages of the battle.

On both sides the airmen were young. A study of the rolls of honour of either the *Luftwaffe* or the RAF reinforces the words of one Fighter Command pilot, who said that men were becoming old at 21. At the age of

25 they certainly were. Douglas Bader, who commanded No 242 Squadron, was a senior figure, aged 30. Killing in the skies was a young man's contest.

At the start, the Germans' air fighting tactics were generally superior. From the Spanish Civil War they had

**ABOVE:** The standard German single-seater fighter during the Battle of Britain, the Messerschmitt Bf 109E was unforgiving for novices but fast, hardhitting and highly manoeuverable. Successive versions would serve in the frontline until 1945.

**LEFT:** A formation of the infamous Junkers Ju 87 Stuka dive bombers. Their low level attacks sapped the morale of Allied soldiers during the campaign in France, but in the Battle of Britain they proved highly vulnerable to British fighters. They were withdrawn, but continued to wreak havoc in the Mediterranean and on the Russian Front in later years.

**LEFT:** A Dornier Do 17 plunges to earth. Dornier's so-called 'flying pencil' was replaced by the Heinkel He 111 and Junkers Ju 88 in the bomber role, but many were converted into specialist night-fighters as the RAF stepped up its attacks on Germany.

**RIGHT:** The Supermarine Spitfire was already a legend in 1940. Developed by its designer with precious little help from the British government, its excellent all-round performance came as a disagreeable surprise to German fighter pilots used to enjoying a technological edge over their opponents.

**LEFT:** Spitfire production exceeded British losses throughout the battle. Over-claiming by German aircrew and underestimates of British manufacturing rates led German intelligence to predict the imminent collapse of British resistance.

developed the 'finger-four' formation, with four fighters flying roughly in line abreast, about 150yds apart. Pilots then could look inwards and outwards, up and down, to guard the rear and flanks of comrades. In action, the four broke into two pairs, each having a leader and a wingman, whose task was to guard the former's tail. The system worked well.

The RAF from pre-war days had trained on 'vic-threes', with a triangle of three aircraft – a leader and two wingmen. The latter had to look inwards, holding position close by the leader's tail, and avoiding each other. Some pilots felt that the formation was good for the Hendon Air Display but of little use in combat. The 'vic-three' was designed to meet formations of unescorted bombers and against those would have been effective. However, dealing with enemy fighters demanded a different pattern. During the battle, some squadrons evolved their own tactics, but others failed to change and suffered heavily.

Concerning intelligence, in general the RAF tended to overestimate the numbers and strength of the *Luftwaffe*. The Germans, generally, wrongly estimated their opponents in two particular aspects. The first was the British use of radar, which became the 'eyes' of Fighter Command. During the battle, the *Luftwaffe* made no concerted onslaught on RDF stations; had they done so, the defences would have been 'blinded'. The second was their wide overestimate of RAF losses, so that by mid-September some senior intelligence officers believed that Fighter Command had only 50 aircraft left to defend London. In spite of some later claims, Fighter Command did not have the benefit of information from 'Ultra', the Enigma machine, to give immediate knowledge of when and where German raids would be aimed. RAF commanders had to rely on other sources of intelligence, which makes their efforts all the more praiseworthy.

The cost of the battle was high for both sides, although exact figures are not easy to assess. The number of *Luftwaffe* aircraft destroyed is usually given as 1,733 and, as most were bombers, the loss rate of aircrew was considerable. For example, between

July and September 955 medium bombers were destroyed or damaged, 69 per cent of the initial strength. Flying over Britain lacked much of the easy attraction of earlier campaigns. In the same period the *Luftwaffe* had over 1,000 fighters destroyed or damaged. The customary figure for Royal Air Force fighters destroyed is 915, although adding other types of aircraft hit on the ground raises RAF losses above a thousand. Of over 2,900 pilots who gained the Battle of Britain clasp with Fighter Command, 487 were killed by the end of October and 833 others did not survive the war.

For many nations, the Battle of Britain would prove to be the most important struggle of the war. Here was an 'either/or' campaign. Either Britain did not lose and could stay in the war, or, by losing, she would have been forced out. Later in the war British forces suffered defeats, for example in North Africa and the Far East. By then, however, Britain had allies who, even if the United Kingdom had been overrun, could have contin-

ued the struggle. In the autumn of 1940 Britain stood alone, and her defeat would have brought dire international results.

Firstly, by not losing, Britain gave hope to many European countries already occupied by the Nazis; for the rest of the war she was a beacon of light amid the darkness of oppression. Secondly, had Britain been defeated, Germany could have invaded the USSR earlier in 1941. As it was, German troops reached the gates of Moscow and Leningrad. With extra forces released from the West at Hitler's disposal, there is every chance that his attack would have had greater success in his effort to overthrow Bolshevism. Next, in the Far East, Japan would have been in a position to make earlier demands on the old European empires of Holland, France and Great Britain in her search for economic and political benefit. War in the Far East might well have taken a different course. What of the United States? Probably, with Britain defeated, the US would have become more isolationist, if only for the

reason that there would have been no European springboard from which to hit back at Nazi Germany. Gradually, the United Kingdom became a 'floating aircraft carrier', naval base and military barracks from which the D-Day operation would be launched. Without this, the 3,000 miles of Atlantic Ocean would have precluded US intervention and American eyes would have turned elsewhere.

In Britain an enemy victory would have been followed by a severe regime. Undoubtedly, as in all occupied countries, a few people would have collaborated, but under harsh German military law. For example, the German Army Order of 9 September 1940, signed by General Halder, ordered the removal of all men aged from 17 to 45 from Britain to the Continent as soon as possible, obviously for the purposes of slave labour. The *Gestapo* produced a 'black book' with names of prominent people who were to be arrested. These varied, bizarrely, from Churchill and his Cabinet to H. G. Wells, and from Noël Coward to Virginia Woolf.

**ABOVE:** Dorner Do 17s flying in tight formation to provide mutual support from their defensive machine guns. The British tracked their approach by radar as they crossed the Channel and also visually from observation posts along the bombers' likely routes.

# The Night Blitz

With the avowed aim of finally removing the British thorn from their flesh, from September the Germans stepped up a night bombing offensive. This had been carried on to a small, yet gradually increasing, degree since June 1940, as the French Campaign was ending.

The new offensive opened in Wagnerian style on 7 September. Late that afternoon, Göring came to the Channel coast to watch the despatch of 348 bombers, protected by 617 fighters, aiming for the first heavy raid an London. Their main target was Dockland, in the east of the city. By the time they had finished, about 6 p.m., the largest blazes seen since the Great Fire of London in 1666 were burning out of control. The *Luftwaffe*'s declared intention was to hit economic targets – docks, factories, warehouses and shipping – and this they did. However, they also, inevitably, destroyed or damaged hundreds of nearby civilian buildings. As night came on, a further 250 bombers arrived to continue the attack. By the next morning over 2,000 Londoners had been killed or seriously injured. The intensive Night Blitz was under way.

The campaign, in its main phase, lasted until June 1941, far longer than the daylight battle. There were two main aims. The first was to destroy Britain's industrial capacity by bombing factories, transport centres, shipyards and ports. The Germans hoped to cause so much damage that Britain would be unable to continue the struggle. As most of those targets were situated in or near large cities, a second aim followed. This was to break civilian morale, so that the British people would compel their government to make peace. As events unfolded, the Night Blitz became largely a battle between *Luftwaffe* aircrew, who were trained in war, and British civilians, who were not.

Several *Luftwaffe* leaders later suggested economic reasons for the change in strategy. After the first tentative plans for possible air raids on Britain were laid late in 1938, two main objectives were selected. One was shipping, both merchant and naval, while the other was a series of industrial and transport centres on the mainland. These had not been raided during the daylight battle, when the prime targets had been airfields. Now, with the erroneous belief that Fighter Command was on its last legs, the pressure could be turned on Britain's economy. At the same time, the Germans believed that an erosion of civilian morale, together with widespread destruction, would show British people the futility of further resistance. Douhet's theories would be put into practice.

However, a more potent reason for the change to the Night Blitz came from German bomber losses. By late August they were so heavy, with so little result for the effort involved, that they could not be easily sustained. An obvious solution was to fly under the

cloak of darkness, escaping the depredations of Hurricanes and Spitfires and giving aircrew the opportunity of rebuilding morale. One German pilot wrote on 25 August that 'the losses suffered by our bombers must be terrible', while a senior fighter commander admitted that the change came 'because of severe losses in daylight raids'. All German medium bombers had a weak defensive armament to counter Hurricanes and Spitfires, while the double crossing of the Channel became an increasing peril.

Subsequently, the change to night bombing certainly reduced the *Luftwaffe*'s casualties. In the three months from 1 October to 31 December 1940 bomber losses due directly to British action fell to 140. At the same time, widespread destruction and heavy casualties were caused across the United Kingdom. Several months elapsed before the defences were able to find raiders accurately and inflict heavier casualties on them.

German air formations associated particularly with night bombing were part of *Luftflotte III*, under the command of *Feldmarschall* Sperrle, and flew from bases across the north and north-west of France. Many of the airmen were experienced flyers; one bomber pilot over London on 7 September was making his 69th raid of the war.

As with the daylight campaign, the largest German aircraft was the Heinkel He 111, with a five-man crew. Wide use was also made of the speedy Junkers Ju 88, in which the *Luftwaffe* invested great faith. The Dornier Do 17, often used by day, was seldom employed at night. Paradoxically, the Stuka dive-bomber, so ineffective in the daylight battle, was twice used to open raids in darkness.

It seemed remarkable that, in spite of the 'black-out' and often in bad weather, bombers were able to reach British cities unerringly. By early 1940 the Germans had developed methods of guiding aircraft along radio beams, emitted from transmitters on the mainland Continent, to cross the target. Basically, pilots were led on the correct course along, or parallel to, the beam, then other cross-beams indicated the position of the target and bombs could be released. British scien-

tists were aware of these beams from June 1940 and soon a secret contest developed between them and their German counterparts. Churchill called this 'The Wizard War'. German beams were aimed at cities across the United Kingdom, while British scientists tried to jam or distort them with counter-signals. In this contest, both sides

enjoyed victories – and suffered defeats.

To meet the threat of night bombing were two types of defence – the armed services and civil defence. At ground level, the services had anti-aircraft guns, searchlights and balloons, whilst in the air were night fighters. All, however, suffered for some months from

**ABOVE:** St Paul's emerges through the smoke and fire during a German bombing attack on 29 December 1940. By the end of 1940, the *Luftwaffe* had dropped over 13,000 tons of bombs on London and about a million incendiaries.

**LEFT:** Over 500 firemen and members of the London Auxiliary Fire Fighting Services, including many women, combined in a war exercise over the ground covered by Greenwich (London) Fire Station.

WOMEN OF BRITAIN

COME INTO THE FACTORIES

ASK AT ANY EMPLOYMENT EXCHANGE FOR ADVICE AND FULL DETAILS

and airborne radar. For the British this was the Beaufighter, but few of them were operational until March 1941. By then cities across Britain had been deluged with bombs by the thousand. Consequently, for six months service defences were on the back foot and attackers struck when and where they chose. There were dividends for the *Luftwaffe*. Bombers caused widespread damage, while their losses fell.

The Second World War is sometimes called 'The People's War' because civilians were closely involved in their own defence. Their position in war occupied the thoughts of many strategists after 1918. Were they legitimate targets during a conflict? Yes, asserted some writers. The man constructing a rifle in a factory is as dangerous as the soldier who fires it; so too is the woman who makes the bullet. It is as lawful to bomb them at their workplaces as to bomb soldiers on the battlefield. If they are at home, they are still proper targets because they are providers of weapons, and therefore equal to servicemen who are always legitimate prey. Other leaders believed that striking at civilians, whatever their standing, was immoral. Such actions were just not cricket. Wars should be fought on battlefields,

or in the skies, or on the oceans. Civilians and their homes should be spared. At the start of the war, both sides pledged that cities and civilian targets would be immune from aerial bombardment. These statements, however, included the escape clause that parties would not attack civilians unless their opponents did. There was the rub. In bombing, blast respects no boundaries and does not stop at the factory gate. Soon, civilians and their homes were affected and pledges collapsed in a welter of mutual recrimination. In reality, there are no non-combatants in modern war.

Thousands of British civilians had experienced air attack before 1940, a point often overlooked. Many aged over 30 had suffered raids during the First World War, especially at night, from Zeppelins and bombers as Germans pioneered the aerial bombing of civilians. Although attacks were comparatively light, the nature of assault was similar: guns, searchlights, fighters and death from the skies – in Biblical terms, the terror that walketh in darkness.

Between 1918 and 1939 the fear of air raids grew dramatically. Until the late 1930s bombers were often as fast as fighters, carried more guns and were

**ABOVE:** Facing national extinction, the British moved much faster than the Germans in the complete mobilisation of the civilian workforce. Women replaced male workers in the factories, releasing more men for the armed forces. In contrast to Britain's post-war industrial problems, the wartime economy was managed with such success that production rates surpassed that of Germany for a while.

**RIGHT:** Barrage balloons were raised over key targets to frustrate low level attacks and dive bombing. Here, WAAF (Womens' Auxiliary Air Force) teams assemble in a hanger for instructions.

one cardinal weakness. The combination of radar and the Observer Corps, excellent for tracking daylight raids, could not work at night. Radar scanners faced seawards and could not follow aircraft past the coast; observers could not see in darkness. Not until early 1941, when the Blitz had been running for several months, was ground radar improved for guns and searchlights, bringing about more accurate fire. Until then thousands of shells were fired into the night sky – good for public morale but not very effective.

The Royal Air Force had problems through a lack of night fighters. People wondered why Hurricanes and Spitfires could not defend them at night. The answer was that they were day fighters, not designed for the 'cat-and-mouse' game of combat in darkness. The ideal night fighter, as the Germans discovered for themselves later in the war, needed a two-man crew, a good speed, a heavy armament

considered unstoppable. When Stanley Baldwin told Parliament in 1932 that 'the bomber will always get through', people believed him. The Air Ministry, prophets of doom, offered alarming predictions of casualties and damage, with cities shattered, their panic-stricken inhabitants shrouded in gas.

In this atmosphere, preparations were made for civil defence as Nazi power grew from 1933 and the clouds of war approached. By the time of the Munich Crisis of 1938 over 1.14 million men and women were serving in Air Raid Precautions (ARP) organisations. The development of aircraft changed the nature of war, placing civilians in the front line. They had to train to defend themselves and their homes.

Householders prepared for the anticipated onslaught. Gas-proof rooms were set up in houses, with all cracks sealed, to which families and pets could retire. Gas masks were issued. Windows were taped to prevent flying glass and, by law, 'blackout' had to be complete. Small Anderson shelters, costing £5 each but issued free to families with an income of less than £250 per annum, were installed in gardens or backyards. Later, householders received small stirrup pumps, useful for tackling incendiary bombs – or greenfly in the garden!

The Blitz fell into several phases. The prime target throughout was London. For the Germans, this was the capital of the British Empire, the seat of enemy government, the world's largest city and Britain's biggest port, transport and industrial centre. It was clearly marked and easily reached. Taking day and night raids together, by 31 December 1940 the city was bombed 126 times. From 7 September London was hit on 54 consecutive nights, and 67 night raids had occurred by 14 November. A major raid was one in which at least 100 tons of high explosives were dropped, apart from incendiaries. By May 1941 the capital had suffered 71 of these; the next highest total of major raids on any city was eight. Over 18,000 tons of high explosives fell there in addition to hundreds of thousands of fire bombs.

A few examples will suffice. On 17 September the *Luftwaffe* unloaded more than 350 tons of bombs on the

capital – more than the total dropped on the whole of Britain throughout the First World War. Three weeks later, Göring ordered that London was to be annihilated, and shortly afterwards some 1,200 civilians were killed or injured in seven hours. The last great raid of the year, on 29 December, was a heavy incendiary attack on the square mile of the City. In that night, eight Wren churches were destroyed or damaged and fire temperatures reached 1,000°C. Towards the end of the Blitz there were four great raids; in each of three of them over 1,000 civilians died. Their intensity can be judged from the last two. On 19 April 1941 the Germans dropped, for the first time in one raid, over 1,000 tons of high explosives, together with 153,000 incendiaries. The greatest

total of civilians killed in any raid on Britain – 1,436 – came from the *Luftwaffe*'s final kick on 10 May, when over 2,000 fires were started and 5,000 homes destroyed.

The places hit are familiar at the end of the twentieth century as some of London's exceptional buildings – Buckingham Palace, the Tower of London, St Paul's, Westminster Abbey, the Mansion House and the Law Courts. The list could go on. By mid-February 1941, 94,000 houses had been destroyed across Britain, with a further 1.4 million damaged; about two-thirds of these were in the capital. Churches and hospitals, schools and shops and houses and flats were turned into cataracts of masonry.

What of other cities? From mid-November, industrial centres were pin-

ABOVE: An electrical fitter at work in a partly completed British bomber. Only in the air could Britain take the war to the enemy and the experience of German bomber attacks in 1940 spurred the British to develop their strategic bombing force into the devastatingly powerful weapon it would become by 1943.

RIGHT: The failure of the Blitz did not end Hitler's determination to flatten London. It led to redoubled efforts to produce 'vengeance' weapons. In 1944 they were unleashed. Here is a V1 flying bomb pictured just before impact in London. These 'vengeance' weapons had no military value since they were unable to hit a target smaller than a city, and even then often missed. But their terror effect was enormous and post-war British estimates suggested it cost the British four times as much to defend the country against the V1s as it cost the Germans to build them.

pointed, for example, Birmingham, Sheffield, Manchester and Coventry. This phase opened with the Coventry raid on 14 November, an attack which became infamous in aviation history. Because local industries were closely intermingled with civilian and historic buildings, great devastation occurred, with 568 civilians killed. A new verb, 'to 'coventrate', entered both the German and English languages.

Ports also were bombed: in the south, Portsmouth and Southampton; in the west, Plymouth, Bristol, Cardiff, Swansea, Merseyside, Clydeside and Belfast. At the end of the Night Blitz, ports in the north-east, especially Hull, were raided. The Germans claimed that aiming points were economic targets but, in reality, from the aspect of

the nation's ability to fight on, no crucial damage was caused to factories and docks, transport centres and supplies. The widest destruction occurred in central civic areas. Today, a visit to some cities shows how their centres were rebuilt in the 1950s and 1960s, areas where homes, offices, shops and places of worship had become deserts or bonfires. The *Luftwaffe* rearranged British architecture. Hitler did more for slum clearance in eight months than local authorities had achieved in 50 years.

Raids on western ports intensified early in 1941 as part of the Battle of the Atlantic. The Germans aimed not only to hit shipping in the Western Approaches, but also the ports receiving cargoes. Thus Merseyside, which

had been raided at night even before London, suffered heavy assaults in which dock and civilian areas alike were blasted. Towards the end of the Blitz the area received 'The May Week', when an onslaught was launched on the first seven nights of the month, killing almost 2,000 and leaving 70,000 homeless.

Clydeside was raided from March to May, with great destruction resulting. Of Clydebank's 12,000 homes, only eight escaped damage. Although shipyards and docks were hit, the Germans failed to halt their operation and could not prevent vital supplies arriving from overseas. The long arm of the *Luftwaffe* reached out to Belfast in April and May. The region was considered by many to be immune to attack because of its distance from *Luftwaffe* bases. They were wrong, and in two major raids over 1,000 civilians were killed.

Some of the most intense bombing occurred in Plymouth, a comparatively small city. Of its eight major raids, five fell within one week at the end of April. Great areas of the city and nearby Devonport were simply wiped out, including 50 churches or chapels. Such suffering and devastation occurred to a greater or lesser degree in every city raided. It also was seen in hundreds of smaller towns and villages across the land. For example, in one small town to the south of London, of the 720 hours, day and night, in September 1940, the population were under 'Red Alert', that is attack, for 300 of them.

Overall, the Night Blitz failed in its main aim, to break Britain's capacity to make war. Supplies of gas, coal, oil, electricity and water seldom stopped. Food losses were minimal and weekly rations were sustained. These were, for the average adult, 1lb meat, 4oz bacon, 2oz butter, 6oz fat, 8oz sugar and 2oz tea. British people then suffered neither from malnutrition nor obesity.

Three other factors prevented German success. First, through the growing strength of night fighter and anti-aircraft defences, between March and May 1941 the *Luftwaffe* lost about 200 aircraft. The second factor was poor German strategy, with a lack of concentration and a switching from target to target. Occasionally they launched *Doppelgänger* raids, hitting

LEFT: Many children were evacuated from London at the outbreak of war, but had returned by the time of the Blitz a year later. Some families took to pre-fabricated bomb shelters dug in their gardens, others famously took cover in the London Underground. Families were told that the safest place was under the stairs, but Victorian terraced housing was not built to withstand such damage and whole city blocks could be levelled by a 1,000 kg 'fat Herman' bomb.

one target on consecutive nights, but that policy was not sustained. The greatest success came from concentrating on a city for several nights, for example Plymouth or Liverpool. The third factor was the *Luftwaffe*'s lack of a heavy bomber. Had the Germans possessed truly heavy aircraft, Dresdens and Hamburgs would have been suffered in Britain. As it was, between May and November 1940 Bomber Command killed 975 German civilians; in the same period the *Luftwaffe* killed 15,000 British civilians. Between September 1940 and May 1941 the casualty rate was heavier than at any other time of the war. An average of about 180 civilians a day were killed, bringing a total of 42,000, half of whom died in London. About 60,000 were seriously hurt.

The Night Blitz also failed to achieve its second aim, namely to break public morale. Overall, the population reacted stoically and proved Douhet wrong. Those in ARP rose to the challenge. Dire pre-war predictions of enormous casualties and psychological breakdown were wide of the mark. 'Mass hysteria was feared,' wrote a medical correspondent in 1941, 'but nothing of the sort happened – anywhere.' He added that women suffered less than men from bomb shock, but were more likely to discuss it. Overall, British reserve was broken down. 'Death is a great leveller,' commented one writer. 'It has smashed the silence of the railway carriage.' The best remedy was to take part in civil defence. Civilians were scared by bombing, and devastated by the loss of loved ones or their homes, but generally they got on with it. They saw their friends doing their duty – so they did theirs.

The techniques of making raids were studied carefully by RAF commanders. The subsequent intensive bombing of Germany owed much to what they learned from the *Luftwaffe* over Britain during the Night Blitz.

ABOVE: Two ladies among the rubble of a row of almshouses in Newbury. Through poor intelligence or bad navigation, German raids struck many small towns as well as the big cities.

LEFT: Heavy anti-aircraft batteries seen on a pre-war exercise in Hyde Park. Londoners knew the guns fired more for the effect on morale than with any serious hope of hitting a bomber and some resented the noise that was often louder than the bombs detonating. *Luftwaffe* bomber losses in the Blitz were a mere 1.5 per cent per sortie in 1940 although they climbed steeply later in the war as night-fighters were developed.

RIGHT: Having failed to overcome Britain's defences, the Germans increased their efforts to sever the Atlantic 'lifeline' across which came many of the raw materials for British war industries as well as a high proportion of foodstuffs. Fortunately for the British, the weather in the North Atlantic was bad even by its normal standards in the winter of 1940–41 and the merchantships enjoyed a brief respite from U-boat attacks.

RIGHT: Admiral Karl Dönitz was a veteran submarine captain from 1914–18 who inspired enormous loyalty from his crews in the Second World War. Had his pleas for a 200-boat force been listened to in the 1930s, Germany might well have won the Battle of the Atlantic.

Having failed in their strategy to force a British surrender either from the daylight battle or from night bombing, the Germans tried another form of attack. This was the third campaign against the United Kingdom and is generally known as the Battle of the Atlantic. Hitler believed that Britain could be defeated through an assault on seaborne supplies. This would be achieved by a combination of air and submarine attacks on imports. By August 1940, many units of the *Luftwaffe* and the *Kriegsmarine* were ready to exert a blockade on the United Kingdom. Through the employment of warships, armed merchant raiders, U-boats, mines and bombs, they would implement a strategic aim laid down before the war.

They operated particularly from the west coast of France, aiming for the Atlantic convoys, whose supplies were essential for Britain. The *Luftwaffe* moved Condor long-range bombers there, from where they could range over the Western Approaches, either striking directly at ships or reporting their position to U-boats in the area. They enjoyed some successes, but were hindered by bad weather from November 1940 until February 1941.

With the coming of spring, both the *Luftwaffe* and the *Kriegsmarine* intensified their efforts. The German Navy believed that the Air Force alone could sink 300,000 tons of shipping each month, a figure almost achieved between March and May. The Navy, under Admiral Dönitz (who had never been in favour of 'Sealion'), reckoned that if 750,000 tons of shipping could be sunk each month for a year, by the combined efforts of the *Luftwaffe* and the *Kriegsmarine*, Britain would be defeated. Consequently the campaign launched by bombers and, more particularly, by U-boats caused great concern to the British government.

Between 31 March and 31 May 1941 U-boats sank 142 ships, grossing over 800,000 tons. Of those, 99 were British. In the same period *Luftwaffe* aircraft sank another 179 vessels. A further 77 were destroyed by surface vessels or mines. Such losses were heavy for Britain, because the sea link with the United States was threatened. This link, as Churchill well appreciated, was vital for diplomatic as well as economic reasons. Therefore a vigorous campaign to meet the threat was launched by the Royal Navy, with some success in the sinking of U-boats. Nonetheless, the danger to Britain's supplies was not removed by the summer of 1941 and remained for much of the war.

At the end of May 1941 there occurred one of the most dramatic incidents in the Battle of the Atlantic, one which, for Britain, almost spelled disaster. Admiral Raeder, Commander-in-Chief of the *Kriegsmarine*, had fewer surface vessels than the Royal Navy, but one of them was the recently built *Bismarck*. This vessel was, at the time, possibly the world's most powerful battleship. Raeder moved *Bismarck*,

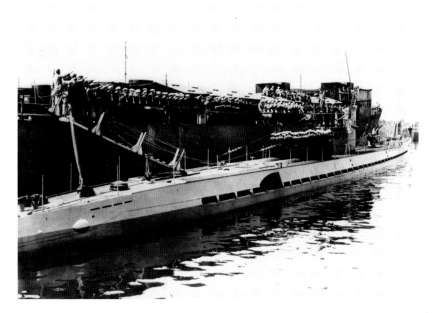

LEFT: Nazi salutes all round as *U-42* prepares to sortie. She was an early casualty but other Type IX boats made astonishingly long patrols, reaching into the Indian Ocean and even as far as Japanese-held Singapore and Indonesia later in the war.

accompanied by a cruiser, from the Baltic Sea, via the Norwegian coast and the Arctic Circle near Greenland, out into the North Atlantic. Once there, rich pickings awaited in the form of convoys sailing to and from the United Kingdom. The threat to Britain's maritime trade was ominous.

Ships of the Royal Navy's Home Fleet were despatched to intercept the German vessels and an action was fought in the Denmark Strait early on 24 May. In this, HMS *Hood*, the pride of the Royal Navy, blew up with the

loss of 1,400 lives. Only three men survived. The ship was 'one of our most cherished naval possessions,' Churchill wrote. 'Her loss was a bitter grief.' *Bismarck* sailed on. At the British Admiralty there were mixed emotions – sorrow over losing *Hood*, fear of the threat to merchant shipping, and a desire to avenge. Naval units were quickly gathered to confront the German vessel before it could reach the safety of a western French port. So much was at stake.

Salvation for the British came first

BELOW: In the first part of the war U-boats made frequent use of their deck guns to conserve torpedoes, just as they had in 1914–18. However, once most shipping was concentrated in convoys and lone targets became rarer, the guns became superfluous and were removed from late-war boats.

ABOVE: Two young sailors and their pet dog aboard the British battlecruiser *Hood*. In action with the *Bismarck* on 24 May 1941, *Hood* blew up with the loss of all but three of the 1,419 officers and men aboard.

the battleship's fate by jamming the starboard rudder and wrecking her steering gear. The vessel then was 400 miles from the French port of Brest, but could move only slowly in circles.

The end came next morning, 27 May. A British fleet arrived, including two battleships. For two hours *Bismarck* was battered with shellfire, then torpedoed. Eventually she turned over and sank, with the loss of over 2,200 men. The loss of *Hood* had been avenged and a threat to convoys removed. The whole episode, however, had been a close-run business, and without the intervention of air power *Bismarck* might well have escaped. The Germans reverted to waging maritime war with U-boats and, to a decreasing degree, Condor bombers.

What finally reduced the *Luftwaffe*'s involvement in the Battle of the Atlantic by mid-1941 was the approaching campaign against the USSR. Many bomber units were moved eastwards across Europe and the pressure on the United Kingdom eased. By then, the Night Blitz on British ports was also slackening. In June 1941 the British government and

not from the sea but from the air. This was a lesson learned, sometimes at great cost, by all of the world's navies later in the war. When Royal Navy ships lost contact with *Bismarck*, she was located by a reconnaissance aircraft of Coastal Command. Then she was attacked twice by torpedo-bombers from a carrier and hit three times altogether. One torpedo sealed

RIGHT: Seen from the German cruiser *Prinz Eugen*, *Bismarck* fires on HMS *Hood* during their brief but deadly action in the Denmark Strait. The *Hood* was sunk and the *Prince of Wales* driven off, but the Royal Navy was determined to intercept the German squadron before it could dock in France.

people could look back on a hard year. From the collapse of their French ally, when defeat appeared to be imminent, they had experienced three major German attempts to force them out of the war. Throughout the Battle of Britain, the Night Blitz and the early stages of the Battle of the Atlantic, they had suffered heavily. Yet they were undefeated. In spite of many predictions of an early demise, they were still alive and kicking.

**ABOVE:** *Bismarck* in Norway shortly before her fatal maiden voyage. Admiral Raeder's decision to send her into the Atlantic owed more to the need to reassert the navy's importance to his *Führer* than the battleship's potential to sink merchantships. The loss of the *Bismarck* led Hitler to order his remaining heavy units back to Germany and leave the Atlantic battle to the U-boats.

**LEFT:** The Fairey Swordfish was an obsolete biplane torpedo-bomber and reconnaissance aircraft, but it was a flight of such aircraft that damaged the *Bismarck* enough to slow her down. The *Bismarck* was brought to action by the British battleships *King George V* and *Rodney* and sunk within a few hours of safety.

Soviet power was an enigma. Here was the world's largest nation geographically, spanning two continents and covering one-sixth of the Earth's land surface. Living under Stalin's iron grip was a population of not far short of 200 million people, providing a vast supply of recruits for the fighting services. The Russian Air Force was numerically the world's largest. The nation's people were used to hardship and privations beyond the experience of most of the inhabitants of Western Europe. Across the main battle areas in western Russia, the vastness of space and harsh climate could be devastating to armies. Why, then, historians have since asked, did Hitler invade the Soviet Union?

Some view the move as a product of Hitler's megalomania. He had plans – a Grand Design – for world domination, and overcoming the USSR was an important step towards that end. According to Bullock, the invasion came 'for the simple but sufficient reason that he had always meant to establish the foundation of his thousand-year Reich by annexation of the territory between the Vistula and the Urals'. His further expansion could surpass the successes of Alexander the Great by driving into India and sweeping down through the Caucasus to meet with his forces advancing through North Africa. Others believe that he wanted no more than to consolidate Germany's position as Europe's greatest nation, with power and influence across the east and south-east of the continent. As Russia was a rival there, a contest of arms was inevitable.

There were also compelling economic reasons for the invasion. A military dictatorship is a hungry animal, needing to be fed with the materials of war. Without them, the state's strength is rapidly exhausted. Germany's maritime trade had been largely cut off by the British blockade. However, an extensive network of land routes enabled supplies to be imported from neighbours and the conquered territories. Oil was transported from Rumania. Nickel and timber arrived from Finland, while the iron ore trade with Sweden had been safeguarded by the Norwegian Campaign. Many goods also arrived from the occupied

countries as the Germans took the spoils of victory, plundering the defeated nations. These places also provided slave labour.

A vital supply line came from Russia, with whom, since the Nazi-Soviet Pact of August 1939, Germany had been at peace. In February 1940 a commercial agreement with the USSR allowed Hitler to receive a steady flow of supplies from the East. Over the following year the Russians undertook to send 900,000 tons of oil and one million tons of cereals. In addition, they provided chrome, iron ore, cotton, rubber and phosphorous. A year later the agreement was renewed, much to Germany's benefit, because it bypassed the British naval blockade.

There was, however, one snag which concerned Hitler and his advisers. As the supplies reached Germany from the USSR, the Russians exercised control over one of the Reich's main lifelines. It would be possible for the Soviets to close the frontier overnight, thereby strangling their neighbour. All would depend on the mutual attitudes of two great dictatorships – which hardly shared a common outlook. One way of overcoming the uncertainty of this position, Hitler estimated, would be to conquer the Soviet Union and take over the supply of vital materials. By invading the USSR the *Führer* would also be seeking *Lebensraum*, or living space, for his people. Vast areas of Russia could provide settlements, while, at the same time, there would be the bonus of oil from the Caucasus and wheat from the Ukraine. For him, this brought recollections of 1918, when those areas had been occupied by the German Army after the defeat of Russia.

Underpinning these motives for attacking the USSR was Hitler's deep-seated hatred of Communism – probably his fiercest conviction. The Nazis' resolve to overthrow 'Jewish Bolshevism', to which they had been opposed since the political street battles of the 1920s, was ingrained in their philosophy. They hated the 'Red butchers' of Moscow, which was regarded as the home of Marxism.

As with all gamblers, the *Führer* assessed the odds before making a decision. How strong were the Russian armed forces? Would they be

**RIGHT:** A German supply column crosses yet another river in northern Russia, September 1941. The bulk of the German army's transport units remained horse-drawn throughout the war but German horses would fare badly in Russia where the fodder supplies dwindled and only local ponies could survive the winter temperatures. Hitler had persuaded his commanders that a lightning summer campaign could overcome Russian resistance in a matter of weeks. For a time, it seemed he might be right.

able to withstand a pounding from the German Army which had so quickly overrun Western Europe? With memories of the collapse of Russia in 1917, Hitler estimated that the numerical masses available to the USSR could count for little. During the war with Finland in late 1939 Stalin's men had often performed badly. The Germans believed that their own troops were the best in the world. The Red Army in western Russia, if hit by a panzer *Blitzkrieg*, would probably collapse as quickly as the Allied forces had in France. With careful planning, all Russian armies to the west of Moscow

could be surrounded, cut off and annihilated by a swift offensive. The war
could be over in about six weeks.

All of these compelling reasons
fermented in Hitler's mind, but there
was another, equally powerful factor
sometimes overlooked. This was the
failure to defeat the United Kingdom.
With a strange logic, he estimated that
the stubborn British could receive help
only from Russia or the United States.
If the USSR were defeated, the
Americans would be unwilling or
unable to become involved in
European affairs. 'Should Russia,
however, be smashed,' noted General

Halder in his diary, 'then England's
last hope will be shattered.' After overwhelming the Red Army, the Germans
would turn back to Western Europe.
Britain then would either see sense and
make peace, or would be invaded and
defeated in an updated version of
Operation 'Sealion'.

The treaty made with the Russians
in August 1939 certainly did not lead
to an era of happy cooperation
between the two dictatorships. The
treaty had agreed that the Baltic states
of Latvia, Lithuania and Estonia
should be placed in the Soviet Union's
sphere of influence, but on 15 June

1940, as France was in its death-
throes, Stalin acted. He announced
that the three states had 'asked' to be
incorporated into the USSR; needless
to say, he had agreed. Hitler and his
advisers, busy in the West, were uneasy
over what was happening in the East.

Worse was to come. About a week
later the Germans were informed that
the Red Army was about to recoup
parts of Rumania which Russia had
lost in 1918. The news was a blow to
Hitler because the Russians were now
uncomfortably near to the Rumanian
oilfields on which Germany relied
greatly for supplies.

# The Balkan Campaign

Hitler's active planning for this attack had begun in July 1940, after the French Campaign. The onslaught would open in spring 1941. Before then, however, the actions of his ally, Mussolini, in south-eastern Europe caused a change of plans as Hitler was forced to intervene to rescue the Italians from the morass into which they had blundered. The *Führer* found, much to his annoyance, that his hand was being forced by Mussolini's grandiose attempts to ape the Germans, set in motion late in 1940.

On 28 October, the Italians declared war on Greece, launching their invasion from Albania. Mussolini was trying to gain prestige from a rapid victory, proving that he was a great war leader with dynamic armed forces. He never consulted his ally over his plans. '*Führer*, we are on the march,' he told a surprised and angry Hitler when they met on the day of the invasion. 'Victorious Italian troops crossed the Greco-Albanian frontier at dawn today!' The Greeks, however, refused to fit into the Italian timetable. They fought in mountainous terrain with a skill and resilience that heartened friends and dismayed enemies. By mid-November the Greek Army had counter-attacked, forcing the Italians to retreat some fifteen miles into Albania. The greatly trumpeted victory march had turned into a shambles.

Of five nations in the Balkan region, three soon submitted to Hitler's wishes and plans. They were Rumania, Hungary and Bulgaria, whose leaders were influenced by what the Germans had done to Poland – and that country had started with greater armed forces than any of them possessed. To oppose the Nazis could severely damage a nation's health. Consequently, their governments came increasingly to agree with Hitler's demands. In September 1940 German troops were 'invited' into Rumania; soon afterwards they entered Hungary. In March 1941 the German Twelfth Army crossed into Bulgaria, where a Nazi military mission had been operating for two months. All three of these small countries had lost their independence without the Germans having to fire a shot. Now they were Hitler's vassals.

However, Yugoslavia and Greece were unwilling to cooperate with Hitler's plans for controlling the entire Balkan area before launching an invasion of Russia. For his part, the *Führer* was not prepared to open operations against the USSR until they were. Hence, in April and May 1941 he launched a short, savage campaign to bring both into line.

The actions consisted of two operations, 'Punishment', to deal with Yugoslavia, and 'Marita', to crush Greece. German forces were ordered by Hitler 'to make all preparations to destroy Yugoslavia militarily as a national unit'. They were to employ 'pitiless harshness'. The capital, Belgrade, 'will be destroyed from the air by continual day and night attack'. Both actions started on Palm Sunday, 6 April 1941. Aircraft units had been withdrawn from France, Germany and the Mediterranean and the offensive opened with a paralysing Stuka raid on Belgrade, which was packed with pilgrims. The attack was devastating, with possibly 17,000 people killed. Within a week the Yugoslav Air Force had been smashed and the army overrun by invading forces sweeping in from Italy, Austria, Hungary, Rumania and Bulgaria. After twelve days, Yugoslavia surrendered.

The German advance into Greece was inexorably swift and Athens was captured in just three weeks. German use of air power, combined with armoured thrusts, could not be matched on the Allied side. Panzer warfare

## THE BALKAN INVASION

The German invasion of Yugoslavia and Greece was another *Blitzkrieg* showcase: fast moving armoured columns supported by aircraft raced ahead of the infantry to isolate the defenders and seize key strategic points. Belgrade was subjected to a terror bombing that killed 17,000 people. The invasion of Greece involved a parachute drop to seize the Corinth canal and the British Expeditionary Force soon found itself in full retreat. Only much later would it become apparent that the German victory was a mixed blessing: many vehicles taking part in the invasion of Russia in June would begin that campaign with high mileages and in urgent need of maintenance.

The Balkans
6–30 April 1941

→ German attacks
⇢ Allied evacuation
⌒ German front line
〰 Allied fortified line

① German front line 16 April
② German front line 20 April
③ German front line 23 April
④ British evacuation 22–28 April

0        100 km
0        100 miles

2000
1500
1000
500
200
0 m

LEFT: The invasion of Yugoslavia was launched from Hungary, which had joined the Tripartite Pact in 1940. Hungary was rewarded with the Magyar-speaking territory between the Drava and Tisza rivers where these German troops are seen in April 1941.

scored again. Defensive positions were quickly bypassed or outflanked. On 28 April the last British forces were evacuated by the Royal Navy, being taken either to Crete or back to Egypt. Over 7,000 men were left behind, to become prisoners, while the Germans collected 100 tanks, 400 guns and several thousand abandoned vehicles.

When the triumphant *Wehrmacht* reached the southern Peloponnese at the end of April, Hitler's Balkan Campaign had gained all the areas he had intended to control. Now, in the forthcoming confrontation with Russia, his right flank was secure. The German empire had grown rapidly in less than a year. Although the tenacious British were still refusing to submit, his forces had subjected them to three defeats – Norway, then France, then Greece. Unknown to the British, a fourth defeat was on the way.

### Crete

To the south of Greece lay the island of Crete, occupying a strategic position in the eastern Mediterranean. Even before the British evacuation from Greece had started, Hitler had added it to his shopping-list. The island contained Suda Bay, which could be used by the Royal Navy. More important in the *Führer*'s mind were the aerodromes from which RAF bombers could reach Rumanian oilfields, which were of such importance to the German economy.

An Australian division and two brigades of New Zealanders, evacuated from Greece, became the main part of a defence force of some 30,000 men, together with 11,000 Greek troops. Although not well equipped, they held good defensive positions and were protected by ships of the Royal Navy. Any attempted German seaborne invasion would suffer severely. However, the Germans, always innovative in war, overcame the drawback by employing airborne forces as a large component of the 23,000 troops used. With complete air superiority, the *Luftwaffe* was able to control the skies, ferrying in men over the top of the Royal Navy.

After several days of intensive bombing, the main attack opened on 20 May when hundreds of German parachutists and glider troops landed. The first waves suffered heavy casualties and for a time the operation was in jeopardy, but soon an airfield was captured and reinforcements were flown in. Slowly but surely the Germans extended their positions. Within a week the Royal Navy were once again preparing an evacuation of ground troops. Thousands of soldiers were taken off successfully, but 5,000 were left behind to face captivity.

On the British side another costly lesson was learned: air cover was vital for successful land or sea operations. The Mediterranean Fleet had unflinchingly placed itself in the firing line to carry out the evacuation, but without the protection of fighters overhead its losses were heavy. Three

RIGHT: British tanks abandoned in Greece after the hurried evacuation of the expeditionary force. Yet again, the Royal Navy found itself rescuing 'the evacuees' from hostile shores with no air cover to protect the ships from determined attacks by *Luftwaffe* bombers.

RIGHT: An SS gun detachment in action in Greece. The military arm of the SS would expand rapidly once the invasion of Russia was in progress, eventually becoming an army in its own right, over a million strong.

cruisers and six destroyers had been sunk by the *Luftwaffe*, while seventeen other vessels, including three battleships, had been damaged. Over 2,000 sailors had been killed or wounded – a heavy price to pay for courage in the face of disaster.

### OPERATION MARITA

The island of Crete was prized by both sides for its airfields that could dominate the eastern Mediterranean. Although the British had only a handful of aircraft there, they made no effort to block the runways and, when Maleme airfield was captured by German parachutists on 21 May, they failed to counter-attack before German reinforcements were flown in. However, it was a very close-run battle and the losses among the German airborne forces were so high that Hitler forbade another parachute operation on such a scale.

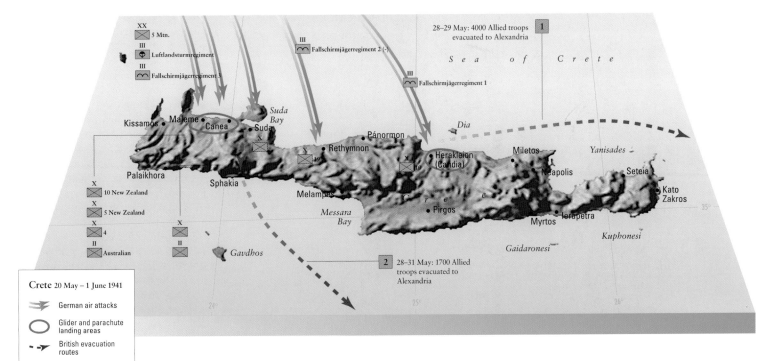

XX
5 Mtn.

III
Luftlandsturmregiment

III
Fallschirmjägerregiment 3

III
Fallschirmjägerregiment 2 (-)

III
Fallschirmjägerregiment 1

28–29 May: 4000 Allied troops evacuated to Alexandria  **1**

*Sea    of    Crete*

*Dia*

Kissamos • Maleme • Canea  *Suda Bay*  Suda

*Pánormon*

Rethymnon

Miletos  *Yanisades*

Herakleion (Candia)

Neapolis  Seteia

Palaikhora

Kato Zakros

Sphakia

Melampes

*Messara Bay*  • Pirgos

Myrtos  Ierapetra

X  10 New Zealand

X  5 New Zealand

X  4

II  Australian

*Gavdhos*

*Gaidaronesi*

*Kuphonesi*

**2**  28–31 May: 1700 Allied troops evacuated to Alexandria

Crete 20 May – 1 June 1941

German air attacks

Glider and parachute landing areas

British evacuation routes

# Planning 'Barbarossa'

**RIGHT:** A German transport column in Russia during the early winter of 1941–42. The troops learned to copy the Russian methods, relying on local ponies pulling sledges. Unfortunately for the soldiers, the generals' assumptions of a quick victory meant that only small quantities of winter clothing had been ordered.

**BELOW:** The 1941 campaign was determined as much by horse-teams like this as by the grand sweep of strategy. As pre-war wargames had shown, the real limit on the pace of the German advance was the slow process of repairing the railways. The gauge of the track had to be changed to match that of Germany's. Until that was achieved, supplies had to be brought forward by truck or wagon.

Early plans for an attack on Russia were crossing Hitler's mind in July 1940, while the Battle of Britain was in its first stages. By the end of the month preparations were under way for an operation in the following spring. The aim was to defeat in four to six weeks a Russian Army then estimated to include 50 to 75 'good' divisions. Planning went ahead in increasing detail over the following months. There were two main problems. The first was logistical. In an undertaking of this size arrangements had to be made to supply three million men fighting in the East. They would have half a million motor vehicles requiring fuel and maintenance. The German Army still relied heavily on the horse, and 300,000 animals needed fodder and equipment. Who was to provide ammunition and clothing, food and oil? In Russia, vast areas of space stretched to an apparently unending horizon. The battle front was about a thousand miles long. Troops would have to cover greater distances than any previously tackled by the *Wehrmacht*, crossing areas where few good roads or railways existed. Where should supply centres be established? What effect would the weather have on movement? How many airfields would be needed by the *Luftwaffe*?

The second problem also related to the size of the USSR. What and where were the main targets for the invasion? Was the priority to capture key cities, such as Leningrad, Kiev or Moscow, or to destroy the enemy's armies? Or, could the two be achieved simultaneously? In November and December 1940 the General Staff played several war games to assess the strengths and weaknesses of both sides. By then they agreed that there should be three main thrusts into Russia. A northern push would aim for Leningrad. In the centre, forces would drive towards Moscow. The city of Kiev in the south

would be the target for the third force. Which should be the main thrust? The strongest units on the ground, they decided, would be allocated to Army Group Centre, which had the Russian capital in its distant sights.

In early December, however, after inspecting the draft plans, Hitler began to make alterations to suit his own judgement. On 18 December he issued Directive No 21, setting out orders. This was to be Operation 'Barbarossa', named after the medieval warrior emperor Frederick I ('Red Beard'), whose physical vigour was to be emulated in the new crusade. The document ordered the forces 'to crush Soviet Russia in a rapid campaign'. The Red Army would be destroyed 'by daring operations led by deeply penetrating armoured spearheads'. The final optimistic objective was 'to create a barrier against Asiatic Russia on the general line Volga–Archangel'. The attack would open on or about 15 May 1941. Here was a man re-planning the garden before ensuring that he had sufficient cash to buy the property.

Worries for the General Staff came when Hitler changed the balance of the offensive. He now wanted Leningrad, not Moscow, to be the first main target. Only after its capture 'will the attack be continued with the intention of occupying Moscow'. He went on to claim that only a 'rapid collapse of Russian resistance could justify the simultaneous pursuit of both objectives'. In amending the plans he inserted fatal flaws which would eventually undermine the whole campaign. So much for his opinion of the General Staff, an organisation which 'was positively stunned; it remained, however, definitely silent.' Faced with the mesmeric *Führer*, opponents usually did.

Further changes came early in February. Hitler now wanted to strengthen the attacks made towards Leningrad in the north, but also towards the wide, grain-growing areas in the south. While these two flanks were upgraded, the armies in the centre were to be put on hold. The taking of Moscow was a reduced priority.

Large-scale plans were made for administering the occupied regions. For example, how would the *Wehrmacht*, hundreds of miles from its homeland, be fed? Either supplies would have to be sent from Germany or, like a force of medieval mercenaries, soldiers would have to live off the conquered lands. A report by economic staff suggested that all armed services should be fed by the USSR in the third year of the war. 'There is no doubt that many millions of people will starve to death in Russia', but that was unavoidable. Göring was to be in charge of the economic exploitation of the Soviet Union. On 23 May he explained that the local population would suffer famine. Any attempt to relieve this 'would be at the expense of supplies to Europe. It would reduce Germany's staying power in the war.' Planning for the subjugation of Russia was as great and detailed as for that nation's military defeat. Some German generals later claimed that such moves offended their honour, yet they still connived at Nazi aims and methods.

For this greatest of trials ever faced by the Germans, the *Wehrmacht* had at its disposal over 200 divisions. Of these, 120 were to make the preliminary attack, with 28 others in reserve. From Finland, Rumania, Hungary and Croatia, all partners in the venture, came about 30 extra divisions. On the main front, the Northern Group had 29 divisions, the Central Group 49 and the Southern Group 42. Altogether, seventeen panzer and twelve motorised divisions, including over 3,000 tanks, faced the Russians. Protection from above was offered by three air fleets, consisting of some

2,700 aircraft. The movement of this mass of men and material to the East was a huge operation, remarkable for the efficient and secretive manner in which it was carried out.

Ironically, some of the most severe wounds suffered by the Red Army at the outbreak of hostilities had been caused between 1937 and 1939. The

**ABOVE:** Russian refugees pass a German field kitchen during the early stages of the invasion. Thousands of Russian soldiers, cut off by the pace of the German advance, simply melted away into the forests. The Germans found themselves plagued by guerrilla attacks and whole areas behind the lines remained in control of the partisans.

**LEFT:** A German reconnaissance unit seen taking directions from a local guide. Unfortunately for all concerned, Nazi propaganda led many Germans to treat the civilian population with great brutality. Many peoples within the Soviet Union had had their fill of Communism and looked on the invaders as potential liberators.

nation then was wracked by a series of minor revolutions and purges, affecting all levels of life in general and the armed services in particular. Vigilance was exercised against anyone who failed to carry out the Communist Party's plans, as secret police arrested thousands across the USSR. The effect on the armed forces was exceptional, with most of the Army's General Staff being imprisoned or shot, accused of plotting a fascist military conspiracy. The speed of action was frightening. On 11 June 1937 Moscow announced that eighteen senior officers of the High Command had been charged with treason; on the following day came the statement that they had been tried and shot. About 35,000 officers were removed, including three of the five Marshals of the Soviet Union. The effect on the leadership of the Red Army was catastrophic. At the top afterwards were men who had served with Stalin since the Bolshevik Revolution but whose ideas were outdated. Furthermore, all officers became fearful for their positions and therefore hesitant to recommend necessary changes. Military leaders of other nations believed that the forces of the Soviet Union had been turned into a second-rate team.

Facing Germany's three main armies attacking the Russian frontier in June 1941 were four Soviet army groups, with a further group covering Leningrad. The first was stationed in

### OPERATION BARBAROSSA

'We have only to kick in the door,' Hitler told his generals, 'and the whole rotten edifice will collapse'. Hitler's strategy for the invasion of the USSR was grounded in the belief that the Russian army would collapse again, just as it had in 1917. Its recent performance against Finland spoke of an army commanded by political generals ignorant of modern warfare. Three German army groups invaded Russia on 22 June 1941. Army Group North headed for the cradle of the Bolshevik revolution, the former capital of St Petersburg re-named Leningrad after the Communist victory. Army Group Centre drove straight for Moscow, following much the same route as Napoleon in 1812. Army Group South advanced into the Ukraine. From the beginning there were disputes over objectives: Hitler changed his mind several times, uncertain which was the vital target, the Russian army, Moscow or Leningrad, or the industrial heartland of the Don Basin.

**BELOW:** MiG-3 fighters near Moscow, winter 1941. The Russian air force was the biggest in the world when Germany attacked, but few of its aircraft were modern and the training of its aircrew was lamentably bad. Its communications were dismal and it lacked radar, but as the Germans outran their supply lines that winter, the Russians were finally able to counter-attack in the air as well as on the ground.

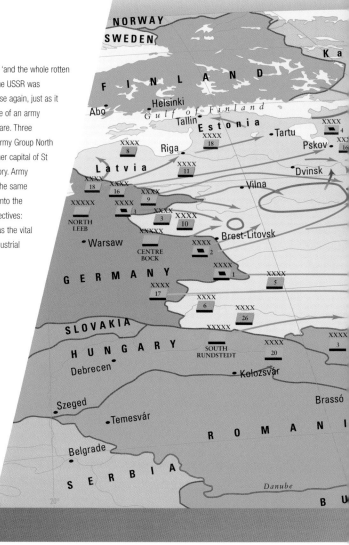

the Baltic Military District, where 26 divisions, of which six were armoured, defended mainly the regions of Latvia and Lithuania. To the south of this came the Western Military District, where 26 infantry and ten armoured divisions guarded the area to the north of the Pripet Marshes. South again was the Kiev Military District, protecting the northern Ukraine. Fifty-six divisions, six of them armoured, covered a frontier zone some 500 miles long. Facing the Rumanian frontier was the Odessa Military District, in which twelve infantry and two armoured divisions gave cover.

On paper, the USSR could put out almost 166 divisions, 34 of them armoured or motorised, for the immediate defence of western Russia. For years, the cloak of secrecy has not

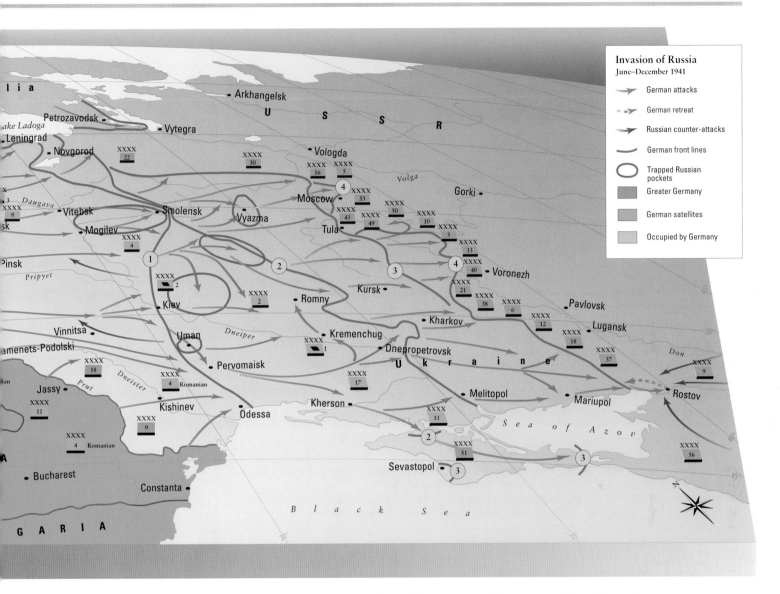

**Invasion of Russia**
June–December 1941

- → German attacks
- ⇢ German retreat
- → Russian counter-attacks
- ⌒ German front lines
- ◯ Trapped Russian pockets
- Greater Germany
- German satellites
- Occupied by Germany

helped historians to make precise judgements of Soviet power at that time, but probably in total the Red Army had nearly 240 divisions under arms in June 1941. Not all, however, were at full strength and readiness. Guarding the skies above Russia was the world's largest air force numerically. At the time of the invasion, nevertheless, it was caught unprepared. To find figures of the exact number of aircraft ready for action is not easy, but most machines were either obsolete or lacking in quality when compared with the *Luftwaffe*. Some Germans estimated a total of 8,000 aircraft, of which 6,000 were in European Russia; others suggested figures of 7,400 and 4,000 respectively; further estimates gave the total as 12,000. Russian secrecy at the time kept a veil over true

totals. The fighters, many designed by Polikarpov, comprised the greatest numbers confronting the *Luftwaffe*, but were generally outclassed. Most of the bombers also were obsolete at the start of the war, being too slow and under-gunned. They were able to offer little support to ground troops.

The German invasion of 22 June 1941 caught the Russian armed services by surprise. Since the war, many people have wondered why. In more recent times, Soviet intelligence and espionage departments have been renowned for their capabilities, so what was lacking in that summer? Much of the answer lies in the power exercised by Josef Stalin. The final authority over almost every part of Soviet life rested in his hands, and he had absolute control over military

matters. The extent and awfulness of Hitler's authority in Germany often occupies the minds of people so greatly that they overlook similar qualities of dictatorship exercised by Stalin in the USSR.

Stalin was certainly provided with ample evidence that an invasion was coming. In March 1941 a Communist spy sent microfilmed German documents to Russia, giving details. Russian officials hotly denied reports passed on from Britain and the United States and accused those governments of trying to force a rift between Germany and the USSR. When one senior Russian intelligence officer, believing that Hitler was about to attack, argued with Stalin, he was arrested and shot the next day. That encouraged others to keep their counsel.

German front lines:
1. end of August 1941
2. early October 1941
3. 15 November 1941
4. 5 December 1941

# 'Barbarossa': The Attack

At dawn on 22 June 1941 Nazi armies crossed into Soviet territory stretching from the Baltic to the Black Sea, while overhead the *Luftwaffe* began relentless attacks. Under the cover of artillery bombardments, the three main drives planned by Hitler began their advance.

One of the first targets was the Soviet Air Force. German strategists appreciated that Russian aircraft would have to be overwhelmed if the familiar *Blitzkrieg* tactics of Stukas and panzers working closely together were to be carried out. *Luftwaffe* aircraft crossed the frontier and then descended to raid airfields where, in many cases, Russian planes were lined up in rows. Few Soviet aircraft managed to get airborne, and most of those that did were soon shot down. By midday, the Russians had lost over 500 aeroplanes on airfields in the central area alone; more than 1,200 Soviet aircraft had been destroyed in all battle areas by the early afternoon.

Army Group North was allocated the task of driving north-eastwards from East Prussia, penetrating into Lithuania, Latvia and then Estonia. The High Command at the start of the year had ordered it to destroy 'enemy forces fighting in the Baltic theatre', before taking the Baltic ports, then Leningrad and Kronstadt. These moves would neutralise the Russian Fleet and open the ports as supply bases for further advances. In overall command was Field-Marshal von Leeb, with three panzer, three motorised and twenty infantry divisions at his disposal, and two other divisions in reserve. Russian forces opposite were more concentrated than on any other front, and he knew that his panzers would have to hit them speedily to achieve success. Distances were daunting. The first target, the river Divina, was 185 miles away, while the second, the town of Ostrov, lay 150 miles further on.

In the long run, the drive of the Northern Group was aimed to join up with the offensive launched from Finland by the Finnish Army, old opponents of the Russians, with German support. At first the Finns enjoyed some success, but Soviet troops fought strongly and gradually halted their advance.

German troops made rapid progress. The Divina crossing was reached in four days, followed by the capture of Ostrov on 4 July. In less than three weeks advance forces reached the river Luga, only 60 miles from Leningrad. Thousands of Russian prisoners were taken and hun-

BELOW: I-16 fighters proved themselves during the Spanish Civil War, but by 1941 they were obsolete compared to the latest Messerschmitt Bf 109s. Many of them were destroyed on the ground in the opening days of the German invasion since Stalin had refused to allow any defensive preparations.

dreds of tanks destroyed as the German progress seemed unstoppable. Panzer forces drove the Red Army out of Estonia before the end of August. They then planned a dash for Leningrad, with the aim of capturing the second city of the Soviet Union – which would have been a severe blow to Soviet morale.

At that stage, Hitler's intervention altered the balance of the offensive. As Army Group North moved to isolate Leningrad, the *Führer* decided to post-

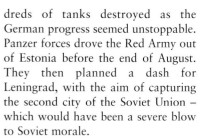

pone the taking of the city. He was now turning his attention back to Moscow. Most of the panzers in the north were therefore moved to Army Group Centre and the siege of Leningrad was left mainly to infantry. Shelling of the city had begun on 1 September, and over the next fortnight the Russians there were cut off. A number of German soldiers there believed that a glorious opportunity of success had been thrown away as they dug in. One of history's greatest and most costly sieges then began. Lasting for 900 days, it probably cost the lives of 900,000 Russians in the city. On Christmas Day 1941 alone, 4,000 starved to death there. Such suffering meant little to Hitler. In an earlier directive he ordered Leningrad to be 'wiped off the face of the earth'. It would be razed 'to the ground by artillery and by continuous air attack'. He was not concerned by the problems of feeding civilians. 'In this war for existence we have no interest in keeping even part of this great city's population.'

Some of the greatest early victories in the Russian Campaign were won by Army Group Centre, under the leadership of Field Marshal von Bock. At his disposal were 51 divisions, including two panzer armies, whose task was to launch the main thrust against the Red Army. From the start, all went well. The Army Staff were aiming forces at Minsk, then Smolensk, then finally the great prize, Moscow. Minsk was taken

**ABOVE:** Over two million Russian soldiers were taken prisoner in 1941 but few of them were alive by the end of the winter. The Germans herded the men into gigantic camps with little food, water or shelter and no medical support. Captured officers, Commissars and Jews were often executed on the spot.

ABOVE: More Russians emerge to surrender, summer 1941. The early stages of the campaign appeared to suggest that Hitler was right: Russia seemed poised to collapse and the German spearheads met only light resistance.

RIGHT: A German anti-tank gun is ferried across a Russian river. The prime mover is one of many captured French vehicles taken over by the German army. All sorts of captured lorries, half-tracks and armoured vehicles were pressed into service, bulking out the numbers but creating a logistics problem: they required so many different spare parts.

on 30 June as the *Wehrmacht* put into brilliant effect the carefully laid plans. Russians were outflanked and surrounded by the full force of the panzer aggression which had devastated Western Europe. By 9 July, Army Group Centre claimed to have taken 300,000 prisoners, together with 1,400 guns and 2,500 tanks.

The Germans pushed further forward. A week later they entered Smolensk and soon had captured a further 300,000 Russians. The way to Moscow beckoned many senior strategists, but Hitler had different ideas. 'The proposals of the Army for the continuation of the operations in the East do not accord with my intentions,' he responded. The new objectives were to be the isolation of Leningrad in the north, and aiming for grain-growing areas, oil supplies and

coal-mining regions in the south. Moscow was no longer the most important objective. Guderian's panzers were therefore drafted to Army Group South to assist the campaign around Kiev.

On the central front, the drive towards Moscow did not regain momentum until 2 October with Operation 'Typhoon'. At first there were again great successes, with over 650,000 more prisoners taken, but the coming of rains, together with intense Russian resistance, slowed down the advance. When early frosts came in November, the offensive restarted, but it ground to a halt only twenty miles from Moscow. By the end of the month the great prize was tantalisingly close, but still out of the Germans' reach.

Many of the most spectacular advances in the early Russian Campaign were made by Army Group South, where 33 divisions were commanded by Field-Marshal von Rundstedt. In launching the third onslaught into the USSR, his immediate target was the ancient city of Kiev, third largest in the Soviet Union. Beyond that lay further wide grain-growing lands of the Ukraine.

German forces moved with customary speed. By early July they had broken through Russian defences, taking 100,000 prisoners at Uman. Further south, Rumanian armies advanced towards Odessa, on the Black Sea coast. Then Guderian's panzers were brought in from Army Group Centre to open the way to Kiev, afterwards driving towards the great industrial region of Kharkov. In a brilliant campaign from late August to early September the *Wehrmacht* cut off enormous numbers of Russians around Kiev which were then methodically ground down. Altogether over 500,000 Soviet troops were killed or captured in the worst defeat ever suffered by the Red Army. By the end of September the Russians had lost about one-third of their original strength.

With such overwhelming victories under their belt, von Rundstedt's forces pushed on. They aimed for Kharkov and Rostov, which were taken in October and November respectively. By then another 100,000 Russian prisoners were in the bag.

Consequently, by the end of November, in the space of five months, 'Barbarossa' had achieved astounding success. German troops had occupied thousands of square miles of Soviet territory, reaching to the outskirts of the USSR's two largest cities. The Russians had lost some 7,000 aircraft. Over four and a half millon men of the Red Army had been killed or wounded, with a further 3,800,000 captured.

However 'Barbarossa' had failed in its first objective of annihilating the Red Army: in spite of tremendous losses, the Russians appeared to have an inexhaustible reserve of manpower which could be produced at crucial moments.

Secondly, neither Moscow nor Leningrad was taken. The capture of either would have been a devastating blow to Soviet spirit, but they now lay frustratingly just out of reach. Here, German generals later apportioned blame to Hitler's interference and change of aims. Should Leningrad be taken first? Would it be best to strike towards the industrial and oil producing regions in the south? Could Moscow be occupied before the end of the year? Vacillation led to failure on all three fronts.

So much is often made of the extent of Russian losses that the effect of battle on the German armed services is overlooked. By the end of 1941 the *Wehrmacht* had suffered almost one million casualties; about 150,000 of these occurred in three weeks from mid-November. By the same token, the *Luftwaffe* had taken heavy casualties during 'Barbarossa', with an average loss of 750 aircraft and 300 aircrew each month. The air support so vital for the German campaign had diminished seriously at the end of the year.

Another factor affecting the *Wehrmacht* was distance. 'The spaces seemed endless,' wrote a German general, 'the horizon nebulous.' The landscape was depressingly monotonous, with endless vistas of marshland, plains and forests. For best effect, as in Poland and France, panzer warfare required more limited areas. Because of Russia's geography, the front widened as German forces advanced. Consequently, even enveloping pincer movements which trapped thousands of soldiers of the Red Army allowed

many others to slip through the net. And all the time the *Wehrmacht* was moving further from its sources of supply.

Behind the *Wehrmacht* came Himmler's SS *Einsatzgruppen* (killing squads), whose task was to subjugate the defeated people. Apart from slaughtering those who were viewed as political opponents, which they did ruthlessly, they mounted an immediate

hunt for Jews. In same cases, as in the Baltic states where anti-Semitism was strong, they encouraged local people to do the killing. Elsewhere the SS did the job themselves. They experimented with various forms of elimination, from shooting to gassing, searching for the most economic method. The business had to be cost-effective. The SS murder squads followed the Army's advance like a virus.

**ABOVE:** Russian 'partisans' are hanged in reprisal for guerrilla attacks on the German forces. From the very start of the invasion, the Germans resorted to indiscriminate killing to terrorise the population into passivity.

**LEFT:** Another execution: army commanders had to repeat orders to their troops not to send pictures like this home to Germany. For a long time after the war, the SS was blamed for all such atrocities, but the involvement of many army units is now uncomfortably clear.

ABOVE: A Sturmgeschutz assault gun kicks up the snow together with some infantry in half-track armoured personnel carriers. The assault guns were crewed by artillerymen and proved so successful in 1941 that many more were manufactured and they became a key element in the German army.

RIGHT: In the Baltic States, the local population turned on their Russian occupiers, attacking all the symbols of the Communist regime as the Germans arrived. The statues of Stalin would be repaired after 1945 however, and it would be another fifty years before they won their freedom again.

As the Russians retreated, they removed or destroyed industrial and economic resources. They had seen the way in which the Germans had taken over the productive capacity of occupied nations in Europe – for example, the Czech armament industry. This would not be allowed to happen in the USSR. More than 1,500 factories, with industrial plant and workers, were moved east, usually by rail, beyond the Ural mountains. There they re-started production to service the armed forces. In areas of occupied Russia, Stalin ordered a 'scorched earth' policy, so that anything of use to the invaders was burnt or destroyed. Not a single railway engine, loaf of bread or can of oil should be left.

Towards the end of the year the Germans faced a new opponent – 'General Winter'. The lack of good roads in the western USSR now became a benefit to the Russians. The coming of rains had already slowed up the advance, turning battlefields into quagmires. Then the temperature fell rapidly and snow arrived. 'Death came with icy pinions and stood at our elbow,' wrote a German soldier. Men clothed and equipped for a summer campaign suffered from frostbite, while machinery would not operate. Guderian noted that fires had to be lit under tanks in order to start the engines, while fuel froze. By 13 November the temperature had dropped to –8°F; on 4 December, near Moscow, it had fallen to –31°F. An American correspondent in the city noted that the cold was paralysing. 'The cold was inside our clothes. It was inside our bones.'

What happened to the hundreds of thousands of Russian prisoners who had been collected so easily during the great advance? Some German economists wanted them to be drafted to the Reich as farm labourers or factory workers, but Hitler refused. They were kept in the East in vast, poorly equipped prisoner-of-war camps, where many froze or starved to death. Communists and Jews were shot. One *Wehrmacht* officer believed that he could hear packs of dogs howling. Upon investigating, he discovered thousands of Russian prisoners at the point of death, their faces dried up as they moaned for food. By the following

February, of the 3,800,000 prisoners taken, just over one million were still alive. The dead were dumped in mass graves.

Then, in December 1941, two events occurred, thousands of miles apart, which were to have a lasting effect on Nazi Germany and on the course of the war. On the 5th an unexpected and unwelcome blow fell on forward units of the *Wehrmacht* in the vicinity of Moscow. Out of the blue, the Russians launched a great counter-offensive. Their new commander was General Zhukov, then a virtually unknown officer, yet a supremely competent leader. Over the previous weeks, undetected by German intelligence, the Red Army had gathered a force of 100 divisions, many fresh to battle, which were well equipped and warmly clad. Zhukov now unleashed this force, gathered from the seemingly inexhaustible supply of manpower, on to tired enemy divisions over a front of 200 miles. Their success was immediate. In places the Germans were rolled back over 100 miles during a campaign that lasted into the following month. The threat to Moscow was lifted.

Two days into the offensive, thousands of miles away in the middle of the Pacific Ocean, an air raid occurred which ultimately brought disaster to Hitler and his 'Grand Design' for the Third Reich. On the early morning of Sunday 7 December Japanese aircraft attacked the American Pacific Fleet at Pearl Harbor, launching those two nations into war. Hitler, angered by the aid increasingly given to the British by the Americans, decided to honour the Tripartite Pact and support Japan. Therefore, on 11 December, in front of a cheering *Reichstag*, he declared war on the United States. Noticeably, however, the canny Japanese did not reciprocate by taking up arms against Russia.

**ABOVE:** A Panzer III supports German infantry at Toropec, January 1942. The Russian winter offensive drove the Germans back from Moscow but failed to create a major rupture in the frontline. Nevertheless, German casualties in Russia exceeded 750,000 by the end of 1941 and both sides recognized that the next summer campaign would be decisive.

**LEFT:** A Panzer 38t in winter camouflage. This was one of two types of tank captured from the Czech army and used by several panzer divisions in the invasion of Russia. Most were lost by the summer campaign in 1942.

# 1942 and Stalingrad

**ABOVE:** A Panzer III tows a Sturmgeschütz out of a snowdrift, winter 1941–42. The first winter in Russia took a heavy toll on the German tank forces which lacked special lubricants for cold weather operations or track extensions to cope with the snow.

With the resignation of von Brauchitsch, made a scapegoat for failure, Hitler became Supreme Commander of the Armed Forces in December 1941. From then until the end of the war he controlled all activity, dismissing senior officers who disagreed with his policies or bullying others into submission, and appointing men who were prepared to follow his orders without question. That in itself was quite an achievement for a man who had served as a corporal on the Western Front in the First World War. However, this led the German nation into deeper trouble as he ignored or rejected wise advice given by senior officers whose lifetimes had been spent studying the science of war.

One of these, Halder, the Chief of Staff, noted on 25 March 1942 the extent of German losses in the Eastern Campaign. Casualties totalled over 32,000 officers and one million other ranks, which was about one-third of those who had started 'Barbarossa' only nine months earlier. Of the 162 German divisions in Russia, only eight were in a position to take the offensive immediately. Losses of equipment had also been heavy, with almost 3,500 tanks destroyed, while only 873 replacements had arrived. At that time, on the whole of the Eastern Front, only 140 tanks were ready for action.

Hitler had developed a form of megalomania for overthrowing what he termed 'Jewish Bolshevism'. In spite of all difficulties and setbacks, he set down his plans for action in 1942 during a conference held in the previous November. 'First of all the Caucasus. Objective: Russia's southern borders. Time: March to April,' he announced. 'In the north after the close of this year's campaign, Volgoda or Gorki, but only at the end of May.' He had decided to put his offensive back on the rails as soon as possible, still convinced that the *Wehrmacht* had the power to defeat the USSR. This was written before the opening of Zhukov's counter-offensive which saved Moscow. Yet by the end of February 1942 that offensive, after early successes, had come to a halt. Hitler's hopes rose again.

On 5 April he issued Directive No 41, setting goals for each of the three main Army Groups on the Eastern Front. This order showed clearly his priorities for the next stages of the war. Army Group North was to launch a limited offensive against Leningrad, aiming to link up with the Finnish Army. Inside Leningrad, where hundreds of people starved to death weekly, and some survivors ate vegetable scraps or wallpaper, the siege would continue. Army Group Centre was to be largely on the defensive,

with the capture of Moscow now no more than a distant hope. The main action was reserved for Army Group South, who were given distances to cover which evoked memories of the campaigns of Alexander the Great.

The reason for this new policy becomes obvious through a study of Hitler's fears at the time. His particular concern was that the German war machine was running short of oil. That was the message impressed on him by economists, so he therefore looked away to the south as well as to the east. His directive spoke of 'destroying the enemy before the Don, in order to secure the Caucasian oilfields and the passes through the Caucasus mountains themselves'. Later in the year he told a senior general that if oil were not obtained, 'then I must end this war'. What he appeared to overlook were the vast distances involved in reaching the oilfields. The nearest, at Maikop, lay over 200 miles away from his forward troops, while the furthest, at Baku, were over 700 miles ahead.

Before the great drive south could begin, other military moves were necessary. In May and June the German Eleventh Army finally overran the Crimea, capturing Sevastopol and the Kerch peninsula, after savage fighting. Then, when Marshal Timoshenko's armies counter-attacked near Kharkov, their moves ended in disaster. Almost 200,000 were taken prisoner and many tanks were lost. Consequently, just before the great German offensive to the south, codenamed Operation 'Blue', began, the *Wehrmacht* was in good heart. In the field, German soldiers believed that they could gain a good result.

In July, Hitler's Directive No 45 divided Army Group South into two – a north and a south battle group. Both were to launch simultaneous offensives. The former was to drive eastwards towards the Don river, having in its sights a city whose name would soon echo round the world and ring a death-knell in German ears. This was Stalingrad. The latter group was to sweep southwards into the Caucasus, towards the distant oilfields. Here, however, lay the seeds of a future disaster. Too much was being asked of too few men, with too few vehicles

**TO THE CAUCASUS**

Hitler's plan for the 1942 summer campaign was to strike south, aiming to capture the Russian oil industry in the Caucasus and on the shores of the Caspian Sea. The left flank of the advance would be covered by the 6th Army and allied contingents occupying the west bank of the Volga. The city of Stalingrad was to be occupied as part of this mission, but it was incidental to the main thrust of the campaign. To an extent the Russians played into Hitler's hands as they retained their main strength near Moscow, expecting another attempt to take the capital. The Germans reached the Caucasus but not the oil fields, and the struggle for Stalingrad seemed never ending. German intelligence failed to notice the major transfer of Russian units to the Stalingrad front at the beginning of winter.

German front lines:

1 June 1942

2 23 July 1942

3 November 1942

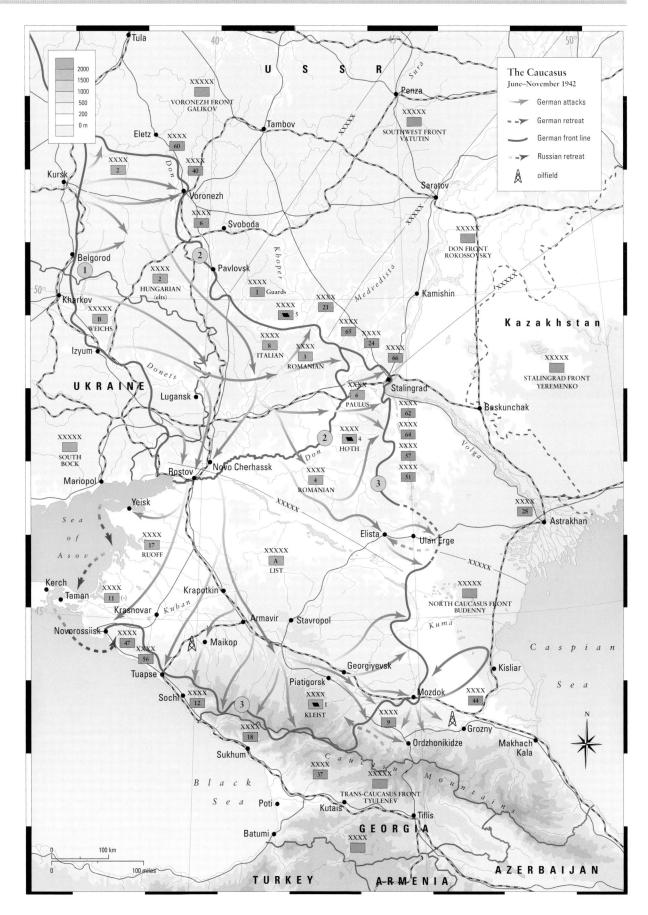

The Caucasus
June–November 1942

→ German attacks
⇢ German retreat
— German front line
⇢ Russian retreat
⚑ oilfield

**ABOVE:** German heavy artillery in action, winter 1942. The guns are deployed in the open, without camouflage: a luxury only possible because of the relative inactivity of the Russian air force at this stage in the war.

**RIGHT:** The Italian 8th Army fought alongside the Germans in the Stalingrad campaign despite being very badly equipped for the task. As the fighting in the city sucked in all available German troops, the long flanks either side were protected by Italian, Rumanian and Hungarian units of much lower fighting power. The Russians made their plans accordingly.

over too great a distance. Although the southern group made advances over hundreds of miles into the Caucasus, its supply lines were quickly over-extended. In places the group came to a halt. 'The prime causes,' wrote a historian later, 'were a shortage of fuel and an abundance of mountains.'

To the student of the map it appeared that the German Army was occupying vast tracts of the USSR, but the reality was ominous. The northern group, advancing towards Stalingrad, found the going increasingly tough. For both sides the city came to represent an icon of Communism. Stalin, who had fought there in 1919 during the Russian Civil War, was adamant that the place should not fall to the enemy. Hitler was equally determined to occupy and hold it, before driving on further east. In August, the Germans were sufficiently close for the *Luftwaffe* to launch heavy raids on the city, reducing the centre to rubble. Half of all German aircraft on the Eastern Front were employed in that area.

The *Führer*'s tunnel vision over Stalingrad brought increasing pressure to his troops on the ground. At first, the move towards the city was to be only a holding operation, guarding the flank of the advance into the Caucasus.

Then obsession took over. The benefits of panzer warfare were thrown aside. Panzer divisions enjoyed success when they had space to manoeuvre, racing forward to outflank or surround opponents. At Stalingrad, however, the army was slowly sucked into the vortex of a small space, where the grinding attrition of infantry fighting suited the Russians. Throughout September and October the struggle increased in intensity and German losses rose. For example, between 21 August and 16 October the Sixth Army alone suffered 40,000 casualties. By late October most of the devastated city had been

captured, but the Russians held on doggedly. Increasingly the *Luftwaffe* was called on not only to attack the enemy but also to carry supplies to the *Wehrmacht*.

At the start of operations General Paulus, commander of the Sixth Army, led seventeen divisions, comprising about 250,000 men. Although their great fortitude and skill carried them right into the city, their final lack of progress put them increasingly in a dangerous position. Supply lines were difficult to keep open. Yet any suggestion to Hitler that it would be prudent to withdraw the Sixth Army was met with scorn. It was ordered to fight until victory – or death. The *Führer* now treated the taking of the city as a matter of personal prestige. Opposite the Germans, the Russians slowly and methodically gathered some of their enormous reserves of soldiers. The Russian 62nd Army, under General Chuikov, which had fought desperately to cling on, had been reinforced with six fresh divisions by the end of October. New tanks, aircraft and guns were drafted in.

The crippling blow fell on the Germans on 19 November, when Russian armies advanced in a large pincer movement to surround Stalingrad. One reason for their success was that some attacks fell on nearby areas held by troops of Germany's allies. The Third and Fourth Rumanian Armies and the Italian Eighth Army were strong on paper, but some lacked the fighting spirit and skill of German soldiers. Soon they gave way under pressure, and by the 23rd of the month Russian

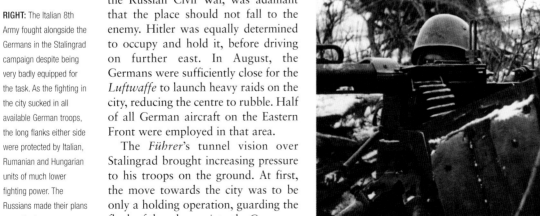

## THE SIEGE OF STALINGRAD

Cut off by the Russian counter-attack, the German 6th Army clung to the ruined city and its positions along the frozen steppe in vain hope of a German counter-attack. Hitler forbade any thought of withdrawal, although the army had little transport left and was in no state to fight its way free. In the most grisly conditions imaginable, the 6th Army defended its shrinking perimeter until the end of January 1943 when there was no choice left but to surrender.

**The Battle for Stalingrad**
January–February 1943

- → Russian attacks
- → German counter-attacks
- →→ German retreats
- —— German front lines
- —— limit of Russian artillery
- ⇢ Russian air support

German front lines 1943:

| | | | |
|---|---|---|---|
| ① 9 January | | ④ 23 January | |
| ② 12 January | | ⑤ 28 January | |
| ③ 20 January | | ⑥ 29 January | |

spearheads had closed the trap round the Sixth Army. Hitler made much of leading a European crusade against Bolshevism and, as the war progressed, contingents from a number of nations served on the Eastern Front. Apart from Italians, Hungarians and Rumanians, the Spanish sent a division. Some volunteers appeared from France, Belgium, Holland and other lands to serve with the SS as auxiliaries. Under front-line pressure, few could match the fighting qualities of German troops. At Stalingrad this was an important factor in sealing the fate of the Sixth Army.

**LEFT:** Men of the 6th Army among the ruins of Stalingrad before the first snows and the Russian counter-attack that left them surrounded. The Germans continued attacking the last fraction of the city still held by the Russians right up to the massive Red Army offensive that turned the tables.

RIGHT: A Sturmgeschutz and men of the 6th Army in the wooden suburbs of Stalingrad, summer 1942. Most of the outer districts were burned to the ground by the time the Germans had to create defensive positions here in the winter.

BELOW: In the street-by-street fighting at Stalingrad, the Germans made extensive use of their assault guns, firing at point blank range into Russian strongpoints. This was the first time in the war that the Germans had tried to storm a city rather than simply surround it with their panzer divisions. The tanks were divided between operations on the Moscow front and the charge to the Caucasus: there was no armoured force available to outflank Stalingrad.

Subsequently, eleven weeks of purgatory followed for the trapped men. The Red Army fed in extra forces to tighten the python grip exerted on their prey. The *Luftwaffe*, in spite of wild promises made by Göring, was unable to fly in sufficient supplies. An attempted relief offensive by panzers in mid-December ended in failure. By then the Sixth Army lacked the power to break out from the crushing pressure, which grew by the day. From January 1943, the southern battle group's earlier drive forward into the Caucasus was in full retreat as its flanks were threatened by Russian advances near Stalingrad. No help could come from that direction.

On 8 January 1943 the Russians invited Paulus to surrender. His situation was desperate, they pointed out. His men were 'suffering from hunger, sickness and cold. The cruel Russian winter has scarcely yet begun.' Paulus again asked Hitler for freedom of action in dealing with his opponents. The *Führer* refused. Two days later, the Red Army launched the final phase of the attack on the depleted and dispirited Germans. The desperation of the trapped men can be judged from the Sixth Army's daily situation reports. On 14 January they announced that 'only half of the forces now have 200 grams of bread.' One German prisoner told his captors, 'We've eaten our cavalry.' Men were fighting with bare steel because ammunition was exhausted. A later report mentioned 20,000 wounded 'uncared for [and] seeking shelter in ruins', together with starving and frostbitten soldiers without weapons. Again, the Russians offered an opportunity to surrender. Hitler would not be moved. 'Surrender is forbidden,' he told Paulus. Troops were to make 'an unforgettable contribution' to 'the salvation of the Western world' by fighting 'to the last man and the last round'.

About a week later, most of the trapped army surrendered, being incapable of further resistance. A few were defiant to the end, sending messages of support to the *Führer*. Of the quarter of a million men who had started out on the campaign, about 90,000 went into captivity, including 24 generals. Most never again saw their homeland.

**Stalingrad and the Allies**

By 1942 the Russians believed – and they made their opinion forcefully known – that they alone were carrying the main burden of war. Why, they demanded, did American and British forces not invade the Continent at the western end, opening a Second Front? This would take the pressure off the Red Army. Their argument sounded powerful – but was it?

The Russians, being a mainly land-based nation, failed to see that the United Kingdom and the United States, with different geographical and historical backgrounds, had world-wide commitments and interests. By the end of Stalingrad both had been heavily engaged in the war with Japan, a campaign in which the USSR played no part. Already, the Americans had negotiated one of the Second World War's main turning-points by not losing the Battle of Midway. British, Commonwealth and American troops had gained victories in North Africa, the most notable being the Eighth Army's triumph at El Alamein. They were within a few months of clearing Axis forces from the continent and taking about 170,000 prisoners. The unceasing Battle of the Atlantic, crucial for supplies reaching the United Kingdom, was causing heavy Allied losses. Bomber Command's offensive against the German homeland was developing. Such contributions, however, cut little ice with the Russians, who thought in terms only of a land war of attrition on the continental mainland.

In the meantime, both Britain and the United States were sending large quantities of vital war materials to the USSR. Some travelled by the hazardous sea route via the North Cape to Murmansk, while others travelled overland through Persia. Up to 1 July 1943 the US despatched 81,000 vehicles, 3,200 tanks and 2,600 aircraft; Britain sent 2,000 planes and 2,600 tanks. Many other items, from food to telephones, and from aluminium to rubber, were conveyed. Through the exigencies of war, not all arrived, but

those numbers were provided.

To have opened a poorly planned Second Front would have courted disaster. A second Dunkirk could well have followed. Such an undertaking required extensive and thorough preparation, using greater resources than were available in 1942. Some British people were stung by the demand for a Second Front. By February 1943, they recollected, the United Kingdom had been at war for 41 months and Russia for only nineteen. They asked where the First Front had been when there was a Second Front in 1939 and 1940. The Russians then had readily cooperated with the Germans to overrun Poland, while Britain and France were fighting Nazism. The controversy over the Second Front continued until it was launched in June 1944.

**ABOVE:** The pitiful end of the once proud 6th Army: 100,000 men were captured, of whom half died within months. Disease, malnutrition and hypothermia accomplished what Russian bullets had failed to do. A scant 5,000 veterans survived the Russian prison camps to return to Germany in the 1950s.

**LEFT:** One of the remaining Panzer IVs of the 14th Panzer Division taking part in the final German assault on Stalingrad, October 1942.

# CHAPTER 5: The Far East, 1941–42

At the outbreak of the European war in September 1939, most Americans believed far more strongly in the cause of France and Britain than they did in Germany's. They had watched the expansion of Nazi power and could see that Hitler's ambitions were worrying, especially to smaller nations. There was a widespread moral support for the Allies. And there the concern ended. Most Americans were adamant that the United States should not enter the war. Many felt that their nation's duty had been performed in 1917, when the United States went on the march against Germany. The Europeans themselves, they believed, had made a hash of peace settlements and had created conditions which led to the disagreements of the 1930s.

In September 1939, as war began, Roosevelt said that the United States 'will remain a neutral nation'. However, knowing that many Americans favoured the Allies, he added that they would not remain detached in their thoughts. 'Even a neutral cannot be asked to close his mind or his conscience.' The president also appealed to each combatant government, asking it 'to affirm its determination that its armed forces shall in no event and under no circumstances undertake bombardment from the air of civilian populations and unfortified cities' – provided that its opponents did likewise.

This attitude was sustained throughout the last months of 1939 and the first five months of the next year. The Americans continued as distant watchers while Hitler overran Poland, the Finnish War occurred, then Norway and Denmark were invaded. Their outlook changed, however, when the Germans launched their Western Campaign in May 1940. The *Wehrmacht*'s steamroller success, followed by the Dunkirk evacuation and the collapse of France, brought a new dimension to the war. The Atlantic Ocean was the new frontier with Nazism. The only nation now standing between Germany and total success in the Western Campaign was the United Kingdom. If Britain should fall, Hitler's forces would be facing the eastern seaboard of the United States. They might invade South America. From bases in, say, the Azores, German bombers could be within range of New York.

Consequently, the reasons for helping Britain were not entirely altruistic: they also were prompted by reasons of security for the United States itself. At that stage, many Americans knew in their hearts that their nation was bound eventually to be drawn into the war. The great worry was that their own armed forces were small in number and unprepared. Therefore, the sleeping giant of industry in the United States was roused to begin a massive production of war materials. While the Germans were advancing through France, Roosevelt pressed Congress to vote $5 billion to modernise the army and expand aircraft production. As the British were withdrawing from Dunkirk, the president warned that 'not one continent or two continents, but all continents, may become involved in a world-wide war'. Congress then agreed to spend a further $1.7 billion. Although slow at the start, the overall competence and size of American industry, especially with its experience of vehicle production, gradually overtook the output of any other nation. Where the United States had produced 5,800 aircraft in 1939, the figures for 1940 and 1941 were 12,800 and 26,200 respectively. Nevertheless, although American society was being put on a war footing, popular feeling was still against taking the final step of active combat.

Instead, the United States channelled its growing dislike of Nazi policy into providing help for Britain, although, for the British, the assistance could not come quickly enough. Rifles, aircraft and food were sent, and 50 old American destroyers were exchanged for some British bases in the Western Hemisphere. At all times, especially as a presidential election in November was in the offing, Roosevelt had to step carefully for fear of offending isolationists. However, American public opinion sided increasingly with Britain, especially after the latter's powers of resistance were demonstrated during the Battle of Britain and the Night Blitz.

Fighting wars is a costly business, and soon Britain's financial resources were virtually exhausted. By December 1940 the United Kingdom had less than half of the money needed to buy the arms required. Therefore a system of Lend-Lease was devised to ensure that Britain could fight on. The move, which broke the spirit but not the letter of the Neutrality Laws, was opposed by isolationists. When eventually it was passed, the plan suited both sides, but was a step nearer war for the United States. 'We must be the great arsenal of democracy,' Roosevelt announced on 29 December 1940, pleased that his nation was still at

RIGHT: The Imperial Japanese Navy based its strategy on a powerful fleet of battleships. The Pearl Harbor raid was supposed to be the prelude to a fleet action in which the Japanese and American battleships would decide the issue. In the event, carrier-borne aircraft would determine almost every battle of the Pacific war and such mighty vessels as the *Haruna*, seen here on pre-war trials, would be relegated to the support of the aircraft carriers. *Haruna* was one of the few Japanese major units to survive until 1945 when she too was sunk by US carrier aircraft.

peace although contributing to the fight against Hitler. Cooperation between Britain and the United States, both in war planning and in the provision of materials, grew at a fast rate.

The event which finally drew the United States into war had nothing to do with the occurrences in Europe or North Africa, or the unrelenting Battle of the Atlantic. Instead, it occurred in the Far East and has been registered as one of the most deadly blows ever suffered by the Americans.

## PACIFIC SITUATION

Japan's army was already deeply engaged in Manchuria and China when she attacked the USA in 1941. Throughout the war a huge Japanese force remained on the Asian mainland while comparatively smaller armies were landed in the Philippines and Burma. The Japanese strategy was to seize the resources required for war, above all, oil, then establish a perimeter that would cost the USA too much to break into. As a purely military exercise it made sense, but took no allowance of US determination to avenge the treacherous attack on Pearl Harbor.

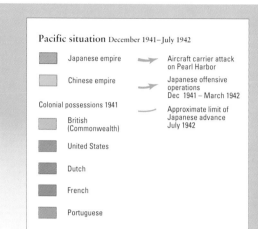

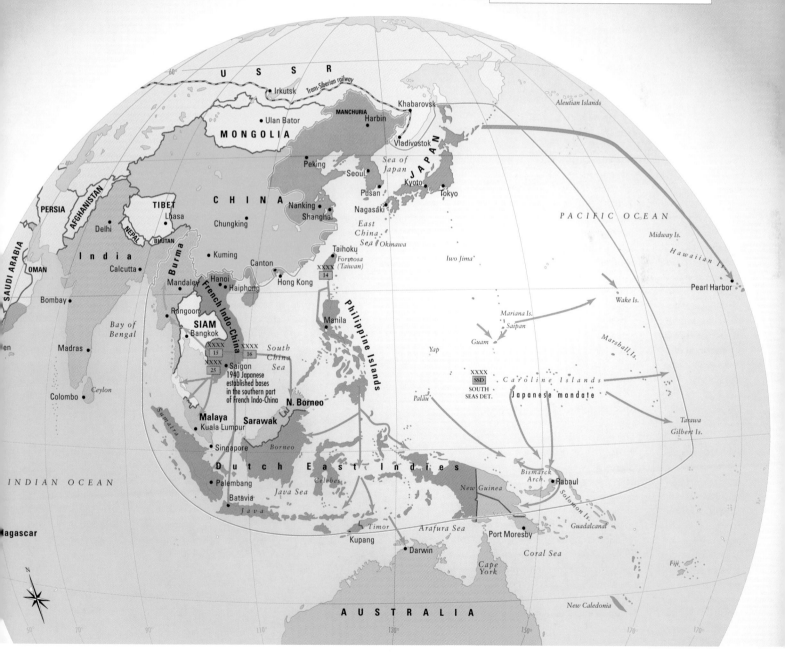

# Why the Japanese Attacked

Japan's hopes of becoming Asia's super-power became brighter when the European war began in 1939. Senior officers of the Army and Navy anticipated benefits coming their way. France, Britain and Holland, all colonial powers, would have to concentrate their attentions at home and that could provide openings for the Japanese on the other side of the world. That had happened in the First World War: it could occur again.

In less than a year, these ambitions came closer to realisation. By the end of June 1940 the Germans had over-run Holland and France; Britain appeared ready to receive the last rites. The Japanese Army, locked in the throes of a grinding conflict with China, saw opportunities of obtaining new bases for that war. The first European nation to be brought under pressure was France. The new Vichy government, which had no power left to oppose anyone, soon gave way, on 29 August 1940, by allowing Japanese forces to occupy towns in the north of French Indo-China. They were also permitted to build eight airfields there, within range of Chinese Nationalist targets. The British, who were under intense threat in Europe, agreed to

close the Burma Road, a supply route for China, and withdrew garrisons from Shanghai and Tientsin. Japanese aims were being achieved without the firing of a shot.

The landings in Indo-China altered US policy. The United States decided to fight by employing economic, instead of military, measures. An embargo was enforced on the export of scrap steel and of oil, both of which were vital to the Japanese economy:

about three-quarters of the scrap steel and four-fifths of the oil used in Japan came from supplies controlled by the United States. The embargo shocked and angered Japan's government, but certainly did not cause them to withdraw. Such a move would have involved too great a 'loss of face'.

On the contrary, Japan's power was further extended in September 1940 by the signing of the Tripartite Pact with Germany and Italy. This

Rome–Berlin–Tokyo treaty promised help from the other two for any one of them attacked by a state not already involved in the European war. For example, the Japanese could now be assured of backing from Germany and Italy in the event of trouble with the Americans. The strength of this new type of insurance policy gave Japan confidence in pushing harder for its aims.

By then, various other powers were growing increasingly worried over Japanese policy in the Far East. The war in China was seen as an example of aggression and repression. As the conflict continued, nearby territories were threatened. Therefore, over the next months, defence talks were held by British, Australian and Dutch officials, with the Americans joining in during January 1941. The British re-opened the Burma Road, while the USA sent a volunteer squadron, the 'Flying Tigers', to help Chinese air defence. Both the Dutch and the Americans refused to sell extra oil to Japan.

Two events in 1941, nevertheless, gave the Japanese further confidence to go for their aims. In April, they signed a neutrality agreement with the Russians, which eased the pressure for

them on the Manchurian border. Then, in June, came Hitler's onslaught on the USSR. With the Red Army now heavily engaged in Europe, Japanese forces were released for further operations in south-east Asia.

Japanese minds were concentrated on two main themes. The first was the seemingly endless war with China, waged ruthlessly by the Army and Air Force. Connected with this came the second, which was the thirst for oil required, particularly, by the Imperial Navy, to drive ships' engines. The nation's supply of 50 million barrels in 1939 had dropped to 40 million barrels by mid-1941. By then, 12,000 tons were being consumed each day. A turning point came at the end of July 1941 when the French government allowed Japanese troops into southern Indo-China. Roosevelt froze Japanese assets in the United States, and Britain and Holland followed suit. There was now an even more powerful economic stranglehold round the neck of the Japanese government, whose response would come through open war. One Japanese admiral later admitted that when they had signed the Tripartite Pact, then had entered southern Indo-China, they 'had already burned the

bridges behind us on the march towards the anticipated war with the United States of America and Great Britain'.

As the American government adopted a stronger resolve, a note was despatched to Tokyo on 17 August 1941. If the Japanese government tried to dominate neighbouring countries by force, then the Americans would 'be compelled to take immediately any and all steps' which would be required for 'the safety and security of the United States'. In particular, the US wanted four moves from Japan, all of which were inherently unacceptable to her military and naval commanders. They were told first to end the war against China, then to renounce the Tripartite Pact, then to evacuate Indo-China, and lastly to employ peaceful means to solve problems. As the US set out to enforce these demands through economic sanctions, not by armed force, the solution for the Japanese was easier. All they had to do was to take the raw materials they required from local sources by military power – problem solved! To Japanese eyes, American sanctions were a form of blackmail used against proper and legitimate ambitions.

**ABOVE:** Japan's secret weapon: the super-battleship *Yamato* was (with sistership *Musashi*) intended to give the Imperial fleet a decisive advantage in the gun-duel with US battleships that they anticipated would decide the war. They were the most powerful battleships ever built, constructed in enormous secrecy and at incredible cost. Yet they spent their brief lives swinging idly at anchor in a war dominated by aircraft and submarines.

# Pearl Harbor: Planning and Execution

and here was a problem: across the line of communications lay two barriers which could interrupt the supplies. At the southern tip of Malaya the British held Singapore, which had been developed as a strong naval base from the 1920s; and the Americans had a powerful force of troops, aircraft and ships in the Philippine Islands. These two areas would have to be brought rapidly under Japanese control before the scheme could succeed.

Japanese expansionist ambitions were aimed in two directions. The first, launched by the Army against China, had become costly and slow by 1940 and also had led to troubles with the Russians on the Manchurian border. The second, favoured particularly by the Navy, looked south for oil and other raw materials. By 1940, both armed services saw the second option as the better choice. Plans were laid accordingly.

Several difficulties faced them. Many units of the Navy and the Air Force would be closely involved, together with about fifteen Army divisions, all attacking to the south. They would aim at an early stage to take the oil wells of Java, Borneo and Sumatra, which produced over 60 million barrels annually. Of course, these targets would have to be taken before defenders could destroy them. Furthermore, it was essential to have a clear route for transporting the oil back to Japan,

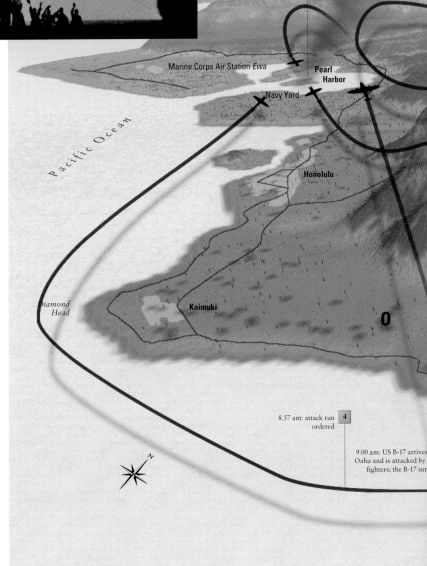

9.00 am: smoke from fires started after first attack and anti-aircraft fire hamper second wave

Marine Corps Air Station *Ewa*

Pearl Harbor

Navy Yard

*Pacific Ocean*

Honolulu

*Diamond Head*

Kaimuki

8.57 am: attack run ordered

9.00 am: US B-17 arrives Oahu and is attacked by fighters; the B-17 sur

## PEARL HARBOR

This map shows the second wave attack on Pearl Harbor, 7 December 1941. The raid on the US Pacific Fleet inflicted spectacular damage on ships unprepared for battle. Luckily, not one of the US aircraft carriers was present when the Japanese bombers swooped on the base that Sunday morning. Also, the Japanese failed to destroy the vast stores of fuel kept there, a surprising oversight in an otherwise brilliantly executed attack. A simultaneous raid by Japanese mini-submarines was a complete failure and nearly betrayed the whole operation. Japan had begun her war with Russia in 1904 in exactly the same way: before war was declared, Japanese torpedo boats raided the Russian fleet anchorage at Port Arthur in an attempt to sink the Russian battleships at anchor.

Japanese leaders planned for their great southern offensive to achieve rapid success through the seizure of several territories. They knew that the response from the US would be slow, because the Americans had no rapid deployment force. By the time the United States had recovered from the shock and had gathered and trained sufficient forces to intervene, the Japanese intended to be firmly established in their conquests. Possession is nine parts of the law. The Americans,

they hoped, would then appreciate the futility of waging a long war and would accept the *status quo*, after diplomatic discussions.

How best to achieve their aims? First would come attacks on Malaya, leading down to Singapore. A second assault would be made on the Philippines, then would follow invasions of Burma and the Dutch East Indies. Originally, naval planners anticipated that when the Philippines were attacked, the Americans would

despatch the full might of their Pacific Fleet from Pearl Harbor to intervene. The Japanese, like a matador in front of a bull, would draw the fleet on to destruction by air, submarine and surface attack. Such losses, in the Japanese view, would bring the Americans to their senses and a readiness to talk.

However, in August 1939 a new commander came to the Japanese Fleet, carrying with him a radically different scheme for starting the war. He was Admiral Yamamoto, a sailor

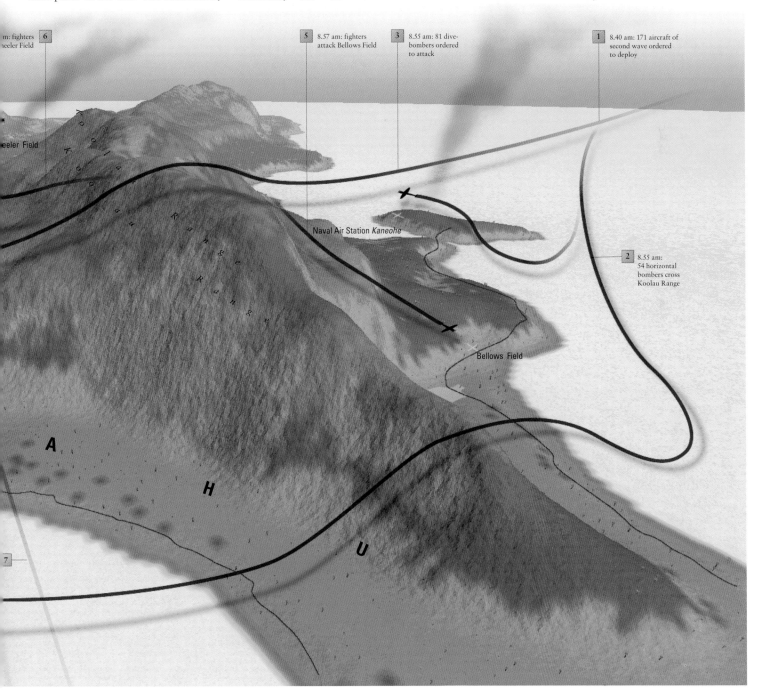

**ABOVE:** This photograph was taken from one of the Japanese aircraft over Pearl Harbor during the attack. Many of the US fighters normally stationed in Hawaii had been sent to Wake and Midway islands to cover the transfer of bombers to the Philippines where the Japanese attack was expected. When the Japanese aircraft appeared over Pearl Harbor the US shore-based anti-aircraft guns had no ammunition ready, none of the fleet's 5-in guns were manned and many key personnel were ashore.

of considerable foresight and imagination. Yamamoto had lived in the United States and was well aware of the immense industrial power which the Americans could raise, even though slowly, in war. Therefore, he reasoned, Japan would have to achieve a rapid success before American reinforcements could arrive. The crux of the question for him was how to deal with the American Pacific Fleet. Most Japanese naval commanders were content to tackle the vessels as they sailed towards the battle area after war had begun, but Yamamoto wanted to be one step ahead. In his unorthodox view, US ships should be eliminated at the very start of hostilities. The best way of achieving that would be to attack them at their home base at Pearl Harbor. The whole operation would be a gamble, but in Yamamoto's view the risk was entirely justified.

In December 1940 Yamamoto ordered preparations for a masterstroke to be launched against the American Pacific Fleet as it lay at its main base. Plans were made in great secrecy and airmen experienced in fighting over China were drafted in to practise attacks. Some were to drop torpedoes specially designed to run in shallow water. Others worked on dive-bombing of pin-point accuracy. Others

again flew in simulated high-level raids. Photographs and models of Pearl Harbor were studied, with detailed observations of ships' moorings and shore installations. After many practices and rehearsals, the scheme was ready.

When the plan was unfolded to the Naval General Staff, it was widely criticised. The dangers of failure were great. Six of Japan's carriers would be needed for the operation and one fatal slip could bring the destruction of the Navy's most powerful weapon. Yamamoto's faith in the venture, however, finally overcame opposition. As diplomatic talks with the Americans were near breaking point in mid-November 1941, a Japanese task force slipped away quietly into the northern Pacific Ocean, heading east. The fleet consisted of two battleships, nine smaller warships and eight oil tankers; their trump cards, however, were the six aircraft carriers, embarking almost 400 aeroplanes. The ships sailed on through fog and heavy seas until on 6 December they lay undetected only 500 miles to the north of Pearl Harbor.

On Sunday 7 December 1941 the Pacific Fleet was anchored in Pearl Harbor. US naval commanders, although suspecting that the Japanese were about to launch aggressive action

somewhere, had no idea that they were the selected victims. They were amazed when, at about 8 a.m., the first wave of Japanese aircraft, launched from the carriers at first light, appeared, dropping bombs and torpedoes in their meticulously planned operation. Before the defences could respond, American fighters were shot up on airfields and shore establishments were hit. Far worse, in the harbour five battleships were immediately torpedoed, while others were struck by heavy bombs. Within half an hour the complete battleship strength of the American Pacific Fleet had been destroyed, together with various other vessels. The whole base was a mass of sunken or stricken vessels, huge fires and destroyed aircraft. An hour later, a second wave of 170 Japanese aircraft arrived, adding to the damage and carnage below. The assault finished about 10 a.m. By then the Pacific Fleet had lost, either sunk or badly damaged, eight battleships, seven other vessels, 188 aircraft and almost 3,500 men. This stunning result was gained for the loss to the Japanese of nine fighters and twenty bombers.

The results of Pearl Harbor were more widespread than its planners could have imagined. Overnight, what had been largely a European war was transformed into a world-wide conflict. All continents were now involved. At first the Japanese people were exultant. Their Navy had struck a blow whose planning and daring were soon to become a legend. The way was open for the launching of the programme of expansion into the south-west Pacific, with no great threat to oppose them.

There were, nevertheless, two distant clouds which would throw shadows on their success. First, although they had demolished the American Pacific Fleet's battleship strength, they had failed to sink two aircraft carriers which, at the time of the attack, were at sea. Nor had they destroyed the large supplies of oil kept at the base. Both were costly omissions. Secondly, few Japanese leaders appreciated the degree of anger roused in the United States by what was seen as a treacherous act. When President Roosevelt addressed Congress, he referred to 'a date which will live in infamy',

LEFT: Of the eight battleships present when the Japanese raid took place, six were sunk and two damaged. However, they went down in shallow water and the Japanese did not attack the repair facilities, enabling the Navy to have six of the battleships back in service eventually.

because diplomatic talks were still in progress when the blow fell.

On 11 December Hitler and Mussolini declared war on the USA. In part this was to meet their commitment to Japan under the terms of the Axis Tripartite Pact, but the *Führer* had also been exasperated by the help, short of war, which the Americans had been giving to Britain. He had a low opinion of the fighting services of the United States, but his study of America's potential strength was obviously limited. By taking on the Americans he had signed his nation's death-warrant. At the end of the year, during a conference held in Washington, American service leaders were now faced with a double threat – Germany and Italy in Europe and Japan in the Pacific. Which should be tackled first? Their answer was explicit. 'Our view remains that Germany is still the prime enemy and her defeat is the key to victory. Once Germany is defeated the collapse of Italy and the defeat of Japan must follow.'

# The Two Sides

On paper, there was little difference in the strengths of the two opposing sides in December 1941. On the one hand were the combined forces of the United States, Great Britain and her Commonwealth, and Holland; against them were the armed services of a single country, Japan. In reality, several factors gave the Japanese a great superiority of strength.

First, the forces of the United States were divided. Through their geographical position, the Americans had a double responsibility. On their eastern seaboard lay the Atlantic, where trouble with Germany had been developing since mid-1940. That area required the cover of the American Atlantic Fleet. Beyond the west coast lay the Pacific, where another fleet was stationed at Pearl Harbor, in Hawaii. Altogether, the US Navy had nine battleships, three aircraft carriers, 24 cruisers, 80 destroyers and 36 submarines available in the Pacific region.

As for Great Britain, by late 1941 the bulk of her armed forces were serving in areas far distant from the Far East. At home, naval units were still employed against the possible threat of a German invasion. The Battle of the Atlantic required many warships as escorts for convoys. In the Mediterranean, in the struggle with the Italian Navy, further forces were needed, working from Gibraltar, Malta and Alexandria. Other vessels were guarding the route round the Cape of Good Hope. Consequently, although the Royal Navy was the world's largest, there were insufficient ships to form a powerful Far Eastern Fleet. At the start of the Pacific War, Britain could spare for service there no more than two capital ships, eight cruisers and thirteen destroyers. Holland, overrun by the Germans in May 1940, was undergoing the ordeal of occupation eighteen months later. Therefore, to protect the Dutch East Indies only ten surface vessels and a dozen submarines were deployed. Both Australia and New Zealand had home-based warships, but these were comparatively few in number and of small size.

Consequently, the Allies employed a combined force almost equal in numbers to that of Japan. For them, how-

ever, several disadvantages appeared. The main one was the lack of aircraft carriers, vessels whose vital role became increasingly obvious as the Pacific War developed. Another was the lack of a unified system of command for vessels of separate nations, each with its own particular traditions and methods. Affecting the Dutch was the difficulty of not sharing a common language.

On the other side, the Japanese had a unified command whose vessels were generally more modern and more heavily armed than those of their opponents. They possessed ten capital ships, 36 cruisers, 113 destroyers and 63 submarines. The prizes of their collection were ten aircraft carriers, the most powerful weapon in their armoury. This navy was well-trained and highly skilled in carrying out the planned operations.

In air power, the Japanese enjoyed a clear superiority both in numbers and quality, together with the experience of aircrew. About one half of their 1,500 Army aircraft were used for early operations, but these were supported by 1,400 naval aeroplanes. They were of excellent quality. The best known was the A6M2 Zero-Sen fighter, a superb, lightweight machine with great manoeuvrability and long range, which could comfortably cover 1,500 miles. In the early stages of the war, no Allied fighter could match its performance. Together with the 'Kate' torpedo-bomber, the 'Val' dive-bomber and the 'Betty' medium bomber, these machines offered an air superiority to cover landing operations.

Opposed to this formidable force, the Americans, British and Dutch altogether had about 650 aircraft in the Far East. Many were obsolete, underpowered or under-gunned; thus the Brewster Buffalo, Curtiss P-40 and Lockheed Hudson offered little threat to Japanese aircraft. Once again, there was a lack of centralised command in their operation.

Japan's powerful naval and air forces prepared the way for the landing of troops. These were mainly highly experienced men, many of whom had seen service in the Chinese campaign. Most of the 50 divisions available were kept either in China or for

the protection of the homeland, but eleven were employed in the great drive into the south-west Pacific. All were well-seasoned soldiers, whose weapons and training were excellent.

Against these powerful land forces were ranged about 360,000 Allied troops. These, however, not only belonged to several nations, but also were spread wide in the territories to be defended. Just over 130,000 British and Commonwealth troops were in Malaya, Burma and Hong Kong. The

Dutch kept 25,000 regular soldiers in the East Indies. In the Philippines the Americans had about 30,000 men, together with 110,000 Filipino troops. Although much of their equipment was satisfactory, these forces were generally poorly trained and lacked the fighting experience of the battle-hardened Japanese.

Consequently, at the start of the Pacific War, the armed services of Japan held many advantages. The auguries for the Allies were bleak.

ABOVE: The *Chiyoda* was a seaplane carrier designed to operate up to 24 aircraft in the long range reconnaissance role. Seen here as built in 1938, she was later converted to carry midget submarines and modified again as a light aircraft carrier, thus spending almost as much time in the dockyard as on operations.

LEFT: The British battleship *Resolution* seen off Madagascar in 1942. When Japan attacked British colonies in 1941 the Royal Navy was at full stretch in the Battle of the Atlantic and, in any case, simply did not have a battlefleet capable of taking on the Japanese. The British fell back across the Indian Ocean where a squadron of modernised First World War battleships was maintained for a while.

# The 'British Pearl Harbor'

ABOVE: The British battlecruiser *Repulse* was a veteran of the First World War whose size and sleek lines disguised her vulnerability. She had the range and speed to respond to the crisis in the Far East but the lack of British aircraft in Malaya left the naval squadron hideously exposed to Japanese air attack.

On 10 December 1941 Britain suffered its own version of Pearl Harbor, although on a reduced scale. In August 1941, after oil and trade embargoes had been placed on Japan, the Royal Navy despatched the battleship *Prince of Wales* and battlecruiser *Repulse* to Singapore, as a show of strength in the Far East. As soon as the raid on Pearl Harbor had finished, the Japanese launched attacks by air, sea and land on the two main targets which they had planned to take on the great drive south. These were Singapore and the Philippines.

Instead of making a direct frontal assault on Singapore, Japanese troops were landed on the Malay peninsula, far to the north. Their intention was to approach the great naval base overland, from the rear. When the British learned that a Japanese convoy was putting men ashore on the north-east coast of Malaya, the two capital ships were despatched to intercept them. Japanese bombers flying from Indo-China attacked and sank the *Prince of Wales* and the *Repulse*. Only three of the 85 aircraft were lost.

On the other side, Japanese service chiefs were exultant. In two strokes they had removed the major naval strength of the Allies. A majestic drive south would now follow, in search for raw materials, especially oil. A further blow to Britain's imperial power in the Far East was suffered on Christmas Day 1941. The territory of Hong Kong, a possession for a century, was isolated on the coast of China. To the Japanese it represented an example of European intrusion into Asia, therefore from 7 December they employed an army division to take the port. A small defence force of local civilians, Canadians and British held out strongly, but were overwhelmed, surrendering on 25 December. The Japanese had notched up another success.

Over the following six months, the Japanese put into operation their dynamically planned great southern drive. This involved them in five main campaigns. In the first, they aimed to secure Malaya and the powerful naval base at Singapore from the British.

RIGHT: A British 25-pounder field gun in action in a jungle clearing. The British had been at war for over two years when Japan attacked Pearl Harbor and their best forces were in North Africa or Britain itself. The disaster that followed in Malaya and Burma during 1942 was the greatest in British military history.

The second was action to occupy the Philippines, conquering American forces there. With these two areas taken, the Japanese would have a clear route home for oil supplies. These were to be obtained from the third campaign, after landings in the Dutch East Indies. The first of the other two areas of action was to be Burma, aiming to cut supplies reaching China via the Burma Road, and also to threaten India, the 'Jewel in the British Crown'. The second was far across the Pacific to the east, in New Guinea: the Japanese hoped to isolate Australia and New Zealand from any help arriving from the United States, thereby forcing them out of the war.

In proposing these campaigns, the Japanese showed a breathtaking sweep of strategy, fired by a double determination. They would seize the raw materials needed for war or peace while establishing themselves as the leading nation in the Far East. The industrial and military potential of the United States was apparent to them, but they hoped to make conquests before the Americans were ready to strike back. Then Japan would be able to bargain from a position of strength. That was a gamble. Would it work?

**ABOVE:** Japanese Mitsubishi G3M bombers flew from Saigon to attack the British naval forces off the coast of Malaya. The British did not know these aircraft had a range of over 3,500 miles and failed to coordinate their few fighter aircraft with the two battleships sent to attack the Japanese beachhead.

**LEFT:** The *Prince of Wales* was one of four 'King George V' class battleships completed by the British. Although the most modern in the Royal Navy, the design was dogged by numerous problems with the main armament and the ship was rushed into battle with the *Bismarck* before completing her trials.

# Malaya and Singapore

During the months following Pearl Harbor, Britain suffered some of the worst blows received during the whole of the Second World War. The most humiliating was the loss of Singapore, which had, since the 1920s, been developed as an 'impregnable' fortress for the British Empire in the Far East.

On the Japanese side was the 25th Army, commanded by General Yamashita. This included some of the nation's most experienced troops, numbering over 100,000 men. The bulk of the force advanced overland from French Indo-China, through Thailand, to link up with those put ashore on the Malayan coast. With them came 200 tanks and 560 aircraft. Opposed to these forces were some 88,000 British, Indian, Malayan and Australian troops, under the command of General Percival. Compared with their adversaries, they were inexperienced and badly equipped, having no tanks and few aircraft. They lacked the morale that comes from a coherent force working together.

An unequal contest began, with the Allied forces showing no lack of bravery and fighting spirit but being constantly outwitted and bypassed by more experienced men. British soldiers were unprepared for fighting in the environment of Malaya. One officer commented that his men's heavy equipment, including blankets and great-coats, gas masks and haversacks, made them look like Christmas trees. On the other side were lightly equipped troops, using bicycles for rapid progress. They avoided strongpoints and commandeered motor boats along the coast. Their progress south was bewilderingly fast. The Japanese had good maps, complete air cover and the will to win. They made flank attacks or infiltrated defensive positions. After one engagement, a Japanese officer expressed surprise over how quickly Allied troops retreated. 'We now understand the fighting capacity of the enemy,' he reported. The only things he had to fear were 'the quantity of munitions he had and the thoroughness of his demolition'.

By the end of January 1942 towns and villages across Malaya had fallen into Japanese hands, together with rich rubber plantations. The contest had lasted only 54 days. General Percival then ordered his army to withdraw across the causeway into the city of Singapore. There they were joined by British, Australian and Indian troops who were still being ferried into the battle area. For example, the British 18th Division, intended originally for the Middle East, was diverted to Singapore. The men had barely time to disembark before the storm of battle broke.

On 8 February Japanese infantry launched heavy attacks on the island.

General Percival had large numbers of men at his disposal but there had been little time to coordinate a defence. Over the following week Allied troops were progressively outfought. By then the city was packed with thousands of refugees as well as with soldiers. Food and water supplies were running low, and Percival believed that the end was not far off. On 15 February he sought an armistice. When he met Yamashita, the Japanese general insisted on unconditional surrender, and when Percival prevaricated, he threatened to resume the assault. At that, the British commander surrendered.

The scale of the Japanese victory resounded across Asia. Europeans had been defeated decisively. Seeds were undoubtedly sown for post-war Asian nationalist movements struggling against European domination. However, those people in the Far East who looked to the Japanese as saviours from colonial government were soon to be disillusioned. The 'Greater East Asia Co-Prosperity Sphere' proved to be no more than an airy phrase of false hope. Japanese treatment was more brutal and murderous towards them than anything they had known. Atrocities and persecution, exploitation and neglect were their legacy from the Japanese victory.

### THE JAPANESE INVASION OF MALAYA

This invasion was the greatest achievement of the Imperial army during the war. With some 60,000 men, General Yamashita attacked the peninsula that was occupied by 88,000 British and Commonwealth troops. Two of the three Japanese divisions were veterans of the war in China, whereas few of their opponents had experienced modern battle. The Japanese advanced 600 miles in just over 50 days and drove the British over the straits into Singapore by 31 January 1942. Overextended, outnumbered and running out of supplies, Yamashita attacked once more and to his delight and surprise Singapore surrendered. The British, who had reinforced the so-called fortress, surrendered over 130,000 men: more than the Germans lost at Stalingrad.

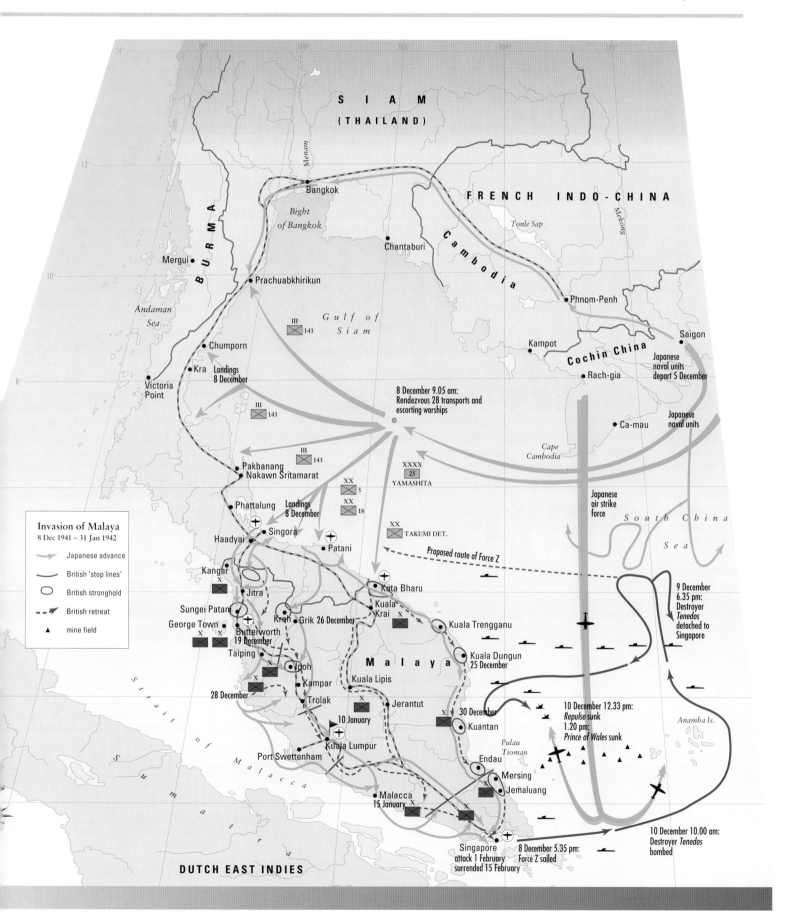

S I A M
(THAILAND)

FRENCH INDO-CHINA

BURMA

Menam

Bangkok

Bight
of Bangkok

Chantaburi

Cambodia

Tonle Sap

Mekong

Mergui

Prachuabkhirikun

Phnom-Penh

Andaman
Sea

Gulf of
Siam

III 143

Kampot

Cochin China

Saigon

Chumporn

Kra

Rach-gia

Japanese naval units
depart 5 December

Victoria
Point

III 143

8 December 9.05 am:
Rendezvous 28 transports and
escorting warships

Ca-mau

Japanese
naval units

Pakbanang
Nakawn Sritamarat

III 143

Cape
Cambodia

XXXX 25 YAMASHITA

XX 5

Phattalung

Landings
8 December

XX 18

Japanese
air strike
force

South China

Sea

Haadyai

Singora

XX TAKUMI DET.

Patani

Proposed route of Force Z

Kangar

X

Jitra

Kota Bharu

Kuala
Krai

Sungei Patani

George Town

Kroh  Grik 26 December

X

Kuala Trengganu

9 December
6.35 pm:
Destroyer
Tenedos
detached to
Singapore

Butterworth
19 December

M a l a y a

Kuala Dungun
25 December

Taiping

Ipoh

Kuala Lipis

X

Kampar

Jerantut

Anamba Is.

28 December

Trolak

X

10 January

30 December

10 December 12.33 pm:
Repulse sunk
1.20 pm:
Prince of Wales sunk

Kuala Lumpur

Kuantan

Pulau
Tioman

Port Swettenham

Strait

of

Malacca

S
u
m
a
t
r
a

Malacca
15 January

X

Endau

Mersing
Jemaluang

X

X

Singapore
attack 1 February
surrended 15 February

8 December 5.35 pm:
Force Z sailed

10 December 10.00 am:
Destroyer Tenedos
bombed

DUTCH EAST INDIES

## Invasion of Malaya
8 Dec 1941 – 31 Jan 1942

→ Japanese advance

⌐ British 'stop lines'

◯ British stronghold

- - - British retreat

▲ mine field

# The Philippines

A second barrier standing in the path of Japanese expansion in late 1941 was the Philippine Islands. The United States' interest there dated from 1898 when, as a Spanish colony, they were invaded and conquered by American forces. The Philippines then became a US colony, but had been promised full independence by 1946. From the 1930s they had their own army, as well as the American forces stationed there. When war with Japan approached, all were placed under the leadership of General Douglas MacArthur, Commander-in-Chief of US forces in the Far East, with his headquarters at Manila. Consequently, although 5,000 miles distant from Pearl Harbor, the Philippines constituted a stumbling block to Japanese ambitions.

In December 1941 there were about 110,000 Filipino and 31,000 American troops there, with artillery support. In the main, these men had not seen action and were not well trained. Covering them were just over 300 aircraft, the most valuable of which were some B-17 Flying Fortress bombers, which had the range to reach Japan itself from Philippine bases. Many other planes, however, were outdated. In addition, a US naval force of three cruisers, thirteen destroyers and 29 submarines was stationed in the islands. Pitted against this combined force at the start of hostilities were 57,000 men of the Japanese Fourteenth Army, commanded by General Homma. They included tank and artillery formations. Sections of the Japanese Navy's Third Fleet were to cover landings. Above them flew nearly 500 fighters and bombers of V Air Group.

On the first day of war, the Japanese seized an early advantage, destroying more than 100 American aircraft on the ground in a sudden raid. At a stroke, the balance of fighting power between the two sides was altered. With little naval or air protection, American and Philippine forces were always at a disadvantage. Japanese landings were made on the main island of Luzon on 10 December, continuing over the next twelve days. Other smaller islands were quickly occupied. Then, at Christmas time, large-scale landings took place near the chief city, Manila. Although some defenders fought bravely, they were no match for their experienced opponents. Enjoying complete air cover, Japanese infantry, well supported by their gunners, pressed forward remorselessly. As his men retreated, MacArthur decided to fall back towards the Bataan peninsula, a mountainous area. He was prepared to make a last stand there from January 1942, by which time the Japanese had occupied most of the remainder of Luzon.

Here, however, both sides were confronted with a common enemy – malaria. It struck the two armies without discrimination, but MacArthur's forces suffered heavily. Fighting went on throughout March and April 1942, with the invaders slowly grinding their way forward. On 12 March, under orders from President Roosevelt, MacArthur left the battle zone to take up a new appointment in Australia and was succeeded by General Wainwright. MacArthur's words on leaving were, 'Keep the flag flying. I shall return' – a promise which he kept towards the end of the war. By early April a further 20,000 Japanese reinforcements arrived, with more heavy artillery and the inevitable air superiority. On the 9th the remaining Americans surrendered and over 75,000 men went into captivity. This began with an infamous forced 'death march' of 65 miles, under a blazing sun, during which some were bayoneted, beaten or died from exhaustion.

With a rugged perseverance, about 15,000 troops retreated to the last bastion in the Philippines, the island fortress of Corregidor, 3½ by 1½ miles in extent. It lay only two miles off Bataan. Concrete emplacements were awesome in size and the forts contained over 60 coastal guns and good anti-aircraft defences. Of the thousands of troops there, however, few were battle-trained infantry, the type needed to combat the enemy. Throughout April and early May, the defenders held on doggedly. The Japanese then brought up several 240mm guns, whose shells gradually smashed down even the strongest concrete, while bombs rained down from aircraft. On 6 May, Japanese infantry got ashore and, after bitter fighting, the defenders surrendered.

RIGHT: The heroic resistance of the US forces on Corregidor lasted until 6 May 1942. Its fall signalled the end of conventional warfare on the Philippines (guerrilla fighting would continue until the US forces returned in 1944). Only a month after the garrison was forced to surrender, the Japanese advance received its decisive check at the Battle of Midway.

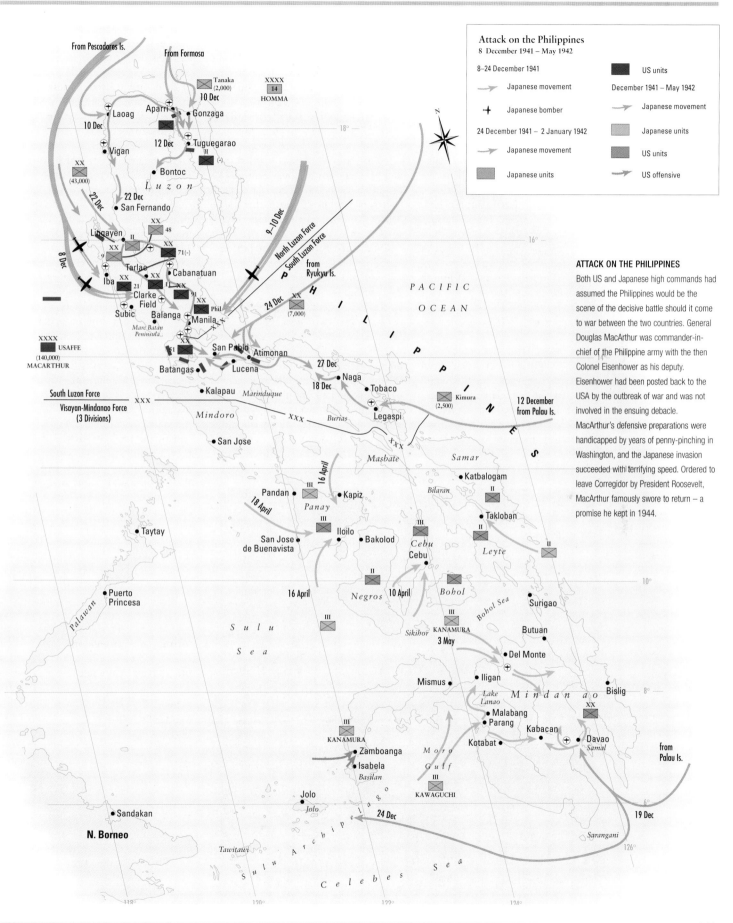

**Attack on the Philippines**
8 December 1941 – May 1942

**8–24 December 1941**

→ Japanese movement

✛ Japanese bomber

US units

**24 December 1941 – 2 January 1942**

→ Japanese movement

Japanese units

**December 1941 – May 1942**

→ Japanese movement

Japanese units

US units

→ US offensive

From Pescadores Is.

From Formosa

Tanaka (2,000) · 10 Dec

XXXX 14 HOMMA

• Laoag · 10 Dec
Aparri · • Gonzaga
12 Dec · • Tuguegarao
• Vigan
• Bontoc
XX (43,000)
*Luzon*
22 Dec · San Fernando
Lingayen · XX 48
XX 9 · XX 71(-)
Tarlac · • Cabanatuan
Iba · XX 21 · XX 91
Clarke Field
Subic · Balanga · Manila · Phil
*Mare Batan Peninsula*

North Luzon Force
South Luzon Force
from Ryukyu Is.

9–10 Dec
24 Dec · XX (7,000)

PACIFIC OCEAN

XXXX USAFFE (140,000) MACARTHUR

San Pablo • Atimonan
Batangas • • Lucena
• Kalapau · *Marinduque*
27 Dec · • Naga
18 Dec · • Tobaco
Legaspi
Kimura (2,500) · 12 December from Palau Is.

South Luzon Force
Visayan-Mindanao Force (3 Divisions) · XXX

*Mindoro* · XXX · *Burias*
• San Jose
*Masbate* · *Samar*

• Taytay

• Katbalogam
*Bilaran* · II
16 April
Pandan • · III · • Kapiz
18 April · *Panay* · III
San Jose de Buenavista · • Iloilo · • Bakolod
*Cebu* · Cebu · III · II · • Takloban
II · *Leyte* · II

• Puerto Princesa
*Palawan*
*Sulu Sea*
16 April
III
*Negros* · 10 April · *Bohol*
*Bohol Sea* · • Surigao

III · KANAMURA
3 May
*Sikibor* · • Butuan
• Del Monte
Mismus • · • Iligan
*Lake Lanao* · *Mindanao* · • Bislig
• Malabang
• Parang · Kabacan
Kotabat • · • Davao
*Samal*
III · KANAMURA
• Zamboanga
• Isabela · *Moro Gulf*
*Basilan*
III · KAWAGUCHI
Jolo · *Jolo*
• Sandakan · *Sulu Archipelago* · 24 Dec
**N. Borneo**
*Tawitawi*
from Palau Is.
19 Dec
*Sarangani*
*Celebes Sea*

**ATTACK ON THE PHILIPPINES**

Both US and Japanese high commands had assumed the Philippines would be the scene of the decisive battle should it come to war between the two countries. General Douglas MacArthur was commander-in-chief of the Philippine army with the then Colonel Eisenhower as his deputy. Eisenhower had been posted back to the USA by the outbreak of war and was not involved in the ensuing debacle. MacArthur's defensive preparations were handicapped by years of penny-pinching in Washington, and the Japanese invasion succeeded with terrifying speed. Ordered to leave Corregidor by President Roosevelt, MacArthur famously swore to return – a promise he kept in 1944.

# The Dutch East Indies

ABOVE: In the naval battles that took place during Japan's victorious advance, the British and US navies were astonished at the firepower of Japanese destroyers. The *Ushio* was one of the 'Fubuki' class built in the 1930s: carrying 12 of the deadly 'Long Lance' torpedoes, they were superb ships manned by highly trained crews.

Covetous Japanese eyes had been cast for some time on the Dutch East Indies. From the seventeenth century, the Dutch had traded there in what Europeans knew as the Spice Islands, and gradually the area had become part of Holland's Far East empire. To the Japanese, however, other local resources drew them on. The main commodity was oil, although deposits of coal were also mined, which made the islands the richest prize. That was the view held by the Japanese Navy, whose fuel supplies were running dangerously low. In addition, the taking of the East Indies was of strategic importance in the plan of conquest, presenting the opportunity of isolating Australia and bringing Japanese forces within 500 miles of Darwin.

Allied forces, small in number, were already outclassed both in strategy and quality by the Japanese. Nonetheless, on 10 May 1942, to meet the increasing threat, a combined organisation was set up to counter the advance. This was known as ABDA, for American, British, Dutch and Australian Command. What appeared to be the strength of a unified organisation, however, was also a weakness. Ships, aircraft and army detachments had received no coordinated training in planning for battle. The difficulties proved to be immense.

On the other hand, the Japanese had three powerful army forces at their disposal and had prepared meticulously. A Western Force, including the Sixteenth Army, sailed south from bases in French Indo-China, while the Eastern and Central Forces left from the occupied southern Philippines.

RIGHT: Another Japanese secret weapon: the 5,000 ton cruiser submarines of the I-400 class. With a range of 37,000 miles at 14 knots, far greater than any contemporary design, they carried three aircraft and were intended by Admiral Yamamoto to carry out an attack on the lock gates of the Panama Canal. Had such an attack succeeded, it would have seriously handicapped the US Navy.

Carrying and protecting them were two fleets of the Imperial Navy. Overhead, operating from captured airfields, were large detachments of the Air Force, which rapidly established aerial supremacy over all battle zones.

The invasion of the Dutch East Indies occurred between December 1941 and March 1942. Operations took a customary pattern. First came heavy air raids, followed by well-protected seaborne landings. In places the defenders fought fiercely, but to little avail. The invaders were soon seizing airfields and oil installations, occa-sionally using paratroops. In some places the defenders were able to destroy oil refineries but in others the latter were captured intact. Even when damage occurred, Japanese engineers worked rapidly to restore production. Allied naval units had a few successes, sinking several transports and war-ships. In general, nothing could halt the advance.

What really settled the issue was an overwhelming sea victory won by the Imperial Navy at the end of February 1942 in the Battle of the Java Sea. After that, the position of Allied ground forces on various islands of the East Indies became untenable. Faced with overwhelming odds, they were unable to continue and were finally compelled to surrender unconditional-ly on 9 March. Once again, Japanese forces, combining well in attack, had been victorious. Some of the richest regions economically in the Far East had fallen to them. Their search for sources of oil had been rewarded. Now the Imperial Navy would have fuel to continue its Pacific conquests while, in the long run, the Army would be able to complete the crushing of China.

# Burma and Ceylon

**ABOVE:** Widely regarded as the best British general to emerge from the Second World War, General Bill Slim rose from humble private to end his career as a Field Marshal.

For the Japanese at the end of 1941, an invasion of Burma was a vital move. As part of their plan to establish and guard the Greater East Asia Co-Prosperity Sphere, they hoped to protect its north-west boundaries by occupying Burma. That would serve two purposes. First, any attempted Allied counter-attack from India would be blocked. Secondly, the Burma Road, the only route for moving supplies to China overland, would be cut. In addition, the country had a number of valuable resources needed by Japan – rubber, tin, tungsten, rice and oil. Thus, for the Japanese, the Burma Campaign was a component in prosecuting their war aims.

The British, for whom Burma was an outpost of empire, bordering on India (from which it had been separated in 1937), had never believed that action there was likely. Therefore few defences had been prepared. Nevertheless, from December 1941 the storm clouds rolled nearer. Even before the fall of Singapore, Japanese troops pushed into Burma from Siam (Thailand), moving towards the capital, Rangoon, and taking airfields on the way. When Malaya and Singapore were lost, the Burma Campaign opened in earnest. On 16 February 1942 the governor of Burma received a message from Churchill, warning him that, with the fall of Singapore, 'more weight will assuredly be put into the attack upon you.'

In the early stages, two Japanese divisions, under General Iida and protected by an air brigade, launched the assault. Only small forces opposed them, composed of Indian, British and Burmese troops. As was so often the case at the time, the invaders were well-trained and well-equipped, while the defenders were not. No amount of bravery could redress the deficiencies in skill, tactics and equipment. To help the defence, the Indian 17th Division was sent in late January 1942, but its men were generally only semi-trained. In addition, the Chinese drafted in a division from their Fifth Army, commanded by the American General Stilwell. Overhead, sixteen Buffalo aircraft of the RAF were joined by a squadron of Tomahawks flown by American volunteer pilots who had been helping the Chinese.

The fighting of war in Burma was totally different from the type of conflict experienced in Europe. There were no sweeping panzer drives, nor enormous artillery barrages. Often men were struggling as desperately against the harsh environment as against the enemy. Few roads existed and there was only one main railway, running from north to south. The great rivers, like the Irrawaddy and the Sittang, were widely used for transport. In places there were thick jungle and high mountains, where well over 200in of rain fell annually. The heat in the rice-growing plains could be intense. Soldiers also had to compete with insects and leeches, malaria and dysentery. Allied troops received little support generally from the Burmese people, of whom General Slim wrote, 'The vast majority had no feeling that the war was their business; they wished to avoid it.' In fact, some cooperated with the Japanese, who claimed that they were freeing them from white colonialism.

Between December 1941 and May 1942 the Allies were in almost regular retreat. Japanese troops advanced quickly, often bypassing or outflanking defensive positions. They then suddenly appeared to attack from the rear. Their engineers made rapid repairs to blown bridges, while infantry made speedy progress through even the thickest jungle areas. Overhead, the Japanese had air superiority, bombing and strafing to harass defenders. On 8 March 1942 the Japanese entered Rangoon, which had already been evacuated by Allied forces. For the remainder of the month, and also throughout April, the retreat northwards continued. By 29 April the invaders had achieved one of their main ambitions by cutting the Burma Road link, forcing Chinese forces to pull back. In May, during the monsoon season, the last of the Indian and British troops reached the Indian frontier. Their thousand-mile retreat was the longest ever known in the history of the British Army; and they had suffered three times as many casualties as their enemy. Slim described the end of the retreat: 'All of them, British, Indian and Gurkha, were gaunt and ragged as scarecrows.' Nonetheless, he added, 'they still kept their arms and kept their ranks. They might look like scarecrows but they looked like soldiers too.' With them went thousands of Indian refugees who feared being left to the mercy of the Burmese.

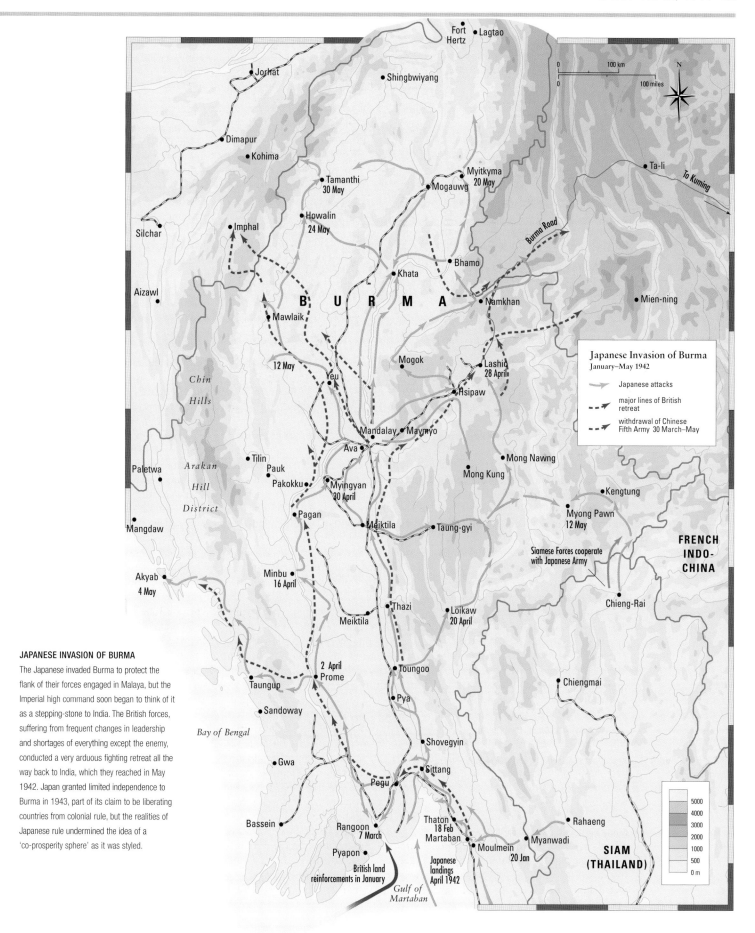

Japanese Invasion of Burma
January–May 1942

→ Japanese attacks

-→ major lines of British retreat

-→ withdrawal of Chinese Fifth Army 30 March–May

**JAPANESE INVASION OF BURMA**

The Japanese invaded Burma to protect the flank of their forces engaged in Malaya, but the Imperial high command soon began to think of it as a stepping-stone to India. The British forces, suffering from frequent changes in leadership and shortages of everything except the enemy, conducted a very arduous fighting retreat all the way back to India, which they reached in May 1942. Japan granted limited independence to Burma in 1943, part of its claim to be liberating countries from colonial rule, but the realities of Japanese rule undermined the idea of a 'co-prosperity sphere' as it was styled.

Fort Hertz • Lagtao

• Jorhat

• Shingbwiyang

• Dimapur
• Kohima

• Tamanthi 30 May

Myitkyma 20 May

Mogauwg

• Imphal

• Howalin 24 May

• Silchar

• Khata

• Bhamo

Burma Road

• Ta-li

To Kuming

• Aizawl

B U R M A

• Namkhan

• Mien-ning

• Mawlaik

Chin Hills

12 May

Yeu

• Mogok

Lashio 28 April

• Hsipaw

• Paletwa

Arakan Hill District

• Tilin
Pauk
Pakokku •

Mandalay • Maymyo

Ava •

Myingyan 30 April

• Mong Nawng

• Mong Kung

• Kengtung

Myong Pawn 12 May

• Mangdaw

Pagan •

Meiktila

• Taung-gyi

Siamese Forces cooperate with Japanese Army

FRENCH INDO-CHINA

• Akyab 4 May

Minbu 16 April

Meiktila

• Thazi

Loikaw 20 April

Chieng-Rai

Taungup

2 April Prome

• Toungoo

• Chiengmai

• Sandoway

• Pya

Bay of Bengal

• Shovegyin

• Gwa

• Sittang

Pegu •

Bassein

Rangoon 7 March

Thaton 18 Feb
Martaban

• Rahaeng

Pyapon •

Japanese landings April 1942

Moulmein 20 Jan

• Myanwadi

British land reinforcements in January

Gulf of Martaban

SIAM (THAILAND)

5000
4000
3000
2000
1000
500
0 m

0   100 km
0   100 miles

N

# Turning Points

ABOVE: The USS *Saratoga* was one of two aircraft carriers converted from battlecruisers in the 1920s. Her sistership *Lexington* was sunk during the battle of the Coral Sea but the *Saratoga* survived the war after participating in many of the greatest battles of the Pacific War.

By April 1942 the powerful Japanese drive had enjoyed amazing success. Within four months Malaya and the Philippines, the Dutch East Indies and Burma had been conquered. China had been isolated from the Allies. In the whole of history, no other expansion had gained so many territories covering such a wide area in a similar time. Moreover, all had been achieved at low cost. The price paid for conquest amounted to about twenty small warships, 67 merchant vessels, fewer than 400 aircraft and about 15,000 servicemen. The Japanese people were exultant.

The original intention of Japanese planners was that after these successes their forces should sit tight. The United States was still far from prepared to hit back, while the British were unable to provide further resources for the Far East. This would be the time when the Allies, having suffered so many reverses, would be compelled to accept the new balance of power in the Pacific and East Asia. The next fighting would be at the conference table.

In conflict, though, winners are not always satisfied by success. They suffer from the 'Victory Disease'. Often they press for one or two further objectives, reaching just beyond their grasp. This was particularly true of the Imperial Navy's General Staff, who were influential in deciding policy. Their victories had been stupendous and the drug of triumph now affected the balance of their reasoning. For them, in the Grand Scheme, two more ambitions beckoned. The first was to force Australia out of the war. The second was to have a final showdown with the US Fleet in the Pacific, so that its destruction would inevitably compel the Americans to talk peace. The Japanese knew that they still had a greater number of aircraft carriers than the United States. As that vessel was now the linchpin of success at sea, they would use their superiority before the USA, with its enormous industrial potential, could build enough to draw level.

Then, on 18 April 1942, a comparatively small action occurred whose repercussions echoed world-wide. For

RIGHT: A Japanese aircraft plummets out of control after taking hits from US anti-aircraft fire. American anti-aircraft weapons and tactics developed continually during the war while the Japanese remained much the same. Japanese aircraft were capable of flying vast distances but at the expense of protective features such as self-sealing fuel tanks and armour to protect pilots.

the Japanese people here was an ominous forerunner of later disasters; for the Allies, a shaft of light shone briefly in a general darkness. The event also influenced Japanese policy and affected the great naval battles which took place over the next seven weeks.

Until mid-April 1942 the Allies had been constantly on the defensive in the Pacific War. Yet the Americans, who had suffered so devastatingly at Pearl Harbor, were determined at the earliest opportunity to hit back with an avenging operation. A blow of that type would raise Allied morale everywhere and remind the Japanese that even their homeland was not free from retribution. Thus, one of the war's most daring and remarkable raids was planned. The strike would have to be made by aircraft flying from a carrier, as no Allied airfields were within return-flight range of Japan. The aircraft carrier *Hornet*, carrying sixteen B-25 bombers, was part of a task force which would sail to within 450 miles of Japan. After taking off, each aircraft would drop a small bomb load on Tokyo, then fly on a further 1,200 miles to land in China.

In reality, the American ships were spotted by a Japanese vessel when about 800 miles from the coast, on 18 April. Therefore, the bombers took off

immediately. Under the command of Colonel Doolittle, the sixteen aircraft, basically unsuited for carrier work, were airborne ten hours earlier than planned, rising into a 40mph gale. They arrived over Tokyo after midday, flying at 1,000ft and catching the defences by surprise. After dropping their bombs, all escaped to fly on

towards China. There, the crews had to crash-land or bale out. Most were rescued by the Chinese, but some were captured by the Japanese, who later executed three men on charges of deliberately bombing civilians – a grim irony, considering the countless civilians who had suffered at the hands of the Imperial forces.

**ABOVE:** President Roosevelt and the architects of victory in the Pacific: General MacArthur (left) and Admiral Nimitz (right). Roosevelt's military leaders argued for two different strategic approaches to the war, MacArthur wanting to return to the Philippines as fast as possible, while Nimitz advocated an 'island hopping' attack across the central Pacific. In the event, the US was sufficiently powerful to undertake both.

**LEFT:** A Japanese merchant ship seen sinking through the periscope of a US submarine. Japan's rapid conquests left her with a widely scattered collection of island garrisons that relied on sea transport for all their supplies. No-one in Japan had planned how to guard these sea lanes against determined submarine attack.

# The Battle of the Coral Sea

To the Japanese, the Dominion of Australia represented a double threat. First, it was a fortress against the great drive south; secondly, the country could be used by Allied forces, especially the Americans, as a springboard for a counter-offensive in the Pacific. Therefore Japanese forces were despatched into New Guinea and the Solomon Islands to establish a ring of bases to the north-east of Australia. They would isolate her from the United States.

Australia had already come within range of attack. While action was being launched against the Dutch East Indies in February 1942, Japanese aircraft, both land-based and carrier-borne, attacked the northern town of Darwin. On 19 February, 135 aeroplanes caused widespread destruction to the port and shipping, while 400 civilians were either killed or injured.

In May, the Japanese planned a double thrust against Australia. First, they intended to capture Port Moresby in New Guinea, from where they could raid the whole of northern Australia. The second aim followed.

As soon as their ships moved into the Coral Sea on this mission, they believed that the US Navy would react with its own fleet. Japanese commanders felt that they could land a blow on the Americans by winning yet another maritime victory.

What the Japanese failed to appreciate was a point that would cost them dearly for the rest of the war. Code-breakers in the United States had cracked their naval codes and thus Japanese plans were known in advance to American leaders, especially General MacArthur, by then the overall Commander-in-Chief, and Admiral Nimitz, the naval commander. The difficulty for the Allies, nonetheless, was that although they knew Japanese intentions, they lacked sufficient forces to counter them adequately.

The Japanese prepared an invasion force, carried in eleven transports, to take Port Moresby and a lesser one to occupy one of the Solomon Islands. These vessels would be covered by warships, including a small aircraft carrier. The main strike force com-

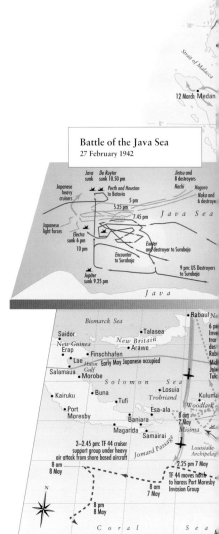

prised two powerful carriers, both veterans of the Pearl Harbor raid, supported by other vessels. Their task was to deal with any American naval units which tried to prevent the seaborne landings. They believed that the US Navy had only one carrier available in that area. That was a serious mistake. As a result of the code-breakers' work, the Americans employed two 'flat-tops', carrying 140 aircraft and supported by other units. Both fleets of ships were deployed into the Coral Sea in early May.

**THE RISE AND FALL OF THE JAPANESE NAVY**

Japan's run of victories at sea continued into February 1942 when they inflicted a stinging defeat on an Allied British-Dutch-US squadron off Indonesia. In May the Japanese were checked at the Battle of the Coral Sea, their widely dispersed forces deployed with little regard to US reaction. This was the first naval battle in which neither surface fleet made visual contact with the other: the whole action was fought in the air.

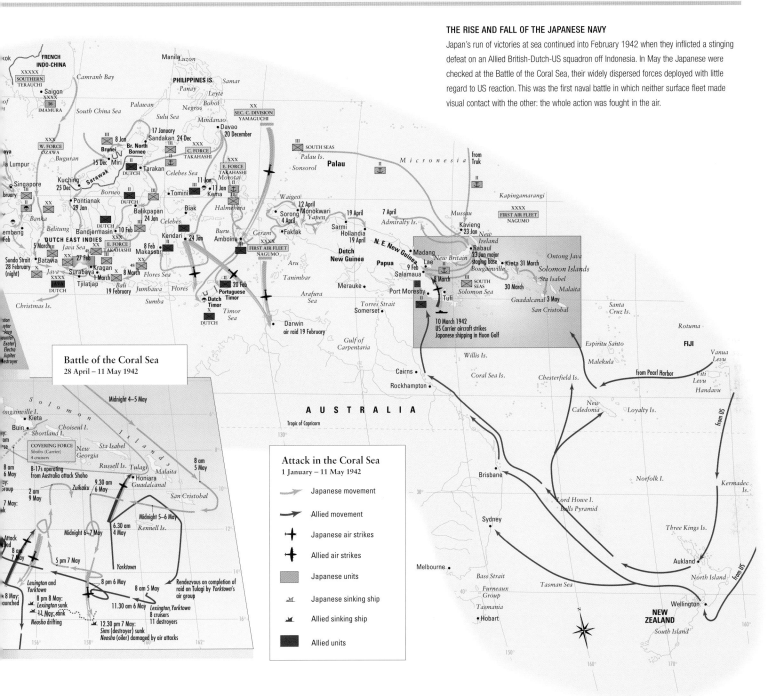

Battle of the Coral Sea
28 April – 11 May 1942

**Attack in the Coral Sea**
1 January – 11 May 1942

→ Japanese movement

→ Allied movement

✚ Japanese air strikes

✚ Allied air strikes

▨ Japanese units

⚓ Japanese sinking ship

⚓ Allied sinking ship

■ Allied units

Action opened on the 3rd. Each fleet despatched reconnaissance aircraft, but some of their reports were inaccurate or misunderstood. In fact, the whole battle was remarkable for the number of errors made. Then, on 7 May, American bombers sank the small carrier which was part of the Port Moresby invasion force. As a result, the Japanese postponed that operation, ordering the transports to turn back.

The main action took place next day, with both fleets equally balanced in strength of ships and aircraft. In each case, attacks by dive- and torpedo-bombers were primarily aimed at enemy carriers, with ships turning desperately to avoid them. By that evening, one of the powerful Japanese carriers was damaged, while the other lost many experienced aircrew and had to re-form its units.

On the other side, the Japanese sank the carrier *Lexington* and two other vessels, but the Americans lost fewer aircraft. At first, the Imperial Navy appeared to have won the day, but in the long run the Battle of the Coral Sea proved to be a strategic defeat for Japan. The invasion of Port Moresby had failed – the first real setback of the war in the great drive south. The Australians were fighting on. Two Japanese carriers were temporarily out of action, but at a time when they were badly needed. The Americans also learned many lessons from a contest in which all action came from carrier-borne aircraft. For the first time ever, the ships involved in a sea battle never even sighted each other.

# The Battle of Midway

The Imperial General Headquarters in Tokyo had laid plans to achieve the second part of the Japanese Grand Design. This was to effect the complete destruction of American naval power in the Pacific, so that the United States would be vulnerable up to the western coastline. This would be achieved particularly by sinking every US carrier. With air cover gone, other American vessels could be eliminated at leisure.

The great operation intended to use almost the entire Japanese Navy. Eleven capital ships were involved, including the world's newest and largest battleship, the 70,000-ton *Yamato*, equipped with 18in guns. With them went 22 cruisers, 65 destroyers and 21 submarines. But the jewels of the Imperial Fleet were the carriers, of which eight were to be employed. In support were 600 aircraft. In the opinion of Japanese naval leaders, this force would be sufficient to overwhelm American opposition. The US Pacific Fleet's main battleship strength was lost at Pearl Harbor, and it had three carriers, with about 230 aeroplanes, to oppose Japanese might. There was also a collection of smaller warships, but only some 75 vessels in total – far fewer than the number mustered by the Imperial Navy.

From the start, Yamamoto made the error of splitting forces in his over-complicated plan. A transport group, heavily escorted, was to land 2,500 troops on Midway Island, an American base lying 1,100 miles to the north-west of Hawaii. A base would be established there to give warning of any future raids being made against

Japan, a need underlined by the shock caused by Doolittle's attack on Tokyo two months earlier. The assault on Midway would be supported by a strike force, including four powerful carriers. The main body, with seven battleships and supporting vessels, would wait to engage the American Fleet when it arrived for battle. As a decoy, the Japanese intended to send a northern force to land in the Aleutian Islands, far away in the north Pacific.

### THE BATTLE OF MIDWAY

The Japanese invasion of Midway involved enormous forces split into numerous squadrons and took little account of possible US reaction. The US fleet was badly outnumbered but had the priceless advantage of reading the Japanese signal traffic and could position its carriers to take the Japanese by surprise. Nevertheless, it took a combination of coincidences, accidents and the cold courage of US aircrews to shatter the Japanese attack. Significantly, the Japanese withdrew after the loss of their carriers, recognising that their overwhelming superiority in battleships was now virtually irrelevant.

**ABOVE:** *Yorktown* lists heavily after a desperate last strike by the *Hiryu*'s surviving airgroup. The battle ended with all four Japanese carriers on the bottom, together with over 350 aircraft and most of their aircrew.

The Americans viewed the forthcoming contest in a different light, especially as they were forewarned by their decoders. Admiral Nimitz therefore decided on another course of action. He would keep his smaller Pacific Fleet away from a head-on confrontation, while using every occasion of hitting back. By 3 June the US force was already at sea, coming well to the north of Midway, ready to intercept the Japanese.

Far away to the north-east on the same day, the northern force went into action against the Aleutian Islands. The Japanese claimed the operation as a success, but it failed in its main objective. Nimitz would not be drawn and sent no extra forces in support. A hole had appeared in the Japanese plans.

The main and deciding part of the battle occurred near Midway on 4 June and the Americans concentrated their attention there. First, Japanese carriers of the strike force launched aircraft to attack the island base, where they caused heavy damage. Many ground-based US bombers and fighters attempting to defend Midway were destroyed either on the airfield or in aerial combat, while Japanese aircraft suffered few losses. By 8.30 a.m. the Japanese were confident of victory and the carriers prepared their aircraft for a second strike against Midway, to finish off its defences.

Just then, however, Admiral Nagumo, commander of the strike force, was confronted with a dilemma. He suddenly learned that the American task force had been discovered roughly 200 miles away. What should he do? Many of his Zero fighters were on patrol. His torpedo planes were loaded with bombs for the next raid on Midway. Aircraft from the first raid there now needed to land. Should the second raid go ahead? Or should he launch an immediate torpedo-bomber raid on the US ships? In the confusion of battle, with unclear messages arriving and different advice being offered, Nagumo hesitated. He then decided first to land his returning aircraft before ordering preparations to attack the American task force. That move settled the outcome of the battle.

The US carriers had learned of the Japanese strike force's whereabouts at 6 a.m. Within two hours they were in position to have their torpedo- and dive-bombers airborne, searching across the ocean for enemy ships. These were discovered about 9.30 a.m. The Devastator torpedo-bombers were slow and vulnerable to defending fighters. They came in low, trying to gain position for the attack, but Zero fighters and anti-aircraft guns on the ships massacred them, shooting down 35 out of 41 aircraft. Not one torpedo struck home, and the carrier crews felt triumphant. At that moment, disaster struck the Imperial Navy, altering the whole course of the Pacific War in ten minutes.

All eyes on the Japanese vessels and in the defending Zeros were concentrated on the low-level torpedo-bomber attack. No one noticed that, high above, 35 Dauntless dive-bombers had gathered, ready for the kill. 'At that instant a look-out screamed "Hell Divers!"' a Japanese officer recounted. 'I looked up to see three black enemy planes plummeting towards our ship.' Four hits on the carrier Kaga quickly turned her into a blazing wreck. Two bombs struck Akagi, starting fires and explosions that shortly destroyed her. Soryu was soon engulfed in flames. All three vessels stayed afloat for several hours, but were now funeral pyres of the supremacy of the Imperial Navy.

In the afternoon, aircraft from the remaining carrier, Hiryu, struck back at the US task force, hitting the carrier Yorktown, which later sank. Retribution followed. At 5 p.m. 24 American dive-bombers found the Japanese vessel, their bombs destroying her flight deck and setting the ship ablaze from stem to stern. As night came on, both sides took stock of the events of a momentous day in naval history.

The costs of battle stood comfortably in favour of the Americans. They had lost one carrier and about 150 aircraft, but four Japanese carriers, with 330 aircraft, had been destroyed in return. Together with them went many highly trained seamen and aircrew.

The Battle of Midway certainly did not stop Japanese efforts at launching further ground attacks in the Pacific – for example, on New Guinea and the Solomon Islands – but the Americans had shattered the notion of the invincibility of the Imperial Fleet.

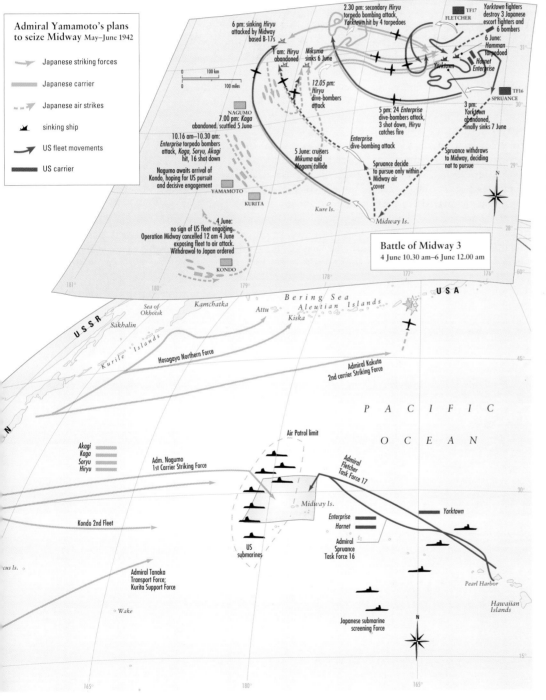

# CHAPTER 6: Africa and the Mediterranean, 1940–43

The campaigns in North and East Africa both finished long before the end of the war in 1945. By then, Axis forces had been swept from the continent. In East Africa, Mussolini's empire collapsed in the summer of 1941 when his forces surrendered in Eritrea. The North African campaign ended almost two years later, when Axis armies capitulated in Tunisia.

Servicemen from those two theatres of war recollect not only the hardships of battle common to conflict anywhere in the world, but also the harsh environment in which the fighting occurred. This was especially true of the campaigns fought between June 1940 and Christmas 1942 in the area generally known as 'The Western Desert'. That zone of action lay mainly between the northern extremity of the great Sahara Desert and the Mediterranean coast, a wild, barren wasteland, inhospitable for living in, let alone fighting in. Many servicemen in both armies remember mainly the lack of water, searing winds and countless flies, 'a filthy, pertinacious, excruciating pestilence'. Distances were vast. For example, Tripoli in Libya and Alexandria in Egypt were as far apart as Moscow and Berlin.

In June 1940 the odds of war were stacked heavily against the British. After the collapse of France, and with the threat of an impending invasion of the United Kingdom, few forces could be spared to serve in the Middle East. Most of Britain's land and air resources were needed to defend the homeland. Having lost the support of the French Fleet, the Royal Navy alone was not strong enough to exercise control over the whole of the Mediterranean Sea, especially the route from Gibraltar to Alexandria. The Italians, at their late entry into the war, appeared to hold the whip-hand. They no longer had to fear attack by French forces coming at them from Tunisia or Algeria. They had no world-wide entanglements and could commit large resources to a conflict in Africa, where they had altogether half a million men.

Commanding their forces in North Africa was Marshal Graziani, an experienced soldier. At his disposal he had the Tenth Army in Cyrenaica and the Fifth in Tripolitania. There were nine divisions of regular soldiers, three Blackshirt divisions and two of Libyan recruits. With this huge force to manoeuvre, Graziani's main target was the Egyptian Canal Zone, lying to the east. This step appeared easy to

take for well-equipped and well-supplied forces.

Opposite these formidable numbers stood 36,000 British and Commonwealth troops in Egypt, under the overall leadership of General Wavell. He had been Commander-in-Chief Middle East for less than a year. His army at the time consisted of a British armoured division, together with an Indian and a New Zealand division. Assisting them were fourteen British infantry battalions and two small regiments of artillery. Wavell could also call on 27,000 Commonwealth and British troops of various categories who were stationed in Palestine. Nevertheless, the total force appeared to be quite inadequate to fend off an overwhelmingly power-

**RIGHT:** The British army spawned a bewildering number of special forces units during the desert war. Some regular officers regarded these 'private armies' with distaste, but one was to achieve lasting fame: the 22nd Special Air Service or SAS. Here, an SAS patrol, returns to base after three months in the desert.

ful Italian army. For example, the 7th Armoured Division 'only had four regiments of obsolete tanks. There was a shortage of ammunition and most of the tanks had only two of the three machine guns they were meant to have.' In addition, no tank transporters were available, which shortened 'the lives of both tracks and engines'.

In East Africa, the imbalance of numbers and strength was even more marked. Mussolini's forces, both Italians and colonials, in Eritrea and Abyssinia totalled over 200,000 men. On the opposite side were about 9,000 British and local troops in the Sudan and 8,500 soldiers in Kenya. The Italians, it seemed, could walk into British territory whenever they chose.

The same inequality of numbers was evident in air power. Air Chief Marshal Longmore controlled 29 squadrons, comprising 300 aircraft, many of which were old, or even obsolescent. With these he was required to defend 'Egypt, Sudan, Palestine and Transjordan, East Africa, Aden and Somaliland, Iraq and adjacent territories, Cyprus, Turkey, Balkans, Red Sea, Mediterranean Sea, Persian Gulf'. In Egypt at the start of the desert campaign he could call on 94 bombers and 64 fighters, only a minority of which latter were Hurricanes. Further south, in East Africa, were 85 bombers and a handful of fighters. His responsibilities were as breathtaking as his resources were inadequate.

On the other side lay the full might of the *Regia Aeronautica*, consisting of 2,600 aircraft. Of these, the Italians kept 200 fighters and 200 bombers in Libya, while in East Africa they had twice as many aeroplanes as the RAF. Among these were highly manoeuvrable biplanes, CR.42 fighters, to match British Gladiators, and SM.79 bombers, among the best aircraft of the war.

On paper, at least, the future in the Middle East looked bleak for Britain and the Commonwealth. 'In every department of modern warfare,' wrote a correspondent, 'especially in such equipment as tanks and guns, we were pitifully, hopelessly weak.' With all of these advantages in their favour, where would the Italians strike? Which territory would be added first to Mussolini's new Roman Empire?

**ABOVE:** British soldiers from the Rifle Brigade watch as a supply dump burns on the horizon. The rival armies swept back and forth across the Libyan desert in a series of advances and retreats that cynics dubbed the 'Benghazi handicap'. With few urban areas or other obstacles, the war was often described as a tactician's paradise but a logistics officer's nightmare. All supplies had to be delivered to the front by lorries, often over enormous distances.

# East Africa

ABOVE: A British Universal Carrier, also known as the Bren Gun Carrier but seen here armed with an anti-tank rifle for good measure, lurches across the desert at top speed. Even after local modification, few vehicles could withstand the desert environment for long.

BELOW: An Italian officer stands on top of his armoured car for a better view. The comparative immobility of the Italian forces initially despatched to invade British-held Egypt proved to be their undoing.

Italy's entry into the war threatened Britain's ability to supply forces in Egypt in two respects. First, the usual Mediterranean maritime run from Gibraltar, via Malta, to Alexandria was now at risk from air or naval attack. Consequently, ships carrying supplies had to sail the old pre-Suez route round the Cape of Good Hope, then up to Egypt by way of the Red Sea. This introduced a second threat, which occurred near the Horn of Africa. Both Italian Somaliland and Eritrea bordered the route. Aircraft flying from the Italian naval base at Massawa on the Red Sea would easily be able to launch raids on convoys sailing towards Suez.

The biggest territory in Italy's East African empire was Abyssinia, conquered four years earlier. The country covered over half a million square miles, but lacked good roads and com-munications. In war, however, the terrain made life difficult for defenders and attackers alike. To the north lay Eritrea, only one-tenth the size of Abyssinia but bordering the Red Sea. Again, the hinterland was harsh, an area of desert and mountains. Further to the south lay Italian Somaliland, fringing the Indian Ocean, but a barren land of no natural resources.

In Abyssinia, 91,000 Italian troops were stationed, supported by 200,000 Abyssinian levies. Their particular disadvantage was that, being cut off from Italy, they could receive no supplies or reinforcements. Nonetheless, such a large, well-armed force posed a formidable threat to British interests: it could invade the Sudan or Kenya and change the balance of power in Africa. Opposed to the Italians were comparatively small British and Commonwealth forces. Only two or three battalions of troops were in British Somaliland, although a force eventually totalling 75,000 Commonwealth soldiers was gathered in Kenya to defend the colony.

British Somaliland was not invaded until 3 August, when 26 Italian battalions, well supported by guns, tanks and armoured cars, moved against a small force of defenders. Although greatly outnumbered, these men fought back magnificently for over two weeks before being evacuated by sea to Kenya. In this time they suffered 250 casualties, but inflicted over 2,000 on the invaders. The Italians devel-oped a healthy respect for the fighting qualities of Commonwealth soldiers and this slowed up even further their desire to launch offensives.

In the aftermath of Dunkirk in June 1940, the Middle East was the only zone where British and Axis land forces were in immediate conflict. The eyes of the British government were therefore turned sharply to North and East Africa. The débâcle of the French Campaign strongly underlined the need for Britain to enjoy a success somewhere in the world, to raise the morale of a public growing accus-tomed to defeat. By late 1940, realis-ing that a sizeable army had been gath-ered in Kenya under General Wavell's overall command, Churchill pressed strongly for an offensive to be launched against the Italians. When cautious generals were unwilling to start attacks until every preparation was made, the prime minister could be like a sheepdog, snapping at the heels of a reluctant flock.

Eventually, in February 1941, Commonwealth troops entered Italian Somaliland, then Eritrea and later Abyssinia. The manoeuvre started as a counter-measure to protect Kenya, but success was so rapid and unexpected that it turned into a full-scale invasion. Troops from South Africa, the Gold Coast and East Africa raced ahead, usually meeting little resistance. Although the Italian Air Force had superior numbers of aircraft it failed to offer much defence to the Army; on the other side, the RAF gave good support to Commonwealth troops. Neither the Italian soldiers nor their levies showed much stomach for the fight.

By the end of February 1941 Italian Somaliland had been overrun, so the invaders swept forward to Abyssinia and Eritrea. Although transport was a particular difficulty, Commonwealth forces pushed on with great vigour, finally driving the Italians out of the country they had conquered five years earlier. By 19 May the Italian com-mander surrendered. British and Commonwealth forces within a few months had occupied the whole of Mussolini's much vaunted, yet largely barren, East African empire. At the same time they captured large quantities of military supplies, including stocks of oil, and took 230,000 prisoners.

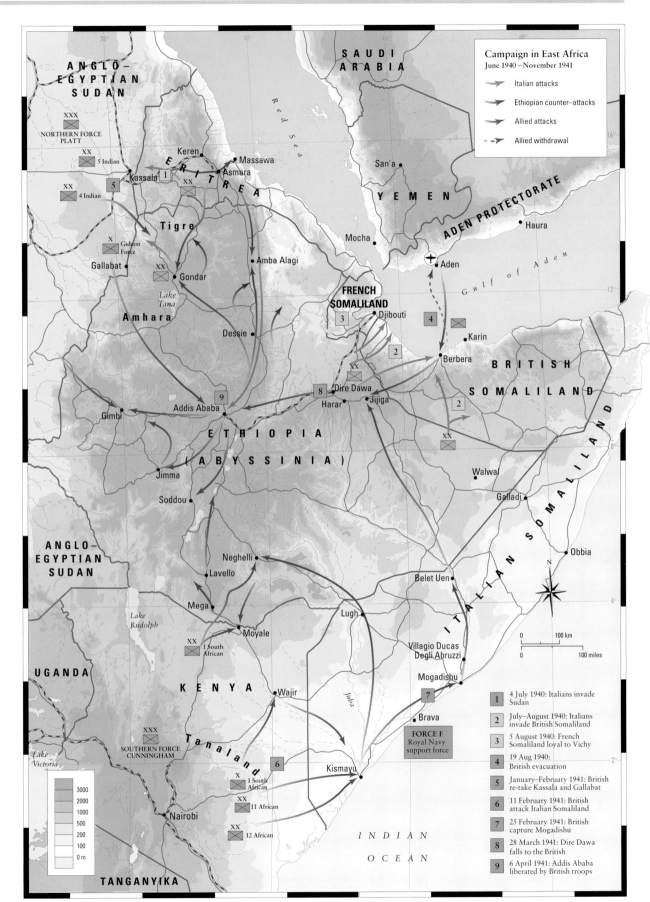

## Campaign in East Africa
### June 1940 – November 1941

→ Italian attacks

→ Ethiopian counter–attacks

→ Allied attacks

⇢ Allied withdrawal

**EAST AFRICA**

Italy had invaded Abyssinia (Ethiopia) in 1935 and launched attacks on British-held Kenya and Somaliland in 1940. However, the British counter-attacked despite only having 40,000 troops (half of them locally raised) against 92,000 Italians and 250,000 Abyssinians in Italian service. The British captured Mogadishu in February and reached Addis Ababa in April having covered 1,700 miles. The main Italian army surrendered in May although some pockets of resistance remained until November. With the Red Sea no longer a 'war zone' for American purposes, US shipping could now sail directly to Egypt with war supplies for the British.

**ANGLO-EGYPTIAN SUDAN**

XXX NORTHERN FORCE PLATT

XX 5 Indian

Keren

Massawa

Kassala

1

ERITREA

Asmara

5

XX 4 Indian

Tigre

X Gideon Force

Gallabat

XX Gondar

Lake Tana

Amhara

Dessie

Amba Alagi

Red Sea

SAUDI ARABIA

San'a

YEMEN

Mocha

ADEN PROTECTORATE

Haura

✈ Aden

Gulf of Aden

FRENCH SOMALILAND

3 Djibouti

4

XX Karin

2 Berbera

BRITISH SOMALILAND

XX Dire Dawa

8 Harar   Jijiga

2

9 Addis Ababa

Gimbi

ETHIOPIA (ABYSSINIA)

Jimma

Soddou

XX

Walwal

Galladi

ITALIAN SOMALILAND

Obbia

ANGLO-EGYPTIAN SUDAN

Neghelli

Lavello

Belet Uen

Lugh

Mega

Villagio Ducas Degli Abruzzi

Moyale

XX 1 South African

Mogadishu

UGANDA

KENYA

Wajir

Juba

7

Brava

FORCE F Royal Navy support force

SOUTHERN FORCE CUNNINGHAM

Lake Rudolph

Lake Victoria

Tanaland

6

Nairobi

X 1 South African

XX 11 African

Kismayu

XX 12 African

INDIAN OCEAN

TANGANYIKA

3000
2000
1000
500
200
100
0 m

0    100 km
0    100 miles

1  4 July 1940: Italians invade Sudan

2  July–August 1940: Italians invade British Somaliland

3  5 August 1940: French Somaliland loyal to Vichy

4  19 Aug 1940: British evacuation

5  January–February 1941: British re-take Kassala and Gallabat

6  11 February 1941: British attack Italian Somaliland

7  25 February 1941: British capture Mogadishu

8  28 March 1941: Dire Dawa falls to the British

9  6 April 1941: Addis Ababa liberated by British troops

# North Africa

Contrary to most expectations, British forces made the first moves in desert fighting. Wavell, a commander of underestimated ability, ordered General O'Connor to form a Western Desert Force and to harry Italian frontier positions in Libya. This he did with patrols of mobile, well-trained columns in raids made by troops who were used to movement in the desert. During June and July 1940 they gained a series of small, but important, successes, catching their enemies by surprise, before retiring to defensive positions in Egypt. Throughout this time, Wavell was already planning counter-strokes against the Italians when, as he knew they would, they began to advance into Egypt.

In August, Graziani's armies had still barely moved. Wavell was called to London. There he learned that, in spite of the ominous threat of invasion, Churchill was arranging for strong reinforcements, including 150 tanks, to be sent immediately to Egypt. This most courageous act, in the prime minister's words, 'was at once awful and right. No one faltered.' Wavell returned to the Middle East, heartened by the government's support. The convoy carrying the equipment, after travelling round the Cape, reached Egypt in mid-September.

Churchill certainly hoped for a military success in the Middle East. So did Mussolini, who pressed a reluctant Graziani to make a move. However, the Italians' cautious advance did not start until mid-September. They occupied Sollum on the 13th, taking four days to cover the 65 miles to Sidi Barrani – hardly an inspiring overture.

His policy played into the hands of Wavell, who prepared a counter-offensive, Operation 'Compass'. This was to open as no more than a large sortie but if successful would be carried further. Wavell knew the risks involved, but had great faith in his men, believing them to be superior to the Italians in everything but numbers. 'We must

accustom our minds to the offensive which alone can bring victory,' he wrote to a general in November. Subsequently, O'Connor's troops trained hard and prepared to strike the enemy an unexpected blow. They were helped particularly by information from excellent signals intelligence in Cairo. By the start of the assault, 'British knowledge of where the Italian Army was strong and where it was weak, and of its administration layout, was very comprehensive, and this determined the final shape of the British plan.'

The counter-offensive opened on 9 December, with 30,000 British and Commonwealth troops, employing 275 tanks, attacking 80,000 Italians. Their success was immediate and remarkable. They fought with skill and energy, so that within three days most Italians had been driven out of Egypt and 38,000 prisoners captured. Once on the retreat, Graziani's forces had little desire to stop. O'Connor kept moving on. First Bardia and then Tobruk were taken, and a further 65,000 prisoners, with mountains of equipment, fell into British hands as Graziani's men surrendered in droves.

O'Connor would not let the enemy off the hook. By early February 1941 he had reached the coast road running from Benghazi westwards, cutting off the retreating Italians. They were forced into battle at Beda Fomm. Few people have heard of this contest, which became one of the most important of the whole war. Within two days Graziani's Tenth Army was shattered, the important port of Benghazi had been captured and O'Connor's victorious troops were ready to push on to the west, into Tripolitania. In ten weeks the British had snared 130,000 prisoners, about 1,300 guns and 400 tanks. 'The Army of the Nile,' wrote Churchill, 'had advanced 500 miles, [and] had destroyed an Italian army of more than nine divisions.' This astounding victory had been gained at the cost of 2,000 casualties. A war correspondent reported seeing an entire Italian division marching into captivity, 'tired and dispirited beyond caring'. He noticed them, 'first in hundreds, then in thousands, until the stupendous crocodile of marching figures stretched away to either horizon.'

**LEFT:** An Italian anti-tank gun in action. The Italian forces were woefully ill-equipped compared to their German allies and, with some notable exceptions, were not prepared to fight to the death for Mussolini.

**RIGHT:** The campaign in North Africa was decided by mechanized forces: without transport, infantry could only defend static positions. Here, an Italian infantry formation deploys in the open desert.

**LEFT:** An Italian infantry gun in action. Many Italian divisions were equipped for fighting in the mountainous terrain of northern Italy, but pack artillery and animal transport was of little value in mobile warfare.

LEFT: A lorry unloads its vital cargo. Fuel and water arrived in tins for both the British and German armies. The latter had the better kit and captured 'jerrycans' were widely used (and copied). While tanks looked more glamorous, generals knew they could never have too many lorries.

RIGHT: An Italian 75 mm self-propelled gun kicks up the sand as it fires. Based on the lightly protected hull of an obsolete tank chassis, this combination offered greater firepower although the main armament had very little ability to traverse.

ABOVE: British troops arrive in Greece on their ill-fated attempt to halt the German invasion. The withdrawal of British troops from North Africa had a disastrous effect there, but the British government could not bring itself to abandon Greece to its fate without a struggle. The Greeks had resisted Italy's treacherous attack with tremendous skill and courage.

In the distance gleamed the main prize – the port of Tripoli. O'Connor knew that with the impetus his men had built up, he could keep the Italians on the run. There was every chance that he could drive them completely out of North Africa, gaining a victory of giant proportions, worthy to stand beside the greatest. However, at the moment of triumph, two factors intervened to change the balance of success. Wavell and O'Connor, who controlled neither of them, suffered as a result.

The first emanated from the Italian invasion of Greece in October 1940. A few months later, the British wanted to help the Greeks who had fought back vigorously and successfully against the invaders. To do this, it was decided to halt the British advance in North Africa and to despatch troops under Wavell's command to the Balkans. Just as O'Connor had won his remarkable victory at Beda Fomm and was preparing to press ahead, he was ordered to stop. The bulk of his successful army was withdrawn, leaving only a holding force. Before long, contingents of Australian, New Zealand and British troops were sent to Greece.

Churchill has been criticised since for halting the efforts of a victorious general and for posting men to a Balkan campaign which ended in fail-

ure. Hindsight, of course, lends a clarity unavailable at the time. The decision certainly puzzled some German commanders. 'We could not understand at the time,' General Warlimont, who was on the *Führer*'s staff, said later, 'why the British did not exploit the difficulties of the Italians in Cyrenaica by pushing on to Tripoli. There was nothing to check them.'

The second factor intervening in North Africa early in 1941 and altering the balance in the Western Desert was the arrival on the scene of a German general. His name was Erwin Rommel.

General Erwin Rommel had proved to be a successful and skilful leader during the French Campaign when commanding the Seventh Panzers, 'The Ghost Division'. He understood the merits of armoured warfare and was already renowned as a hard-driving commander. On 6 February 1941 he was instructed personally by Hitler to lead a small force of two divisions into North Africa, to help rescue the Italians. Six days later he flew to Tripoli and immediately began organising his resources as they arrived by sea. He was a man in a hurry. Although the British learned of the arrival of German units in North Africa, they believed that several months would elapse before they would be ready for battle. Rommel soon proved them wrong.

By this time, many of O'Connor's victorious men had been sent to Greece or East Africa, or were back in Egypt refitting. Their places had been taken by under-equipped and untried

divisions led by new and inexperienced commanders. On 31 March Rommel suddenly advanced with no more than a small force against British and Commonwealth positions. By skilful use of limited resources, plus bluff, he soon had his adversaries retreating faster than they had advanced. After just twelve days, he had swept the British out of Cyrenaica, recaptured Benghazi, taken O'Connor prisoner and reached the Egyptian border. The only Commonwealth troops left in Libya were a small, mainly Australian force holed up in Tobruk. Rommel, the opportunist, halted only because of fuel and supply shortages.

Within a fortnight, the legend of the 'Desert Fox' was born. Here was a leader experienced in armoured warfare, supremely confident and commanding well-trained troops. Overall, he had greater vision than his opponent and kept in closer touch with his men, whom he pushed relentlessly. Italian units which came under his command also fought far better than they had earlier. Rommel used them well, but still believed that they were mainly 'designed for a colonial war against insurgent tribesmen'. He became an inspiring figure to his own men, who enjoyed some remarkable successes stemming from his leadership.

Rommel started his desert command with some advantages over his enemies. The Germans were far more experienced in armoured warfare, had superior staff organisation and possessed better equipment. In the Western Desert they displayed these superiorities for about eighteen

months after Rommel's arrival. Another German general was specific about the advantages of the *Afrika Korps* over the British forces which eventually became the Eighth Army. First, the Germans had superior anti-tank artillery, especially the 88mm gun, which could be used against aircraft or tanks or as a field-gun. The British equivalent, the 3.7in anti-aircraft gun, was not used to target tanks. In addition, the 50mm high-velocity anti-tank gun, which always accompanied panzer tanks, was a far better weapon than the 2pdr carried by British armoured vehicles. Second was

'our systematic practice of the principle of cooperation of arms'. Third came, 'last but not least – our tactical methods', in which Rommel and his troops were very experienced. Consequently, although the *Afrika Korps* was sometimes outnumbered in tank strength, he used his limited numbers skilfully, often handing out heavier casualties than he received. One could also mention the generally better quality of the Germans' tanks, their more effective system of battlefield tank recovery and even the superiority of their petrol cans –'jerrycans' – over the British equivalent.

**ABOVE:** Rommel's *Afrika Korps* soon became a self-conscious elite with its own emblems, uniform and song. Both the British and the Germans would be adopted 'Lile Marlene' after the German controlled Radio Belgrade broadcast Lale Anderson singing it. Ironically, the German propaganda ministry had originally sought to ban it for its unpatriotic message.

**LEFT:** German Panzer IIs and Panzer IIIs in the open desert. German tank forces enjoyed repeated success against the British, luring their opponents on to concealed lines of anti-tank guns, a tactic it took the British a long time to recognize.

# Desert Campaigns, May 1941 – August 1942

By the end of April 1941, when Rommel had evicted British forces from Cyrenaica, he was left with a thorn in the side of his advance. This was the enclave of Tobruk, whose 30,000 defenders, mainly Australian, held out grimly, although surrounded and attacked by Axis forces. Rommel came to respect the way they 'fought with remarkable tenacity', adding that even their wounded 'stayed in the fight to their last breath'. These self-styled 'Rats of Tobruk' deprived the *Afrika Korps* of a vital supply port. Between April and November 1941 they kept back four Italian divisions and three German battalions from the main forces. Their siege lasted until the end of the year.

From May 1941 to June 1942 Axis forces faced three main offensives in North Africa. These were made at various times by units from South Africa, India, Australia, New Zealand and Britain, as well as by Free French, Greek and Polish troops. One of the difficulties for senior commanders was to weld these disparate formations into a cohesive army. This task was not always made easy by demands from the home governments of the formations. For example, by September 1941 the Australian government asked for the withdrawal of their soldiers from Tobruk, citing worries over their health and powers of resistance – or, as one soldier cynically suggested, 'before their mothers, fathers, wives and sisters voted in the forthcoming elections'. The British government acceded and, with some difficulty, the Australians were replaced, by sea, with British and Polish detachments taking over.

In his Egyptian headquarters, Wavell was assailed with demands on his limited forces throughout the desperate period from March until June 1941. During that time, his men were suffering disaster in Greece and Crete; he was trying to bring the East African Campaign to a successful conclusion; in Iraq he was confronted with a revolt which threatened local oil supplies; an operation against Vichy-controlled Syria had begun, to forestall Axis intervention there; and he was confronted by the mercurial Rommel in

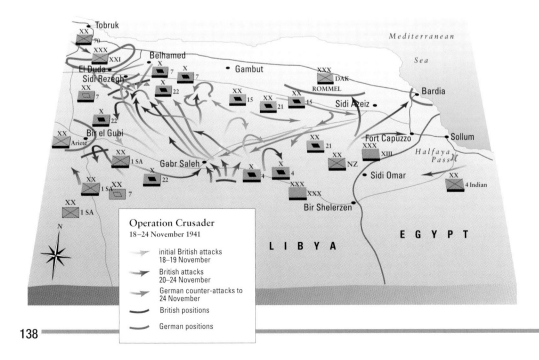

**Operation Crusader**
18–24 November 1941

→ initial British attacks 18–19 November
→ British attacks 20–24 November
→ German counter-attacks to 24 November
━ British positions
━ German positions

the Western Desert. Throughout the war, few commanders had to meet similar responsibilities, spanning such diverse areas, with such limited resources. In Churchill's words, 'the extraordinary convergence of five or six different theatres, with their ups and downs, especially downs,' were a strain 'to which few soldiers have been subjected'.

In early May 1941 Wavell intended to push the *Afrika Korps* from its positions inside the Egyptian frontier. In achieving that he would have an entry point back into Cyrenaica, especially through the escarpment at the Halfaya Pass. However, that region was just as important to Rommel: the pass marked his way into Egypt. Therefore, between 15 and 27 May 1941, a small yet fierce battle developed in the frontier region as Operation 'Brevity' was fought. After a series of skirmishes inside Cyrenaica, the British withdrew. Then the Germans counter-attacked and they regained the Halfaya Pass. 'Brevity' marked another failure. F. Hinsley remarks that one reason, and 'the most important indeed, was the technical superiority of the German equipment, particularly armour and anti-tank guns'. It would take a heavier offensive to defeat the *Afrika Korps*.

The onus was on Wavell to do that. He planned a new and larger campaign, code-named Operation 'Battleaxe'. Churchill hoped that it would lead to the complete defeat of Rommel and the removal of Axis armies from North Africa. However, Wavell's aims were more modest: he hoped to drive enemy forces back and relieve the garrison in Tobruk. To help his preparations, convoy 'Tiger' was sailed boldly through the Mediterranean to Alexandria, bringing 238 tanks and 43 Hurricane fighters. The ships arrived on 12 May.

Wavell's offensive did not open until 14 June. By then Rommel, warned by his intelligence services, had moved forces into position to blunt 'Battleaxe'. His plans were carefully laid to demonstrate mobile defence to the greatest effect. British armour was used in a more stilted way, through a number of slow, head-on assaults, with the intention that tanks should fight each other almost like ships-of-the-line engaging individually in the eighteenth century.

Such a contest was not for Rommel. Using anti-tank guns to great effect, he quickly knocked out large sections of British armour before bringing his own machines into action. The German 50mm gun was well employed at short range, but the heaviest damage came from a few 88s. These were well dug in, with a clear field of fire over open terrain. They could fire up to eight rounds a minute with shells which punched holes in the 77mm frontal armour of the Matilda tank at 2,000yds. Of thirteen Matildas attacking the Halfaya Pass, only one escaped the deadly fire of four defending 88s. The previously

named 'Queen of the Battlefield' was dethroned. The new Crusader tanks which had arrived in the 'Tiger' convoy were untried and suffered both from mechanical troubles and enemy guns. At the end of a three-day battle, in which Wavell went to the front line trying to help his generals, he had lost 91 tanks; the Germans lost 25. Once again, Rommel had shown his mastery in the use of armour.

The failure of the armour rang Wavell's death-knell. Churchill and the Imperial General Staff in London decided to replace him on 21 June, the very night when the Germans attacked

**THE 'DASH TO THE WIRE'**
Rommel ended the battle with a typical piece of bluff, charging towards Egypt in an attempt to stampede the British into a premature retreat as he had managed to do in the past. This time the British did not panic with the 'Desert Fox' behind them and Rommel was compelled to pull back.

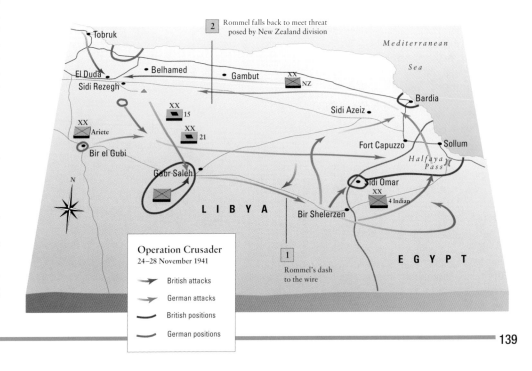

**Operation Crusader**
24–28 November 1941

→ British attacks
→ German attacks
⌐ British positions
⌐ German positions

**LEFT:** The frontline positions at Tobruk were built around dug-in artillery and anti-tank guns and tens of thousands of land mines. At the time Tobruk fell, many of the defensive mines had been lifted in preparation to be re-laid elsewhere.

Russia. Rommel, the victor, was highly praised by Axis leaders; the loser was posted to India.

In a straight exchange, Wavell swapped positions with General Auchinleck, Commander-in-Chief India. The new man was a highly competent professional soldier, popular and respected. How would he cope with the 'Desert Fox', who had the habit of seeing off British generals? Unfortunately for the prime minister, the exchange proved to be another case of 'SOS' (Same Old Story). 'Auchinleck had every soldierly quality,' wrote a military historian, 'except the killer instinct.' In battle, that was a mortal deficiency.

After the various batterings received by British forces in the Western Desert, Auchinleck was in no mood for hasty action. Instead, he looked forward to a period of reorganisation and re-equipment, while planning his offensive, Operation 'Crusader'. His forces, renamed the Eighth Army in September, were built up methodically over several months. New divisions and tanks were provided and Churchill waited with impatience to see them in action. However, preparations were slow, including as they did

1. 21 January: Rommel feints toward Mechili while the bulk of his forces head for Benghazi
2. 29 January: Rommel reaches Benghazi
3. 26 May: the Battle of Gazala
4. 21 June: Rommel takes Tobruk
5. 28 June: Rommel reaches Mersa Matruh
6. 30 June: Rommel poised to take El Alamein

### ROMMEL'S OFFENSIVE

Driven back at the end of 1941, Rommel mounted a determined offensive in January, catching the British off-guard. Despite their successes in Operation Crusader, the British proved unable to deal with Rommel again and were driven back so quickly that the Axis forces were able to storm the vital port of Tobruk against only minimal resistance. The fall of the port that had sustained such a long siege the previous year was a terrible blow and by June Rommel was threatening Egypt once more.

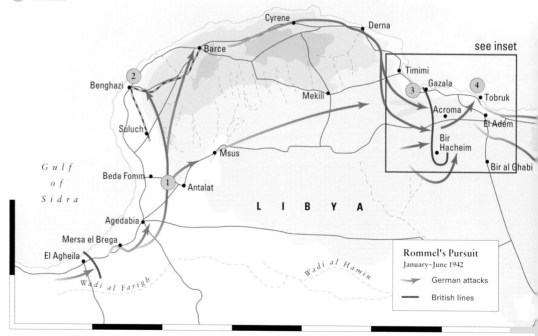

the laying of a 150-mile extension of a water pipeline westwards from Alexandria.

Auchinleck had six main divisions and several brigades, with a reserve division, including the Tobruk garrison. Altogether there were 760 tanks. Their main objective was to capture Cyrenaica and relieve Tobruk. By mid-October the prime minister, worried by the slow start, was telling

Auchinleck, 'It is impossible to explain to Parliament and the nation how it is our Middle Eastern armies have to stand for months without engaging the enemy while all the time Russia is being battered to pieces.'

The British offensive opened on 18 November and at first appeared to have some success. However, Axis troops responded strongly, with Rommel's generalship playing an

important part. The battle continued with a series of confused engagements over the next four weeks. Gradually, the Allied superiority in numbers of armoured vehicles was whittled down and the longed-for complete victory over the *Afrika Korps* disappeared. However, by mid-December, 'Crusader' represented a sort of victory, the first gained by British and Commonwealth forces against the

**GAZALA AND THE FALL OF TOBRUK**

Classic Rommel: the panzer divisions sweep deep into the desert to outflank the British while Italian infantry batter the Gazala defences. Once the fighting became fluid, Rommel was able to react faster and impose his grip on the battle while the British high command collapsed into rival factions. Rommel was promoted to Field Marshal for taking Tobruk. For the British, the loss of nearly 40,000 men was their second greatest defeat of the war.

1  26 May: Italians attack north end of Gazala Line while Rommel takes a wide outflanking move to the south

4  14 June: British withdraw towards Tobruk

**Battle of Gazala**
26 May – 14 June 1942

2  28 May: Rommel's forces are trapped in the 'Cauldron'

3  10 June: Free French withdraw from the fortress at Bir Hacheim

**ABOVE:** A German *kubelwagen*, their equivalent to the US jeep, ploughs through the sand. If a vehicle broke down and could not repaired, it was often cannibalized and the hulk left in place. Many such vehicles are still lying in remote parts of the desert, as are some of the landmines.

Germans since the start of the war. Yet it was mainly a victory over territory, not over men and *matériel*. Tobruk was relieved and Axis forces were pushed out of Cyrenaica. Rommel, with considerable skill, extricated the *Afrika Korps* and retreated westwards to El Agheila.

By the end of 'Crusader' the Germans and Italians had suffered 38,000 casualties and had lost 300 tanks; the figures for Auchinleck's forces were 18,000 and 278 respectively. Although Auchinleck himself was a fine commander, several of his generals were not. 'Crusader's' high hopes were unrealised. The situation

was thrown into greater perspective on 7 December 1941, the day that Tobruk was finally relieved; that victory was overshadowed by the news that the Japanese had attacked Pearl Harbor.

Both sides had fought themselves to a standstill. Axis forces had lost Cyrenaica, while the Eighth Army was in no condition to advance towards Tripoli. How long would the stalemate last? The surprising answer came on 21 January 1942. Having received some tank reinforcements, the resilient Rommel took the offensive, catching the Eighth Army detachments unprepared. With a few powerful thrusts

he recaptured Benghazi and drove Auchinleck's forces back. They quickly lost much of the ground so painfully gained in 'Crusader'.

In the spring of 1942 both sides again prepared forces for an offensive. By then, Auchinleck was hampered by events in the Far East. Two divisions destined for his command were redirected to oppose the Japanese. Furthermore, he was now wary of the 'Desert Fox', knowing that any small error of judgement would be heavily punished. Yet, in spite of their difficulties in the Pacific, the US authorities despatched large quantities of war material to the Middle East. By May 1942 the Eighth Army included 850 tanks, of which 170 were Grants, from America, equipped with 75mm guns. In addition, 420 tanks were held in reserve. Auchinleck controlled six main divisions, of which two were armoured, as well as tank and motorised brigades. His artillery outnumbered his opponents' by 50 per cent and included a number of the excellent new 6pdr anti-tank guns. In the skies above, the Desert Air Force had 600 aircraft. Auchinleck's total forces were certainly larger than those of the Axis.

At Rommel's disposal were three German and six Italian divisions. Of his 560 tanks, only half were German medium tanks which had done so well in the desert. Above them flew 530 Axis aircraft, 120 of which were Bf 109s. What would count in action, however, would be not so much the overall size of forces on each side as the use made of them. Judged by previous experience, Rommel therefore still held a strong hand.

Once again, Churchill tried to press Auchinleck into action. 'There are no safe battles,' he wrote on 21 May, when 'Ultra' intelligence reported an imminent German assault. He added, 'We have full confidence in you and your glorious army.' That confidence was put to the test four days later, when Rommel's offensive opened.

Over the following four weeks an intensive battle occurred in the Western Desert, in which the 'Desert Fox' showed a mastery of armoured manoeuvre. With numerically inferior resources, he outfought poorly positioned and managed defences. General

**RIGHT:** Local Arabs, seen here with some Italian troops, were mainly pro-German but were not disposed to get involved in the fighting. As both sides were prepared to pay for information and also littered the desert with useful kit, the conflict afforded considerable commercial opportunity for those prepared to seize it.

Ritchie, Commander-in-Chief of the Eighth Army, failed to use his stronger armoured power thoroughly and a number of positions were overrun. Worst of all, when Rommel drove at Tobruk, its defences were quickly smashed and 38,000 prisoners fell into his hands on 21 June. Hitler at once promoted him to the rank of Field Marshal, the youngest in the *Wehrmacht*. For the British, the loss was a military disaster second only to the surrender of Singapore. When Churchill received the news, 'a bitter moment', he was with Roosevelt in Washington. The American president's reaction summarises the relationship of the two allies at the time. 'What can we do to help?' he enquired. The immediate result was that the United States despatched 300 Sherman tanks and 100 howitzers of 105mm calibre to Egypt.

Axis forces then poured into Egypt, reaching the old 1940 defences on 25 June. Five days later they were at El Alamein, only 60 miles from Alexandria. They paused then only

because forces of armour and men were depleted and weary; by 2 July Rommel had only 40 tanks operational. The retreating Eighth Army, 80,000 men fewer than a month earlier, managed to take up a defensive position. In the eyes of most observers, this was the last ditch: another defeat and the *Afrika Korps* would be in Cairo. In reality, British and Commonwealth troops held strong positions and were being constantly reinforced; being so close to the Nile Delta, their supply lines were greatly reduced in length.

By this time Churchill wanted new leaders in the Middle East. He could not comprehend why Auchinleck had achieved so little with the 700,000 men who were on the ration strength of his command. Auchinleck was undoubtedly an able commander-in-chief, but he was often poorly served by subordinate commanders. In those circumstances, the buck stopped at the top. The prime minister flew to Egypt on 4 August to weigh the situation for himself. Auchinleck was replaced by General Alexander, while General Montgomery

took over the Eighth Army. Once again, Rommel had 'seen off' a chief opponent. Yet Auchinleck's swansong during July was to fight a last and successful battle, staving off a further German effort to break through.

During August, both sides re-formed their forces, with the Eighth Army gaining more than its opponents. Rommel required one more victory and on the last day of the month he launched his army into an attack towards Alam Halfa. Montgomery had inherited Auchinleck's defensive plan, which worked well. German and Italian units pushed hard but found the defences too strong to crack; they were suffering from a severe fuel shortage. Within a few days, the *Afrika Korps* was forced to pull back, raising the morale of Eighth Army troops, who were growing in confidence.

The need for a victory in the desert was paramount, so that Britain could share the admiration accorded to the Russians on the Eastern Front and the Americans at Midway. However, it would not be enough merely to regain

**ABOVE:** German soldiers reach the Egyptian frontier, June 1942. Rommel had out-run his supplies and had very few operational vehicles but he was only 60 miles west of Alexandria and the British had once again sacked their commander-in-chief. Rommel's next opponent was due to be General Goff, but he died in a plane crash and the position went to General Montgomery.

ABOVE: A knocked out British Matilda lies abandoned in the desert. This type of 'Infantry Tank' was heavily armoured but could only carry a 2-pounder gun firing solid shot but not the high-explosive needed to take on anti-tank guns. The British were saved by the arrival of American M3 and M4 medium tanks in large numbers.

being particularly well-gunned and strongly armoured. In artillery, the Eighth Army was far stronger, with 900 guns. Ample supplies could be brought along the short distance from the Canal Zone. Against this might, Rommel had about 100,000 men, half of whom were German. Of his 540 tanks, half were obsolete Italian machines. There were 500 guns. Shortages of ammunition and fuel existed, especially as much had to be brought 1,200 miles from Tripoli. In addition, Rommel himself fell ill before the battle opened and had to return to Germany for treatment.

Montgomery had neither Rommel's experience nor his dash in handling armour in the desert. Fortunately for his men, he recognised that. Therefore he decided to open his campaign with a large-scale artillery bombardment of forward troops. With his overall advantages in strength, he knew that a pounding match would sap the Axis forces more than his own. The barrage, fired from 450 guns, started on the night of 23 October and a 'dog-fight' began, with slow, grinding advances through minefields by infantry. They discovered the effects of concentrated shellfire on the enemy. 'Whole gun crews were lying dead round their guns. Even in the slit trenches and dug-outs many had been killed.' An officer was dead with his telephone to his ear. 'A man who had been about to light a cigarette was dead with a cigarette in one hand and a box of matches in the other.'

Montgomery had planned the battle in three phases. First came the break-in, secondly the 'dogfight' – a 'hard and bloody killing match' – and thirdly the break-out. Over the following two

territory, as had happened before: Axis forces, particularly the *Afrika Korps*, had to be given a beating from which they would not recover, thus removing the potential threat to the Canal Zone which had existed ever since Rommel's arrival. Montgomery, noted for his addiction to efficiency, determination and training, was to be the man for the job. Before long, soldiers in the Eighth Army, who had sought a general with charisma to match the 'Desert Fox', knew that they had a true leader. A staff officer wrote of his clarity of mind and physical bravery, his dogged perseverance and directness: 'Whether on paper or in speech,' he added, 'he is always crystal clear.' The Eighth Army certainly had not lost morale, but wanted inspirational guidance to overcome bewilderment. Montgomery

gave them that. After his first staff conference on 13 August, an officer wrote, 'We all feel that a cool and refreshing breeze has come to relieve the oppressive and stagnant atmosphere. The effect of the address was electric – it was terrific.'

Nonetheless, like his predecessors, Alexander, through Montgomery, would not launch an offensive until he was fully prepared. The process took ten weeks of reinforcement, training and planning. This time Churchill was prepared to wait. By mid-October the imbalance in size between the opposing forces was more marked than ever. The Eighth Army's strength stood at 195,000 men, with over 1,000 tanks and hundreds more in reserve. About 500 of the machines were American-built Grants and Shermans, the latter

RIGHT: Junkers Ju-87 dive-bombers on an airstrip in the desert. With the frontlines so fluid, airmen had to be ready to move at a moment's notice and it was not unknown for aircraft to find their escape blocked by an enemy tank. The Ju-87 'Stuka' remained a potent weapon in the desert war, right up to the final campaign in Tunisia.

weeks, Australian, South African and Free French troops, together with British, all fighting tenaciously, gradually broke the German and Italian defences. Even Rommel's hasty recall from convalescence in Germany to take command could not halt the tide. By 29 October he was writing to his wife that little hope was left. 'At night I lie with my eyes open, for the load that is on my shoulders. In the day, I'm dead tired.'

At several stages of the battle, Churchill, together with military leaders in London, became uneasy over slow progress. Surely the Eighth Army could do it this time? From 'Ultra' reports, which landed on their desks as fast as information reached Hitler's headquarters, they knew what desperate straits confronted the *Afrika Korps*, which was short of fuel, food and ammunition. 'Alamein was lost before it was fought,' wrote a German general. 'We had not the petrol.' Montgomery's advance was slow, yet methodical, as he exercised a masterly control over his divisions on the battlefield. By 2 November the enemy were retreating, with Rommel trying hard to extricate as many men and machines as possible.

In the midst of impending disaster, most of the *Afrika Korps*, still falling back out of Egypt ,were unaware of the importance of events on 8 November. That day Operation 'Torch', the Anglo-American landings in north-west Africa, started far to their rear, marking another step towards Axis defeat in the Middle East. By then, the Battle of El Alamein had been won – and lost.

As far as he could, Rommel kept his depleted forces together while retiring. They were constantly bombarded by the Desert Air Force as they followed the coastal road to the west. He soon found that Hitler was as anxious for the *Afrika Korps* to stand and fight to the last man as Churchill had been for the Eighth Army to do likewise a few months earlier. On 4 November a message from the *Führer* ordered him to 'show your troops no other way than that which leads to victory or to death'. Lacking reinforcements, the 'Desert Fox' knew that impossible demands were being made on his weakened forces, equipped as they were with barely 80 tanks. For him,

the main aim was to retain an army in being. After reaching Benghazi on 20 November, the Germans made a stand on a defensive line at Wadi Zem Zem for three weeks from Christmas 1942. A week after that Rommel reached Tripoli, after a memorable retreat.

El Alamein was one of the war's great turning-points. The *Afrika Korps* had been well and truly beaten. At last in a great land battle British and Commonwealth troops had triumphed over the Germans without suffering a humiliating counter-attack. Churchill commented that 'it may almost be said, "Before Alamein we never had a victory. After Alamein we never had a defeat."'

**ABOVE:** The German retreat and British pursuit that followed the decisive Battle of Alamein took place during winter rains that washed away the roads. These German vehicles lie abandoned to the flood.

**LEFT:** As they fell back westwards the Germans poured troops into Tunisia ahead of the Allied forces advancing from Morocco. Among them was a small unit of Tiger tanks, the first the western Allies had encountered.

**LEFT:** A German 75 mm infantry gun team in action. German infantry battalions had considerably more organic firepower than their British equivalents including a battery of light howitzers and increasingly larger numbers of heavy mortars.

# Operation 'Torch'

German military leaders were puzzled when, in early November 1942, reports came of an armada of Allied ships gathering under strong air cover off the north-west coast of Africa and at Gibraltar. Where were they heading? Some believed that the convoys were taking supplies to the beleaguered island of Malta; others estimated that they would put men ashore near Tripoli, to cut off Rommel's retreat. The answer was revealed on 8 November when thousands of troops landed in two of France's North African territories. One force invaded the Atlantic coast of Morocco; two others went ashore on beaches in Algeria, in the Mediterranean. Significantly, no troops were landed in Tunisia, a little further east. The whole venture was code-named Operation 'Torch'.

To understand the reasons for the campaign, the relationship among the Allies – the USA, Russia and Britain – has to be weighed. Each nation had laid out its own agenda for the continuation of the war, based on its own special needs, strengths and weaknesses. These points were discussed at length by their leaders, Roosevelt, Stalin and Churchill. A noticeable feature of the Second World War was that Allied leaders worked together far more closely and met more frequently than those of the Axis powers. Hitler, Mussolini and Tojo often appeared to be running separate and independent campaigns. Never once in the war did the three of them confer together. However, when Allied leaders met, there were bound to be differences over the crucial question: what shall we do next?

For Stalin, both problem and answer were straightforward. The only effective means of taking pressure off the Red Army on the Eastern Front was for the British and Americans to invade Western Europe. The Germans then would have to withdraw forces from Russia. Nothing less was acceptable. He wanted this Second Front to open in 1942 and believed that his allies were dragging their feet.

Churchill was cautious. He knew that in the long run the only way to overthrow Hitler was to defeat the *Wehrmacht*, preferably in its homeland. There would have to be a Second Front. However, with his experience of what the German war machine could achieve on the battlefield, he believed that an under-prepared invasion would end in disaster. Therefore

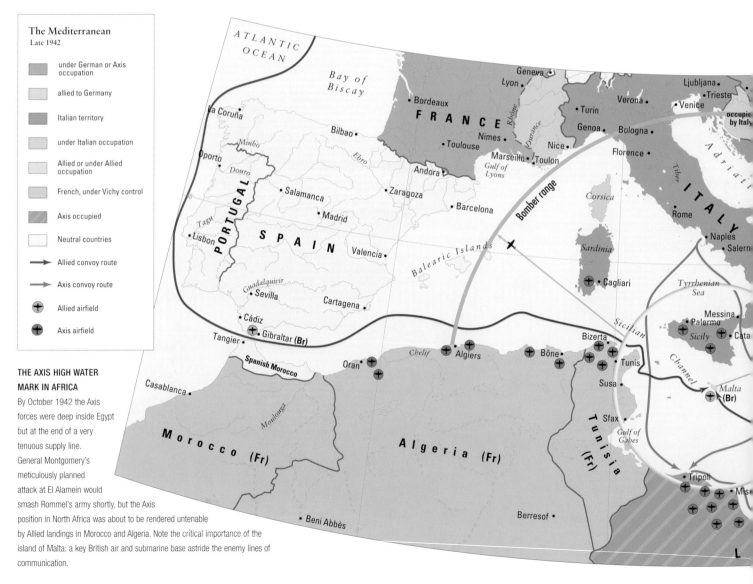

**THE AXIS HIGH WATER MARK IN AFRICA**

By October 1942 the Axis forces were deep inside Egypt but at the end of a very tenuous supply line. General Montgomery's meticulously planned attack at El Alamein would smash Rommel's army shortly, but the Axis position in North Africa was about to be rendered untenable by Allied landings in Morocco and Algeria. Note the critical importance of the island of Malta: a key British air and submarine base astride the enemy lines of communication.

he preferred to 'tighten the noose' round Germany, weakening the Axis powers by peripheral attacks – for example driving them out of Africa and then invading Italy. He also had to allow for the British commitment to fighting the Japanese, a problem which did not affect the Russians.

The Americans had a double responsibility, taking on both the Japanese and Germans. Some of their service leaders wanted to despatch the bulk of their forces to fight in the Far East, to take immediate revenge for the attack on Pearl Harbor. Roosevelt and Churchill, however, had agreed on a policy of 'Germany first'. As a result, General Marshall, the US Chief of Staff, was willing to commit American forces to the European war but wanted them used as soon as possible in

**ABOVE:** British aircraft carriers *Argus* (left) and *Eagle* (right) escorted by the battleship *Malaya* (far right) seen from the cruiser *Hermione* in March 1942. The only way to get more fighters to Malta was for the Royal Navy to undertake a series of hazardous voyages that led to intense aerial battles with the German and Italian air forces.

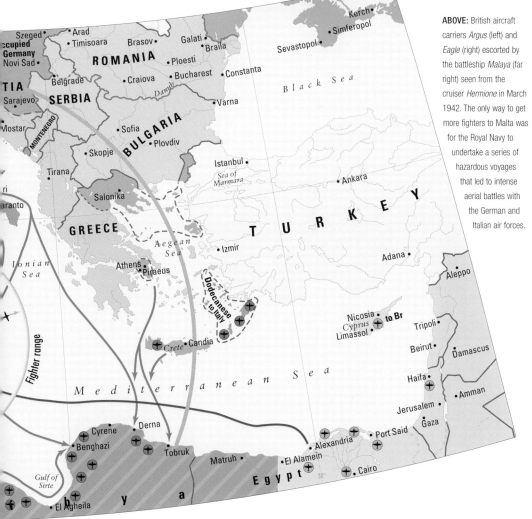

opening a Second Front. The best opportunity, he believed, would come from large-scale landings in France during 1942. Gradually Roosevelt and Churchill became convinced of the impracticability of such landings. Marshall was persuaded to agree, somewhat unwillingly, to landings in North Africa first.

These factors help to explain the landings of Operation 'Torch' in November 1942, to the puzzlement of Axis leaders. Why choose French North Africa? What advantages lay there? And, particularly, why were the great majority of the invaders American, not British?

In answering the last question, the reasons why British forces kept a low profile became apparent. At root lay the troubled relationship between France and Britain since the French collapse in June 1940. Controversies over the evacuation from Dunkirk and the shelling of the French Fleet at Oran led to differences between the two formerly allied governments. There followed disagreements over the role of General de Gaulle and the Free French movement, based in London. To the British they were brave patriots; to the French government at Vichy they were renegades or traitors, with de Gaulle acting like a loose cannon.

Throughout this period a kind of

bitter civil war was being fought between the French forces controlled by Pétain and those led by de Gaulle. The latter knew that, with the German occupation, he could have no influence in metropolitan France. The French Empire, nevertheless, offered him scope for raising forces to continue the war. In Tunisia, Algeria and Morocco there were 120,000 French troops; in Syria and Lebanon were a further 38,000. De Gaulle's policy was to persuade colonial territories to join him, putting forces there in a dilemma. Some admired his courage in fighting on and were prepared to serve under his badge, the Cross of Lorraine. Others saw themselves as servants of a government which had signed an armistice with the Germans and therefore had to abide by its terms. Whether they regarded de Gaulle as upstart or patriot, his actions compelled them to make a choice.

In September 1940 he failed in an expedition to Dakar, West Africa, attempting to claim Senegal for his cause. Then in May 1941 the Germans used Syria as a base for their aircraft which were supplying an anti-British rebellion in Iraq. This posed a threat to the rear of Suez at a desperate time, so a British and Commonwealth force entered Syria in a three-week campaign which crushed the resistance of Vichy French troops.

Consequently, although Operation 'Torch' contained Free French troops, the bulk of the forces were Americans, regarded generally by the French as not responsible for previous controversies. The British, suspected as 'perfidious Albion', played a smaller military role, although they provided most of the naval escorts for the operation.

Over 60,000 Allied troops took part in the opening stage of the operation. Some 24,000, arriving directly from the United States, were put ashore in Morocco, with a further 36,000, sailing from the United Kingdom, landing at two places in Algeria. Coastal regions were soon taken. There was less resistance from Vichy-controlled forces, the *Armée d'Afrique*, than had been feared.

Hitler, embittered by what he viewed as Vichy's duplicity, ordered his army into the Unoccupied Zone of France on 11 November. At a stroke, the whole of the country came under his control. The Allies feared that the French Fleet at Toulon, still a powerful navy, would fall into Axis hands. They were relieved, therefore, when the fleet was scuttled by its own sailors about two weeks later. Three German divisions were quickly despatched to Tunisia. By the time the First Army began to advance, it was confronted by solid resistance. This increased when Rommel, continuing his westward retreat with the *Afrika Korps*, reached Tunisia in late January 1943. Significantly, his forces, though depleted, were still in good fighting order.

Consequently, opportunities of a speedy removal of Axis armies from Africa were missed and a bitterly fought campaign ensued. And yet, ironically, this loss of initiative worked to the benefit of the Allies in the long run. Hitler now believed that he could maintain the Tunisian bridgehead and poured increasing numbers of troops and amounts of equipment into Africa, under the cover of the

BELOW: British sailors operating an Oerlikon 20 mm anti-aircraft gun, March 1942. The ammunition handler holds the next magazine as the gunner peers through the sights. Anti-aircraft fire relied more on volume than accuracy.

**OPERATION TORCH**

At the time the greatest amphibious assault in history, the Allied landings in Morocco and Algeria met fierce resistance from the French. This, and the inexperience of many of the Allied commanders involved, slowed the subsequent pace of advance, enabling the Germans to hurry troops into Tunisia. Instead of a rapid knock-out blow, the Allies were faced with a winter campaign that would last well into 1943.

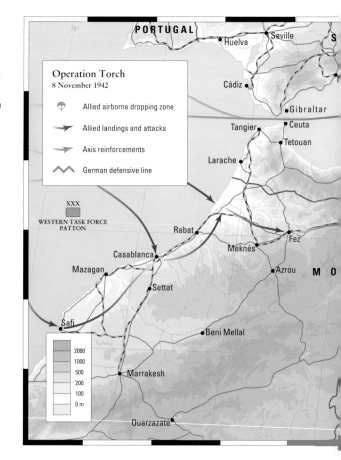

Operation Torch
8 November 1942

🪂 Allied airborne dropping zone

➤ Allied landings and attacks

➤ Axis reinforcements

〰 German defensive line

XXX
WESTERN TASK FORCE
PATTON

*Luftwaffe*. Their aircraft, including formidable Focke-Wulf Fw 190s, flew from local airfields and from Sicily, to give better air support than Allied ground troops received. By February 1943 German and Italian divisions in Tunisia totalled 100,000 men.

By then, Rommel's troops had linked up with other forces and the whole group occupied strong defensive positions, including the old French defences at the Mareth Line, where they faced the advancing Eighth Army. The terrain offered advantages to defenders – and not only that. The Germans used their experience to launch several sharp counter-attacks further north, against less battle-hardened troops. They were able to push British and American soldiers back, for example, at the Kasserine Pass in mid-February. Such reverses extended further the timetable of success laid down by the Allies.

The end came in early May 1943 as the superiority in numbers and equipment of the Allies was made to tell. On 7 May both Bizerta and Tunis were taken; by 13 May Axis forces had been

completely overwhelmed and all surrendered. About 250,000 Germans and Italians became prisoners-of-war, far more than had been taken at Stalingrad; their commanders-in-chief, Generals von Arnim and Messe, went into the bag with them. Hitler, still reeling from disasters in Russia, had received a heavy blow in Africa. His tide of success was receding.

With the completion of the African campaigns, people wondered where the Allies would strike next. So did

Hitler. Would it be through the Balkans, or Italy, or southern France? Or would the armies be taken back to Britain, then launched on the long-awaited Second Front? In reality, as the Tunisian campaign had dragged on for longer than expected, Churchill knew that landings in north-west Europe could not take place in the second half of 1943. In spite of disapproval and frustration from various American commanders, the Second Front would not now be ready until 1944.

**ABOVE:** HMS *Argus* flies off fighters to Malta where daily air battles with the *Luftwaffe* and *Regia Aeronautica* were taking place. By June 1942 the island's population was close to starvation as supplies by sea could not get through the German blockade.

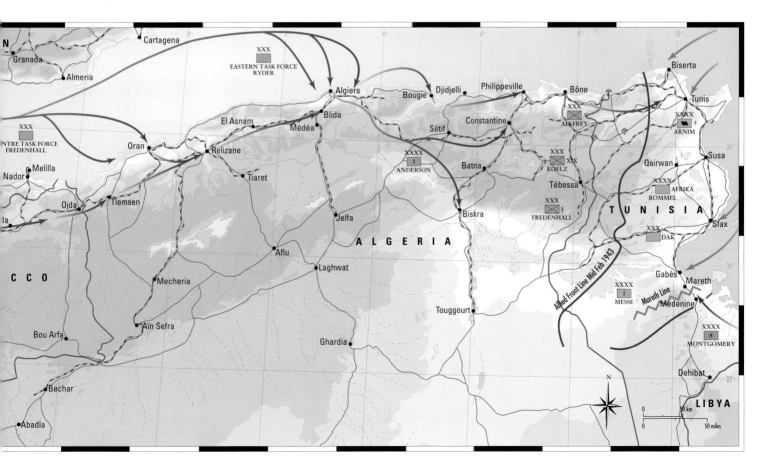

# Malta

Most people today know 'The Friendly Island of Malta' as a holiday resort, providing sunshine, comfortable hotels and a welcoming population. Some go there to appreciate a fascinating history, dating from Neolithic times to the Carthaginians, thence to St Paul's shipwreck and, later, the knights of St John who survived a Turkish siege in 1565. There is a particular attraction for the British, whose legacy can be widely seen, the island having been a possession since 1814.

From the perspective of the Allies during the Second World War, nonetheless, the most important episodes in Malta's story occurred between 1940 and 1943. The island then played a cardinal role in the struggle for North Africa. In that period, the people of Malta, under the immense strain of aerial assault, were shown a less than friendly face by their tormentors. Together with the defending British and Commonwealth forces, they exhibited an amazing spirit of resistance to almost constant attack.

What made the resistance more remarkable was Malta's position close to the enemy. It lay only 60 miles south of Sicily and directly on the route from Italy to its North African empire in Tripolitania. Help for the garrison was far distant. Gibraltar lay 1,000 miles to the west, while Alexandria was 800 miles to the east. The island is small, only 17 miles long by 9 miles wide. Together with neighbouring Gozo, the land surface covers only 143 square miles. This generally rocky area housed 270,000 inhabitants, whose economy was not completely self-supporting and relied on seaborne supplies. With them were defending service personnel.

During the period from January to May 1941 the Germans, despairing of Italian inaction, sent aircraft of *Fliegerkorps X* to Sicily and air raids on Malta intensified. On many days only about ten RAF fighters were serviceable. In that time, with heavy German raids on shipping, only thirteen vessels reached the island with supplies. By the end of the year over 2,500 buildings had been destroyed and the pressure on civilians, who spent much of their time in caves and excavated tunnels, was great. They

**LEFT:** The cruiser *Penelope* struggles to tow the *Breconshire* into Valetta after repeated bomb hits left the merchantship sinking within sight of home. This convoy, in March 1942, was the first for nearly two months and the islanders' rations were reduced to subsistence levels already.

showed no sign of cracking. In the same period more aircraft, including 70 Hurricanes, reached the defences. RAF bombers flew from the island to attack Axis convoys, proving that the defenders could hit back. In August 1941, one-third of Rommel's supplies never reached the *Afrika Korps*, a figure rising to two-thirds in October.

Malta's worst days came during 1942, especially while Rommel was flourishing in the Western Desert. The *Luftwaffe* built up its strength in the Mediterranean until almost 1,000 aircraft were available. By February, the islanders were taking up to ten raids a day, and food, fuel and ammunition were in short supply. As each side recognised increasingly the island's importance in relation to North African campaigns, greater efforts were made. In recognition of the civilians' courage, on 15 April King George VI awarded Malta the George Cross, a unique appreciation. Supply convoys, sailing through under intense Axis air attack, suffered heavily. It was not until the end of the year, with the Eighth Army's success at El Alamein and the 'Torch' landings, that Malta's situation eased and the days of siege passed.

'Without Malta,' Rommel com-

**ABOVE:** The last voyage of the *Breconshire*: her forward guns are manned as a destroyer lays a smoke screen to shield the convoy. Of 86 merchant vessels carrying supplies to Malta, 31 were lost to enemy action. *Breconshire* finally succumbed just south of Grand Harbour.

**LEFT:** British destroyers lay smoke during the second battle of Sirte, one of several incidents when the Italian navy failed to capitalize on its superior numbers and was driven off by aggressive British tactics. The British had to employ four cruisers and 17 destroyers to escort four vital merchantships to Malta.

**LEFT:** HMS *Legion* in action in heavy weather against the Italian fleet off Sirte, March 1942. An Italian task force built around the battleship *Littorio* was beaten off, but subsequent air attacks sank two of the four ships the British were trying to get to Malta.

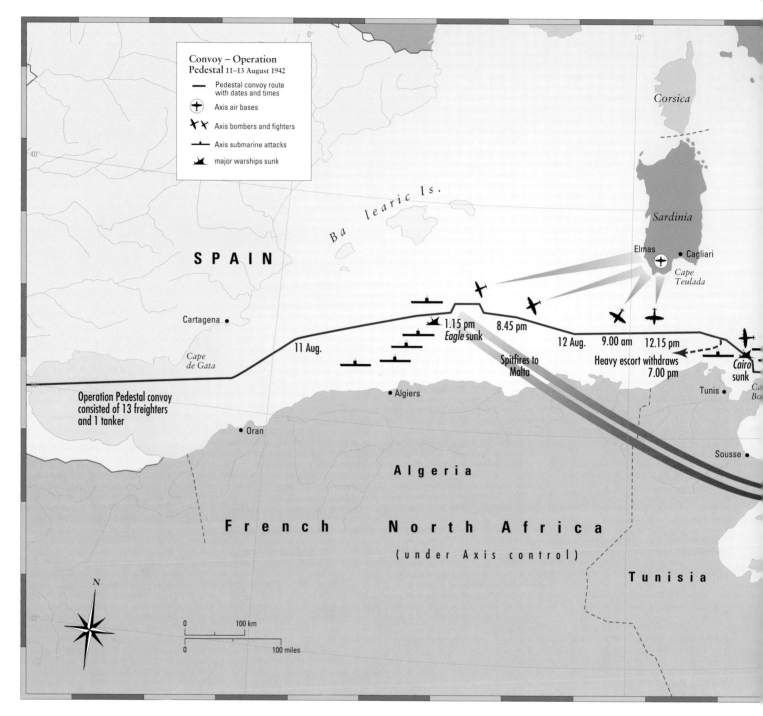

Convoy – Operation
Pedestal 11–13 August 1942

— Pedestal convoy route
with dates and times

✈ Axis air bases

✕✕ Axis bombers and fighters

Axis submarine attacks

major warships sunk

*Corsica*

*Sardinia*

Elmas • Cagliari

*Cape Teulada*

**S P A I N**

*Balearic Is.*

Cartagena •

✈ 1.15 pm
*Eagle* sunk

8.45 pm

12 Aug. 9.00 am 12.15 pm
Heavy escort withdraws
7.00 pm

*Cairo* sunk

11 Aug.

*Cape de Gata*

Spitfires to
Malta

Tunis •

• Algiers

Operation Pedestal convoy
consisted of 13 freighters
and 1 tanker

• Oran

Sousse •

**A l g e r i a**

**F r e n c h   N o r t h   A f r i c a**

(under Axis control)

**T u n i s i a**

N

0    100 km

0    100 miles

## OPERATION PEDESTAL

By July 1942 the island of Malta was starved of food, fuel, ammunition and medical supplies. The British risked a major operation to escort a convoy to the island, and although more than half the supply ships were sunk, enough arrived in Grand Harbour to sustain resistance a little longer. The Germans launched another series of air raids in October 1942 but the loss of their airfields in Cyrenaica in November brought the air assault to an end.

mented in February 1941, 'the Axis will end by losing control of North Africa.' So why was there no invasion attempt? After Italy's initial hesitation to act, the Germans did consider landings in 1942, but had been worried by the high casualty rate among paratroops during the Battle of Crete in the previous year. For the British, in one sense, the loss of Crete led to the saving of Malta. Axis leaders also learned that the island's ground defences were

a formidable system of emplacements, barbed wire, coastal and anti-aircraft guns. They were not prepared to try until it was too late.

By the end of 1942 over 14,000 tons of bombs had been dropped, averaging nearly 100 tons for each square mile of the island. Almost 1,500 civilians had been killed and 24,000 buildings destroyed or damaged. In defending Malta, 568 aircraft of Allied air forces were lost. Was such

ITALY

■ Rome

● Naples

Trapani ● Palermo

*Sicily*

E-boat attack
3 Aug.

E-boat attack

12.00 noon

4.00 pm

*Malta* to Britain

Arrives Malta 13 Aug.
(4 freighters
and 1 tanker)

● Tripoli

**Libya**
to Italy

Moreover, operating from Valletta's Grand Harbour, British submarines and destroyers were able to inflict losses on Axis shipping carrying supplies to North Africa. This feature worried Rommel during his campaigns. For example, on 16 April 1941, the Royal Navy destroyers sank a complete convoy carrying components of the 15th Panzer Division to North Africa. Malta was an 'unsinkable aircraft carrier' from whose airfields not only defending fighters but also attacking bombers operated. Torpedo-, heavy and light bombers carried out day and night raids on shipping and on ground targets in Sicily and Italy. In addition, the island became an important centre for gathering intelligence, from using reconnaissance aircraft, to the 'Y' Service, listening to enemy reports. Not the least value of retaining the island was its role as a symbol of resistance. The bravery of the defenders, civilian and service personnel alike, often under extreme danger, served as an example to all the Allies.

By May 1943 things were looking up. Axis forces had finally been removed from Africa, yet only the perspective of later years proved what a crucial part had been played in that victory by Malta's unyielding stand.

**ABOVE:** A formation of Junkers Ju-52s flies grimly on as the lumbering transports are picked off by American P-38s and B-25s. Scenes like this were enacted throughout April/May 1943 as the Axis bridgehead in Tunisia was squeezed to extinction. Very few Axis troops escaped and the scale of losses was so high, Germans called it 'Tunisgrad'.

a high price worth paying? Why go to such lengths to retain a small blob of territory in the Mediterranean? The answer is that the retention of Malta repaid the Allied war effort many times over.

The island was an important naval base and link between Britain's two fleets in the Mediterranean, Force H at Gibraltar and the Mediterranean Fleet at Alexandria. Malta was a vital point of contact for both groups.

**LEFT:** HMS *Formidable* flies off aircraft while escorting a convoy to Malta. The Royal Navy's lack of modern aircraft proved a serious handicap in this part of the war: it had no carrierborne fighters able to take on German or Italian shore-based aircraft.

# CHAPTER 7: War on Three Fronts, 1943–44

ABOVE: Russian tank crews collect their new KV-1 heavy tanks from the factory. The German invasion and the barbarities it entailed quickly fostered a sense of national unity in Russia. The recovery of Russian industrial production that followed the wholesale transfer of factories to the Urals could never have succeeded without such a committed workforce.

## The Russian Front, 1943–44

Until the collapse and surrender of the German Sixth Army at Stalingrad in January 1943, the Russians had fought a mainly defensive war against a ruthless invader. Hitler's forces had won some spectacular victories, taking hundreds of thousands of prisoners. Stalingrad, however, was a watershed. During the remainder of the war, the Red Army experienced further setbacks, but, in the main, it was now launched on a westward advance destined to end in Berlin in May 1945.

Following the German invasion of the USSR in June 1941, the Russians had, with remarkable enterprise and success, moved complete factories far to the east, beyond the Ural mountains. Out of range of German bombers, these industrial centres then worked flat out to produce war materials. The upsurge in production, nevertheless, started only in the later months of

1942. Before then, the industrial capacity of the Soviet Union had been savaged, reaching a low ebb in February 1942. The Russians, careful accountants in keeping balance sheets, registered losses to industry, and these included the destruction of 239,000 electric engines, 31,850 industrial enterprises, 65,000km of railway track and electric power plants capable of generating 5,000,000kW. The ability of the Soviet Union's economy to rise, phoenix-like, from the ashes of such disaster demonstrated both the determination of the Russian people to survive and the power of Stalin's dictatorship to control the nation.

Tanks and guns, rifles and ammunition, aircraft and bombs began to come off production lines in a steady flow. Russian weapons manufacture easily outstripped that of the Germans. In 1942, Soviet factories produced three and a half times more aircraft and

almost six times as many tanks per million tons of steel as did German factories; by the summer of 1943 the same factories were turning out 750 aircraft and 500 tanks and self-propelled guns weekly. At that time, in spite of catastrophic losses, the Red Army had twice as many mortars and guns as the *Wehrmacht*. Its tanks numbered 10,000; the Germans fielded less than 6,000. The Russians' particular advantage lay in the size of the fighting army, men and women. In mid-1943 Stalin could call on personnel totalling 6.5 million, while Axis troops, mainly German, numbered 5.3 million.

In addition, aid from the United States and Great Britain arrived in increasing quantities; for example, thousands of American lorries were sent via Persia. All supplies helped to build a Russian superiority in the *matériel* of war.

As well as having the equipment to

fight the Germans, the Russians had learned from bitter experience the best methods of taking on the enemy. The boost given by the victory at Stalingrad was immense, and morale, so important in war, rose sharply. Reorganisation of the Red Army had taken place and troops were filled with a new determination. The 'unbeatable' Germans had been beaten. That could be done again.

The Russians were operating solely in their homeland. On the other side, Hitler's attention was drawn to areas other than the USSR during 1943 in his catalogue of commitments. Britain, supported by her Commonwealth, had never surrendered, tying down German forces in Western Europe. The British Isles were becoming a store-house of men and *matériel*, preparing to hit back. Personnel were arriving from the USA in an increasing threat. At sea, the Allies were beginning to win the Battle of the Atlantic. In North Africa the defeats at El Alamein and, finally, in Tunisia, were costly in lost manpower. These were followed in the summer by the invasion, first, of Sicily, then of the Italian mainland and the subsequent overthrow of Mussolini, before Italy changed sides and joined the Allies. The *Führer*'s world was crumbling. Ominously, air attacks on Germany by the RAF and the USAAF

were increasing. Further large forces had to be maintained in Occupied Europe, to control and administer the defeated countries. All of these extra factors obviously affected Hitler's ability to fight the Russian Campaign.

In February and March 1943 Russian offensives pushed the enemy back. German forces which had penetrated south into the Caucasus had to beat a hasty retreat to avoid being trapped after the fall of Stalingrad. In a sense, the sacrifice of their comrades at Stalingrad saved von Manstein's troops in the Caucasus by holding a gap open for their withdrawal. War has its swings and roundabouts. Cities were retaken from the Germans. Kursk fell on 8 February and Kharkov was re-occupied eight days later. On the northern front, Russian advances relieved the siege of Leningrad, enabling more supplies to reach the beleaguered city. These successes, however, led the Red Army to overstretch its resources. They were reminded of the ability of the Nazis to hit back when in March a sharp German counter-attack retook the embattled city of Kharkov. A lull followed. The wet season following a spring thaw halted military activity, so both sides planned ahead for the summer.

For Hitler, there would have to be another offensive, aimed once again at

**ABOVE:** Cossacks in German service: as they had fought on both sides during the revolution, so the Cossacks divided again during the war. Anti-Communist leaders recruited two divisions of Cossack cavalry that served in Russia and Yugoslavia from 1943–45.

**LEFT:** Russian cavalry charge, sabres in hand for the benefit of the camera. They did charge for real during the winter campaign of 1943–44, cutting down German troops retreating from a number of 'pockets' formed as the Russians drove steadily west.

**LEFT:** SS men in their distinctive camouflage uniforms seen during the Battle of Kursk. Fought in the full heat of the Russian summer, the battle was punctuated by terrific thunderstorms each afternoon.

### THE BATTLE OF KURSK

Hitler's decision to attack the Kursk salient made military sense but it was delayed so long that the Russians were able to prepare their defences to meet it. For the first time the Russian army managed to stop a full-strength summer offensive led by the most powerful panzer forces in the German army. Although the experience cost the Russians enormous losses, they had sufficient troops in reserve to counter-attack once the German offensive was halted. The Germans, forced to despatch troops to Italy after the Allied landings in Sicily, did not.

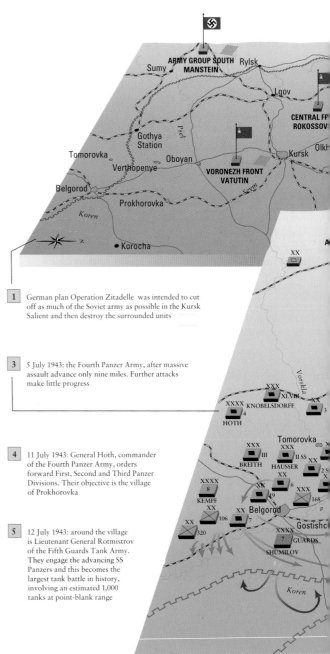

1. German plan Operation Zitadelle was intended to cut off as much of the Soviet army as possible in the Kursk Salient and then destroy the surrounded units

3. 5 July 1943: the Fourth Panzer Army, after massive assault advance only nine miles. Further attacks make little progress

4. 11 July 1943: General Hoth, commander of the Fourth Panzer Army, orders forward First, Second and Third Panzer Divisions. Their objective is the village of Prokhorovka

5. 12 July 1943: around the village is Lieutenant General Rotmistrov of the Fifth Guards Tank Army. They engage the advancing SS Panzers and this becomes the largest tank battle in history, involving an estimated 1,000 tanks at point-blank range

smashing the Red Army. In each of the two preceding years, mighty summer assaults had gained victories, sweeping the Russians back and making great gains. Surely the dose could be repeated? The question to be settled was the location where the huge attack should be launched. After discussion with his generals – and it was noticeable that after the débâcle at Stalingrad, the *Führer* was more receptive to their opinions – the region around Kursk was chosen for Operation 'Citadel'.

The Russians knew that the attack was coming. Detailed information of Hitler's plans came to them from, among other sources, spies inside the German High Command itself. Stalin and his generals had their own strategic aim for smashing the *Wehrmacht* and were able to respond to the secrets received. Marshal Zhukov cannily suggested that his forces should first be on the defensive against the panzer onslaught. 'It would be better to make the enemy first exhaust himself against our defences, and knock out his tanks,' he wrote to Stalin on 8 April, 'and then, bringing up fresh reserves, to go over to a general offensive.' Shades of Rommel! He intended to build strong anti-tank defences to slow the Germans up. Subsequently Russian troops and 300,000 civilians dug lines of trenches and ditches, laying over 5,000 mines on each mile of frontage. About 6,000 anti-tank guns were positioned, together with 20,000

other guns and nearly 1,000 'Katyusha' rocket launchers. Artillery, the Red Army's 'God of War', was ready for 'Citadel'. For further protection of the salient, over a quarter of the army's personnel and half of its tanks were moved into position. All was ready for a big show.

Against this formidable army, the German General Staff posted some of their best formations. For the pincer movement, they allocated seventeen panzer, three motorised and eighteen infantry divisions. At the start, these contained about 2,700 tanks, an armoured force greater than any previously employed. Overhead, the *Luftwaffe*, although inferior in numbers to the Red Air Force, managed tactically to gather good support. The stage was set for a clash of Titans.

At dawn on 5 July the greatest armoured battle yet seen in war opened, and before long the German attack had foundered on the intricate defensive position. Losses grew, and by 10 July only small advances had been made. The great panzer armies had been held. Then, on the 12th, the Russians hit back. Near Prokohovra some 7,000 tanks and assault guns from both sides were locked in conflict. Fighting swayed back and forth as giant formations of armour engaged in close combat. The whole area was soon littered with burning vehicles. The Panthers burned easily and suffered huge losses. On the other hand,

RIGHT: German tanks at Kursk, a mixture of Panzer IVs with long 75 mm guns and late model Panzer IIIs. Kursk revealed the shortcomings of the original T-34 that was no longer a match for the Panzer IV but newer German tanks, like the Panther and Elefant, were rushed into battle prematurely and suffered frequent mechanical failure.

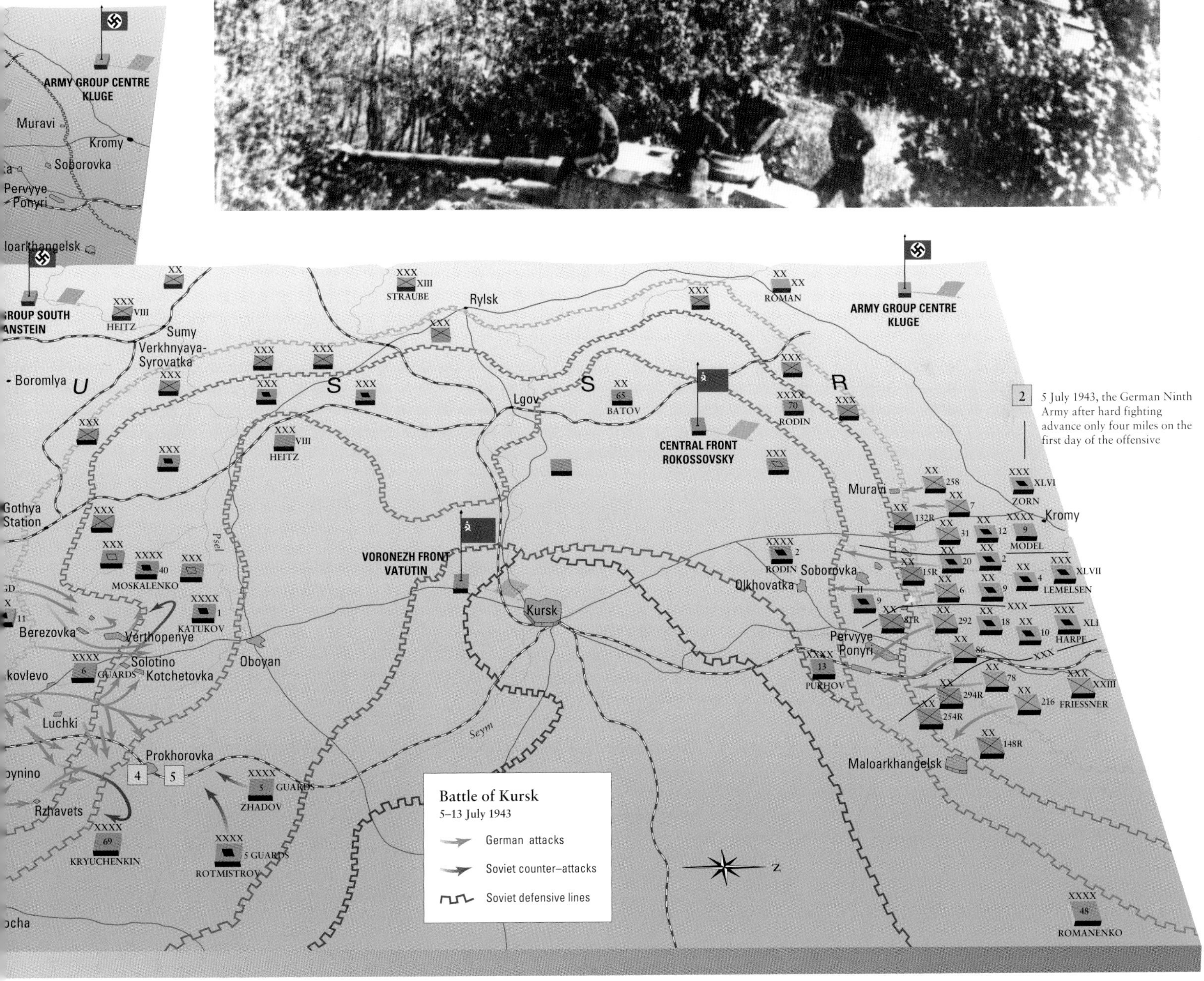

ARMY GROUP CENTRE
KLUGE

Muravi
Kromy
Soborovka
Pervyye
Ponyri

loarkhangelsk

GROUP SOUTH
ANSTEIN

HEITZ VIII
Sumy
Verkhnyaya-
Syrovatka

Boromlya U

STRAUBE XIII
Rylsk

ROMAN

ARMY GROUP CENTRE
KLUGE

S

S

R

Lgov

BATOV 65

RODIN 70

2  5 July 1943, the German Ninth Army after hard fighting advance only four miles on the first day of the offensive

CENTRAL FRONT
ROKOSSOVSKY

Muravi

HEITZ VIII

ZORN 258 XLVI
Kromy
132R 7
31 12 9
MODEL

Gothya
Station

VORONEZH FRONT
VATUTIN

RODIN Soborovka
Olkhovatka

2

20 2
15R XLVII
6 9 LEMELSEN
8TR 9
292 18 10 HARPE XLI

MOSKALENKO 40

KATUKOV 1

Berezovka
Verthopenye
Oboyan

Pervyye
Ponyri
PURHOV 13

86
78 FRIESSNER XXIII

GUARDS 6
Solotino
Kotchetovka

kovlevo

294R
254R 216

Luchki

148R

Prokhorovka

Maloarkhangelsk

4  5

oynino

GUARDS 5
ZHADOV

Rzhavets

KRYUCHENKIN 69

5 GUARDS
ROTMISTROV

**Battle of Kursk**
5–13 July 1943

→ German attacks
→ Soviet counter–attacks
ⵎⵎ Soviet defensive lines

Z

Seym

ROMANENKO 48

ocha

the Russian T-34 tank, carrying a rapid-firing 76mm gun, proved itself in combat. Of simple, revolutionary design, it was also rugged, with wide tracks. These could traverse soft ground, even snow, while shells often glanced off the sloping front armour. Some included women in their crews – a further example of the manner in which the whole population of the USSR was expected to fight actively.

Most of the Battle of Kursk ended on 15 July. The terrain was like a desert where bushes and trees had been devastated by shellfire. The battlefield was littered with the skeletons of burnt out tanks and aircraft. The stench of death from thousands of unburied corpses pervaded the air. The Russians had lost about half of their tank force as well as thousands of troops; the German toll included 70,000 dead and almost 3,000 tanks. In all history, there have been fewer harder-fought, bloodier battles.

One of the roots of German problems during the Russian Campaign was Hitler's reluctance to permit withdrawals. He could not stomach the idea of relinquishing even the smallest parcel of land. Perhaps an element of vainglory entered his decisions. In late 1941 this resolve had helped to strengthen the *Wehrmacht*'s position

when the first Russian counter-attacks were launched – and brought to a halt. Later, though, the *Führer*'s policy led to disaster. At Stalingrad the Sixth Army, ordered to stand fast, was slowly ground to destruction. Hitler's outlook denied flexibility of choice to commanders on the spot, who could have re-grouped and hit back. These rigid orders sometimes led to a paralysis of decision-making at local level, where officers dared not carry out movements they knew to be in the best interests of their men.

As the Red Army moved forward, the Germans were compelled to abandon a number of cities that had been taken at such high cost. By the end of August 1943 Orel and Kharkov had both been recaptured. The general advance then aimed for the line of the Dneiper river, which was reached in late September. Blows fell on Axis troops along the whole of the Eastern Front. On 25 September the Russians entered Smolensk, which had been an important target for Hitler's forces in the early stages of 'Barbarossa'. Then, early in November, the great city of Kiev was restored to Russian control. How could this flood be held back? Hitler hoped to build a great defensive system in the east, comparable to the 'Western Wall' being prepared in

**ABOVE:** With its wide tracks and low ground pressure, the Russian T-34 had excellent cross-country performance. It's sharply sloped armour made it almost invulnerable to frontal attack by the anti-tank weapons used by the Germans at the beginning of the war.

Western Europe to stave off the anticipated Allied invasion. He had little hope. The steady, unrelenting power of Russian forces offered him neither the manpower nor the time to construct the necessary fortifications. The coming of the winter of 1943 brought no respite for the *Wehrmacht*: the Russians rolled on.

In January 1944 many observers believed that Hitler's great European empire would not last until the end of the year. With the Russian steamroller coming from the east, Allied forces battling their way forward in Italy and preparations going ahead for the opening of the Second Front, surely the *Wehrmacht* would be overwhelmed? The aerial bombing of Germany, night and day, was intensifying. How much longer would the Nazi regime last? The answer was, 'Quite a time.'

During the early part of the year, Russian pressure in the northern sector finally broke the siege of Leningrad. There, an epic defence for a thousand days had cost the lives of about a million civilians. Further pushes carried the Red Army out of its homeland when it crossed the old Polish frontier, yet it was still facing fierce resistance. Then cracks appeared in Hitler's alliances. The Finns, who had joined what they envisaged as a crusade against the USSR, saw the writing on the wall. In February they started to negotiate a separate peace. Talks with the Russians dragged on for several

**ABOVE:** The famous Tiger tank performed well at Kursk, small numbers of them inflicting huge losses on the Russians in long-range fire-fights. Its 88 mm gun could knock out any Russian tank at up to 2,000 yards.

months, but Finland's example was carefully noted by other nations, for example Rumania and Hungary, both satellite states of Germany. Concentration of their minds on impending doom came in April and May when the Red Army re-took the Crimea and big advances were made in southern Russia.

The Russians' success was all the more remarkable considering the battering they had taken in the early stages of 'Barbarossa'. During the winter and spring of 1944 the Red Army freed about 330,000 square kilometres of Soviet territory, home to 19 million people. Russia's frontiers were re-established for 400km, and Rumania was invaded. As far as Stalin and his generals were concerned, nevertheless, such achievements were mere staging-posts on the way to the end target – the Nazi homeland.

German intelligence officers learned of Russian plans. 'By 28 March we had assembled enough *Abwehr* [intelligence] material to report that the Soviet offensive would be conducted without respite on every sector of the Eastern Front,' General Gehlen wrote later. He listed their objectives as the occupation of Estonia, Latvia and Lithuania, advancing through Rumania to Hungary, Bulgaria and Yugoslavia and taking possession of Poland. The Russians, now with very powerful armies, could strike at will. They decided to launch a huge summer assault on the main force – Hitler's old Army Group Centre – which stood between them and the heart of Germany. On 20 May the plan was ready and code-named Operation 'Bagration', after a Russian general who had been killed during Napoleon's invasion in 1812.

The battle opened on 22 June. By then, the Second Front of US and British landings in France had been established, while Allied forces in Italy had advanced north of Rome. The German General Staff were having to weigh the balance of conducting three land campaigns simultaneously. Army Group Centre, with 37 divisions available, was subjected to the weight of over 160 divisions of the Red Army, accompanied by 4,000 aircraft. Under such attack, German forces were soon driven into retreat. Many were

trapped. A soldier of the 6th Division remembered the annihilation when they were surrounded and only a handful of troops escaped: 'A hundred from the eighteen thousand men who had marched into Russia under the Bielefeld crest. Sixth Division, the heroic Regiment 18, had ceased to exist.' Army Group Centre, in which Hitler had pinned such faith three years earlier, was eradicated as a coordinated fighting force. It had lost over

200,000 men when 'Bagration' finished in mid-July.

In August, the Red Army entered Rumania, which rapidly surrendered, then changed sides by declaring war on Germany. The Russians took the capital, Bucharest, on 30 August. Bulgaria had cooperated with Hitler, yet had not taken part in the conflict against Russia. The arrival of the Red Army in September caused the Bulgarian government to think quick-

**ABOVE:** A German Tiger tank commander scans the snowfields for his next target. Note the corrugated effect on the side of the turret: this was a paste applied all over German vehicles to prevent magnetic mines from adhering. Fixing a mine to a live Tiger tank was a fast track to a posthumous Order of Lenin but enough Russians were prepare to try for this to become standard issue.

**LEFT:** Russian light tanks led by a T-60 in the far north of Russia. The Red Army proved capable of fighting in Arctic conditions that rendered most German equipment inoperable.

ABOVE: The Ilyushin Il-2 'Sturmovik' ground attack aircraft was built in enormous quantities and expended to good effect against German troop concentrations. These missions were so hazardous that the position of rear gunner in an Il-2 was a disciplinary posting in the Red Air Force.

ly and join forces against Germany. In the far north, Finland signed a peace treaty with the all-conquering Russians on 19 September. The three Baltic states, Lithuania, Latvia and Estonia, also fell to the irresistible advance. The Hungarians had given good support to Hitler. As the Russians approached, the Hungarian authorities tried to reach terms with them, but in October the Germans stepped in to occupy the capital, Budapest. The city was not taken by the Russians until February 1945.

Trouble also broke out for the Germans in the two countries of the Balkans which they had ruthlessly conquered in 1941 – Yugoslavia and Greece. By October 1944 the Germans had to evacuate their occupying forces from Greece, where a civil war soon started between pro- and anti-Communist forces. In Yugoslavia, the Germans met fiercer resistance. Since the German invasion of 1941, various groups of partisans had fought a guerrilla war against the invaders in the mountains. Tito, commander of the Communist partisans, gradually emerged as a national leader, accepted by all of the Allies. Russian troops entered Belgrade on 20 October.

One of the war's greatest controversies occurred in August 1944 and

was a precursor of troubles that would arrive at the end of the conflict, when Russia imposed Communist governments across Eastern Europe. The tide of the Russian advance, sweeping westwards, reached the river Vistula, close to Warsaw. In Poland's capital were the Home Army, underground forces loyal to the exiled government in London but not recognised by Stalin. His support was given to Polish Communist forces, who were part of the Red Army. The Home Army, believing that liberation was at hand, rose in revolt against the Germans on 1 August, expecting Russian troops to arrive at any moment. None came. Whether the Russian advance had run out of steam at that point or whether Stalin wished to see potential opponents crushed is unclear. The Germans cashed in on the Red Army's hesitation to smash the Warsaw Uprising with unbridled ferocity. By the time the revolt had been defeated by SS troops under Himmler, 200,000 Poles had been killed and much of the city destroyed. The Russians did not take the city for another five months. People still wonder why not.

Hitler's troubles of raising manpower were proving insuperable by the end of the year. Boys as young as fifteen and men of sixty years were being called up. As Hitler's defeated forces were driven from the USSR, and were now faced with the prospect of holding off the Red Army from the German homeland, they left behind a double legacy. One was a trail of destruction unequalled in history. Possibly a quarter of Russian property had been destroyed. The inventory included 70,000 villages, 17,000 towns, 84,000 schools, 40,000 miles of railway track and 45 million farm animals. Over 25 million people were left homeless, living in cellars and dugouts, huts and pits.

This led to the second legacy – one of hatred for the Germans and a resolve for revenge. 'I am on my way to Berlin. True, we may not get there in time, but Berlin is precisely the place we *must* reach,' a Russian soldier wrote home in November 1944. 'Our fellows' fury and thirst for revenge after all we have seen are more intense than ever.'

RIGHT: Panzer IVs in Zhitomir, late 1943. Their turrets are shrouded by additional spaced armour designed to detonate anti-tank rockets before they strike the vehicle itself. The changed shape of the vehicle led many Allied soldiers to misidentify them as Tiger tanks.

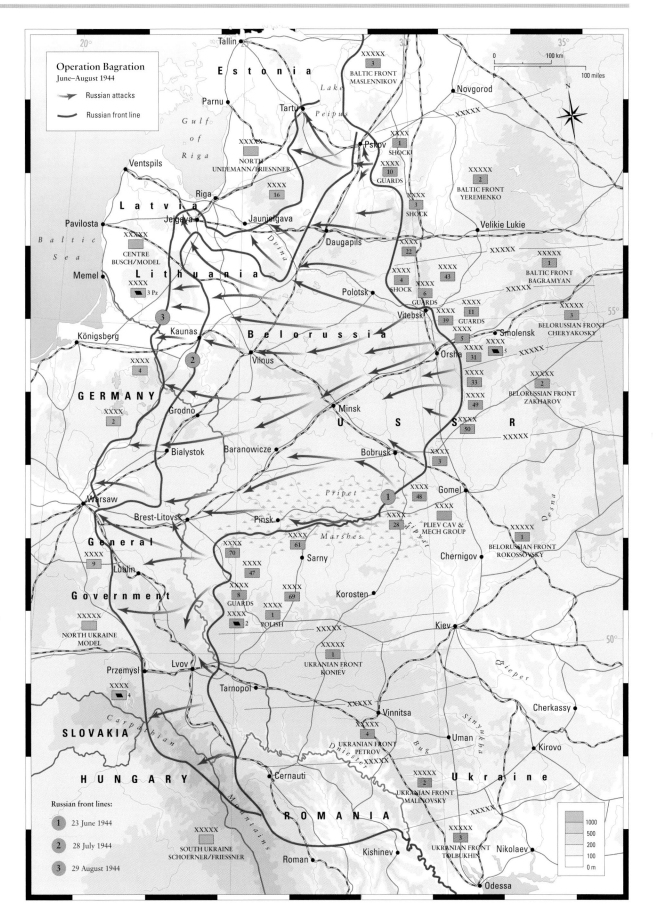

**OPERATION BAGRATION**

An operation of incredible scope, the Russian offensive of summer 1944 involved 2.4 million troops and over 5,000 tanks and 5,000 aircraft. It crushed Army Group Centre and liberated all remaining Soviet territory from German occupation. The Russians entered Poland and then, in one of the most cynical acts of the war, halted operations to give the Germans time to crush the Polish 'Home Army' that had seized control of Warsaw in the name of the government-in-exile. A follow-on invasion of Rumania at the same time overthrew the Rumanian government and, for the second time, destroyed most of the German 6th Army.

Operation Bagration
June–August 1944

→ Russian attacks

↝ Russian front line

Russian front lines:

① 23 June 1944

② 28 July 1944

③ 29 August 1944

# The Italian Campaign

The Italian Campaign resulted particularly from decisions taken by American and British service leaders, meeting under Roosevelt and Churchill. They attended two conferences. The first was held at Casablanca in January 1943 and the second, 'Trident', at Washington in May.

The main purpose of the eight-day Casablanca Conference was to plot a way forward. On the American side were two power groups. One was strongly in favour of sending more forces immediately to the Pacific, speeding up the campaign against Japan. The other wanted a Second Front to be opened in 1943 by means of landings on the French coast. In their view, that would be the most direct route to Berlin – and the demise of Hitler. For the Americans, as soon as the Axis forces had been evicted from Africa, the centre of attack should be moved away from the Mediterranean.

British commanders, under Churchill, disagreed. They believed that Allied forces were far from ready in terms of numbers, training and equipment to launch a Second Front in 1943. There was, for example, a shortage of shipping required for the operation. Landings in France would end in disaster. There was, nonetheless, a need for Anglo-American armies to keep in action somewhere against Axis armies, thereby taking some pressure off the Russians. Italy and the Balkans were possible targets.

Churchill's arguments were persuasive. After much discussion, the Americans agreed that Sicily should be invaded. Its capture would open up the whole Mediterranean sea route between Gibraltar and Egypt. The campaign, code-named Operation 'Husky', would also be a step on the way to an invasion of Italy. The Americans agreed because they hoped that a Second Front could be opened at the same time. In his heart Churchill believed that they were wrong. The Allies were gathering enormous supplies of men and *matériel* on the eastern side of the Atlantic Ocean, but not enough to sustain two great campaigns simultaneously. The opening of the Second Front would not come before 1944.

Two other important results came from the Casablanca Conference. One was Britain's commitment to fight on, beside the Americans, against the Japanese after Hitler had been defeated. The second was an Unconditional Surrender declaration. This did not mean 'the destruction of the German populace, or Japanese populace'; instead, it would lead to the destruction of a policy 'which is based on the conquest and subjugation of other peoples'. These words sounded fine, particularly to the populations of many lands who had been trampled underfoot by Axis powers. Since then, some historians have suggested that

RIGHT: US troops come ashore at Salerno, spelling the end of Mussolini's Fascist regime and opening a new theatre of operations on the Italian mainland. Hopes of a swift capture of Rome faded fast as the Germans occupied the country.

162

the people of Germany, caught between the alternative of total surrender or utter destruction, fought all the more fiercely for the rest of the war.

At the 'Trident' conference in May, American commanders, somewhat unwillingly, agreed that landings in Sicily, then Italy, could go ahead. The proviso was that these campaigns could last until November. After that, the centre of attention would be switched to the build-up for the Second Front. Landings in France, they decided, would be made by 1 May 1944. General Marshall, the US leader of the Combined Chiefs of Staff, feared that unless care were taken, the Italian Campaign would swallow up resources intended for the cross-Channel operation. The agreed compromise was uneasy.

# Operation 'Husky'

BELOW: 'C' company, 2nd
Northamptonshire
Regiment prepare to board
the invasion fleet in Sicily
for the short journey
across to the mainland.
The invasion of Sicily was
a success, but the German
garrison succeeded in
escaping across the straits
despite Allied air and naval
superiority.

Planning for the invasion of Sicily began in February 1943, before the campaign in Tunisia had finished. Although the Allies were building forces of overwhelming superiority in the western Mediterranean, there were many problems to overcome. General de Guingand, Chief of Staff of the Eighth Army, was one of the planners. His difficulties included worries over shipping and assault craft, the lack of experience of amphibious warfare and the fact that some units which had seen long action were short of men and equipment. In addition, British and American naval units had to coordinate convoys coming from seven ports in North Africa, the United Kingdom and the United States: 'Somehow they had to meet off Sicily at the right time.' The importance of Malta was again underlined as troops, ships and aircraft gathered there for the assault. The American General Eisenhower was overall Commander-in-Chief. Under him was General Alexander, who then controlled General Patton's Eastern Force, and the Western Force led by General Montgomery.

On the Axis side there was discussion over where an Allied invasion would be aimed. Corsica and Sardinia were possibilities. In an attempt to persuade the Germans that the target might be Greece or the Balkans, MI5 used 'The Man Who Never Was'. A corpse, that of a man apparently killed in a plane crash, and dressed in a British staff officer's uniform and carrying secret documents, was floated ashore in Spain. The documents soon reached Germany. They showed that Sicily was not the target for invasion and the Germans reacted accordingly. Nevertheless, Field Marshal Kesselring, the German Commander-in-Chief South, estimated that Sicily would be chosen as 'an objective within striking distance of fighter aircraft operating from a fixed base'.

Most Allied troops invaded on a night of rough weather, 13 July. 'The Italian coastal divisions were an utter failure,' wrote Kesselring, whose visit to Sicily 'yielded nothing but a headache'. At that stage, many Italian servicemen were heartily sick of a war into which they had been dragooned by Mussolini's excesses. Little was needed to persuade them to opt out.

Patton's forces soon overran areas in the west of the island, capturing the important city of Palermo on the 22nd. After mopping up resistance, they turned east to support the British. In the east, Montgomery's troops found heavier opposition from the Germans. His plan was to advance rapidly to the port of Messina, lying only a few miles across from mainland Italy. That move was intended to block the retreat of all Axis forces on the island. However, the Germans, with reserves drafted in from the mainland, fought a skilful defensive operation so that Montgomery had to make a radical change of direction in attack.

Messina was not taken by Allied forces until 17 August. Not the least difficulty of the fighting was caused by the weather. 'The troops on both sides,' wrote Kesselring, 'had to face extraordinary exertions in the heat of a blistering summer sun in the rocky and almost treeless regions.'

The taking of Sicily, although a victory, cost the Allies almost 23,000 casualties, of whom 5,500 were killed.

Much was learned from Operation 'Husky', especially concerning the conduct of combined operations. 'In Sicily,' wrote Terraine, 'we may discern all the elements, if not the details, of the amphibious operations that were to come.' The Allies were now ready to step back on to the European continental mainland in real force, for the first time since Dunkirk. The 'toe' of Italy beckoned.

# Fighting in Italy

After the expulsion of Axis armies from Tunisia in May 1943 the Italians knew that active warfare was heading rapidly in their direction. By then their army was weakened through defeats, their navy and air force proven to be inferior, and the solid determination required by a nation in conflict noticeably lacking. Allied aircraft bombed northern cities – Milan, Turin and Genoa – damaging factories but also hitting civilian buildings. Public morale was fragile. The invasion of Sicily realised the inhabitants' worst fears. German troops on the island fought with their customary tenacity; Italians offered little resistance. The Italian people were trapped 'between a rock and a hard place'. The Allies demanded unconditional surrender, allowing no scope for old-fashioned diplomacy and negotiation. 'It is difficult to overstate the depth of depression that has overtaken the members of this unhappy country,' wrote an Englishwoman living in Tuscany. People wanted peace. 'The intransigence of the Allies' terms is only equalled by the firmness of Germany's refusal to remove her troops.' Italy was bound to be a bat-

tlefield, and her people were unsure whether to remain 'half-hearted participants or passive spectators'. The hatred of other nations and races shown by the Germans, for example, to the Slavs and Jews was not shared generally by Italians. In addition, many of them harboured more than a small historic liking and respect for Americans and the British, whose armies were about to land on Italian soil.

The driving force holding Italy in the war was largely one man, Mussolini. Together with his close Fascist associates and backed by Hitler, a fellow dictator, *Il Duce* had, by 1943, lost the confidence of important sections of the nation. 'I feel that all Italians understand and love me,' Mussolini had written seven years earlier. 'I know that only he is loved who leads without weakness.' Those words now had a hollow ring. Kesselring later asserted that 'his sublime self-confidence proved his own worst enemy.' The army and the Royal Family realised that he was an embarrassing burden who would have to go.

Plotting was soon under way. This gathered speed from mid-July when

several leading Fascists secretly planned their leader's overthrow. Their efforts were encouraged by a message to the Italian people from Roosevelt and Churchill. 'Consult your own self-respect and your own interests and your own desire for a return to national dignity,' it said. They should decide whether to 'die for Mussolini and Hitler – or live for Italy and civilization'. A meeting of the Fascist Grand Council was convened on 24 July, at which Mussolini was openly criticised. The next day he was summoned to the Royal Palace. 'At this moment,' the king told him, 'you are the most hated man in Italy.' As he left, *Il Duce* was arrested and later transferred to an isolated mountain retreat at Gran Sasso. Marshal Badoglio became prime minister.

The new government pledged to continue the war at the side of its German allies, but secretly sought peace with the Americans and the British. The world learned of the Italian surrender on 8 September, just as American troops were poised to invade the mainland, to the south of Naples. Five days earlier, Montgomery's forces had occupied Reggio, a port in the 'toe' of Italy, and it appeared that decisive thrusts at the 'under-belly of the Axis' would bring swift results.

Hitler quickly sent Rommel into northern Italy, ostensibly to support Axis forces in the south but really to block Alpine passes. 'Whoever controlled the Brenner and the roads and railways running eastwards into Austria and the Balkans and westwards into France,' Kesselring believed, 'had a stranglehold on Germany.' By early September, the 'Desert Fox', in new surroundings, commanded eight divisions. Forces in the south were under the command of Kesselring. At one time, several German senior staff believed that they would be lost, but Kesselring was sure that he could hold off an Allied invasion to the south of Rome. When Mussolini resigned and the Italians capitulated, German units moved in quickly to take control of the capital and to prepare to resist the anticipated arrival of American and British armies.

The slowness of the Allies played

into German hands. Mussolini was deposed on 25 July and Messina in Sicily captured on 17 August, yet Montgomery's troops did not land at Reggio until 3 September. The main invasion followed six days later. By then, the Germans had been able to establish their forces in Italy, occupying Rome and continuing preparations. Thousands of Allied prisoners-of-war, freed when Italy had surrendered, were rounded up and returned to captivity.

Under the code-name Operation 'Avalanche', the main assault on the mainland went ashore at Salerno, to the south of Naples. Strategists have since queried why landings were made so far south on the 'leg' of Italy. In his memoirs, Kesselring, with the benefit of recollection, believed that 'an air landing on Rome and sea landing nearby, instead of at Salerno, would have automatically caused us to evacuate all of the southern half of Italy'. An important reason for the choice of Salerno was the ability of Allied air forces to offer massive fighter cover in the form of an 'aerial umbrella',

LEFT: The invasion fleet at sea, barrage balloons overhead to discourage dive-bombers. This campaign witnessed the first use of radio-controlled bombs, launched from German aircraft against Allied shipping.

BELOW: US troops landing at Salerno, 9 September 1943. Initial resistance was light but soon stiffened as the Germans poured reinforcements into the area. A determined German counter-attack nearly cut the Allied beachhead in two.

ABOVE: Tracer fire from ships' anti-aircraft guns lights up the sky off the Salerno beaches. Tip and run raids by individual German aircraft were followed by large scale raids on the narrow perimeter held by the Allies. German bombing continued even after the advance inland resumed, one attack sinking an American ship loaded with mustard gas in Naples harbour.

RIGHT: Swazi troops among the South African contingent serving with the British Commonwealth forces in southern Italy. The Allied armies in Italy included soldiers of almost every conceivable race and creed, ranging from the Brazilian brigade to African and Indian troops fighting for the British and French.

were under-equipped, but soon 'revealed the amazing ability of the Germans to resist in apparently hopeless situations'. Over the following days panzer units, supporting motorised infantry, launched several successful counter-attacks, keeping Allied troops pinned largely to the area of the beaches. In fact, on the evening of the 10th, several Allied commanders even contemplated re-embarking some of their men. The line was largely held by artillery fire, both from land and sea, together with close air support. In the view of one writer, 'Without the battleships, Avalanche would have been turned into another Dunkirk.'

Yet the emergency did not pass for another five days. Then Kesselring, accepting the inevitable, pulled his troops back to a defence line as Montgomery's Eighth Army joined up with the bridgehead. Allied soldiers did not reach Naples until 1 October and within a few days they were stretched in a line, 120 miles long, right across Italy. By then, Clark's Fifth Army had suffered 12,000 casualties.

### Rescuing Mussolini

Few events excite public imagination more than stories of derring-do by special forces in war. They become headline news because of the skill and determination of the men taking part. Some end in glorious failure, like the commando raid on Rommel's African headquarters in 1942. Others are brilliantly successful.

One of the best remembered occurred on 12 September 1943, at the isolated Italian mountain resort of Gran Sasso. After Mussolini was deposed in July, Hitler decided to rescue him. Not only was *Il Duce* his friend, but also he could be used to lead a Fascist government set up in northern Italy. When Hitler learned of Mussolini's whereabouts he ordered an operation to be set up for his release.

The task was difficult because the Gran Sasso could be reached only by funicular railway. However, Otto Skorzeny of the SS, with a commando unit, landed by glider outside Mussolini's hotel. Having freed the Italian leader, he spirited him off in a

unavailable for a more distant landing.

Consequently, a huge Allied fleet of 700 vessels, large and small, transported some 170,000 troops, under the command of US General Mark Clark, to the Salerno beaches for Operation 'Avalanche'. From 3.30 a.m. on 9 September, men and materials were landed, with the intention that rapid

success would take them to Naples by the third day. Then a large port would be available for receiving reinforcements. Any thoughts that the defences would be rolled up easily, however, were rudely dispelled. Of Kesselring's eight divisions, two were near Rome and six in the south, four of which had fought in Sicily. All these formations

**LEFT:** M4 Shermans en route north. Its size dictated by the need to ship them by sea or rail rather than strict combat criteria, the M4 was inferior to the later German tanks but more mechanically reliable and available in vastly greater numbers. None of this was any compensation for the crews who had to fight in them. The British called them 'Ronsons' after the cigarette lighter that famously lights every time.

small aeroplane. This brilliant operation resulted in Hitler and Mussolini being reunited within two days. At the *Führer*'s behest, Mussolini became the leader of the 'Italian Social Republic', or 'Salo Republic', in opposition to the Italian government which had deposed him. Nevertheless, *Il Duce* was still a burden to the Germans. He showed no desire 'to wreak vengeance on his betrayers,' wrote Goebbels. 'He is not a revolutionary like the *Führer* or Stalin.' Mussolini was a spent force.

### Fighting On

The Italian Campaign over the following fifteen months, until the end of 1944, became one of the hardest fought of the whole war. For the Allies, progress was both costly and painfully slow, and a study of the map

of Italy helps to explain why. The Appenine mountains are a fearsome barrier to any army advancing from the south. In places they rise to heights

of over 8,000ft, stretching across Italy and leaving on each side strips broken by fast flowing rivers and gorges. Any progress along the coastal plains could

**LEFT:** The Focke-Wulf FW190 fighter-bomber proved highly effective in the Italian campaign, able to carry a useful bomb-load and equally capable in air combat against the latest British and American interceptors.

**ABOVE:** German armour passes through Rome, November 1943. The city endured a grim winter of occupation, its population swollen by refugees and the German and Italian Fascist garrison increasingly jittery. A partisan attack on an SS police unit led to the mass execution of hostages, a war crime for which the perpetrators were not brought to justice for nearly fifty years.

**RIGHT:** German paratroops in the ruins of the monastery at Monte Cassino. From their excellent defensive positions in the mountains, the Germans held up the Allied advance on Rome until the summer of 1944.

be dominated by defence systems situated above on high ground. Here the terrain amply favoured defenders, whose observation posts, carefully sited artillery and determined infantry held the whip-hand. It was quite possible for a well-entrenched company of soldiers, protected by mines, to repel attacks from an enemy twenty times stronger. Assaulting troops had little cover and were frustrated regularly when attempts to move forward were met by withering fire. Allied air superiority was unable to smash deep, carefully concealed German positions on the heights. Moreover Kesselring, who conducted a very clever holding retreat, built defences in depth. They were 'so deepened by the construction of armoured and concrete switch lines and intermediate and advanced positions that even very strong enemy attacks could be intercepted in the back area'. To add to the misery of the Allies, bitter cold in the mountains and heavy rains, with seas of mud, delayed progress everywhere from coast to coast. War in the Appenines and the coastal plains finished in frustration.

In an attempt to break the deadlock, another 'leapfrog' amphibious landing was planned for Anzio, north of the Gustav Line and to the south of Rome. The Allied Sixth Corps of four

divisions achieved complete tactical surprise when its men went ashore, beginning on 22 January 1944. All appeared to be well for a speedy sweep to Rome, but two factors prevented success. One was the over-cautious efforts of Allied commanders to expand the bridgehead. They took so much time in consolidating their positions that no real attempt to push forward was made for a week. The second, almost incredibly, was the

robust response from German units, hastily moved up by Kesselring. No break-out from Anzio took place until 23 May, and three more days passed before Rome was captured.

For the rest of the year, fighting continued on the Italian Front, but by then the efforts were overshadowed by two other Allied offensives. One was 'Overlord', the long-awaited re-entry into northern France which started on 6 June. The other, 'Anvil', opened with landings in southern France on 15 August. Forces were withdrawn from Alexander's command for both operations. Three American and four French divisions were taken for the latter at a time when Hitler was posting a further eight to Kesselring.

In early August German forces withdrew north to new defences in the Gothic Line, which Hitler's Todt labour force had been constructing for a year. These were about 200 miles of defensive strongpoints, stretching across Italy. Every route north was blocked, so that the Allies could not reach Vienna or swing round into the Balkans. In September 1944 the Fifth Army in the centre and the Eighth Army to the east launched heavy attacks on these positions, but unusually bad weather intervened, halting the offensive in thick mud. It was not until April 1945 that the momentum of assault built again, in the dying days of the European war.

**ITALY 1944–45**

A second amphibious landing at Anzio failed to prise the Germans out of their defensive positions and nearly led to disaster when they counter-attacked. General Mark Clark charged straight for Rome once the Germans were forced to pull back. His determination to take the city before the Normandy landings dominated the headlines but let the retreating Germans escape to fight another day. Through the long winter of 1944–45 the pace of the Allied advance slowed to a crawl: the terrain was ideal for the defence and the Germans fought on with tremendous efficiency.

**Italy 1944 – 1945**

→ Allied attacks

- ‑ → German retreat

⌒ Allied front line

- - - German front line

∧∧∧ German fortified defensive line

**Allied front lines:**

1 22 May 1944

2 end of May 1944

3 4 June 1944

4 17 June 1944

5 end of December 1944

6 23 April 1945

Scale:
0   100 km
0   100 miles

Elevation scale (m): 4000, 3000, 2000, 1000, 500, 200, 0 m

Map labels:

AUSTRIA, LICHTENSTEIN, SWITZ, YUGOSLAV, ITALY

Innsbruck, Brenner Pass, Predlidz, Villach, Ljubljana, Bolzano, Belluno, Udine, Trieste, Koper, Novigrad, Fiume, Pola, Trento, Rovereto, Treviso, Vicenza, Varese, Como, Biella, Busto Arsizio, Bergamo, Brescia, Verona, Padova, Venice, Chioggia, Ivrea, Milan, Vercelli, Turin, Casale, Cremona, Piacenza, Mantova, Codigoro, Parma, Ferrara, Argenta, Alessandria, Modena, Bologna, Ravenna, Imola, Forlì, Vergato, Rimini, Savona, Genova, La Spezia, Carrara, Viareggio, Lucca, Pistoia, Florence, Pesaro, Urbino, Pisa, Livorno, Arezzo, Ancona, Iesi, Siena, Cortona, Gubbio, Fabriano, Macerata, Perugia, Fermo, Piombino, Foligno, Ascoli, Grosseto, Orvieto, Terni, Teramo, Viterbo, Rieti, Pescara, L'Aquila, Civitavecchia, Sulmona, Tivoli, Rome, Anzio, Cassino, Terracina, Naples, Salerno

Italian Partisans, Alpine Partisans, Venetian Line, Piave Line, Alpine Line, Gothic Line, Gustav Line

Adriatic Sea, Ligurian Sea

Unit labels:
XXXX 7, XXXX 14 LEMELSEN, XXXX 10 HERR, XXXXX C VIGTINGHOFF, XXXX 1 LIGURIAN (Italian), XXXX 10 VIETINGHOFF, XXXX LXVI, XXXX 14 MACKENSEN, XXX LI (Mtn), XXX XIV, XXXX 5, XXXX 8 McCREERY, XXXX 5 TRUSCOTT, XXXX 8 McCREERY, XXXXX 15 CLARK, XXX Fr Exp, XXXX 14 MACKENSEN, XXXX 10 VIETINGHOFF, XXX V, XXXX 8 LEESE, XXX XIII, XXXX 8 LEESE, XXXXX 15 ALEXANDER, XXX Fr Exp, XXXXX 15 ALEXANDER, XXXX 5 CLARK, XXX III, XXXX 5 CLARK, XXX X, XXX VI, 3, 2, 1, 4, 5, 6

# Operation 'Overlord'

By early 1944 two land campaigns in Europe were exerting pressure on the empire which Hitler had amassed for Germany over the previous six years. In Italy, the combined Anglo-American armies were slowly and painfully pushing on. Far greater success came from Russian effort on the Eastern Front, where Axis forces were being pressed back.

Among the Allies there was a general recognition that the complete overthrow of Germany, together with the unconditional surrender demanded, would come only through the occupation of the German homeland. Some Russians believed, after 1943, that the Red Army could achieve that by itself. Most people knew that the best results would come after the opening of the Second Front, starting on the coast of France. If American and British forces could establish a foothold there, the Germans would be faced with their traditional fear – war on two fronts. Germany would be gradually and relentlessly squeezed in a giant pair of nutcrackers: the eastern arm, the Red Army, and the western arm, the combined American and British armies, would slowly crush the fight out of the defending forces.

The Russians believed that on the Eastern Front they were carrying the main burden of fighting the Germans while their two allies were slow in coming to their aid by putting armies ashore in Western Europe. The Americans, growing impatient with British caution, wanted to start a Second Front as the most direct way into Germany, before turning to the other half of their war, namely to defeat the Japanese. Britain, having already lost in France, and with far smaller resources of manpower and *matériel* than the others, wanted to wait until Allied forces were strong enough not to suffer another Dunkirk. Each of the three leaders – Stalin, Roosevelt and Churchill – appreciated how far his nation depended on the other two. The final breaking of Hitler's Germany would require a joint and coordinated effort.

By early 1944 detailed preparations for the Second Front were being made. The US General Eisenhower was appointed Supreme Commander. Under him, a large number of senior

**RIGHT:** The Normandy landings have been the subject of so many books and films that the sheer scale of the operation can be overlooked. By nightfall on 6 June 130,000 Allied troops were in France at a cost of 5,000 casualties, far fewer than planners had expected. Two weeks later, the Allied bridgehead held 800,000 troops and the Germans had lost their opportunity to drive the invaders back into the sea.

ABOVE: A German machine gun team ready for action. The plentiful use of such automatic weapons gave relatively small German formations fearsome firepower. One well sited machine gun could shoot down a whole Allied section with its opening burst.

officers, both American and British, were posted to lead forces in what would become the greatest seaborne invasion in history. Under their command were some 3.5 million service personnel, whose presence turned the British Isles into an enormous armed camp. So many men and so much equipment were there that, according to Eisenhower, only barrage balloons kept Britain afloat! Of the numbers gathered, about 1.7 million were British and 1.2 million came from the US,

while the remainder were from countries of the British Commonwealth, or from those nations occupied by the Nazis. This gigantic force was poised for a great crusade to land in France.

The venture was complicated particularly by the fact that Britain is an island. To carry the troops, 1,600 merchant vessels of various sizes were required, together with 4,000 landing craft to place them and their equipment on the beaches. Protecting this unprecedented armada were 1,200

warships, varying in size from motor torpedo boats to battleships. In the air, some advance forces would be carried in 3,500 gliders. All would be covered by an umbrella of over 12,000 aircraft, including 5,000 fighters. The crusade would stand or fall by the strength of the integration and adaptability among the three services.

The planners knew that it was vital rapidly to create and hold bridgeheads. They hoped to land 150,000 men on French territory on the first day, about 70,000 of them in the opening assaults. During the subsequent expansion more than two million men would be sent to the Continent within two months, together with 500,000 vehicles. The logistical problems were awe-inspiring.

Two main sites were suitable on the French coast. Allied intelligence went to great lengths to confuse the Germans by making them believe that the likely thrust would arrive at the Pas de Calais, on the short Channel crossing; the real blow was planned elsewhere. Five main beaches were chosen in Normandy, further west. Landing points there were good, but until nearby Cherbourg was captured, the Allies would have no major port. Therefore a giant artificial harbour, 'Mulberry', was built in sections, consisting of floating concrete caissons and piers. This was to be towed across the Channel to a landing beach, then protected by sunken ships. The ingenuity shown to overcome shortages or weaknesses was remarkable.

### The Atlantic Wall

On the further side of the Channel the Germans had been preparing for the invasion. Some time in the war elapsed before Hitler accepted that Anglo-American forces were growing strong enough to pose a threat by making landings in France. Until then he felt, almost disdainfully, that any invasion would result in another Dunkirk. When the danger was appreciated, however, preparations were made by the Germans to strengthen an Atlantic Wall to repel the invaders.

Work had begun on the Atlantic Wall, stretching from the North Cape to the Spanish border, early in 1942. The aim was to build a kind of Siegfried Line to prevent seaborne

RIGHT: German navy plans to disrupt the landings with mini-submarines were a spectacular failure. This is one of several hundred one-man submarines the Germans lost in the Channel during 1944.

invasion. On beaches were laid mines and metal obstructions, followed by belts of barbed wire, concrete bunkers, anti-tank ditches and pillboxes. Behind these were further strongpoints and minefields. The work, often carried out by slave labour, had not been completely finished, but even so it was a formidable obstacle by 1944.

In the west, manning the Wall were a number of static divisions, whose task was to fight invaders at beach level. Far more of a threat to the Allies, however, were mobile panzer divisions, capable of being switched quickly to counter any incursions in the Wall. The employment of all defending troops became a matter of some controversy between their commanders in the West. In overall command was Field Marshal von Rundstedt, who controlled 60 divisions. Ten of these were panzers. He believed that the panzer divisions should be held back at the time of the invasion until Allied moves and plans became apparent, then should be sent in to crush them. Rommel, however, who commanded Army Group B in Belgium, northern France and Normandy, wanted panzers to be employed immediately, hitting the Allies at the beaches and throwing them back into the sea.

The weeks approaching the invasion

were characterised by a heavy bombing campaign on targets in France and the Low Countries by Allied aircraft. Bridges, railways, coastal batteries, radar stations and even individual buildings were raided, while the *Luftwaffe* was heavily battered. Here was 'interdiction' over the battle zone. The Germans had to accept that aerial superiority, so often a factor in their earlier campaigns, was now lost. Before 6 June, Allied air forces had dropped almost 200,000 tons of bombs on these targets, slowing, even paralysing, the Germans' ability to prevent the invasion. The corollary was equally important: hardly any *Luftwaffe* aircraft were able to fly on

reconnaissance missions over Britain, so German intelligence was largely 'blind' to the preparations being made.

German leaders sensed the approach of D-Day. French Resistance forces carried out raids and ambushes. 'There were many derailments of trains that were carrying supplies and reinforcements to the front,' remarked General Blumentritt. 'Beyond this was the planned destruction by air bombing of the railways in France and western Germany – especially of the bridges across the Somme, the Seine and the Loire. All these were pointers.' However, they could not tell exactly when or where the landings would arrive.

ABOVE: Still in action over Russia, the Junkers Ju-87G was fitted with twin 37 mm cannon to attack Russian tanks from above. This further reduced the aircraft's already mediocre performance and they would not have lasted a minute over the western front. One Stuka pilot, Hans Rudel, managed to destroy over 500 tanks in his years over the Russian front. He became the most highly decorated pilot in the German air force.

LEFT: German vehicles in retreat towards the Carpathian mountains. Even when the extent of the Normandy landings became known to the German high command, the majority of the German forces remained on the Russian front. Without the oil supplies from Rumania and Hungary the German war machine would come to a standstill.

# D-Day and After

**LEFT:** HMS *Rodney* opens fire with her 16 in guns on German coastal defences. Bombardments by Allied battleships inflicted massive damage on German army formations assembling to counter-attack the beachheads.

At 9 a.m. on 6 June 1944 the BBC announced that 'Under the command of General Eisenhower, Allied naval forces supported by strong air forces began landing Allied armies this morning on the coast of France.' D-Day and Operation 'Overlord' had arrived. Eisenhower, the Supreme Commander, and Montgomery, commander of the ground forces, had earlier fixed 4 June for the start, but bad weather caused a short postponement for what was to be, in Rommel's words, 'The Longest Day'.

During the night, paratroops from three Allied airborne divisions, and glider troops, were dropping inland to seize strategic points. Then, at dawn, landings commenced on five Normandy beaches. Three were attacked by the British Second Army: 'Gold' and 'Sword' were tackled by British troops, while 'Juno' fell to the Canadians. The other two, 'Utah' and 'Omaha', were assaulted by the US First Army. The landings were preceded by heavy naval bombardments and bombing. Overall, the Second Army suffered few casualties in getting ashore, but the Americans, particularly on 'Omaha', met fiercer resistance. Not the least reason for the difference was the British Army's employment of a variety of weapons, nicknamed 'Funnies', developed specially for the landings. The Americans generally preferred not to use them. These ingenious devices included amphibious Sherman tanks, 'Crabs' equipped with flails for exploding mines, and AVREs, armoured vehicles which could lay metal carpets, or fascines or bridges. Without them, Eisenhower wrote later, 'it is doubtful if the assault forces could have firmly established themselves'.

The men on shore pushed forward, gradually managing to scratch a toehold in France. More ships and landing craft arrived, so that during D-Day 156,000 troops were landed from over 2,700 vessels which crossed the Channel. The cost that day was 11,000 casualties, including 2,500 killed. A blessing for Allied forces – and a curse for the Germans – was the strength of air support, with the *Luftwaffe* almost entirely absent. British and American aircraft flew over 25,000 sorties by 9 p.m. on 6 June; the once powerful German Air Force managed only 319 on the same day.

The *Wehrmacht*'s reactions to the landings were confused, helping the invaders. Rommel was in Germany for his wife's birthday, von Rundstedt still believed that the main attack would come later near Calais, while Hitler, who had slept late, refused to release extra panzer divisions into Normandy. By the time the German forces moved forward from reserve, the bridgehead was being firmly established.

Over the following days the Allied armies were reinforced and their positions extended until all the landing sites were combined into a bridgehead forty miles across yet only up to ten miles deep. Progress was slow. Von Rundstedt and Rommel reacted firmly and German troops fought with their customary stubbornness to contest every yard of territory. Everyone then waited for the great 'break-out', when American, British and Canadian divisions would launch offensives and explode from Normandy across France, into the Low Countries, then Germany itself. And they waited.

All this time, the human price continued to rise. In six weeks the Allies suffered almost 100,000 casualties in killed and wounded. One reason for these and for the slowness of the cam-

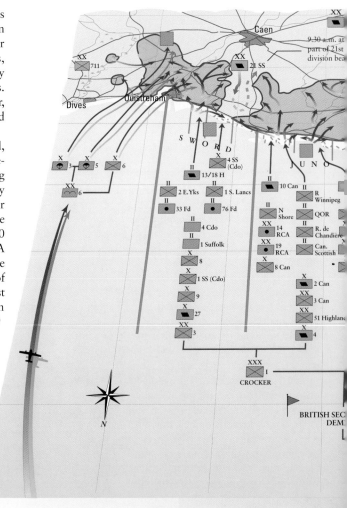

## D-DAY 6TH JUNE 1944

Preceded by the largest airborne operation the Allies had yet attempted, the amphibious landings were a complete success. Most of the German coast defences were smashed by naval and aerial bombardment. General Rommel's plan to counter-attack immediately was frustrated by Hitler and his fellow generals as much as Allied reaction. Only at Omaha beach was the issue ever in doubt, thanks to the recent arrival of a small division of German troops from the Russian front.

**1**

At midnight British airborne troops land around Ranville and seize vital bridges and establish flank defence

**2**

1.30 am: US airborne troops land in groups around the St Mère Eglise area

**3**

6.31 am: US 4th and 90th divisions land at Utah beach

**4**

6.36 am: US 1st and 29th divisions land but run into severe resistance and suffer high casualties

**5**

7.25 am: British 7th, 49th and 50th divisions land, pushing towards Bayeux

**6**

7.35: am British 51st and 3rd Canadian divisions land

**7**

7.45 am: British 3rd division lands and breaks through stiff resistance to meet with the 6th

paign was that hard battles were fought in *bocage* country. This terrain, with sunken lanes, steep earth banks, stone walls and thick hedgerows, was easy to defend with a small number of troops. Tanks and infantry advanced through it at heavy cost and the map of battle changed at an infuriating snail's pace.

Although the Americans captured the port of Cherbourg on 26 June, the great break-out did not come until 56 days after the first landings. While the bulk of the panzer divisions faced Montgomery's army in the east, US forces launched Operation 'Cobra' and swept out from Avranches. Some moved west into Brittany, while others turned east to trap the Germans who were being pushed back by British and Canadian forces near Falaise. This area, the Falaise Gap, then became one of the war's great killing-grounds. The

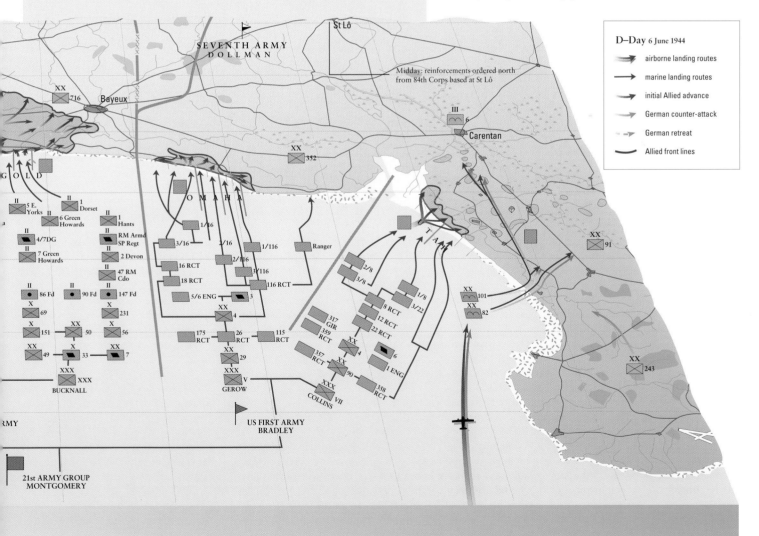

D–Day 6 June 1944

- airborne landing routes
- marine landing routes
- initial Allied advance
- German counter-attack
- German retreat
- Allied front lines

**ABOVE:** British 6-pounder anti-tank guns are towed into action during Operation Goodwood, one of the British offensives mounted in Normandy to draw in the German reserves. British casualties in these battles were so heavy they were losing more men per day than on the Somme or at Passchendaele in the First World War. To be a rifleman or junior officer in a frontline British infantry battalion in Normandy was one of the most dangerous jobs in the war.

Germans attempted counter-attacks and made frantic efforts in the early days of August to escape, but all to no avail. As well as pressure from Allied ground troops, fighters and medium bombers of the Tactical Air Force had a field day. By the end of the battle, the German Army B had been shattered. Some 50,000 prisoners were taken and 10,000 killed. Hundreds upon hundreds of lorries, cars, carts and tanks were smashed, so that only about 110 tanks and assault guns escaped to retreat to the river Seine.

Thus the great invasion and subsequent battle of Normandy were completed, with the German Army retreating eastwards in some disarray. American forces swept forward at panzer pace, especially General Patton's Third Army which aimed

towards Paris. The capital was taken on 25 August when General de Gaulle and French units entered the city, whose humiliating occupation had lasted just over four years. At the end of the month Patton's men reached Verdun and the battlefields of the First World War. Further north, British and Canadian units, under Montgomery, advanced along the Channel coast, while the American First Army took Amiens on 31 August.

Adding to the Germans' troubles, Operation 'Dragoon' opened on 15 August with landings by seven divisions of American and French troops on the south coast of France. Their greatest contribution to the general campaign was to tie up in Provence German divisions which were sorely needed in Normandy. Troops from the

southern invasion force linked up with the American Third Army at Dijon on 11 September. Now a complete Allied front faced Germany from the Channel coast to the Swiss frontier. All rolled forward.

Hitler was assailed on all sides. He barely survived an attempt on his life made by German plotters on 20 July. His forces appeared to be on the verge of collapse. On the Eastern Front, the great Russian offensive, Operation 'Bagration', inflicted 350,000 casualties on the *Wehrmacht*. In Normandy he lost a further 220,000, with thousands more in Italy. Between June and August 1944 the Germans lost 600,000 men at the very least. It appeared that the whole fabric of the Nazi state was bound to collapse within a short time.

them as supply bases to the Allied armies. Thus Le Havre, Boulogne, Calais and Dunkirk were not available. Even when Antwerp was taken on 4 September, the Germans still held fortifications on its approaches, so the port could not be used. This was crucial to the Allies' supply position. Most of the French railway system had been destroyed by bombing, so ammunition, food and fuel had to be transported by road. On reflection, Montgomery's failure to open Antwerp as a supply centre was a costly oversight. Ironically, he was facing problems similar to those which had dogged his old adversary Rommel just

Hesitation over policy shown by the Allies in September gave the Germans unexpected time to re-form and reorganise defences. A considerable contribution was made there by Field Marshal Model, who had to cobble together an army from the broken remains of forces which had been pushed out of France. As the Allied effort slackened in September and October, he gathered men and equipment for what would be a last-ditch stand. Older men and boys were drafted in, together with sailors, airmen and survivors of once triumphant formations. Although inferior in numbers and armour to the Allies, they gradually established defensive positions. In several ways the Allied drive went off the boil. Some servicemen were tired after long periods in the front line without relief. Others, having broken out of Normandy, believed that the war was virtually won. Often commanders, wanting their men to enjoy the forthcoming peace, were careful not to risk too many casualties.

During its retreat through France the German Army, on Hitler's specific orders, had left garrisons in sea ports along the North Sea coast, denying

**ABOVE:** An SS man taken prisoner by US troops. The SS fought with its customary ruthlessness in this campaign, still believing in final victory. Yet many of the SS men in Normandy were not hardcore Nazi volunteers, but conscripted men from all arms of the service, transferred to the SS at the stroke of a pen.

### OPERATION MARKET GARDEN

The Allied attempt to break into Germany and win the war before winter was one of the most optimistic operations of the war. It ended in failure and recrimination but at the time it was planned, the almost total collapse of German resistance suggested it could work. It certainly surprised the Germans who had never expected such an aggressive operation on the front commanded by the notoriously cautious General Montgomery.

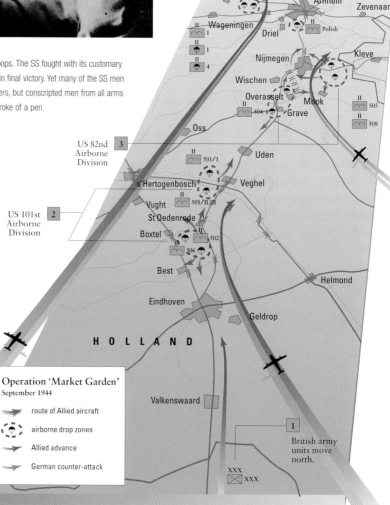

Operation 'Market Garden'
September 1944

➤ route of Allied aircraft
➤ airborne drop zones
➤ Allied advance
➤ German counter-attack

before El Alamein.

Another oversight came with his support of the airborne expedition to Arnhem. The episode is often remembered as one of the war's noble failures. The struggle against odds and the countless acts of heroism shown by paratroops of the 1st British Airborne Division are rightly honoured. So why were they there? Montgomery intended to use two American and one British paratroop division of the First Allied Airborne Army to seize bridges at river crossings which lay ahead of his advance. Operation 'Market Garden' was to open the way into the Ruhr and the north German plain, while outflanking defences along the Rhine. American airborne forces, after hard fighting, took bridges near Eindhoven and Nijmegen. The British, however, were dropped further on at Arnhem and quickly found that their target was 'a bridge too far'. Poor intelligence led to their landing too far from the target in an area where panzer troops were re-grouping. After several days of bitter fighting, in a zone

the Germans called 'The Cauldron' the superiority of panzer equipment led to the failure of the British attempt. Units of Montgomery's main army which had intended to push forward and link up with the airborne troops were unable to do so.

In mid-December came a totally unexpected counter-blow to the Allies which for a short period forced them on to the back foot. On 12 December several German generals were summoned to Hitler's headquarters and learned that he intended to launch a surprise offensive in the West. To sit back defensively, the *Führer* reckoned, would bring inevitable defeat. 'It is essential to deprive the enemy of his belief that victory is certain,' he told them. 'Wars are finally decided by one side or the other recognising that they cannot be won.' He hoped that the Allied coalition, composed of nations with totally different backgrounds and ambitions, would disintegrate.

His aim, resurrecting memories of 1940, was to drive forward through the Ardennes with panzers, which

would then swing towards Antwerp. In his reckoning, the loss of that port would lead to a second Dunkirk, with a rapid evacuation of the Allies from mainland Europe. Afterwards he would turn his attentions to the Eastern Front and deal with the growing Russian menace there. It would be an understatement to say that his generals were surprised at the news, but orders were to be obeyed.

Two powerful armies had been gathered and re-equipped for the offensive and included nine panzer divisions. A cloak of bad weather covered them, preventing Allied air assaults and helping their secret movements. The blow fell on 15 December on four American divisions holding a front of some 90 miles and had rapid initial success. Soon a bulge appeared in the Allied line, with a consequent 'Battle of the Bulge', as mainly American, then British, troops fought to stem the attack. By Christmas Day the offensive had lost momentum. For the Germans there were shortages of fuel and, as the weather improved, increased interven-

BELOW: A German assault gun still smoulders as the Allied advance continues. Allied airpower forced the Germans to move their vehicles under cover of darkness. Any major move in daylight was punished by air attack against which the tanks had little defence.

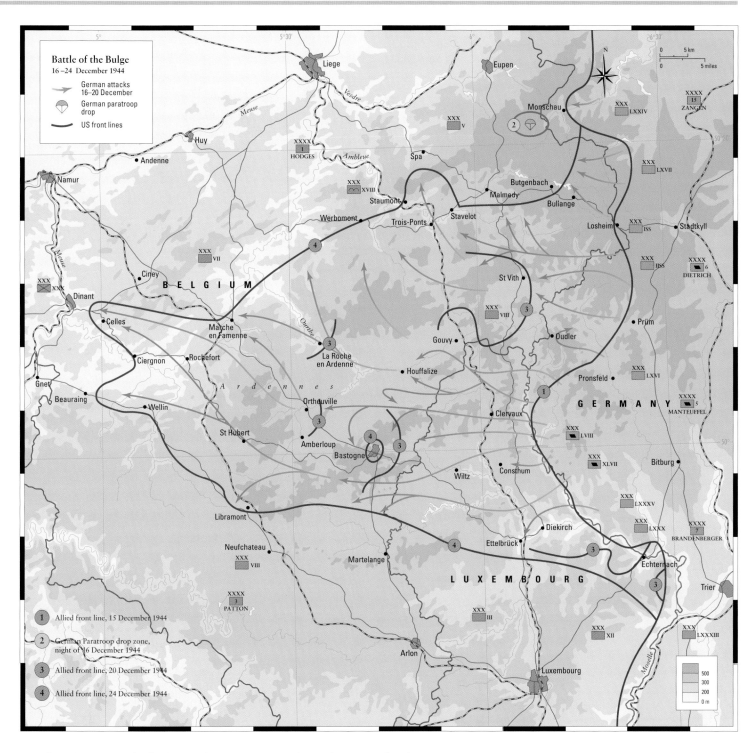

**Battle of the Bulge**
16–24 December 1944

→ German attacks
16–20 December

German paratroop
drop

US front lines

1 Allied front line, 15 December 1944

2 German Paratroop drop zone,
night of 16 December 1944

3 Allied front line, 20 December 1944

4 Allied front line, 24 December 1944

tion from hundreds of Allied aircraft. The panzers were slowly forced to retreat and by 16 January 1945 were back at their starting line.

The unexpectedness of the offensive shattered any complacency on the Allied side. There was still far to go. The cost to the Americans was 19,000 dead and 15,000 men taken prisoner, but the Germans had sustained 100,000 total casualties, as well as losing 800 tanks and 1,000 aircraft. 'It spelt bankruptcy, because we could not afford such losses,' stated General von Manteuffel. As the pincers closed on Germany from east and west, total defeat was in the offing. For Hitler, nevertheless, there would be no capitulation. 'Never! Never!' he told his generals.

### THE BATTLE OF THE BULGE

Hitler's quixotic decision to launch a full-scale counter-offensive in the west in December 1944 played into Allied hands. Although, against all the odds, the attack achieved some initial success, the idea the panzers could break through to the Channel was no more than a fantasy. German commanders knew they would be lucky to reach the river Meuse. When the skies cleared at the end of December, and Allied airpower could intervene again, the game was up. The battle cost the German army its last armoured reserve and hastened the end of the war.

# CHAPTER 8: Bombs and Torpedoes

RIGHT: The Handley-Page Halifax was one of the main four-engined heavy bombers used by RAF Bomber Command in its campaign against German industry. Although British pre-war strategy had made much of the threat of strategic bombing, the outbreak of war caught the British with no real capacity for such a campaign. However, proper heavy bombers like the Halifax and Lancaster were already under development.

BELOW: Bombing-up a Vickers Wellington, the best of the heavy bombers available to the RAF at the beginning of the war. Wellingtons made daylight raids on German ports in 1939 but suffered prohibitive losses to enemy fighters. The RAF concluded that it would have to attack under cover of darkness.

A nation's geography plays a large part in determining its history. This goes some way towards explaining the nature of the aerial campaign which Britain waged, first through the Royal Air Force, then in conjunction with the Americans, against Nazi Germany. Traditionally, Germany was a mighty land power, while Britain had great naval strength. After the collapse of France in 1940 the Wehrmacht was unable to reach the United Kingdom and the Royal Navy could do little to attack the Reich. The common element for both was the sky. Therefore the Germans aimed first for aerial superiority through the Battle of Britain and the Night Blitz. Both campaigns failed. In response, Bomber Command opened a nocturnal aerial battle against Germany which, although comparatively small and ineffective at the start, grew in intensity from 1942. As Churchill wrote in July 1940, Britain's prime hope was 'an absolutely devastating, exterminating attack by very heavy bombers from this country upon the Nazi homeland'.

This night campaign was later complemented by daylight bombing from the United States Army Air Forces after the Americans joined the war. Working together, the two air arms increased the power of their bombing until a crescendo was reached in the early months of 1945. By then no target in Germany was out of reach, as they enjoyed aerial domination, bombing where, when and how they chose.

This position was achieved slowly. In June 1941 Churchill had promised retribution from the air. 'We shall bomb Germany by day as well as by night in ever increasing measure,' he said. This would make 'the German people taste and gulp each month a sharper dose of the miseries they have showered upon mankind'. Few British people, particularly those who had suffered from the Night Blitz, would have disagreed with these sentiments. However, for the first two years of the war Bomber Command experienced several constraints and weaknesses. Its heaviest bombers, Wellingtons, Whitleys and Hampdens, were not large enough for waging a strategic bombing offensive. To escape the attention of fighters, they had to fly at night. Because of poor navigation aids,

they had the greatest difficulty in finding any particular town, let alone a target. Often aircrew believed in all sincerity that they were reaching, identifying and hitting a selected installation, but their inaccuracy was shown in August 1941. A report based on photographs taken at the time of bombing reached some sad conclusions. For example, only one in three aircraft had got within five miles of the target claimed to have been bombed. Over French ports the proportion was two in three, over the Ruhr one in ten. Efforts were therefore made to provide navigation aids to lead bombers directly to their destination.

By late 1941, however, the results achieved were so poor that suggestions were made of abandoning any idea of using Bomber Command in a major campaign to hit limited targets. The alternative was to hit larger areas. At a time in the war when Britain was having little success in overseas campaigns, this policy was chosen as the best – even sole – method of hitting back at Germany. Here was the birth of 'area bombing', a policy that the RAF maintained until the end of the war.

In February 1942 came a sea-change for Bomber Command, when Sir Arthur Harris was appointed Commander-in-Chief. Harris was single-minded in his approach to the task, from which he never deviated. He believed that his Command would have the power, if developed in sufficient numbers, to end the war by its own efforts. Hitler could be defeated by 4,000 heavy bombers. His force would put into practice the heavy

bombing of enemy targets which had been advocated since pre-war days, destroying both industrial capacity and civilian morale. 'There are people who say that bombing can never win a war,' he announced. 'My answer to this is that it's never been tried. We shall see.'

During 1942, as Harris started to expand operations, Bomber Command's hitting power grew. First, the 'Gee' system of navigation was introduced, enabling aircrew to calculate the position of their aircraft after receiving signals from ground stations. The *Luftwaffe* had made good use of radio beams for guiding aircraft during the Night Blitz, and 'Gee' was intended to aid British bombers over Germany. There were weaknesses, but here was a step forward.

In addition, the new generation of RAF bombers began to arrive in larger numbers. The Halifax, Stirling and Manchester (the forerunner of the Lancaster), all carrying heavy bomb loads, were employed increasingly. Several lessons learned from methods adopted by the *Luftwaffe* against British cities were practised. Targets were marked with flares, followed by showers of incendiaries to cause large fires before the bulk of high explosives were dropped. On the night of 30 May 1942 Harris gathered almost every aircraft in his Command, including reserves and training planes, to attack Cologne. For the first time in the war, Bomber Command launched a 'Thousand-Bomber Raid'. Apart from widespread damage caused in the city, this was a fine propaganda *coup* and uplifting for the British people in dark days. Later evidence showed that the raid was not as successful as at first claimed, but at the time it had a positive effect for the RAF. After the raid, Harris pointed out another disadvantage for the enemy. Even at the worst, such attacks would 'force him to withdraw vast forces from his exterior aggression for his own protection'.

For the Germans, 1943 was a bad year. The rising power of the RAF and USAAF to strike with bombers led to massive destruction across Hitler's Reich. Some critics of the Allies' bombing policy have pointed out that, in spite of this aerial onslaught, day and night, German armaments production, under the shrewd leadership of Albert

Speer, actually increased. The fact is that, without the Allies' intensive air attacks, it would have expanded far more; and, in the long run, German production paled into insignificance when set beside that of the United States and Great Britain, let alone that of the USSR. For example, during 1943 the Germans built almost 4,800 bombers and unloaded 2,300 tons of bombs over the United Kingdom; in the same period the US and Britain produced 38,000 bombers and dropped over 225,000 tons of bombs on

European targets, mainly in Germany.

Between March and July 1943 Bomber Command launched the 'Battle of the Ruhr'. Various factors were improving matters for aircrew. Two new aids, 'Oboe' and H2S, were coming into operation, bringing more accurate navigation. A Pathfinder force of Mosquito light bombers was formed to mark targets with coloured flares before the arrival of the main attacking force. Larger numbers of bombers were available as production rose, together with a good supply of

**ABOVE:** British bomber crews had to complete two tours of combat operations. By 1942 the chance of an individual surviving his first tour was only 44 per cent; the chance of surviving both tours, just 2 per cent. Over 50,000 aircrew would die in the British bomber offensive.

# Bombs and Torpedoes

RIGHT: Group Captain Leonard Cheshire VC (centre front) pioneered pinpoint techniques that enabled the RAF to bomb with greater accuracy by night than American bombers could achieve by daylight. US crews, trained in clear Texan skies, often found their targets over Germany obscured by cloud rendering their bombsights useless.

BELOW: With its army driven out of Europe and only able to take on the relatively tiny German units deployed to North Africa, the airmen of RAF Bomber Command were the only force available to the British that could take the war to the enemy.

aircrew, many of whom had trained overseas, especially in Canada.

Over a period of four months, 43 major raids were launched on Germany, about half of them on targets in the Ruhr, the largest industrial area. In this time Essen was raided five times and Cologne four; other towns hit included Aachen, Dortmund and Duisberg. In particular, 'the vast Krupps works, covering several hun-dred acres, had suffered heavy damage to thirteen buildings, with hits on no fewer than fifty-three workshops'.

Goebbels, the propaganda minister, visited Essen afterwards, seeing the damage which was 'colossal and, indeed, ghastly'. The estimate was that it would take twelve years to repair the destruction. Ominously, he added the belief 'that the English could lay a large part of the Reich in ruins, if they go about it the right way'. That, of course, was Bomber Command's aim.

All of this was achieved at a high cost. In those four months, from 18,500 sorties flown, 872 aircraft failed to return and over 2,000 were damaged. German flak could be very accurate over the target and accounted for most of the damaged aeroplanes. More effective in defence were night fighters, which shot down most. The Ju 88, a versatile aircraft, was devel-oped as a night fighter. Carrying its own radar, it could outpace and out-shoot bombers in darkness.

Between April and October 1943, the US Eighth Air Force – 'The Mighty Eighth' – stationed in the United Kingdom began to carry the attack to the enemy, with an offensive launched in concert with Bomber Command. The two air forces had a crucial differ-ence of approach. Bomber Command had learned the lesson that daylight raids for them were too expensive. The Americans, however, had developed their aircraft and techniques specifical-ly for daytime operations. They believed that the B-17 Flying Fortress and B-24 Liberator, carrying a heavy armament of 0.5in machine guns and flying in defensive formations, would be able to meet the challenge of German fighters. In the conditions of 1943 they were wrong. During a raid on Bremen in April, of the 115 American bombers used, 60 were either destroyed or damaged. When Berlin was chosen for a raid in July, 22 bombers were destroyed from the 120 employed. The Americans believed that in daylight they could pinpoint targets and, with good bomb sights, eliminate them without the need for area bombing. Nemesis arrived on 14 October when 291 B-17s raided a ball-bearing works at Schweinfurt. German fighters intercepted them in droves, shooting down 60 of the giant bombers and damaging 138. Such losses could not be sustained.

A main cause of these disasters was a lack of fighter protection. Existing US fighters could cover the bombers for only part of the mission, lacking the range to go the whole way. American air leaders rapidly realised that they must defeat the opposition by attacking German aircraft factories and by introducing a long-range fight-er of their own. One was quickly ready. This was the P-51 Mustang, in some ways the most remarkable fight-er of the war. The aeroplane was American, fitted with a British Merlin engine and carrying extra fuel tanks which eventually provided a range of 1,500 miles. Increasingly, from the end of 1943, Mustangs escorted bombers to and from their targets and had the capability to take on any *Luftwaffe* fighter. The American policy of chal-lenging German fighters and of bomb-ing the factories producing them helped Bomber Command. The RAF

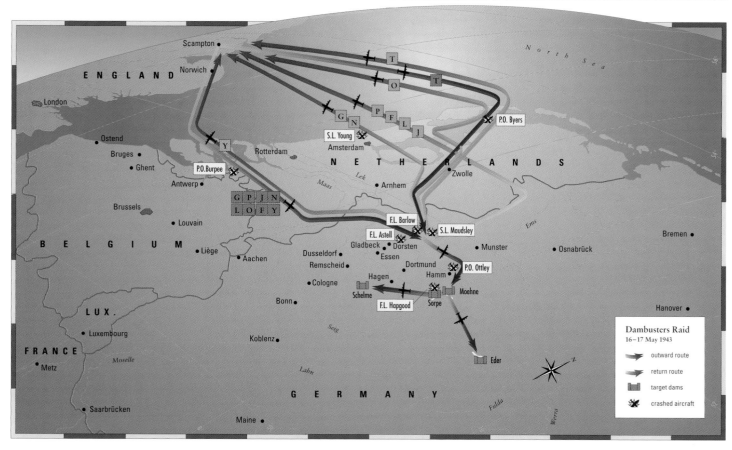

Dambusters Raid
16–17 May 1943

→ outward route

→ return route

target dams

crashed aircraft

still had to confront a formidable and well-organised German defence force of night fighters, which took a heavy toll. Without American efforts, the numbers would have been greater.

At the end of July 1943, over a period of ten days, Bomber Command launched the 'Battle of Hamburg' against Germany's second city and most important port. In four great raids, code-named Operation 'Gomorrah', extensive damage was caused and some 40,000 people were killed. As part of the enterprise, US bombers also raided Hamburg twice in daylight, adding to the destruction.

'Bomber' Harris had seen the effects of the Night Blitz on people and buildings in London three years earlier and appreciated the psychological results of attacking an enemy's capital city. With his stated aim of using the power of area bombing to break both fabric and morale, he launched a new aerial offensive from November 1943. The main target was Berlin, although some other cities were included on the calling list. For four months the Battle of Berlin raged at night, with sixteen major raids. 'We can wreck Berlin

from end to end, if the USAF will come in on it,' Harris told Churchill. 'It will cost between 400–500 aircraft. It will cost Germany the war.'

Berlin, the administrative centre of Nazism, was a city of three million people and contained a number of war industries. In the early stages of the war, as German success blossomed, few bombs fell there and the population generally enjoyed an untroubled

### THE 'DAMBUSTERS' RAID

The 'Dambusters' Raid carried out by specially modified Lancasters in May 1943 was the most famous bombing mission of the war. Using Barnes-Wallace's 'bouncing bomb' they attacked dams that provided power to the German factories in the Ruhr. Two dams were breached and a temporary loss of power affected, but the casualties were heavy. Guy Gibson was awarded the VC for his extraordinary courage and skill in pressing home this attack. RAF reconnaissance aircraft took photographs of the shattered the dams the next day, which were released to newspapers as spectacular evidence of the RAF's ability to strike back at Germany. Tragically, Gibson managed to wangle his way back on to operations in 1944 and was killed over Holland.

**LEFT:** The Dambusters' handiwork: the raid was not followed up with attacks on the repair parties and the dams were eventually restored to working order. The Dambusters (617 Squadron) went on to specialise in attacks on pinpoint targets with specialist weapons including super-heavy bombs.

**ABOVE:** The US Army Eighth Air Force deployed to England in 1942 and stuck to its pre-war commitment to daylight bombing. By 1944 hundreds of brightly coloured bombers were in action over Germany, escorted by long range fighters that wore away the *Luftwaffe*. Most of these B-17s lack the olive green paint scheme of earlier aircraft: simply polishing the aluminium saved weight, adding vital speed.

**RIGHT:** Aircrew being briefed before an attack. Attacks could not be made in formation like the US aircraft attacking by day, but the timing of each 'wave' over the target and the choice of route was critical. The intention was to avoid concentrations of enemy anti-aircraft guns and complex deception schemes were developed to decoy the night-fighters away from the bomber stream.

lifestyle. The vicissitudes experienced in Warsaw and Rotterdam, London and Plymouth, and Belgrade and Leningrad were unknown in Germany's capital. Harris intended to redress the balance. A difficulty for his airmen, however, was the distance of Berlin from Britain's airfields: the round trip for a bomber crew was 1,150 miles. Nevertheless, his crews took the strain of difficult missions. In four months over 9,000 sorties were launched against the German capital, causing heavy damage and many casualties. More than 6,000 Berliners died.

The cost to Bomber Command was immense. Nearly 600 aircraft, most of them Lancasters, were lost to night defences. The long and hazardous flight gave the Germans opportunities to counter with anti-aircraft fire and, more particularly, with night fighters. These were fed into the bomber stream and a deadly cat-and-mouse game ensued, with bombers the victims of a sophisticated radar war. Here was a slogging match with no quarter given. By March 1944 Bomber Command had been badly battered, with unacceptably high losses. 'The Battle of Berlin was more than a failure,' was the judgement of the Official History. 'It was a defeat.' The worst night came on 30 March. Of 795 bombers

despatched to attack Nuremberg, one of the cradles of Nazism, 94 were shot down – the Command's greatest loss in any wartime operation.

From March until December 1944 the strength of the USAAF grew and was increasingly employed in daylight raids over Occupied Europe and Germany. Under the leadership of Albert Speer, many German industries had been dispersed across the nation, especially to the south. In spite of the bombing offensive, production of all weapons actually increased by 250 per cent in two years starting in January 1943. And yet, by 1944, there was 25 per cent absenteeism overall in German factories. Without that, output would have been even higher. However, oil supplies and aircraft factories were less easy to relocate and American bombers concentrated on these, with their policy of picking specific targets. By September 1944 German oil production slumped dramatically and the *Luftwaffe* in particular was affected by fuel shortages. Gradually, the *Luftwaffe* was being ground down in aerial combat, overwhelmed by superior numbers and lack of fuel, equipment and aircrew.

Some relief for Bomber Command came in April and May 1944. Before the opening of Operation 'Overlord', the Command was asked to change the main attack from area bombing to hitting particular targets, especially the transport system leading to northern France. The new policy angered Harris, who maintained his faith in assaulting cities in the German homeland; for him, other requirements were only 'panacea targets'. By June 1944, nevertheless, his Command dropped 65,000 tons of bombs on the transport system, especially in France. Subsequently, after the invasion opened, the *Wehrmacht* had great difficulty in moving men and supplies for ground action. By the end of 1944 Bomber Command had an immense force of 1,500 aircraft and, with the decline of the German fighter arm, these were able to operate safely in daylight for the first time in the war.

At the opening of the Second Front in June, the Allied air forces had overwhelming control of the air in the battle zone and beyond. On the first day of the landings, the *Luftwaffe* in

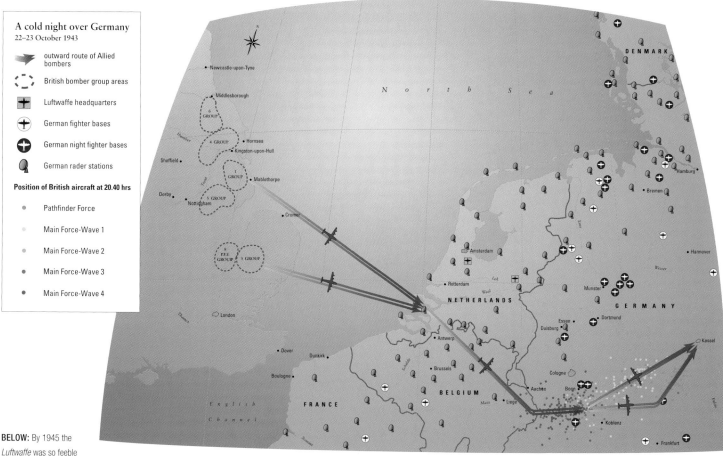

**A cold night over Germany**
22–23 October 1943

- outward route of Allied bombers
- British bomber group areas
- Luftwaffe headquarters
- German fighter bases
- German night fighter bases
- German rader stations

**Position of British aircraft at 20.40 hrs**

- Pathfinder Force
- Main Force-Wave 1
- Main Force-Wave 2
- Main Force-Wave 3
- Main Force-Wave 4

**BELOW:** By 1945 the *Luftwaffe* was so feeble that British heavy bombers were employed in daytime raids on certain targets, especially the ports still holding out after the advance of Allied ground troops had cut them off from German-held territory.

France had only 300 aircraft to oppose a force of nearly 13,000. Without support from the air, Allied ground forces could never have established bridgeheads and made their later advances.

Within a few months, by dint of massive production of aircraft and through the resourcefulness and brav-

ery of their aircrews, Allied aircraft had seized the initiative in the skies. The Americans, their aircraft escorted by Mustangs and Thunderbolts, could choose targets at will. Their daylight bombing, especially of oil targets, dramatically affected the economics of the German war machine. RAF Bomber

**A COLD NIGHT OVER GERMANY**

A typical Bomber Command raid on Germany's industrial power base in the Ruhr. The Pathfinder Force located and marked the target for the following waves of bombers. By late 1943 the bomb loads began with high explosive to blow off roofs then followed with incendiaries to start fires. The development of new explosives in 1944 vastly increased the destructive power of late-war air raids.

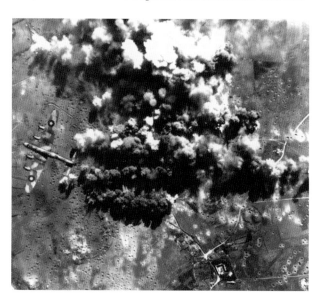

**RIGHT:** RAF heavy bombers over a burning German city. Germany began the war with what Air Marshal Harris called the 'naive view that they would bomb everyone else while no-one would bomb them'. As he declared at the time: 'they have sown the wind; now they shall reap the whirlwind'.

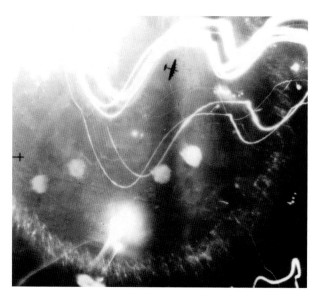

ABOVE: The glare from fires, searchlights and exploding anti-aircraft shells lit up the sky above the target cities. This was often the only time RAF aircrew saw other aircraft during their lonely missions, all too often watching the demise of one of their own.

Command, carrying a heavier weight of bombs, had prepared the way for this superiority through area bombing. Although achieved at great cost, the destruction wrought across Germany affected Hitler's ability to stay in the war. At the end of 1944 the Allies were poised for a final push under the protection of an overwhelmingly powerful air umbrella.

In assessing the value of the double-pronged Allied policy of 'round-the-clock' bombing, several critics have been scathing of area attacks. Sir Arthur Harris is often depicted as a wicked ogre, given to destruction for

its own sake. Such judgements are unjust and inaccurate. Harris was implementing national policy and, as the victims of Nazi aggression found, civilians are not exempt from disaster in war. 'It is often argued,' reckoned an eminent aviation historian, 'that the Allies could have executed the bombing offensive more effectively, but these are judgements from hindsight.' He added that historians have to deal with 'actual effects' rather than 'possible effects as armchair strategists'. One air historian who served in the campaign wrote that bombing was not wanton or indiscriminate. It was

an organised plan to break German military power, which, he added, nothing else appeared able to stop. The question must be viewed through the eyes of the time, when there were few critics. And of those who objected, none could offer a viable and practical alternative. Most people in the Allied and occupied countries viewed the campaign as bringing home to an evil regime some of the miseries it had inflicted on others.

No alternative policy would have caused the Germans to divert to defence resources which otherwise would have been used in land warfare, especially on the Eastern Front. A German historian offers the opinion

RIGHT: By 1945 almost every major German city had been pulverised from the air. The German economy had come to a standstill and rail communications had all but broken down.

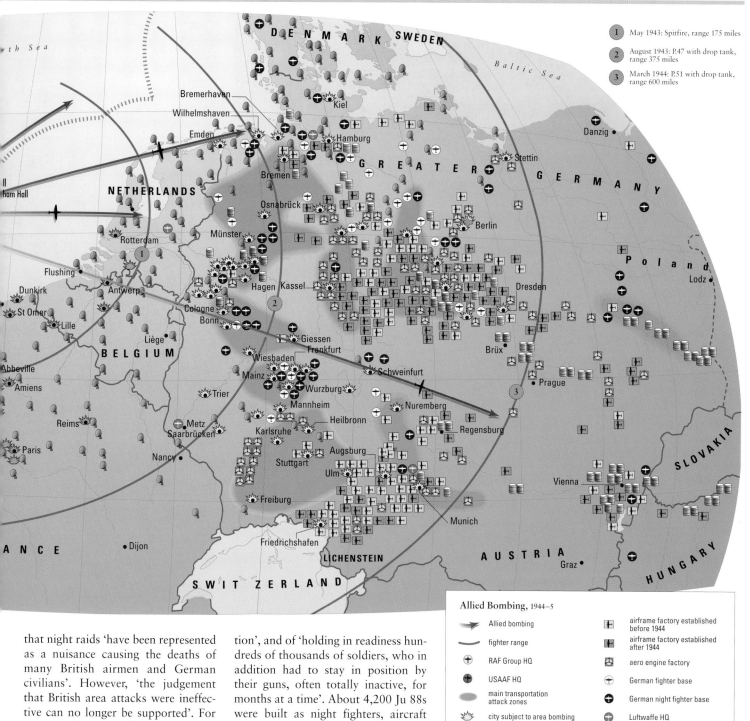

1 May 1943: Spitfire, range 175 miles

2 August 1943: P.47 with drop tank, range 375 miles

3 March 1944: P.51 with drop tank, range 600 miles

**Allied Bombing, 1944–5**

| | |
|---|---|
| ➤ Allied bombing | ⊞ airframe factory established before 1944 |
| ⌣ fighter range | ⊞ airframe factory established after 1944 |
| ⊕ RAF Group HQ | aero engine factory |
| ✚ USAAF HQ | ⊕ German fighter base |
| main transportation attack zones | ⊖ German night fighter base |
| ✺ city subject to area bombing | ⊖ Luftwaffe HQ |
| ✺ USAAF target outside Germany | German radar station |
| oil targets attacked by Bomber Command | limit of German radar |
| oil targets attacked by USAAF | neutral territories |

**ALLIED BOMBING, 1944-5**

This map shows the main bases and targets of the American strategic bombing campaign against Germany. The increasing range of successive fighter aircraft was the critical factor: the P-51 Mustang was equal to or better than any German interceptor yet had the range to escort bombers to Berlin and back. The German air force tore itself to pieces in battles with the P-51s and was no longer able to intervene in force by the end of 1944.

that night raids 'have been represented as a nuisance causing the deaths of many British airmen and German civilians'. However, 'the judgement that British area attacks were ineffective can no longer be supported'. For example, during the bomber offensive of 1943–44, over a million men were employed in anti-aircraft defence. Add to those the numbers and effort required to build shelters, clear debris and run the complete civil defence services, then the pressure exerted by area bombing becomes more apparent. Speer himself later wrote of the requirement to produce 'thousands of anti-aircraft guns, the stockpiling of tremendous quantities of ammuni-

tion', and of 'holding in readiness hundreds of thousands of soldiers, who in addition had to stay in position by their guns, often totally inactive, for months at a time'. About 4,200 Ju 88s were built as night fighters, aircraft which could have altered the balance of air power if used elsewhere. Thousands of anti-aircraft guns, especially the 88mm, were built for home defence instead of for stopping tanks on the Eastern Front. The Russians benefited far more from the Allied air offensive than ever they have been prepared to acknowledge. 'It made every square metre of Germany a front,' Speer wrote years later. 'It was our greatest lost battle of the war.'

# The Germans Hit Back

ABOVE: German anti-aircraft fire was lethal to the end as all the *Luftwaffe*'s 'flak' was concentrated in the German heartland by late 1944. Here a B-24 Liberator takes its final plunge after being struck by anti-aircraft fire over the German coast.

Considering the awesome power of the *Luftwaffe* in the early stages of the war, it seems remarkable that so few raids against Britain were launched after the main Night Blitz ended in May 1941. Demands on the German Air Force were so widespread, from the deserts of North Africa to the Russian steppes, that large numbers of aircraft were never again gathered for an onslaught against the United Kingdom. In fact – and this a barely credible figure for those who recalled that some 40,000 civilians were killed during the Night Blitz – in the whole of the year 1942 only 27 civilians died from enemy action in London.

The main German air operations against Britain in 1942 are generally remembered as the 'Baedeker Raids'. On 28 March, Bomber Command hit Lübeck, an ancient town on the Baltic coast. Great damage, especially from fire, was caused to both historic and industrial sites. A month later another port, Rostock, was attacked, and once again both historic and industrial targets suffered. Hitler, never a man to turn the other cheek, was livid. 'He shares my opinion absolutely,' wrote Goebbels, 'that cultural centres, health resorts and civilian centres must be attacked now.'

And so they were. The places chosen were those listed in the famous Baedeker guide book as containing buildings and monuments of historic and cultural importance. Most had few anti-aircraft defences. German bombers were despatched on moonlit nights, flying at low level, to hit them in short, concentrated assaults. Exeter, Bath, York, Norwich and Canterbury all suffered in raids stretching from April to June. Altogether, over 1,600 civilians were killed and 1,700 seriously hurt, reminding British people that the *Luftwaffe* could still reach them.

By 1943 the Germans had made progress in the development of two novel forms of aerial propulsion, jets and rockets. Experiments had been conducted on both at Peenemünde, a scientific research centre on the Baltic coast. After many trials, technologists there produced two pilotless weapons for bombarding an enemy. To the Germans these were 'revenge weapons' for the damage which the Allied air offensive was spreading across the Reich.

The first was the V1, a small, pilotless flying bomb, powered by a pulse-jet engine. The 'doodlebug', or 'buzz-bomb' could be fired from a ground ramp, or launched from an aircraft. It flew at speeds of up to 420mph until the fuel cut out at a pre-set distance of up to 250 miles, when the bomb fell to earth. Each V1 carried a ton of explosive which detonated with a wide field of blast. From 13 June 1944 until 1 March 1945 about 10,000 flying bombs were launched, mainly against southern England, and about three-quarters of them crossed the coast. More than 6,000 civilians were killed, mostly in London. As antidotes to the threat, the defences used fighters, balloons and, most effectively, anti-aircraft guns. However, the worst of the danger remained until September, when German land forces were pushed back from launching sites on the north French coast.

The second 'secret weapon' was the V2 rocket. Once again, the Germans were pioneers of rocket development, and at Peenemünde on 3 October 1942 the Space Age began. A test rocket was successfully fired, reaching a height of 50 miles before landing 120 miles away. At Hitler's urgent order the design was rapidly developed as the A4 rocket, a monster 46ft in length, weighing thirteen tons and carrying a ton of explosive at a final speed of 3,400mph. As part of the revenge offensive, the first one was fired from Holland on 8 September 1944. It hit Chiswick in London. The last V2 landed on the capital as late in the war as 27 March 1945. As the Germans retreated in Western Europe,

they also fired many at targets in Belgium. Altogether, 1,115 rockets hit Britain, the peak of the offensive being reached in January 1945 when 60 landed in the first week. In total, over 2,700 civilians were killed.

Both devices were potentially devastating and appealed to Hitler, who tended to think of air power as a terror weapon. They had different effects on public morale. The V1 could be seen and heard. For some people that was an advantage. 'If I'm going to be killed,' one lady remarked, 'I would like to have the excitement of knowing it's going to happen.' No one knew of the V2's approach until an explosion announced its arrival. Others preferred it that way. The blessing for all

was that the end of the war was near and the ordeal would not last. 'If we had had these rockets in 1939,' Hitler told one of his scientists, 'we should never have had this war.' That, of course, is hypothesis. Nonetheless, it is interesting to speculate how Allied governments would have reacted if Hitler had been able to open the revenge bombardment a year earlier.

Meanwhile, at the end of 1944 German civilians were preparing themselves to receive a final Allied onslaught from the air, as well as a land invasion. Despite using revenge weapons against Britain, Hitler's Nazi regime could do little to defend them from aerial attacks either by day or night.

**ABOVE:** Germany retaliated against the Allied bombing campaign by pioneering the use of ballistic missiles. The V1 'flying bomb' proved a cost-effective if misapplied weapon, but the V2 rocket was counter-productive, costing Germany far more to build than the damage it inflicted on the Allies. This section of a V2's powerplant was found on wasteground in London after a rocket strike in 1944.

# Torpedoes and Depth Charges

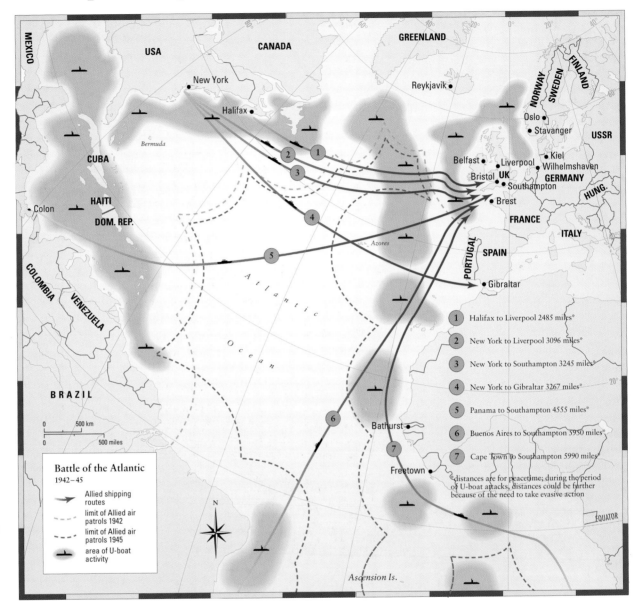

**Battle of the Atlantic**
1942–45

→ Allied shipping routes
······ limit of Allied air patrols 1942
------ limit of Allied air patrols 1945
◣ area of U-boat activity

1. Halifax to Liverpool 2485 miles*
2. New York to Liverpool 3096 miles*
3. New York to Southampton 3245 miles*
4. New York to Gibraltar 3267 miles*
5. Panama to Southampton 4555 miles*
6. Buenos Aires to Southampton 5950 miles*
7. Cape Town to Southampton 5990 miles*

*distances are for peacetime; during the period of U-boat attacks, distances could be further because of the need to take evasive action

In air battles over Germany, the bomb was the supreme Allied weapon; in the war at sea, fought between Allied and German vessels, there were two, the torpedo and the depth charge. The Allies were frequently concerned by the threat from enemy surface vessels, ranging from armed merchantmen to the mighty *Bismarck*. They were apprehensive over the damage suffered by shipping from Focke-Wulf Condor bombers. But their greatest fear was of the depredations caused by submarines, the *Kriegsmarine*'s U-boats.

The U-boat was the main weapon used between 1939 and 1945 to intercept Allied sea trade and cripple Britain's import of supplies. 'The German Navy will conduct mercantile warfare,' the German High Command announced in September 1939, 'having England as its principal target.' In the course of the next year Admiral Dönitz, Commander-in-Chief of the submarine arm, said, 'I will show that the U-boat alone can win the war,' then added that 'nothing is impossible to us'. Such a claim is reminiscent of 'Bomber' Harris's conviction that Bomber Command by itself could defeat Germany. The importance of sea trade to the United Kingdom was appreciated by Churchill: he wrote that 'dominating all our power to carry on the war, or even to keep our-

selves alive, lay our mastery of the ocean routes and the free approach and entry to our ports'.

Nowhere was this mastery required more than on the North Atlantic Ocean. 'The severance of our Atlantic supply lines,' claimed an official pamphlet, 'would have brought us to our knees through the eventual starvation of our war industries and population.' Without supplies of food, war materials and armaments, especially from the United States, as well as the safe transport of hundreds of thousands of service personnel, the Allied war effort would have ground to a halt. Successful campaigns in the Western Desert and Tunisia, the invasion of

Italy, the bombing of Germany and the D-Day landings would have been no more than pipe-dreams. Consequently, the battle to defeat the U-boats became one of the longest-lasting and hardest-fought of the whole war.

What were the features of U-boats which caused such damage and trepidation to a maritime nation for six years? During the crucial period, from 1942 to 1944, there were two main types of submarine operating. The first was the Type VII, with a displacement of about 760 tons. The boat, which was the mainstay of the German Navy, was over 200ft in length and could make a speed of 17kts on the surface, but less than half of that when submerged. At cruising speed, the submarine could travel over some 8,000 nautical miles. In action the official diving depth for vessels with reinforced hulls was 800ft, but in emergencies boats sometimes went deeper. The deadly striking power in war came from five torpedo tubes, which fired the twelve to fourteen torpedoes carried. Mounted on the hull for dealing with enemy ships was an 88mm gun, while anti-aircraft guns were installed on a platform by the conning tower. The crew usually numbered about 44.

On board, living conditions were cramped and unpleasant. The boats were no more than metal tubes packed with men, machinery and explosive weapons. There was barely space to stand upright among the clutter of packed cases, hams and sausages, cans and boxes of food, water and ammunition. The air was dank and foul, with the constant smell of fuel and sweat. Bodies and clothes remained unwashed and there was only one lavatory. In these conditions men lived for weeks on end – and died.

Most U-boat bases were situated on the west coast of Occupied France, facing towards the Atlantic – at Lorient, La Pallice, St Nazaire, Brest and Bordeaux. Others were in Norway and Germany. To protect the installations, giant concrete bunkers were erected by the Todt labour organisation, often with slave workers. Many bunkers had reinforced roofs more than 15ft thick. In general they resisted the penetrative power of bombs dropped by the Allied air forces and provided a safe haven for U-boats

**ABOVE AND LEFT:** To protect them from British bombers, the Germans built enormous concrete shelters in their bases along the French channel coast. Most are still there and the submarine pens at St Nazaire are now open to the public as a museum.

**RIGHT:** *Kapitanleutnant* Bigalk returns in triumph after sinking the British carrier *Audacity* during a convoy battle in December 1941. Awarded the *Ritterkreuz*, he was killed in July 1942 when the *U-751* was sunk with all hands by British aircraft while on a mission to lay mines off Charleston, South Carolina.

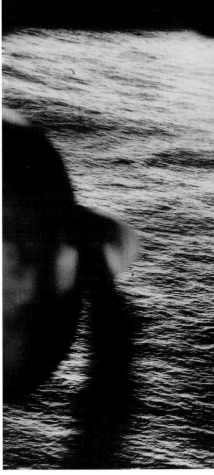

**ABOVE:** The Focke-Wulf Condor provided long range maritime reconnaissance over the Atlantic, locating convoys and vectoring in the U-boats. Sometimes they bombed and strafed merchantships themselves. Fortunately for the Allies there were only a handful of them available at any one time and the growth of Allied airpower drove them from the skies.

to be repaired, refitted and rearmed.

Behind the whole U-boat campaign lay the fertile mind and driving energy of 'Uncle Karl' Dönitz, who moved his headquarters forward to Lorient, close to his crews. From there he maintained constant radio contact with his captains in the campaign. Dönitz had a personal interest in his men, reading their reports and listening to suggestions for improving vessels and the effectiveness of tactics. For example, he helped to evolve the 'wolf pack', where a number of U-boats worked together against a convoy. The German radio monitoring service would decipher Royal Navy codes to estimate a convoy's position. Details were then sent to submarines, which would gather and shadow the ships until night came. Then they would attack. Ironically, although the U-boats were built as submersible weapons, their commanders preferred to stay on the surface and pick off their victims. At first this was done from the side of the convoy, but it was soon discovered that the boats could safely manoeuvre among the lines of merchantmen, hitting from close range. Before daylight, the 'wolf pack' would disperse, keeping well away until the following nightfall.

Generally excluded from convoys at the start were very slow vessels or those fast enough to outrun the U-boats. The great majority, the 'plodders', were gathered round ports or bays on both sides of the Atlantic, then escorted by warships either part, or the whole, way across. Ships were usu-

ally assembled in parallel lines, with, for example, 40 sailing in eight lines of five each. There could be more. Convoy SC.42 contained 64 merchantmen in twelve columns, covering eighteen square miles of sea. At times convoys were escorted by only four small warships. In overall command was the convoy commodore, who had to enforce the strictest discipline over speed, station-keeping, black-out and radio silence. Some convoys crossed the ocean unscathed, but the greatest demands fell on others, especially when ships around them were being sunk. Of PQ.18's 45 ships, thirteen went down; SC.42 lost fourteen.

Nonetheless, it is important to keep the dangers in perspective. For some, the physical and psychological pressures were enormous. Yet in all British-controlled convoys across the Atlantic in the Second World War, while 75,000 merchant ships were escorted, 574 vessels were sunk. That is a ratio of 131:1. The sinkings were tragic, yet there were fewer than might have been expected. Casualties were far heavier among those ships which, for one or another reason, did not sail in convoy.

Protecting convoys were escorts, provided at various times by three navies, the Royal Navy, the Royal Canadian Navy (whose contribution is usually understated) and the US Navy. They sailed from a variety of bases in North America, Greenland, Iceland and the United Kingdom. Unfortunately for the Royal Navy, the government of Eire, which depended heavily on sup-

plies brought in by the Merchant Navy, would not allow the British to use the old 'treaty ports' on the Irish coast. Had they been available, the Royal Navy would have been able to offer 200 extra miles of westward cover for merchantmen, saving both lives and ships. For the Royal Navy, escort groups, or 'minders', were formed, each of about eight vessels, two of which were destroyers. These groups trained in anti-submarine tactics. Their invaluable work was made more difficult in that they had to try to locate submarines which played a deadly cat-and-mouse game, sometimes torpedoing ships in the very heart of convoys.

For the Allies, the war at sea proved extremely expensive not only in lives, ships and cargoes lost, but also in terms of the necessary provision for defence. By March 1941 there were 375 escort vessels, including 240 destroyers. In January 1943 an agreement was made that escorts of a convoy, even with air cover, should consist

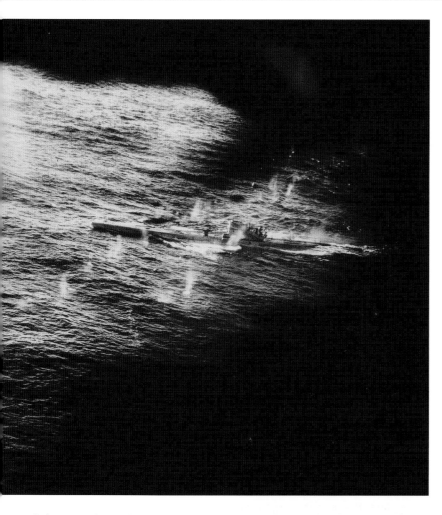

from areas where submarines were gathering – a further example of the 'hunter and quarry' game played across the waters of the North Atlantic. It is possible that in the second half of 1941 alone, re-routing saved 300 ships from destruction.

When close to a convoy and submerged, U-boats could be detected by asdic. An underwater sound signal, emitted from a warship, hit the submarine and bounced back to the receiver. The warship then could be guided to a position directly above the submarine and drop explosive depth charges. However, U-boat captains soon learned that if they attacked on the surface at night, showing only the conning tower, they were safe from asdic. That advantage was overcome when centrimetric radar using a magnetron valve – Type 271 – was fitted, first to aircraft, then to escort vessels. This could detect an 8ft periscope at 1,300yds, a conning tower at over a mile and a half and a surfaced U-boat at 4½ miles.

Submerged U-boats were attacked with depth charges. At the start, these weighed 400lb overall and contained 290lb of amatol, set to detonate at depths between 50 and 500ft. Later the power was increased. A weapon

of three warships plus one extra for every ten merchantmen protected. Without air cover, the figures were to be doubled. In that sense, the U-boat campaign was a highly profitable investment for the Germans. The lethal submarine was small, easily produced and operated, and so was a cost-effective weapon.

Several methods of locating U-boats existed. Sometimes their approximate position at sea could be estimated by ship- and shore-based stations which listened in to their radio signals. The crucial method of detection, particularly of 'wolf packs', was not acknowledged until a quarter of a century after the end of the war. By cracking the code used by the German 'Enigma' machine, British intelligence for much of the time could read the *Kriegsmarine*'s coded orders. Consequently, 'Ultra' information was passed from the code-breakers at Bletchley Park to the Admiralty in London. On many occasions this enabled convoys to be re-routed away

main British base was at Oban, in Scotland. By early 1943 they could range out about 600 miles from their bases before returning. This left an unpatrolled area 'several hundred miles wide in the north-east Atlantic, roughly south of the point of Greenland' and it was there that the heaviest losses were incurred from submarine attack. At length, American Liberator bombers and Catalina flying boats were used to cover 'The Gap', having the range easily to cross the whole region while carrying eight depth charges.

A period of great success for U-boats opened with America's entry into the war at the end of 1941. The East Coast was a soft spot. A local US naval commander reported that he had no force which could offer adequate protection to ships. Many coastal ports had no black-out, while local radio stations continued to broadcast, making submarine navigation easy. Dönitz launched Operation 'Drumroll' right up to the front door of the United States in what U-boat crews termed a 'happy time'. By the end of January 1942 they had sunk 35 vessels in North American coastal waters, a figure which rose to 216 by 31 March. Over half were tankers, carrying the lifeblood of the Allied war effort.

In the Atlantic, the rest of 1942 was a very hard year, which finished with the contest unresolved. The number of U-boats available grew in the first six

**ABOVE:** One of the most effective Allied ASW aircraft, the Short Sunderland flying boat keeps sentinel above a troop convoy also escorted by a British battleship. Sunderlands could remain airborne for 18 hours or more, ranging far into the Atlantic to protect the convoys. Later models carried radar to detect U-boats on the surface by day or night.

**RIGHT:** Photographed from a blimp, USS *Atherton* drops a pattern of depth charges on *U-853*, the last U-boat to be sunk by US forces, 6 May 1945. Caught in shallow water, the submarine was pounded hour after hour until debris rose to the surface. A Navy diver sent down later that day found the *U-853* on the sea bed, 127 feet down, the shattered hull strewn with bodies. There were no survivors.

known as 'Hedgehog' was also employed in the latter stages of the war. This device was a mortar which threw 24 charges, each weighing 32lb, about 250yds ahead of the ship. The effects of these underwater explosions on submarines could be devastating, cracking metal plates and destroying machinery. Some U-boats sank without trace, while others broke up into a mass of debris which floated to the surface. Others again were filled with poisonous fumes and forced up, where they were destroyed by gunfire or rammed. Skilful U-boat captains, however, found ways of evading pursuers, even after the asdic 'pings' had located them.

The Allies soon realised that air power played an important part in the war against submarines. The cover given by aircraft of Coastal Command was vital in locating and attacking them, and speed of assault was crucial as a U-boat could submerge in 25 seconds. In daylight, aircrew could scan miles of sea, while at night a searchlight, the Leigh Light, was used as the aircraft closed in on the target. U-boat crews came to fear attack from the air, which arrived at great speed. One prisoner-of-war said that, when surfaced, if they could see an aircraft it had

already seen them and they were doomed. Sailors on merchant ships were greatly heartened when they could see Allied aircraft overhead.

The value of air cover was underscored by the extent of shipping losses when it was not available. That area was known as 'The Gap' and offered some safety to U-boat crews. Allied aircraft flew from Canada, Iceland and Britain to protect convoys. The

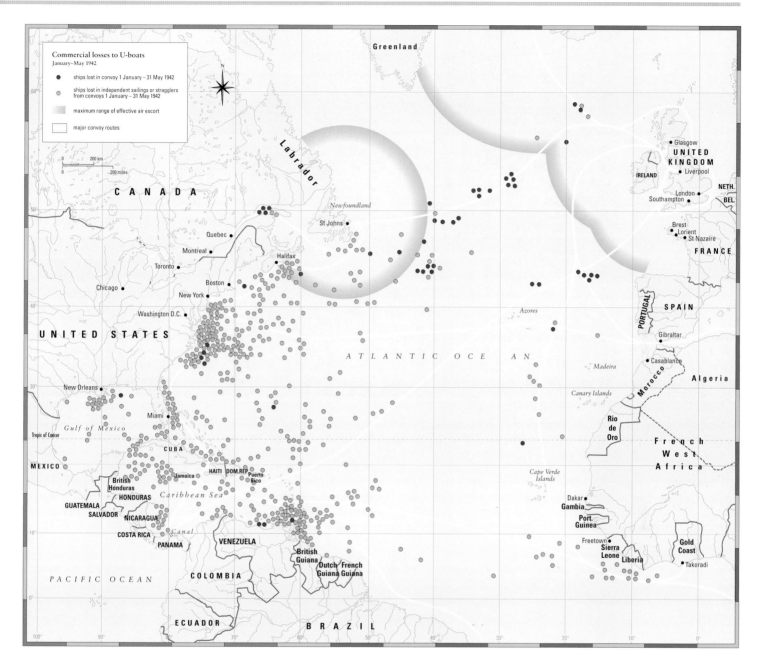

Commercial losses to U-boats
January–May 1942

● ships lost in convoy 1 January – 31 May 1942

○ ships lost in independent sailings or stragglers
  from convoys 1 January – 31 May 1942

maximum range of effective air escort

major convoy routes

0    200 km
0    200 miles

months, so that 140 were operating by the end of June. In that period they sank 585 Allied ships totalling over 3 million tons, and vast supplies intended for Britain finished up below the waves. Gradually the escorts learned new methods of tackling the enemy, but so did U-boat commanders. In early September convoy ON.127 lost seven merchantmen and an escort, while no submarines were hit. Two months later SC.107 had fifteen vessels torpedoed. By the end of the year 1,664 Allied ships had been sunk, 1,160 of them by submarines. In reply, 87 U-boats had been destroyed, but

Dönitz's numbers had grown. He now had an operational strength of 212 submarines.

A crisis for the Allies came in March 1943. 'The Germans never came so near to disrupting communications between the New World and the Old,' noted the Admiralty, 'as in the first twenty days of March 1943.' During those weeks the heaviest convoy battle of the whole war occurred, a turning point in the Battle of the Atlantic. Two convoys, SC.122 and HX.229, were involved as they moved eastwards at different speeds. Their importance to both sides can be deduced from the

### COMMERCIAL LOSSES TO U-BOATS, JANUARY - MAY 1942

When the USA entered the war the U-boats switched their attention to the US east coast where blackout procedures were unknown and convoy systems almost unheard of. A rash of sinkings outside major American ports continued while interservice rivalries delayed the introduction of proper escort procedures. The U-boat service called this their 'Second Happy Time'. However, once escorts were provided and aircraft coordinated with them, the U-boats lost their advantage. From mid-1942 the Allies were building merchantships far faster than the submarines could sink them, while U-boat losses began to mount.

ABOVE: One of the seven survivors from *U-468* is rescued by the Royal Navy. The submarine was sunk off West Africa by an RAF B-24 that pressed home its attack despite being set on fire from end to end by the U-boat's 20 mm AA guns. The U-boat sank but the deck crew survived. The testimony of the German CO and his gunners led to the award of a posthumous VC to Flying Officer Lloyd Trigg.

cargoes. These included oil, meat, grain, timber, ammunition, lorries, aircraft, tanks, invasion barges, food and steel, all desperately needed in the United Kingdom. Soon both convoys, totalling 90 ships, almost merged into one; they were opposed by 38 submarines, which Dönitz had positioned to intercept them. In spite of the presence of 100 escort vessels, the U-boats wrought great destruction. 'The scene was of Wagnerian proportions, with ships and torpedoes exploding in rapid succession.' By 20 March, 22 vessels, grossing 160,000 tons, had been sunk for the loss of one U-boat. The Germans had apparently gained a stupendous victory.

This, however, for the Allies was the darkest hour before the dawn. Two factors now intervened to turn the tide. The first was the presence of more aircraft, some from land bases and others from escort carriers, which began to plague the U-boats. Coastal Command then had some 400 aircraft available and their numbers were a growing threat to submarines on the surface. One of their new weapons was an airborne acoustic torpedo, which homed in on a U-boat's engines. The other was that special hunting groups of warships intensified their search-and-attack tactics, taking the offensive at sea. Under Admiral Horton and, particularly, Captain Walker, they pursued their prey relentlessly. Thus shipping losses in April fell dramatically. In May the pendulum swung further. During that month, 34 ships were lost, but at a cost of 38 U-boats destroyed. For the Germans, such losses were catastrophic. On 24 May, Dönitz ordered his submarines to withdraw. In his memoirs he wrote, 'We had lost the Battle of the Atlantic.'

The U-boat war never again reached such intensity, although, of course, the offensive did not stop. Allied ships were still sunk in the Mediterranean and the South Atlantic, the Arctic and the Indian Oceans – and still in the North Atlantic. During

August only four Allied ships were sunk in the North and South Atlantic Oceans, but then the pace was stepped up. The Germans introduced an acoustic torpedo to be fired at escorts. An example of the devastation brought both to men and to vessels was shown in September. While protecting a convoy approaching North America, a Canadian destroyer was sunk, as was a Royal Navy corvette which went to her aid. Survivors from both ships were picked up by a frigate which was herself hit three nights later. From three ships' companies, only three men survived.

Throughout 1944 the U-boat menace was held at bay, largely through the overwhelming economic power of the Allies, translated into air and sea weapons. Moreover, the production of merchant vessels, especially the American-built 'Liberty ships', was phenomenal both in numbers and speed: as early as October 1942 three Liberty ships were being launched daily, and one was built in 4 days 15 hours. Shipyard workers were opponents whose efforts Dönitz could not touch. Although he wanted his submarines to smash the gigantic armada of shipping which crossed the Channel on D-Day and during the following months, they were hunted so hard that they had virtually no effect.

The cost of the war at sea, especially in the North Atlantic, was heavy. Nearly 2,500 Allied merchant ships were sunk there, totalling almost 13 million tons, the great majority being victims of U-boats. From them the British Merchant Navy alone lost 30,000 dead. The Royal Navy lost 175 warships, and most of its 74,000 sailors killed during the war died in the Atlantic. To them should be added 2,000 men of the Royal Canadian Navy lost in those waters. Nor should the price paid by Coastal Command be overlooked. They lost about 6,000 airmen and 1,800 aircraft in action.

The *Kriegsmarine* also suffered heavily. Of some 1,100 U-boats built, 784 were lost and 220 scuttled. During their campaigns, 41,000 men served in their crews, of whom 26,000 were killed and 5,000 taken prisoner. This was one of the highest casualty rates for any service of any nation at war.

RIGHT: Loading a depth charge on to a 'Y-gun projector' aboard a US Coast Guard cutter in 1942. Depth charges were dropped in a ship's wake, so U-boats would try to turn away as the escort passed over them and they were temporarily hidden from its sonar. Later in the war, forward-firing anti-submarine bombs, 'Hedgehog' prevented this tactic from succeeding.

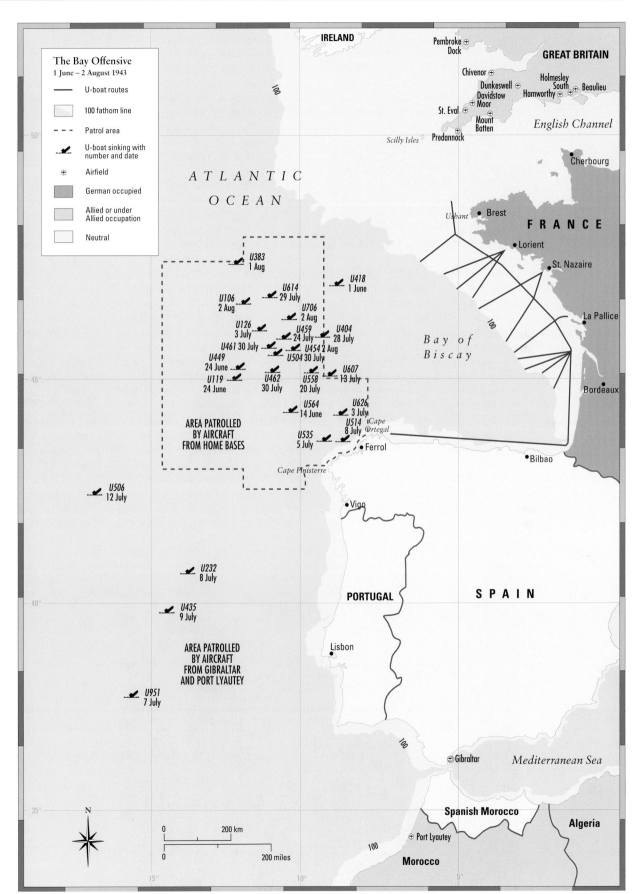

**THE BAY OFFENSIVE,**
The defeat of the U-boats was sealed by the 'Bay Offensive' in summer 1943. Allied aircraft made a concerted attempt to sink the U-boats as they transited Biscay; specialist hunter-killer escort groups, not attached to any convoys also launched raids into the Bay. The Germans experimented with specialist 'flak' U-boats but these proved just as vulnerable to air attack. Ultimately they resorted to schnorkel devices so the submarines could remain submerged, but this kept them to lower speeds and even these could be detected by later airborne radar systems.

The Bay Offensive
1 June – 2 August 1943

U-boat routes
100 fathom line
Patrol area
U-boat sinking with number and date
Airfield
German occupied
Allied or under Allied occupation
Neutral

IRELAND

GREAT BRITAIN

Pembroke Dock
Chivenor
Dunkeswell
Davidstow Moor
St. Eval
Holmesley South
Hamworthy
Beaulieu
Mount Batten
Predannock
Scilly Isles
English Channel

Cherbourg

ATLANTIC OCEAN

Ushant
Brest
FRANCE
Lorient
St. Nazaire
La Pallice
Bordeaux
Bilbao

Bay of Biscay

U383 1 Aug
U418 1 June
U614 29 July
U106 2 Aug
U706 2 Aug
U126 3 July
U459 24 July
U404 28 July
U461 30 July
U454 2 Aug
U449 24 June
U504 30 July
U119 24 June
U462 30 July
U558 20 July
U607 13 July
U564 14 June
U626 3 July
U514 8 July
U535 5 July

Cape Ortegal
Ferrol

AREA PATROLLED BY AIRCRAFT FROM HOME BASES

Cape Finisterre

Vigo

U506 12 July

U232 8 July

U435 9 July

PORTUGAL

SPAIN

Lisbon

AREA PATROLLED BY AIRCRAFT FROM GIBRALTAR AND PORT LYAUTEY

U951 7 July

Gibraltar
Mediterranean Sea

N

Spanish Morocco

Algeria

Port Lyautey

Morocco

0          200 km
0          200 miles

# CHAPTER 9: The End in Europe

As the end of the war approached, a conference was held at Yalta, in the Crimea, by the 'Big Three' – Roosevelt, Churchill and Stalin – to decide on steps to be taken afterwards. Previous meetings, for example, the Teheran Conference in 1943, had been necessary to formulate war strategy. In the main, that need had now passed. In many ways, 'Argonaut', as the Yalta Conference was code-named, was more of a diplomatic pow-pow and game than a council of war. The decisions which were either taken there, or conveniently side-stepped, were to have lasting repercussions on world history over the succeeding half-century.

Churchill was a great admirer of the magnificent fighting spirit shown by the Russians in response to German aggression, and he well appreciated how much the Free World in 1945 owed to the Soviet Union. Nevertheless, like the majority of people in the West, he still had a dislike and mistrust of Communism and of Stalin's dictatorial, bloodthirsty approach to his own people, let alone to his enemies. The prime minister therefore wanted Britain and America to present a united front in discussions with the Russians. He suggested that preliminary meetings could be held in Malta, before they all moved on to Yalta. Consequently, between 30 January and 3 February 1945 various British and American ministers and Chiefs of Staff held talks there, while Churchill and Roosevelt met twice. By then, however, Roosevelt was very ill, with only two months to live. He was into his fourth term as President and the stresses of war had taken a heavy toll of his health. Few people either now or then recollect his polio, his onerous duties being carried out from a wheelchair. Observers saw a pale, drawn, shrunken man. Eden noted, 'He gives the impression of failing powers.'

When they all eventually went to Yalta, the conference lasted for a week, from 4 to 11 February. This was no small, cosy meeting among the 'Big Three', because altogether, with military and civilian officers, diplomats, advisers and ministers, 700 people took part. By the close, there had been intensive bargaining and lobbying, argument and discussion. Eight plenary sessions were held, apart from many deliberations at lower level.

Four main topics were discussed. The leaders, like poker players, kept their cards close to their chests, each striving hard to judge what the others were aiming for. The 'Big Three' had come along with their own claims and were skilled at playing the diplomatic game. Stalin wanted to ensure the safety of his nation's frontiers from any future Western invasion, and therefore was not prepared to give up the gains made by the Red Army in Eastern Europe. They were there; possession

was nine parts of the law. Who could move them?

Roosevelt was very keen to enlist Russian help in the next stage of the war against Japan. He believed that Churchill was, at heart, an imperialist, and the president was therefore prepared to make deals with the Russians in spite of British objections. Churchill wanted Britain and the Commonwealth to be restored as far as possible to the position held in 1939. He knew increasingly, however, that in terms of military muscle, his nation could not match either Russia

**RIGHT:** Churchill, Roosevelt and Stalin pose for the cameras at the Yalta conference in February 1945. The war in Europe was as good as over but the endgame would last another generation as Churchill was acutely conscious. The 'iron curtain' was about to crash down on eastern Europe.

or the United States.

In talks, they first planned for the ending of the war, coordinating steps to be taken from both east and west finally to crush Nazism. They discussed the amount of reparations the Germans would pay, and how to divide Germany into zones of occupation. Churchill insisted that France should be part of the army of occupation, especially when Roosevelt announced that American troops would not be retained in Europe for more than a couple of years. A strong, resurgent France would be needed in

Western Europe as part of a balance against mighty Russia.

When, secondly, they discussed the new United Nations Organisation as a kind of world forum, there was wide agreement. The faults of the old League of Nations were remembered, but this time they would do better. Roosevelt wanted the Great Powers to run the peace as they had controlled the war, but in this a chill wind blew for Britain. There were now only two 'super powers'; Britain, in spite of her prestige, ran third. For agreeing with Roosevelt's plans, Stalin successfully

demanded that the Ukraine and Belorussia, as well as Russia itself, should have membership. He was also granted the right of veto on future United Nations resolutions. That was a right he would frequently employ over subsequent years.

The most controversial arguments came over the fate of Eastern Europe. Having suffered the lash of Nazi invasion in 1941, Stalin wanted the Eastern European states under his control. They would be a barrier between East and West. Poland, Hungary, Czechoslovakia, Rumania, Bulgaria

**ABOVE:** German troops advancing one last time: the offensive in the Ardennes took US forces by surprise and inflicted a sharp reverse on an army that took victory for granted. However, once the skies cleared and Allied airpower could intervene again, the German offensive ground to a halt.

and the Baltic States were all to be turned into Communist satellites. Greece would be left as a British sphere of influence. How far he intended to use them as springboards for spreading a Communist empire across the rest of Europe is still a matter of debate. There is no doubt, nonetheless, that Stalin hoped in the long run to have a united Germany under a Communist-influenced government.

Differences between Stalin and Churchill surfaced particularly over the question of Poland. Britain had gone to war over the Poles in 1939 and, later, a Polish government-in-exile came to London. Their armed forces had fought magnificently beside the Allies throughout the war and now Churchill wanted that government to

be restored in Poland. This did not suit Stalin. On re-taking Poland, the Russians set up their own Communist-friendly administration. Although much talk was heard about 'democracy' and 'free elections' in the liberated countries, the words meant different things to the British and the Russians. Before long, Stalin openly flouted the agreements.

At Yalta, Roosevelt appreciated Britain's weaknesses and was less friendly towards Churchill than he had been earlier in the war. More than anything, he wanted Russian participation in the forthcoming onslaught on Japan. If the all-powerful Red Army, after the imminent conquest of Germany, could be persuaded to cross Asia and attack the Japanese, the American task in the Pacific would be

made much easier. Consequently, the president was prepared to give way to Stalin on such matters as the future of Poland, if Stalin was prepared to send troops to Manchuria. The Russian leader would oblige – at a price. Stalin insisted that certain territories in the Far East would have to be given to the Soviet Union. Roosevelt raised no objections. The Polish government in London, and Churchill, were snubbed. At Yalta in 1945, the Poles were pawns, much as the Czechs had been seven years earlier at Munich.

Churchill knew nothing of these agreements, which were made when the Russians and the Americans held a private meeting on 8 February. Roosevelt may have hoped that Stalin would become a Western-style leader, enjoying the friendly relationships that

**BELOW:** German soldiers are executed by American firing squads in the wake of the Ardennes offensive. Commanded by an experienced SS officer, Otto Skorzeny, detachments of Germans had fought behind Allied lines in US uniforms and using captured US vehicles.

democracies can share. Churchill knew better. His long experience of European politics and his statesmanship gave him a more realistic assessment of how Stalin ran his nation. Churchill's mistrust of the Communist state was shown privately at Yalta when he called the Crimea, where the delegations were staying, 'the Riviera of Hades'.

Statesmen leave the diplomatic gambling-table as winners or losers. Few break even. At Yalta, Churchill lost an amount because his nation's power had declined. Roosevelt, a very sick man, made too many concessions to the Russians. Stalin, playing comfortably on home ground, showed the attributes of a canny operator. He scooped up more winnings than anyone.

**RIGHT:** The firing party prepares another man for execution. The German raiders caused considerable confusion, especially after it was rumoured that assassination squads intended to kill senior US commanders. Fighting in enemy uniform is an offence under international law, punishable by death.

# The Attack from the West

ABOVE: Tiger II heavy tanks assembled on a training ground in central Germany. The 'King Tiger' was the most powerful tank of the war, but fortunately for the Allies they were few and far between. The strategic bombing campaign had crippled German tank production in 1944 and however excellent their tanks, the German panzer forces were so outnumbered they could no longer stop the Allied advance.

Early in 1945 the Allied front line in the West ran roughly along the frontier that France, Belgium and Luxembourg shared with Germany, as well as protruding some way into Holland. The German offensive in the Ardennes, which had started the previous December, had punched itself out. The counter-blow had certainly come as an unwelcome shock to the British and Americans, but it had cost the German Army dearly. Heavy losses had been sustained. There was now much speculation on how long Hitler's fortress could continue to hold out, especially from people in southern England who were still receiving the blast of 'doodlebugs' and rockets. Yet it was feared that the *Wehrmacht*, fighting for its homeland, would resist with unparalleled ferocity.

In January 1945 Eisenhower commanded powerful armies which were steadily growing in strength. Running from the north, along the line, were the First Canadian and Second British Armies. Then came the Ninth US, the First US and the Seventh US Armies. Near the Swiss border, at the southern end, was the First French Army. The three northernmost armies were under the immediate command of Montgomery. The other American armies were controlled in the field by General Bradley. Ahead of all these troops lay two stages of offensive. The first was to drive forward to the line of the river Rhine. After that would come a river crossing which would carry them all into the heart of Germany. In the first stage, they hoped to move

swiftly and cut off German troops before they could retreat across the great river barrier.

The main attack started on 8 February when Eisenhower's 85 divisions went forward against 26 opposing German divisions. Before the battle opened, Montgomery sent a message to all of the troops in his 21st Army Group. As often happened, the words of his order made a comparison with the boxing-ring and referred to the approaching end of the whole contest. 'And so we embark on the final round,' he wrote, 'in close cooperation with our American allies on our right and with complete confidence in the successful outcome of the onslaught being delivered by our Russian allies on the other side of the ring.' Although criticism of Montgomery has appeared since 1945, especially over his relationships with comrades, in the words of his Chief-of-Staff he 'understood this "civilian army" as few before him'. He went on to remind his men of what they were fighting for, quoting words written in Africa by a soldier of the Eighth Army: '"Peace for our kids, our brothers freed, / A kinder world, a cleaner breed."'

The weather was very bad in January and February 1945, with heavy rain leading to flooding and mud. The Germans opened some dykes to impede the Allies' advance, but there was not to be another Passchendaele. Good use was made in the north of tracked amphibious vehicles (Buffaloes) to carry troops and supplies forward, often across difficult terrain. Resistance was sometimes fierce. Thousands of mines had been laid, both anti-tank and anti-personnel, slowing progress. Great use was made by the attackers of the 'Crocodile' flame-thrower, a fearsome weapon against strongpoints and pillboxes. Occasionally they encountered Germans who had had enough, one group being 'found in their best uniforms, cleanly shaved and ready to surrender!' Most defenders, nevertheless, were fighting for their national soil. Although they were outnumbered and outgunned, their resistance was stubborn.

By blowing up dams the Germans held up the American advance for a time, but, further south, by the early days of March Patton's tanks started to move at pace. They advanced 60 miles in three days and reached the Rhine. On 5 March they entered Cologne and soon were in territories previously known only as targets for the bomber offensive. Most importantly for the future of the campaign, American troops took the bridge at Remagen intact and held it. By the end of the month the Germans had been driven back across the Rhine, although a large number were cut off by Patton's men.

Allied forces were now drawn up for the great Rhine crossing by the 21st Army Group in the north, while lower down the river American armies were ready to pour into eastern and southern Germany. 'The strategic

intention,' stated a contemporary summary, 'was for the whole Allied Expeditionary Force to crush the river defences and penetrate deep into Germany to meet the Russians.' There would be a meeting 'on or about the Elbe in central Germany, so divorcing the enemy's northern armies from those in the south'. Patton crossed the Rhine on 22 March, working with the US Seventh and the French First Armies. The next day Montgomery attacked near Wesel with 25 divisions. The full-scale invasion of Germany from the West had begun. He had 3,000 guns and strong air support, while the 18th Airborne Corps were landed ahead, some dropping by parachute from 540 aircraft while others were put down by 1,230 gliders. There was slight resistance only from the five German divisions opposite.

From then on, the four million Allied troops – mainly French, Canadian, British and American – were on an unstoppable roll. German resistance crumbled, having neither the men nor the equipment to hold back such a formidable, well-equipped tidal wave. The advance quickened through April, broken only by the news Hitler received on the 12th when

he learned from Goebbels that Roosevelt had died. 'Fate has laid low your greatest enemy,' the *Führer* was told. 'God has not abandoned us.' Such wild faith in divine intervention was soon proved to be misplaced. By then, nothing was going to defeat either the Grand Alliance or its determination to defeat Germany.

In the north, the British and Canadians drove forward towards Hamburg. Further south, two American armies trapped the German Army Group B in the Ruhr, taking over 320,000 prisoners when it surrendered on the 18th. Patton's Third Army raced down into southern Germany, moving so fast that correspondents failed to keep up with them. 'Jeeps cannot compete,' wrote one on 5 April, 'with Third Army tank columns on the loose.' By the end of the month Patton's men were well into Czechoslovakia and Austria, their sweeping advances reminiscent of the Panzers' old glory days.

For other Americans, the brakes went on. On reaching the river Elbe, they were ordered to stop. 'The enormous implications of this simple statement,' in Terraine's words, 'constitute the fundamental theme of world history ever

ABOVE: US forces advance to the German border in the bitter winter of 1944–45. The war was notable for some extremely harsh winters by western European standards. During the German offensive in December the ground was so hard that trenches could only be dug with the help of explosives.

since that day.' In places they were only 60 miles from Berlin and felt perfectly prepared and able to move on triumphantly and occupy the Nazi capital. However, agreement had been reached previously with the Russians that the great prize of taking Berlin was to be a reward for the Red Army. Therefore, while Montgomery's troops pushed on in northern Germany and American and French armies moved down into Bavaria, the US Ninth Army in the centre marked time. On 27 April it met advancing Russian soldiers on the line of the Elbe. The end could not be far off.

Other features of the Anglo-American advance are worth noting. As Allied troops drove deeper into Germany, they began to uncover evidence of the horrors which the Germans had imposed on some prisoners-of-war and on all inmates of concentration camps. For example, on 15 April British soldiers reached Belsen, finding scenes that dismayed and angered troops who had experienced battlefield carnage. The shoes of the dead were arranged in a heap 20ft high and 50yds long.

'This is the Site of the Infamous Belsen Concentration Camp,' announced a notice-board quickly erected by the British Army. '10,000 unburied dead were found here. Another 13,000 have since died.' Added were the scornful words, 'All of them victims of the German New Order in Europe, and an example of Nazi Kultur.' At the end of the twentieth century, many young people fail to understand the effects that such sights had on those who first saw them.

On 2 May the British 11th Armoured Division took Lübeck, with Hamburg surrendering next day. On the 4th, *Wehrmacht* forces in northwest Germany, Holland and Denmark surrendered to Montgomery on Lüneburg Heath. Further south, American troops had by 4 May reached Munich, Augsburg, Salzburg and Linz. They were not far from Prague in Czechoslovakia. Three days later, in Rheims, the Germans accepted the inevitable and signed an unconditional surrender of armed forces on all fronts. Eisenhower, the supreme Commander, had led his armies to victory.

RIGHT: British troops on the German frontier in January 1945. Unusually, they have received snow camouflage suits. The soldier on the far left has a sniper scope on his .303 rifle; the man beside him has the standard British light machine gun, the Bren gun.

**ABOVE:** The exit from Hitler's bunker and the yard in which he and Eva Braun were incompletely cremated after their joint suicide. His propaganda minister Goebbels and his wife shot themselves here after poisoning their children.

existing between certain British and American military commanders over strategy and procedure; less well remembered are the similar feelings in the Red Army, with both Zhukov and Koniev seeking kudos.

As they prepared for battle, the Russians still had an overwhelming advantage in men and *matériel* on the ground and in the skies. More than 2½ million troops, including reserves, were disposed across the three fronts, 1½ million of them in the front line. Through earlier losses Russian tank strength was probably down to about 3,600, although adding self-propelled guns raised the number to 6,000. In addition, the Red Army were very powerful in artillery. About 8,000 aircraft were also available. On the other side, some 1 million German troops were stationed around the Berlin sector, and the city garrison itself amounted to 200,000 men. They had 1,500 tanks.

The great offensive was opened by Zhukov's front at 5 a.m. on 16 April. A thunderous overture of bombs, rockets and shells deluged forward German positions, then, in a blinding display, 143 searchlights dazzled the enemy and guided the infantry. An hour and a quarter later Koniev's artillery began a devastating barrage

to cover troops of his First Ukrainian Front. By midday the Red Army was pushing on, but already in Zhukov's sector a snarl-up of tanks and armoured vehicles was jamming the roads. Koniev made swifter progress. A message from Stalin, chiding Zhukov, led to a frantic, redoubled effort. Later the Russians drove on to encircle the city, both as a block to any possible American intervention from the West and to prevent German reinforcements arriving.

Fighting was savagely hard, with German units, although greatly outnumbered, defending territory that was specially precious to them. Their anti-tank guns took a heavy toll of Russian armour. Late on the 20th the city was threatened by Koniev's forces from the south and Rokossovsky's from the north. Zhukov, rather needled and anxious for his reputation, pushed his men even harder, fearing that Koniev was about to steal his glory.

As Zhukov's troops forced themselves into the outskirts of Berlin, their tactics changed. Urban warfare now ensued, with each area, then street, then building, being fought for. The Russians, of course, had wide experience of this kind of campaigning, especially those units which had been

involved at Stalingrad over two years earlier. They employed engineers and assault groups, using artillery at close range to blast their way forward. Tanks and flame-throwers were available to back up the infantry drive. Soon wide stretches of the city were marked with burning or gutted buildings and piles of collapsed masonry, all shrouded in dust and smoke. Terrified inhabitants who had never dreamed that war would be so close crowded in cellars, praying for the maelstrom to pass.

It did not. The noose tightened, and by 25 April nine Russian armies had completely encircled Berlin. Inside the burning, shattered city the remaining German formations now awaited the final assault. This began the next day and was made by 460,000 Soviet troops, with 1,500 tanks and supported by overwhelming air power. The boundary lines between Zhukov's and Koniev's forces were close, and eventually, at Stalin's intervention, the latter was compelled to move his line of assault. The accolade of final glory was going to his rival. On 28 April the districts of Charlottenberg and Wannsee came under attack, while on the 30th, at 1 p.m., Soviet infantry opened an assault to take the *Reichstag* building.

By then the crucial question had been answered. Where was Hitler? Had he escaped or was he in hiding? Actually, the *Führer* was dead. On 15 April he had been joined in the bunker by Eva Braun, his long-time secret companion and mistress, of whom Speer later wrote, 'For all writers of history, Eva Braun is going to be a disappointment.' She was a quiet, attractive woman who stayed out of the limelight and was content to be Hitler's companion. During the last days, she stood loyally beside him in the bunker as the tempo of disaster quickened. Early in the morning of the 29th, with the thunder of Russian gunfire creeping ever closer, Hitler married Eva Braun in a small underground conference room. After a wedding breakfast, he retired to another room and there dictated his 'Political Testament'. In this document, he reiterated a catalogue of his beliefs, or delusions. Love of, and loyalty to, the German people had been his inspira-

# The Attack from the East

RIGHT: The *Luftwaffe* had treated the Russian front as a training area for its fighter pilots, so superior were its aircraft and pilots. However, by 1945 the Russian air force finally had the upper hand and bombers like these Il-4s were ranging into eastern Germany.

BELOW: Su-76 assault guns provide close support for Russian infantry attacking German positions in Prussia, early 1945. Russia won the 'battle of the factories', building far more armoured vehicles from far fewer resources than the Germans. By 1945 the disparity in numbers was so overwhelmingly in the Russians' favour that it was only a matter of time before they overran Hitler's Reich.

From this stage of the war, an old boxing maxim comes to mind: 'A good big 'un will always beat a good little 'un.' Time and again from 1939 the German Army had proved itself to be pre-eminent on the battlefield, but in January 1945, on the Eastern Front, it faced a far larger opponent. At his disposal Hitler had almost 3 million men to hold back the Russian juggernaut. There were roughly 185 divisions, fifteen of them provided by the Hungarians. They possessed 4,000 tanks and assault guns, and there were 2,000 *Luftwaffe* aircraft available. Against them the Red Army deployed almost 5 million men. These were arranged in no fewer than 58 armies, with thirteen air armies, comprising 14,500 aircraft, in support. Russian weapons superiority, with 11,000 tanks and self-propelled guns, was overwhelming.

The Russian High Command, or *Stavka*, was in reality another name for Stalin. Ever the dictator – like his opponent, Hitler – final decisions on political and military strategy were taken by the Russian leader himself. Plans were laid to assault at four main points in the East and the battle was to open on 20 January 1945. The date, however, was brought forward when the Germans in the West launched their surprise counter-offensive in the Ardennes and Churchill asked Stalin to help by opening his offensive as soon as possible. Stalin obliged and the Russian advance began on 13 January.

According to Russian estimates, their troops would battle to overwhelm German resistance in six to seven weeks. At first they had some successes, but in places such as East Prussia and Pomerania the *Wehrmacht* resisted strenuously. Progress there was slow. Nevertheless, by the end of February Soviet armies were well into Germany and had reached the line of the rivers Oder and Neisse. Berlin now lay in their sights. In front of them the main defensive system had been broken and men were pouring back for what would be a last-ditch defence of the capital. In March the Russians cleared the right bank of the Oder, took Danzig and, by then, had occupied Poland and much of Czechoslovakia.

On 15 January Hitler moved his headquarters back to an underground bunker below the Chancellery in Berlin. From there he tried to control his forces on all fronts, vainly attempting to hold back the Allied tide. He had lost touch with reality and reacted violently towards those who opposed or disagreed with his decisions. 'His fists raised, his cheeks flushed with rage, his whole body trembling,' wrote General Guderian of a dispute over policy he had with the *Führer* on 13 February, 'the man stood there in front of me, beside himself with fury and having lost all self-control.'

As the Russians pressed on, they began to release thousands of men and women who had been prisoners-of-war or slave labourers. Once free, many of them started to exact a private vengeance on their former captors, robbing, beating and killing, repaying in equal measure the burden of terror under which they had laboured. On 27 January Russian troops in Poland reached a town whose name has echoed down the succeeding years. At Auschwitz they discovered what was left of a Nazi extermination camp – and sights that horrified even the hardiest troops. Some of the worst excesses committed by the Germans were uncovered.

Meanwhile heavy battles continued further south, with other Russian fronts making inroads along the Danube valley and into northern Hungary and Slovakia. Budapest was finally stormed on 13 January. The Red Army moved on into Austria, capturing Vienna on 13 April. By the last days of the month the Russians met up with advancing American troops near Linz. The war on Hitler's southern flank was virtually over, leaving him isolated in the Berlin bunker. He was now commander of crumbling armies, defending a dying Third Reich.

**LEFT:** German troops await the next Russian assault. Massive artillery bombardments would destroy frontline positions before waves of infantrymen charged forwards. Casualties on both sides were at a level unimaginable to the Western Allies.

**LEFT:** After the German airborne forces suffered nearly 50 per cent losses in their attack on Crete in 1941, Hitler forbade further parachute assaults. However, the *Luftwaffe's* parachute forces continued to expand and served as shock troops on all fronts. These paratroops in winter kit are preparing to counter-attack on the Russian front.

**LEFT:** German soldiers deepen a shell hole in readiness for the next attack. Their two key weapons are behind them: on the left, the MG42 machine gun and on the right the panzerfaust anti-tank rocket. Reliable and with a formidable rate of fire, the MG42 was the best weapon of its kind on either side.

# The End in Berlin

ABOVE: Russian IS-II heavy tanks rumble into central Berlin as the battle for Hitler's capital draws to its inevitable conclusion. The US decision to leave Berlin to the Russians was criticized after the war, but it cost the Russians hundreds of thousands of casualties to take the city.

In Stalin's view, only troops of the Red Army were entitled to perform the final act of the European war by taking Berlin, the hub of Nazism which had wreaked devastation across the USSR. By February, three main fronts, still pushing forward at heavy cost, were moving into position for the last rites. Of the three Russian generals, Rokossovsky, Zhukov and Koniev, the latter two had the best positions for a final assault.

At one time Stalin had planned for Zhukov to be the conqueror of Berlin, but Koniev's armies were well handled and wanted to be in at the kill. The Russian leader cleverly encouraged their mutual rivalry, hoping to bring swifter and greater success. 'Whoever breaks in first,' he announced, 'takes Berlin.' As soon as Stalin suspected, in early March, that American and British forces might reach Berlin, his plans were speeded up. The *Stavka* then agreed that all three fronts would advance on the capital, with Zhukov having the prime, central position. Much has been made of the rivalry

1 | 29 April 1945: units of the First Ukrainian advance towards central Berlin

2 | 29–30 April 1945: units of the Second Belorussian Front advance from the northern suburbs, cross the River Spree and capture Gestapo Headquarters, then the Reichstag

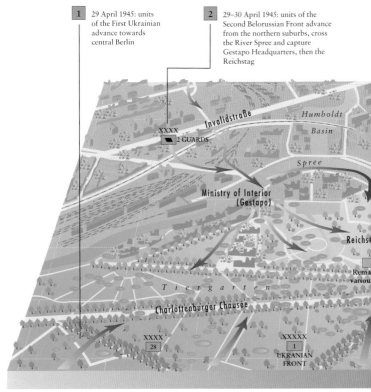

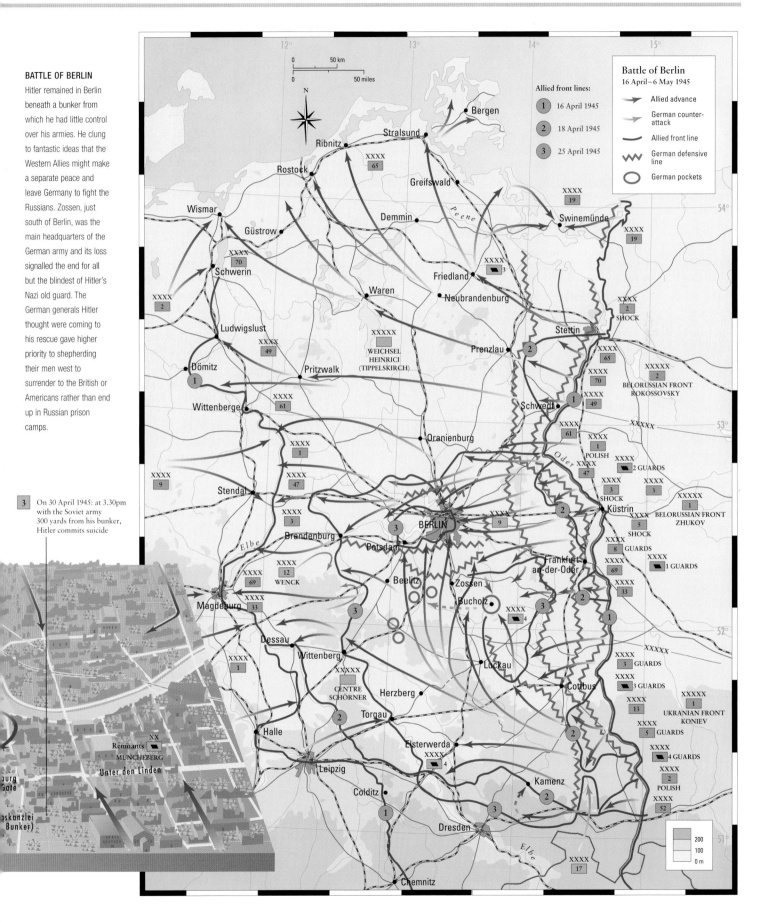

**BATTLE OF BERLIN**

Hitler remained in Berlin beneath a bunker from which he had little control over his armies. He clung to fantastic ideas that the Western Allies might make a separate peace and leave Germany to fight the Russians. Zossen, just south of Berlin, was the main headquarters of the German army and its loss signalled the end for all but the blindest of Hitler's Nazi old guard. The German generals Hitler thought were coming to his rescue gave higher priority to shepherding their men west to surrender to the British or Americans rather than end up in Russian prison camps.

**3** On 30 April 1945: at 3.30pm with the Soviet army 300 yards from his bunker, Hitler commits suicide

**Battle of Berlin**
16 April – 6 May 1945

| | |
|---|---|
| Allied front lines: | |
| **1** 16 April 1945 | Allied advance |
| **2** 18 April 1945 | German counter-attack |
| **3** 25 April 1945 | Allied front line |
| | German defensive line |
| | German pockets |

0    50 km
0    50 miles

N

Bergen
Stralsund
Ribnitz
Rostock
Greifswald
Wismar
Güstrow
Demmin
Swinemünde
Schwerin
XXXX 70
XXXX 2
Waren
Friedland
Neubrandenburg
Ludwigslust
XXXX 49
XXXXX WEICHSEL HEINRICI (TIPPELSKIRCH)
Prenzlau
Stettin
Dömitz
Pritzwalk
Schwedt
XXXX 65
XXXX 70
XXXX 49
BELORUSSIAN FRONT ROKOSSOVSKY
Wittenberge
XXXX 61
Oranienburg
Oder
XXXX 61
XXXX 1 POLISH
XXXX 47
XXXX 2 GUARDS
XXXX 3 SHOCK
Stendal
XXXX 1
XXXX 47
BERLIN
XXXX 9
XXXX 3
Küstrin
XXXX 5 SHOCK
BELORUSSIAN FRONT ZHUKOV
XXXX 9
Brandenburg
Potsdam
Frankfurt an-der-Oder
XXXX 8 GUARDS
XXXX 1 GUARDS
XXXX 12 WENCK
XXXX 69
Beelitz
Zossen
Bucholz
XXXX 4
XXXX 69 SHOCK
Magdeburg
XXXX 33
XXXX 3
Dessau
XXXX 1
Wittenberg
XXXXX CENTRE SCHÖRNER
Herzberg
Luckau
Cottbus
XXXX 3 GUARDS
XXXX 3 GUARDS
Torgau
Halle
Elsterwerda
XXXX 4
XXXX 13 UKRANIAN FRONT KONIEV
XXXX 5 GUARDS
XXXX 4 GUARDS
Leipzig
Coldditz
Kamenz
XXXX 2 POLISH
XXXX 52
Dresden
Elbe
XXXX 17
Chemnitz

Remnants XX MÜNCHEBERG
Unter den Linden

| | 200 |
|---|---|
| | 100 |
| | 0 m |

existing between certain British and American military commanders over strategy and procedure; less well remembered are the similar feelings in the Red Army, with both Zhukov and Koniev seeking kudos.

As they prepared for battle, the Russians still had an overwhelming advantage in men and *matériel* on the ground and in the skies. More than 2½ million troops, including reserves, were disposed across the three fronts, 1½ million of them in the front line. Through earlier losses Russian tank strength was probably down to about 3,600, although adding self-propelled guns raised the number to 6,000. In addition, the Red Army were very powerful in artillery. About 8,000 aircraft were also available. On the other side, some 1 million German troops were stationed around the Berlin sector, and the city garrison itself amounted to 200,000 men. They had 1,500 tanks.

The great offensive was opened by Zhukov's front at 5 a.m. on 16 April. A thunderous overture of bombs, rockets and shells deluged forward German positions, then, in a blinding display, 143 searchlights dazzled the enemy and guided the infantry. An hour and a quarter later Koniev's artillery began a devastating barrage

to cover troops of his First Ukrainian Front. By midday the Red Army was pushing on, but already in Zhukov's sector a snarl-up of tanks and armoured vehicles was jamming the roads. Koniev made swifter progress. A message from Stalin, chiding Zhukov, led to a frantic, redoubled effort. Later the Russians drove on to encircle the city, both as a block to any possible American intervention from the West and to prevent German reinforcements arriving.

Fighting was savagely hard, with German units, although greatly outnumbered, defending territory that was specially precious to them. Their anti-tank guns took a heavy toll of Russian armour. Late on the 20th the city was threatened by Koniev's forces from the south and Rokossovsky's from the north. Zhukov, rather needled and anxious for his reputation, pushed his men even harder, fearing that Koniev was about to steal his glory.

As Zhukov's troops forced themselves into the outskirts of Berlin, their tactics changed. Urban warfare now ensued, with each area, then street, then building, being fought for. The Russians, of course, had wide experience of this kind of campaigning, especially those units which had been

involved at Stalingrad over two years earlier. They employed engineers and assault groups, using artillery at close range to blast their way forward. Tanks and flame-throwers were available to back up the infantry drive. Soon wide stretches of the city were marked with burning or gutted buildings and piles of collapsed masonry, all shrouded in dust and smoke. Terrified inhabitants who had never dreamed that war would be so close crowded in cellars, praying for the maelstrom to pass.

It did not. The noose tightened, and by 25 April nine Russian armies had completely encircled Berlin. Inside the burning, shattered city the remaining German formations now awaited the final assault. This began the next day and was made by 460,000 Soviet troops, with 1,500 tanks and supported by overwhelming air power. The boundary lines between Zhukov's and Koniev's forces were close, and eventually, at Stalin's intervention, the latter was compelled to move his line of assault. The accolade of final glory was going to his rival. On 28 April the districts of Charlottenberg and Wannsee came under attack, while on the 30th, at 1 p.m., Soviet infantry opened an assault to take the *Reichstag* building.

By then the crucial question had been answered. Where was Hitler? Had he escaped or was he in hiding? Actually, the *Führer* was dead. On 15 April he had been joined in the bunker by Eva Braun, his long-time secret companion and mistress, of whom Speer later wrote, 'For all writers of history, Eva Braun is going to be a disappointment.' She was a quiet, attractive woman who stayed out of the limelight and was content to be Hitler's companion. During the last days, she stood loyally beside him in the bunker as the tempo of disaster quickened. Early in the morning of the 29th, with the thunder of Russian gunfire creeping ever closer, Hitler married Eva Braun in a small underground conference room. After a wedding breakfast, he retired to another room and there dictated his 'Political Testament'. In this document, he reiterated a catalogue of his beliefs, or delusions. Love of, and loyalty to, the German people had been his inspiration, he claimed. He had never wanted war with either Britain or the United States, but Russia was not included. All was blamed on 'those international statesmen who either were of Jewish origin or worked for Jewish interests'. He was happy to die in Berlin and from present sacrifices would emerge a 'glorious rebirth of the National Socialist movement of a truly united nation'. Göring and Himmler, both of whom he suspected were trying to usurp his position, were expelled from the Nazi Party; Admiral Dönitz, of U-boat fame, was appointed as his successor. Then came another burst of anti-Semitism: 'I enjoin the government and the people to uphold the racial laws to the limit and to resist mercilessly the poisoner of all nations, international Jewry.' Eva Braun, he added, would die 'with me at her own wish as my wife'.

During the afternoon of the 29th Hitler had poison administered to his favourite dog, Blondi. Then he made his farewells. The following day both Eva Hitler, *née* Braun, and her husband of less than 48 hours committed suicide. Their bodies were laid in a shell crater in the Chancellery garden, soaked in petrol and burned.

At 10 p.m. the next evening Hamburg Radio announced that 'Our *Führer*, Adolf Hitler, fighting to the last breath against Bolshevism,' had fallen 'in his operational headquarters in the Reich Chancellery.' On the following day General Weidling, commanding what was left of the defending forces in Berlin, surrendered. This began a spate of capitulations of German forces right across Occupied Europe, the last being on 11 May.

The cost of taking Berlin had been heavy for the attackers. By the end of the operation the Red Army had lost some 80,000 dead and 280,000 wounded. It is interesting to speculate how large the number of casualties would have been had the Americans and British raced across Germany to arrive at the capital before the Russians, the plan dear to Montgomery's heart. Eisenhower was warned that the total could have been 100,000. The Russians lost almost four times that number. For Stalin, nevertheless, the price was worth paying. 'It was the Soviet people who bore the main brunt of the war, not the Allies,' he told Zhukov in a telephone call on 7 May.

Hitler's dreams and ambitions had brought disaster to the German people. He had predicted that the Third Reich would last for a thousand years; it had crashed into ruins after twelve.

**BELOW:** US soldiers relax in Hitler's mountain retreat in Bavaria where rumour had it the Nazi elite planned to make a last stand. The complex was looted then blown up.

# The End in Italy

While so much activity was taking place in northern Europe, further south the Italian Campaign, with its less well remembered and acknowledged armies, was drawing to its close.

From January to March 1945 the Allied armies which had fought their way northwards through Italy against skilful and dogged German resistance were preparing a final great offensive. For weeks they had wallowed in mud. They now awaited the coming of better weather. Ever since the preparations for the D-Day landings in France had started, these armies had suffered the role of Cinderella. Troops had been withdrawn for 'Overlord'. Seven other divisions were posted to the invasion of southern France. Then, in February 1945, Canadian soldiers were secretly withdrawn from Italy and posted to Belgium, joining Montgomery's forces preparing to attack Germany across the Rhine. By the end of March 58,000 men of the Canadian Corps had reached southern France on their way to Belgium. Their contribution to the Italian Campaign had been magnificent. Nearly 100,000 served there and they had suffered a 25 per cent casualty rate.

Under the overall leadership of Alexander, the American Generals Clark and Truscott and the British General McCreery made their plans for the offensive, Operation 'Grapeshot'. In total they could deploy some 536,000 men, together with 70,000 Italians, both soldiers and partisans. They represented many nations. As well as Americans and British there were Poles, Greeks, Indians, New Zealanders, South Africans and Brazilians. Opposite them were 491,000 German troops, many of whom had fought in Italy for two years, assisted by 108,000 Italian Fascists who had remained loyal to Mussolini. Some of the German formations, for example the 1st Parachute Division, contained battle-hardened troops with great defensive skills.

As planned, the Allied offensive opened on 9 April, preceded by a deluge of bombs, 1,700 tons of which were dropped by heavy bombers alone. Five days later the American Fifth Army, again with enormous air support, began its forward drive. After several days of fierce fighting the American 10th Mountain Division broke out of the mountainous region. When the advance pressed on, the Americans took Bologna, then on 26 April reached Verona. The Eighth Army also moved forward after much

savage combat, especially by infantry. As German resistance began to crumble, New Zealand soldiers took Venice and Trieste. On 2 May, with Allied troops occupying almost all of northern Italy, and harried by a partisan uprising, the Germans surrendered.

Final Allied success in the Italian Campaign owed much to the use of air power. The Mediterranean Allied Air Force had been built to great strength and by 1 April 1945 contained about 3,750 aircraft of all types. Facing them on the same day were about 150 serviceable German and Italian machines. Such a preponderance in numbers gave the Allies almost complete air superiority, with Axis pilots often having no opportunity to become airborne, let alone contribute to the campaign.

Even during the poor weather of January and February 1945 hundreds of Allied bomber sorties were flown both by medium bombers and by 'heavies'. They attacked transport targets such as the extensive railway yards at Verona. At the end of February their bombs blocked the Brenner Pass in nine places. In addition, flying from Italian bases, American heavy bombers were able to hit far distant targets. On 31 January, for example, 625 Liberators and Fortresses raided an oil refinery in

Austria. Closer to the front line, in February over 1,000 sorties were flown by fighter-bombers, often hitting ground positions which soldiers could not easily reach.

An unusual feature of the Italian Campaign was that some senior German staff officers, obviously aware of the direction in which the war was heading by late 1944, started to make peace overtures. Surprisingly, one of the prime movers in this was SS General Wolff. On 8 March he met an American diplomat, Allen Dulles, in Switzerland for secret talks. These continued, on and off, for several weeks, with difficulties on both sides. When the Russians learned of these German overtures they were highly suspicious, demanding that their own representatives should be present. On the German side, a number of officers would do nothing while Hitler was still alive, because of their oath of loyalty to him. Nevertheless, at length their unconditional surrender was signed, coming into operation on 2 May, six days before the main surrender in the West.

During the final days of conflict in Italy, many people wondered what had happened to Mussolini. *Il Duce* had been living in a villa on the shores of Lake Garda but by April 1945, as the war was running towards its end,

he realised that retribution was coming his way. By then he was worn and tired and ready to bargain for his own safety. On 25 April he left Milan in a convoy of cars which two days later merged with German vehicles going north towards the Swiss border. Mussolini had been joined by his loyal mistress, Clara Petacci, both hoping to make their escape. The convoy was stopped by Italian partisans who were trying to prevent Fascists from escaping. Upon searching the vehicles they discovered Mussolini, disguised as a German soldier. He was arrested. At that stage, the partisans were unsure of how to treat their prisoner. Some wanted to hand him over to the Americans, but others believed in instant justice. He would have to die. On the afternoon of 28 April some Communist partisans drove Mussolini and Petacci to the gateway of a villa. Both were shot. Their bodies were taken to Milan and hung upside down on public display from the roof of a garage. With the death of *Il Duce* the era of Italian Fascism had come to an end.

At the close of the Italian Campaign attention turned briefly away from the Second World War to a new contest which would fester in Europe for decades to come. On 2 May 1945 New Zealand troops, in hot pursuit of

BELOW: British heavy artillery bombards another German defensive position in Italy. The Germans built successive fortified lines that the Allies battered themselves against from September 1943 to spring 1945. It is still unclear which side tied down more of its opponents in Italy while the war was being decided in Normandy and Poland.

**LEFT:** Among the multinational forces the Germans assembled to resist the Allies in Italy were the two Cossack corps raised in Russia. Fierce opponents of the Communist regime, the Cossacks fought their former rulers in Russia before being transferred to the Balkans and Italy. These Cossacks, taken prisoner by the Allies, were handed over to the Russians after the war and were either executed immediately or sent to their deaths in the Gulags.

German forces, entered Trieste, requiring the port as a base for future operations into Austria. There they met some of Tito's Yugoslav partisan soldiers. These had fought a bitterly protracted war against occupying Axis forces and had received much material aid from the Allies. Trieste was in Italy, but ownership of the territory had long been contested by the Yugoslavs. For several weeks Tito's forces refused to move out of the area, and in this they were covertly supported by the Russians. There was a danger that

British Commonwealth and American forces would clash with their Yugoslav allies in what could be either the last battle of the Second World War or the first of the Third. Churchill was greatly worried and contacted the new American president, Harry Truman, over Soviet ambitions in that area.

Many people believe that the phrase 'iron curtain' was first used by Churchill at Fulton, Missouri, in 1946; actually, it appeared on 12 May 1945 when he cabled that 'An iron curtain is drawn down upon their

front. We do not know what is going on behind.' The façade of unity among the three Great Powers was beginning to show cracks. A crisis was avoided through the firmness of British and American authorities in refusing to let Tito have his own way. On 9 June, a month after the Second World War had officially ended, the Yugoslavs withdrew. In a sense, the first battle of the Cold War had been won. Over succeeding years such incidents between East and West would recur with displeasing regularity.

# The Air War, January–May 1945

As 1945 opened, three air forces in the West were prepared for the final great battles over Nazi Germany. Bomber Command of the Royal Air Force had about 1,500 aircraft available, over 900 of which were Lancasters. The US Eighth Army Air Force, the 'Mighty Eighth', included over 1,800 bombers, mainly B-17 Fortresses and B-24 Liberators. In subsequent months the number of Allied squadrons grew steadily, with enormous supplies of bombs and fuel. By the end of January on the German side there were 2,200 fighters, but the *Luftwaffe* suffered increasingly from shortages, especially of aviation fuel. The German Air Force then was being run down in numbers as bomber units were disbanded and men were posted to fight in ground regiments, with

infantry or SS detachments. Overall, the numbers serving declined from 2.3 million personnel in December 1944 to some 1.8 million by April 1945.

Although the Germans were now hemmed in, especially by powerful Allied armies advancing from both east and west, they fought stoically to defend their Fatherland. Their revenge weapons, V1 flying bombs and V2 rockets, were still being aimed at southern England, some of the former launched over the North Sea from bombers. Moreover, the *Luftwaffe* was now receiving jet aircraft for operations. Hitler wanted them to be employed as bombers, but many were needed as defensive fighters. Not the least of the *Führer*'s faults, according to the *Luftwaffe*'s last Chief of the Air Staff, was his lack of understanding of

air power. He was 'an infantryman in outlook all his life' and 'had no understanding of the needs of the Air Force'.

After bad weather in early January had cleared, the great bombing campaign against Germany continued and expanded. For example, on 14 January the US Eighth Air Force's 3rd Air Division, protected by 351 P-51 Mustang fighters, raided Berlin in daylight, causing widespread damage. Two nights later Bomber Command despatched 893 aircraft to attack Magdeburg and targets in Czechoslovakia, where their H2S Mk III radar proved to be very accurate.

During February the offensive intensified. On 3 February an armada of 1,200 American 'heavies' dropped 2,267 tons of bombs on Berlin. The size of the aerial battle can be judged

LEFT: The Second World War led to astonishing developments in aviation: ever more powerful piston engines, jet aircraft and the first operational helicopters. This is one of the many odd prototypes developed by the Germans, an asymmetrical reconnaissance aircraft built by Bloehm and Voss.

BELOW: The 'wooden wonder': the two-man British Mosquito bomber could reach Berlin with as big a bombload as a US heavy bomber. Its speed was its protection since it could outrun most German night fighters. Many of the very destructive late war night attacks on Berlin were conducted by Mosquitos.

from the fact that although the formations were escorted by 900 fighters, 27 bombers were lost. Three days afterwards, in selecting transportation targets, 1,300 heavy bombers hit marshalling yards at Magdeburg and Chemnitz.

At the Yalta Conference the Russians asked that Bomber Command and the USAAF carry out attacks on communication centres behind the enemy front line. This would confuse German efforts to reorganise and move supplies. Such bombing would not only help the Russian offensive, but also would fit into general Allied policy concerning the overall campaign. In addition, both Portal and Churchill had been pressing for some time for Bomber Command to attack one or more of the large cities in the east of Germany. At the end of January the former had demanded attacks on 'Dresden, Leipzig, [and] Chemnitz', where confusion would result from 'a severe blitz'. The prime minister asked whether 'large cities in East Germany should not now be considered especially attractive targets'.

Harris obeyed his orders and,

although questioning its value, organised a raid on Dresden, a communications centre of importance. On the night of 13 February 773 'heavies' of Bomber Command dropped 2,659 tons of bombs on the city. There was

little opposition and many closely packed buildings burned furiously. Casualties were particularly heavy, as the city was crowded with refugees. The next morning 316 American 'heavies' added to the raid, returning

**ABOVE:** Bombs fall on Germany from a massed formation of US B-17 bombers. Contrails at high altitude over the Reich were a visible reminder of the American presence and, by 1945, the impotence of the German air force.

the few survivors of Auschwitz. An apt response to those since the raid, from Portal and Churchill onwards, who tried to distance themselves from Bomber Command's success was given in later years by Leonard Cheshire. He was both a highly decorated bomber pilot and devout Christian. When told that the mayor of Dresden had objected to a statue of Harris being erected in London, Cheshire pointed out that the war would not have ended in 1945 without the bomber offensive. 'So what has the mayor of Dresden got to tell me about that? He and his city were supporting extermination camps which were killing a minimum of 10,000 a day.' He recollected that the Germans were 'going to mad lengths using extraordinary methods to kill people in horrible ways'. With such an enemy, 'you have just *got* to get at him'. Criticism of Harris and Bomber Command has failed signally to do justice to men fighting for basic good against basic evil.

By early April the *Luftwaffe*'s resistance was disintegrating, overwhelmed by the sheer numbers and power of aerial bombardment. At that stage Bomber Command could employ 1,609 bombers, of which 1,087 were Lancasters, while the USAAF had 2,018. Hordes of escorting Mustangs and Thunderbolts accompanied the raids, falling on any German aircraft found in the sky. The power of interdiction was so great that from 10 April no further attempts were possible to intercept daylight raids. The once great and vaunted *Luftwaffe* had reached the end of the line. As part of their last-ditch effort, some German fighters rammed American bombers. A total of eight bombers were hit in that way on 7 April, but the *kamikaze* style of defence was too late.

The targets chosen were widespread. Roughly 1,300 US bombers hit airfields to the west of Berlin on 10 April. On the following day the same number raided oil and transport targets as well as airfields. In an attack on pockets of German resistance still holding out back in France, the first napalm bombs were dropped together with high explosives. One of the war's last great raids was carried out in daylight by Bomber Command on 18 April, when 900 'heavies' unloaded

on the 15th to extend the destruction. The result was a successful accomplishment of the task given to Bomber Command and the 'Mighty Eighth'. German communications systems were heavily hit.

So why has the Dresden raid caused such a furore ever since 1945? The bombing has roused some passionate disapproval, especially from those unborn at the time, who never knew the temper and atmosphere of war. International conflict is no picnic. 'The choice lay between the preservation of Allied lives or German lives,' wrote Harris's biographer. 'In the circum-

stances the decision had to be to preserve Allied lives at the expense of those of the enemy.' This was hardly a surprising decision, considering the nature of Nazism and the immeasurable misery spread by the Germans across Europe. The result, nevertheless, has been grossly unfair, especially to Harris and to the airmen of his squadrons.

Death from aerial bombing has an impartial nature. In Dresden, the scale was larger than in many other places, but at the time the citizens of, say, Leningrad or London, Belgrade or Warsaw, were unimpressed. So were

LEFT: Germany developed a true submarine, one designed to operate underwater at all times, designated the Type XXI. Fortunately for the Allies the strategic bombing campaign severely hampered their construction and most were found like this, incomplete in the yards, when the war ended.

BELOW: Another measure of desperation, this German solution to their lack of bombers was to piggy-back a manned fighter on top of a remote-controlled bomber packed with explosive. This example was captured by US ground troops in a typical forest hideaway. With airfields out of commission, the Germans took to using their highways for take off and landing.

5,000 tons of bombs on Heligoland. The American air commander, General Spaatz, announced that the strategic war in the air was now over. Only a few tactical raids remained.

To those who have not experienced conflict, it is paradoxically often difficult to appreciate that war can produce examples of human kindness as well as destruction. Between 29 April and 8 May both American and British bombers were employed on humanitarian missions . The flooding of land in Holland by the Germans as a defence measure had led to food shortages for the civilian population. During the winter of 1944/45, 15,000 Dutch civilians died from starvation. Therefore both Allied air forces used their bombers to drop hundreds of tons of food, which were received with gratitude and saved many lives.

At the end of the European war hundreds of American aircraft and their crews were flown back to the United States. 'Almost all left their youth behind,' wrote one historian, 'in a land they had come to love and respect.' Also left behind were thou-

sands of their comrades who had perished in action over the European mainland. War in the air played a prominent part in defeating Germany, but at a cost. During the whole war, Bomber Command lost 55,000 British and Commonwealth aircrew dead. Between D-Day and May 1945 alone, the Command's casualties were 10,000 killed and over 2,100 aircraft lost. The achievements of Allied aircrew deserve gratitude, not reproof.

# The State of Germany

The ending of the European War in early May brought an outbreak of celebrations across most Allied nations. After inter-governmental consultations and disagreements over timing, Tuesday 8 May was set aside for the luxury of rejoicing. 'New York went wild,' announced the *Daily Mirror*. The London *Evening News* reported that 200 tons of tickertape 'floated like butterflies from the highest windows of Manhattan'. President Vargos of Brazil proclaimed a national holiday, while across much of Occupied Europe lights blazed and bonfires were lit. In London huge crowds thronged the main streets and avenues, singing, dancing and cheering. They were a mixture of civilians finally freed from the fear of attack, and a veritable United Nations of service personnel, representing countries across the world. This was a day of relief, of happiness and of joy. Churchill, broadcasting to the British people, referred to 'the evil-doers, who are now prostrate before us'. In return, the prime minister received acclama-

tion for the manner in which he had led people of the United Kingdom and the Commonwealth through dark days into what he would have called the sunlit uplands of victory. For six years death had sat at the gate and now he was gone. Yet not quite. Above the rejoicing hovered a sobering shadow. The war with Germany was over; the war against Japan was not. How many casualties would the next stage cost?

The population of Germany was in confusion and disarray, living in a national state which had been crushed. Hitler, who had promised his people the earth, had gambled too far. The nation was shattered. Here was an important difference between 1918 and 1945. The end of the First World War had been achieved through an armistice which left the German state intact. The machinery of government then was still in existence, with a civil service and judiciary to control national life. Although the Treaty of Versailles pruned some territory from Germany, the bulk of the nation remained united, physically untouched by conflict. During his twelve years in office, however, Hitler had destroyed

opposition. There could be no alternative administration.

In 1945 the nuts and bolts of government had largely vanished. Many former Nazi officials prudently started running or went to earth; others, like *Oberburgermeister* Freyberg and Chief City Treasurer *Doktor* Lisso, both of Leipzig, together with their wives and daughters, took to the poison bottle. In the words of one newspaper correspondent, 'There is nothing but disintegration. What was once the German State is now a vacuum in the centre of Europe.' The vacuum and its capital were about to be divided into four sectors, ruled and maintained by the three main victorious nations, and by France. And already three of those nations, the United States, Great Britain and France, were experiencing an uneasy relationship with the fourth, the Soviet Union. Over subsequent years a new struggle, the Cold War, would be carried on across the Nazi corpse, where a dictatorship of the East confronted the democracies of the West.

Stalin wanted reparations. Remembering what the Germans had done in the Soviet Union, he was less

inclined to show mercy. In the long run, Stalin foresaw a united Germany whose government was under his influence. His motives have since been debated. Were they merely defensive, by creating a series of buffer-states to protect Russia's frontiers? Or were they aggressive, intending to use a Russian-controlled Germany as a springboard for launching Communism across the rest of Europe? The US government became increasingly aware of Russian intentions and kept forces in Western Europe to counter them. All the time American troops remained on the Continent, the Russians' chances of controlling the whole of Germany were thwarted. Subsequently a 'tennis match' of confrontation opened in which the Russians were usually serving and the Western powers attempting to return the ball across the net.

As British and American troops fought their way across Europe and into Germany, they became increasingly aware of the effects that dictatorship could have on society. They had come from democracies where, in spite of shortcomings, forms of parliamentary government held power. There was a choice of parties. Representatives and their policies could be replaced by the stroke of a pen, not the impact of a bullet. Concentration camps holding thousands of political prisoners did not exist. Other camps dispensing death to 'undesirables' in further thousands were undreamed of. In Eastern Europe, advancing Russian armies found similar manifestations of dictatorship, but were, perhaps, less surprised. The government of the Soviet Union was itself a dictatorship where individuals did not count and sublimation to the state was a national duty. For anyone who offended the official will, which usually meant the opinions of Josef Stalin, death or imprisonment was the result. Across the USSR were scores of prison camps – 'gulags' – where hundreds of thousands of those out of step with the Party line finished their days. A ruthlessness matching that of the Nazis had been shown, for example, in Stalin's pre-war purge of army generals, and by the mass slaughter of Polish officers in the Katyn Forest in 1941.

The Allied entry into Europe uncovered horrors of unimaginable proportions. The hideous apparatus of the secret police, the *Gestapo*, had been clamped on to the German homeland and on the many nations which had fallen under the conqueror's heel. Special squads – *Einsatzgruppen* – of the SS had murdered hundreds of thousands of innocent people, especially in Eastern Europe. Furthermore, the Nazi policy of racial superiority had led to a holocaust of the deliberate killing of 6 million Jews. Their crime? They were Jews. In later years, younger people find it hard to comprehend the loathing of Nazism and the Germans which was ingrained in millions of those who had suffered the arrogance of the 'master race'. They had experienced travails so that the German people should benefit.

Allied forces noted particularly the absence of young men in German towns, cities and villages. Millions of them had gone to fight and were now either dead or languishing as prisoners. Germany appeared to be inhabited almost exclusively by the elderly, together with women and children.

In cities and industrial areas there was a different scene. The devastation caused by bombs and shells was on an unprecedented scale. In the town of Julich, for example, the damage 'was perhaps even greater than that seen elsewhere in Germany. No buildings existed and even walls were non-existent above waist height.' Hamburg, according to a war correspondent, was 'a completely and utterly bomb-ruined city'. Whole areas had been levelled. 'There are miles upon miles of blackened walls and utterly burned-out streets.' In ruins, cellars and air raid shelters over a million people were trying to stay alive. Those who had sown the wind had reaped a terrifying whirlwind.

**ABOVE:** The workhorse of the German panzer forces, a Panzer IV blown up during the Battle of the Bulge. Armed with a long 75 mm gun, the late model Panzer IVs could take on most Allied tanks with confidence. By this stage in the war, many were being abandoned for lack of fuel rather than lost in action.

# A British General Election

**ABOVE:** The Russian victory parade led by IS-II heavy tanks. These enormous vehicles were immune to most anti-tank weapons but their mighty 122mm guns took time to load and only command vehicles had radios. The imposing size and power of these tanks made an immediate impression on the British and Americans.

Soon after the end of the European war, British people became engrossed in a different type of contest which, nonetheless, in the long run had repercussions for the Germans. One basic reason for fighting the war was for Britons to protect their freedom to vote according to the democratic parliamentary system. There would be no one-party state. No general election had been held since 1935, and throughout most of the war the reins of office had been held by a coalition of ministers, under Churchill, representing the three main political parties. Should this government continue until the end of the fighting in the Far East? Or should an election be held as soon as possible? Opinions were divided. After much discussion on the merits of both cases, politicians decided on the latter. Party politics returned with a vengeance in June 1945.

Voting at the ensuing election took place in two stages. First, those entitled to the franchise – that is, those aged at least 21 – voted in Britain on 5 July. But spread across distant parts of the world were thousands of service personnel also entitled to vote. Their choices were made at polling booths set up wherever they were stationed, from Africa to the Far East, from Germany to Italy. Gathering the votes took some time, so the final results were not announced before 27 July. Their publication revealed an unexpected landslide victory for the Labour Party. The totals were Labour 393

# Potsdam

As election fever gripped Britain, plans were laid for the final Allied conference of the war. Churchill particularly wanted a 'Big Three' meeting because several issues remained unresolved. They needed clarifying before the armies packed their bags and went home. Two matters were of particular concern to him. First, the division of Germany had not been clearly settled, and secondly, Poland's frontiers had not been finally drawn, a matter which had brought on the outbreak of war in 1939.

By the time of the conference, codenamed 'Terminal' and held at Potsdam in Berlin, the threat from a mighty and aggressive Germany had gone. Yet for many Western statesmen there was unease over Russian policy. Across Eastern Europe, Communist governments were being installed with a type of political nepotism far removed from the style of democratic elections seen in the West. It soon became apparent that Stalin would not allow the Polish ministers who had been exiled in London during the Nazi occupation to have any role in the new Poland. The Russians pushed their own frontier eastwards to engulf parts of Poland, which itself was told to take territory from the Germans in compensation.

Meetings at Potsdam were held from 17 July until the end of the month and were remarkable for the appearance of new faces. With Roosevelt dead, Harry Truman, the new president, represented the United States. An eminent historian has written that 'Truman was prompter and clearer in decision and more straightforward by nature than Roosevelt.' On the British side, Churchill led the delegation for the first part of the conference but after the general election was replaced by Attlee from 28 July. The fact that a parliamentary system allowed for leaders to be exchanged in mid-discussion was obviously an enigma to the Russians. Opposition to Stalin was often rewarded with a bullet-hole in the head.

On 18 June Truman told Churchill of the successful tests of an atomic bomb which had taken place in the New Mexico desert two days earlier. The news had come to the president via a curt, coded message: 'Babies satisfactorily born.' Truman briefly mentioned the existence of the super-bomb to Stalin, but decided to share no details with him. We now know that, through spies, the Russians had already learned far more of the development than the Americans imagined.

At Potsdam the divisions between East and West became more clearly marked. Each side, although smiling, was wary and suspected deceit. For all, however, there was one major task remaining. The Japanese now had to be defeated.

seats, Conservatives 213, Liberals 12, Independents 22. The complex reasons for this swing to the Left are not to be explored here; suffice it to say that overnight the nation had a change of leadership. Clement Attlee, who had been deputy prime minister in the Coalition Government, now took office; Winston Churchill, leader of the nation through days of disaster and triumph and a man of giant courage and determination, was now leader of His Majesty's Opposition.

**ABOVE:** The winter of 1944–45 left the Netherlands on the verge of starvation, and the Allies resorted to air-drops of food to keep the civilian population alive. Here, a British Lancaster heavy bomber delivers supplies to a cheering crowd.

# CHAPTER 10: The End in the Far East

The Battle of Midway in June 1942 was a remarkable turning point in the Pacific Campaign. It came near the end of a gale of war which had started to blow some six months earlier at Pearl Harbor. Throughout that period Japanese forces had enjoyed spectacular successes on land, at sea and in the air, battering their Allied opponents on the way. The need to gain the raw materials of war was met as Malaya, the Philippines and Burma were overrun. In particular, the Imperial Navy's thirst for oil, which had contributed significantly to the start of the campaign, was satisfied by the occupation of the Dutch East Indies.

Subsequently, the story of the remainder of the Far Eastern war was one of a slow, defiant decline for Japan. That nation had been surprised and exhilarated by the extent and speed of the early conquests. To them, the white imperialists had been humiliated. They were ready to set up their 'Greater East Asia Co-Prosperity Sphere', which really meant a bigger empire with Japan as the chief beneficiary. Now, however, distant thunder clouds formed. Inexorably, over the three years following Midway, Allied forces moved forward towards the Imperial homeland and sufferings increased for all Japanese people, service personnel and civilians alike.

The Japanese were waging two wars simultaneously, a land and sea campaign. Often overlooked is the fact that they were forced to keep a strong army of occupation in China, where they had been fighting since 1937. The Burma Campaign was a related conflict which drew in extensive forces of the Japanese Army, fighting especially against British and Commonwealth troops. This lasted until the end of hostilities in the Far East. A large portion of the Imperial Japanese Army was tied down by land battles and commitments on the continental mainland of East Asia.

The sea campaign also placed demands on national resources. Distances in the Pacific region are difficult for many Europeans to comprehend. Parts of the Dutch East Indies lie 3,000 miles south of Japan; the voyage from Sydney in Australia to Wellington in New Zealand is 1,200 miles; Hawaii is situated almost 3,400 miles from Yokohama and over 2,000 from San Francisco; Hong Kong lies over 1,400 miles from Singapore. Even the great distances covered by Russian and German armies pale beside these.

An idea of the scale of their problem can be gauged by looking merely at the US Navy's expansion in the period from Pearl Harbor until the end of the war. The figures alone are awesome; for the Japanese they were disastrous. Altogether, ten battleships, eighteen fleet carriers, nine escort carriers and twelve heavy cruisers were built. To these were added 110 escort cruisers, 33 light cruisers, 358 destroyers, 504

**BELOW:** Australian troops are landed by the US Navy at Lae, New Guinea in September 1943. The Australians stopped the Japanese advance over the Kokoda trail in New Guinea and by late 1943 had begun a series of counter-offensives.

destroyer escorts and 211 submarines. Supporting them, American factories produced 80,000 naval aircraft and a similar number of landing craft for seaborne invasions. By 1945 the United States had comfortably overtaken the strength of the Royal Navy

and possessed the most powerful maritime force ever known. And the Americans, despite world-wide commitments, never kept less than two-thirds of their naval strength in the Far East. For example, in early 1943 the US Pacific Fleet included six carriers and ten battleships; the US Atlantic Fleet, relying for support on the Royal Navy, had one carrier and two battleships. A further example of the Americans' growing resources in the Far East is seen when comparing their air strength with that of Japan on two dates. In January 1943 the totals of aircraft were 3,200 Japanese and 3,537 US – almost parity; yet exactly one year later the Japanese had 4,050 while the American total had leapt to 11,442. The omens were sombre for Japan.

**ABOVE:** GIs study the imposing bulk of a Japanese Kawanishi H8k flying boat wrecked on Makin atoll in the Gilberts.

227

# China

The size of the armies employed by both sides in the Far East was small compared with the vast number of divisions fighting in Europe. The struggle in China and the defence of the Manchurian frontier with Russia, nevertheless, occupied a large proportion of the Japanese Army. In that sense, the land war against China, which had gone on since 1937, was a constant drain on Japanese resources. There were no great campaigns to match those in Russia and Western

RIGHT: Nationalist Chinese leader Chiang Kai-Shek presided over an uneasy alliance of regional warlords conscious to varying degrees that the real war would start after the Japanese were defeated: against Mao Tse-Tung's Communists.

Europe. No Stalingrads or D-Days occurred, with massive artillery bombardments or tank battles. In the main, Japanese Imperial troops were employed in policing or 'pacifying' the areas which they had invaded, or in 'mopping-up' operations. For many, their service in China consisted of acting as guards in a gigantic, over-populated prison camp. Yet they had to stay

RIGHT: Lt.-General Stillwell was known as 'Vinegar Joe' for his abrasive manner but working with the Chinese forces would have tried the patience of a saint. US support for the Chinese helped tie down some 750,000 Japanese troops in the region until the end of the war.

there to maintain their position as a victorious occupying power. In the north, forces were required to watch the sensitive area in Manchuria opposite the Russians. Thus the Chinese commitment was a burden carried by the Japanese Army, and it was one which could not be easily or swiftly resolved. For much of the early part of the war in the Far East, the Imperial Army was compelled to keep 26 divisions on the Chinese mainland, with a further fifteen at the Manchurian border. An equal number of independent brigades were also maintained there.

ABOVE: With the Japanese astride the main lines of communication between Burma and China, the Allies could only send limited support to the Nationalist Chinese by air. Eventually, the Allies hacked this switchback road link through the mountains, enabling them to supply effective quantities of weapons and ammunition to Chiang Kai Shek's forces.

According to some estimates, as late as August 1945 nearly half of Japan's armed forces were engaged on the mainland of East Asia.

Unlike most states, China had no single army under a unified command. Years of dissension had left the nation divided, with two main groups of Chinese armies. The first comprised Communist forces under Mao Tse-tung, in the north-west, near Yunan, where they had settled after the 'Long March'. The second consisted of Chiang Kai-shek's Nationalist forces around Chunking, 500 miles to the south. These two forces sometimes fought each other and shared only the aim of driving out the Japanese. Early in 1941, for example, the Nationalists defeated a Communist army in eastern China, driving it into a neighbouring province. Neither had much chance

against forces better equipped, trained and led. Between them were the private armies of Chinese warlords who controlled large areas. Some of these, in a climate of anarchy, made their own local peace with the Japanese, while others served them as mercenaries. Many were predatory towards long-suffering peasants. And yet, from the Allies' point of view, Chinese forces had to be supported. In April 1942 Churchill pointed out that the collapse of China would release between fifteen and twenty Japanese divisions to launch a major invasion of India.

The better army for the Allies to back was that under the control of Chiang Kai-shek. In spite of China's enormous population, he had only just over twenty well-equipped divisions at his disposal, probably totalling less

than 250,000 trained men. China's vast reservoir of manpower. which in theory could have provided over 300 divisions, was mainly unused. After Pearl Harbor this was the army that received Allied support. Some was sent along the route of the famous Burma Road, and thus the Burma Campaign, fought by British and Commonwealth troops, became closely linked to the situation in China. Other supplies were flown between Upper Assam and the Yunan plateau, over mountains known as 'The Hump'. From September 1943 about 10,000 tons of supplies monthly were transported over this hazardous air route. In January 1942 General 'Vinegar Joe' Stilwell was appointed US Chief of Staff to Chinese forces, trying to improve the fighting efficiency of Chiang's army. He had a hard task.

**ABOVE:** A Chinese soldier guards American P-40 fighter planes: the most visible sign of US aid to the Nationalist Chinese forces in their struggle with Japan. While the Nationalists displayed depressing tendencies to fight each other or their Communist opponents for much of the war, had the Allies allowed them to be defeated, vast number of Japanese troops would have been released to fight the British and Americans.

# The Burma Campaign, May 1942 – December 1944

**ABOVE:** Gurkhas advance into Rangoon at the culmination of Slim's brilliant offensive that broke the back of the Japanese forces in Burma. The speed and efficiency with which the 14th Army smashed its way past Mandalay was a fitting riposte to the disasters of 1942.

By mid-1942 the victorious Imperial Army had driven British and Commonwealth forces almost entirely out of Burma, cutting the Burma Road link with China. The British Army, after its longest ever retreat, now set up a main base at Imphal, across the Indian border in what was then the state of Manipur. The Japanese, however, did not follow up their success. Those commanders who wanted to press on to Imphal, keeping the British on the run, were ordered to halt. In India, the 'Jewel in the Crown', all was not well for the British. Sir Stafford Cripps, sent to Delhi by the Cabinet in London with an offer of self-government for the Indian people after the war, had failed during talks with the All-India Congress Committee. It wanted independence at once. Congress then ordered acts of civil disobedience, so the British were confronted with some unrest behind them,

as well as a successful enemy in front.

With the arrival of the monsoon season in mid-1942, large-scale military operations came to a halt. Until December, there was, in the main, only patrol activity along the line of the Chindwin river, and thus both sides were given the opportunity of a pause. This was a blessing for Wavell, the Commander-in-Chief, who then began rebuilding his army. The base at Imphal was extended, with fresh troops and supplies drafted in. In particular, air strength was expanded. Between March and June 1942 the air force in India grew from five to twenty-six squadrons; by December there were 1,443 aircraft in the Command.

The first move in this direction, nonetheless, did little to achieve that aim. For six months from December 1942, British and Commonwealth forces went over to the offensive, in the area of the Arakan jungle. Although there were shortages of equipment, Wavell wanted to do something. The offensive foundered against Japanese counter-attacks, and by May 1943 the 14th Indian Division was back at its starting point.

In August 1943, at the Quebec Conference, Allied leaders, both political and military, paid more attention to the land war in the Far East. A South-East Asia Command (SEAC) was formed, with Lord Louis Mountbatten as its Commander-in-Chief. His task was to organise and coordinate the efforts of all three services. The new Command became operational on 15 November and Mountbatten was at once faced with huge tasks. In his reckoning, his greatest problems were the 'three Ms' – monsoon, malaria and morale. For example, during 1943, for every British soldier suffering from wounds, 120 were affected by tropical diseases.

The Japanese High Command appreciated that the Allies were preparing to push back into Burma, so they planned to launch their own pre-emptive offensive. The Imperial Army had forces in the Arakan region in the south, and others facing Stilwell's Chinese in the north. Their main drive, however, was to come in central Burma. There, the Eighteenth Army, under Mutaguchi, a thrusting general, planned to push towards the British base at Imphal, where huge

**RIGHT:** A British 6-in howitzer in action in Burma. In such remote country the employment of tanks and artillery was extremely difficult, yet to break through any fixed defence such heavy firepower was invaluable.

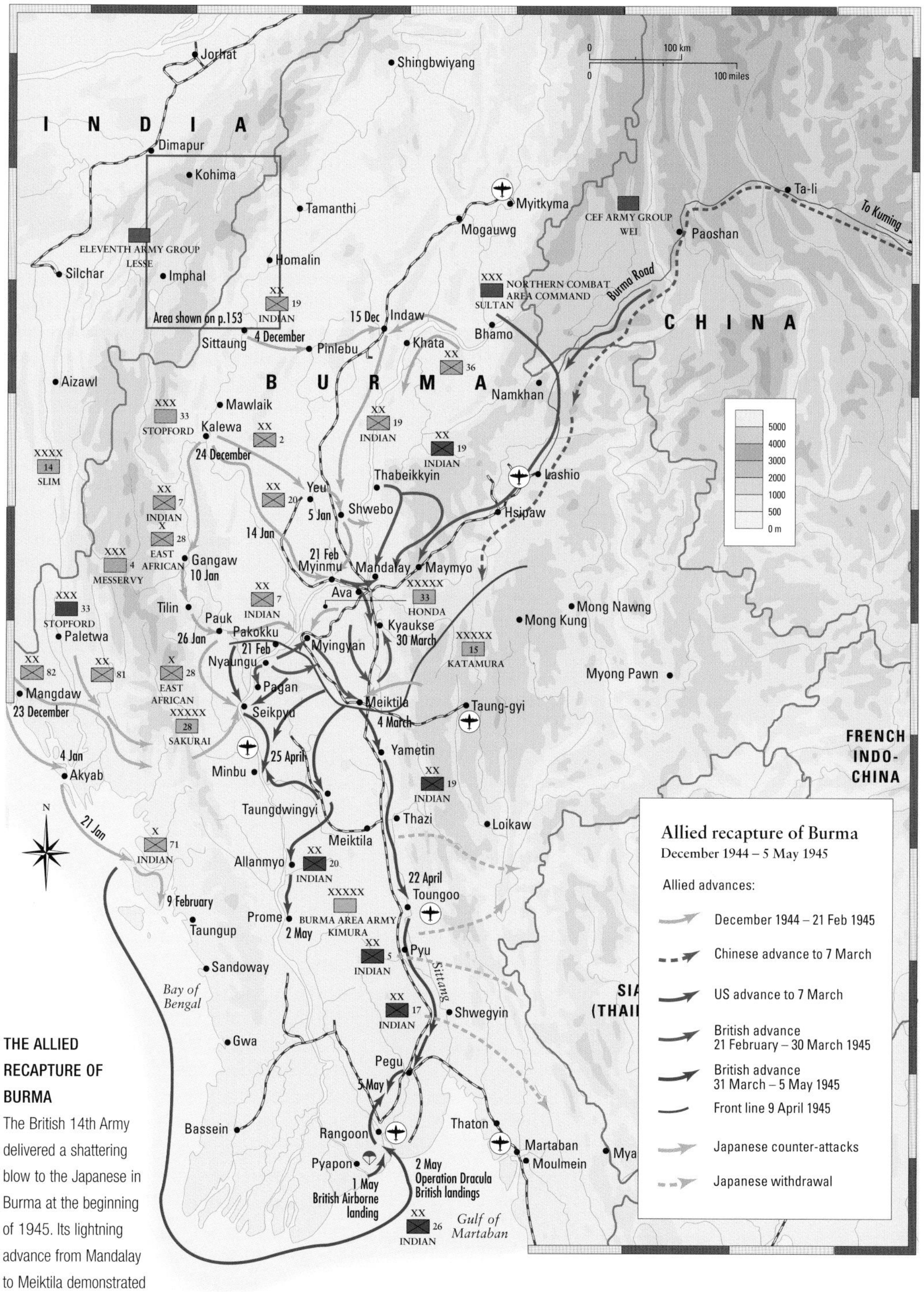
Allied recapture of Burma
December 1944 – 5 May 1945
Allied advances:
December 1944 – 21 Feb 1945
Chinese advance to 7 March
US advance to 7 March
British advance 21 February – 30 March 1945
British advance 31 March – 5 May 1945
Front line 9 April 1945
Japanese counter-attacks
Japanese withdrawal
0 100 km
0 100 miles
5000
4000
3000
2000
1000
500
0 m
I N D I A
B U R M A
C H I N A
FRENCH INDO-CHINA
Bay of Bengal
Gulf of Martaban
To Kuming
Burma Road
Sittang
Jorhat
Dimapur
Kohima
Imphal
Silchar
Tamanthi
Homalin
Shingbwiyang
Myitkyma
Mogauwg
Ta-li
Paoshan
Bhamo
Namkhan
Lashio
Hsipaw
Indaw
Khata
Pinlebu
Sittaung
Aizawl
Mawlaik
Kalewa
Yeu
Shwebo
Thabeikkyin
Gangaw
Tilin
Pauk
Pakokku
Myinmu
Mandalay
Maymyo
Ava
Kyaukse
Mong Nawng
Mong Kung
Myong Pawn
Paletwa
Mangdaw
Nyaungu
Myingyan
Pagan
Seikpyu
Meiktila
Taung-gyi
Yametin
Akyab
Minbu
Taungdwingyi
Thazi
Loikaw
Meiktila
Allanmyo
Prome
Taungup
Toungoo
Pyu
Sandoway
Shwegyin
Gwa
Pegu
Bassein
Rangoon
Thaton
Martaban
Moulmein
Pyapon
ELEVENTH ARMY GROUP LESSE
Area shown on p.153
CEF ARMY GROUP WEI
XXX NORTHERN COMBAT AREA COMMAND SULTAN
XXXX 14 SLIM
XXX 33 STOPFORD
XXX 4 MESSERVY
XXXXX 33 HONDA
XXXXX 15 KATAMURA
XXXXX 28 SAKURAI
XXXXX BURMA AREA ARMY KIMURA
XX 19 INDIAN
XX 36
XX 2
XX 20
XX 7 INDIAN
XX 28 EAST AFRICAN
XX 82
XX 81
X 71 INDIAN
XX 5 INDIAN
XX 17 INDIAN
XX 26 INDIAN
15 Dec
4 December
24 December
5 Jan
14 Jan
10 Jan
21 Feb
26 Jan
30 March
4 March
23 December
4 Jan
21 Jan
25 April
9 February
22 April
2 May
5 May
1 May British Airborne landing
2 May Operation Dracula British landings

THE ALLIED RECAPTURE OF BURMA

The British 14th Army delivered a shattering blow to the Japanese in Burma at the beginning of 1945. Its lightning advance from Mandalay to Meiktila demonstrated a mastery of blitzkrieg in jungle conditions. The Japanese reserves were distracted by a feint and their frontline was torn apart, never to recover.

stocks of supplies had been gathered. His men also would attack Kohima. With these two barriers captured, Mutaguchi intended to break out into the plains and march on Delhi, India's capital. He reasoned that, as he gained successes, many Indians would side with him in overthrowing British rule, welcoming the Japanese as liberators. One group of Indian nationalists, under the leadership of Chandra Bose, had already joined with the Imperial Army, forming their own division. They were now part of his strike force.

The peak of the campaign for Burma was fought between March and June 1944. In the north, Wingate's 'Chindits' went into action behind Japanese lines in early March. They now numbered 9,000 men and were employed on a much bigger scale than on their previous expedition. However, the Japanese reacted strongly and the Chindits had less success. In addition, Wingate, their leader, was killed in a jungle air crash. Mutaguchi's troops entered Assam, trying desperately to take both Imphal and Kohima. The area was mountainous, thickly covered, but even the coming of the monsoon did not stop the fighting. Some contests there were as savage and hard as any experienced during the Second World War. However, General Slim, who commanded the British and Commonwealth forces which constituted the newly formed Fourteenth Army, had brought spirit and confidence to his men. There were to be no more retreats.

The Japanese offensive into Assam was undertaken by a force numerically inferior to the Fourteenth Army. Yet, as the Allies had come to expect, the enemy fought fanatically. In an order of the day, one general told them to regard death 'as something lighter than a feather'. Should any of them fail on the field of action, their commanders would be entitled to use the 'sword as a weapon of punishment'. After several instances of wounded Japanese soldiers shooting British troops who had spared and passed them, a policy was followed of 'Never pass a wounded Jap.' Close fighting became intense in small areas. For example, at Kohima a tennis court became the centrepiece of a desperate struggle. Then, in June 1944, came a turning point. The Japanese had reached the limit of their endurance and began to retreat. Imphal was then relieved after an 80-day siege. In Slim's words, British and Indian troops had mastered , man for man, 'the best the Japanese could bring against them'. And yet the Fourteenth Army was still faced with the enormous burden of the 'three Ms': during 1944 it suffered nearly 25,000 casualties in battle, but over half a million from disease and infection.

Imphal, so long a defensive strongpoint, now became a springboard of attack. Mutaguchi's army, decimated by disease and starvation, and outfought, fell back towards the Chindwin river. All the way they were harried by Allied aircraft and lost about 60 per cent of their initial strength. By the end of 1944 what had started as a Japanese march on Delhi had collapsed into a retreat towards Rangoon.

# Back to the Pacific

The difficulties posed by vast distances caused problems for the Allies. One was the division of responsibilities. There was no overall supremo in the Pacific area, controlling the entire forces of army, navy and air force. Policy was decided by a Joint Chiefs of Staff Committee in Washington. Two main lines of attack were available to them, aiming in the long run to reach the Japanese homeland. One was the northern route, using small islands and atolls of the north and central Pacific as stepping stones towards Japan. The second was a southern route, moving through large island territories, such as New Guinea/Papua and the East Indies, with the same final target in their sights.

After deliberation, the Chiefs of Staff Committee decided on the southern route, but this was also divided into two. They gave to General

MacArthur, whose headquarters were then in Australia, a Command over the South-West Pacific Area. This included Australia, the Philippines, the Solomon Islands, New Guinea, the Dutch East Indies and islands in the Bismarck Archipelago. Some of these territories were already in Japanese hands. The remainder of the southern spaces of the world's greatest ocean, termed the Southern Pacific Area, was passed into the hands of the US Navy, under Admiral Nimitz, who led the Pacific Fleet.

On 2 July 1942 the Chiefs of Staff planned a double attack in the southern zone. The US Navy were offered the island of Guadalcanal in the Solomons as an objective. MacArthur's forces were to advance through New Guinea, then New Britain, aiming for the final target of the Japanese base at Rabaul.

However, the Japanese attacked

first. They particularly needed to take Port Moresby, in southern New Guinea, as part of their plan to isolate Australia. On 21 July Japanese troops landed on the island's northern coast and advanced through the Owen Stanley mountains towards the port. They were opposed mainly by Australian soldiers of the 7th Division, who defended fiercely. By late September the Japanese were within 30 miles of Port Moresby, but then were forced to retreat. From that time until January 1943 the Imperial Army was gradually driven back by the Australians and Americans until the offensive was finally broken. Once again, Allied air power played a prominent part in the defeat of land forces. By the end of the campaign the Allies had suffered 8,600 casualties, nearly 3,000 of them killed. The Japanese had lost 12,000 dead in an operation of attrition. The Imperial Army had been defeated for the first time in the war in a land campaign.

A further blow to Japanese hopes of expansion came in the Solomons, where, once again, they were trying to cut communications to Australia. On 7 August 1942 the American 1st Marine Division landed on several islands. The Japanese responded by pouring in troops, especially to the island of Guadalcanal. For the Allies, the operation was under the overall command of the US Navy. A series of naval actions offshore followed, in which both sides suffered.

On Guadalcanal, fighting continued with unabated ferocity as American Marines refused to yield to fanatical troops of the Seventeenth Japanese Army. In hand-to-hand encounters rifles, grenades, bayonets and boots were employed when foxholes and ridges changed hands in desperate struggles. A main target for the Japanese was Henderson Field, an airfield on the north coast. Throughout September and October both sides reinforced their armies, and suffered further casualties as their warships clashed in nearby waters. On land, each Japanese offensive was held, then repulsed. Although men on both sides lacked nothing in courage, the power of US forces, both in combined support and in *matériel*, gradually told. Yet the epic struggle did not end until

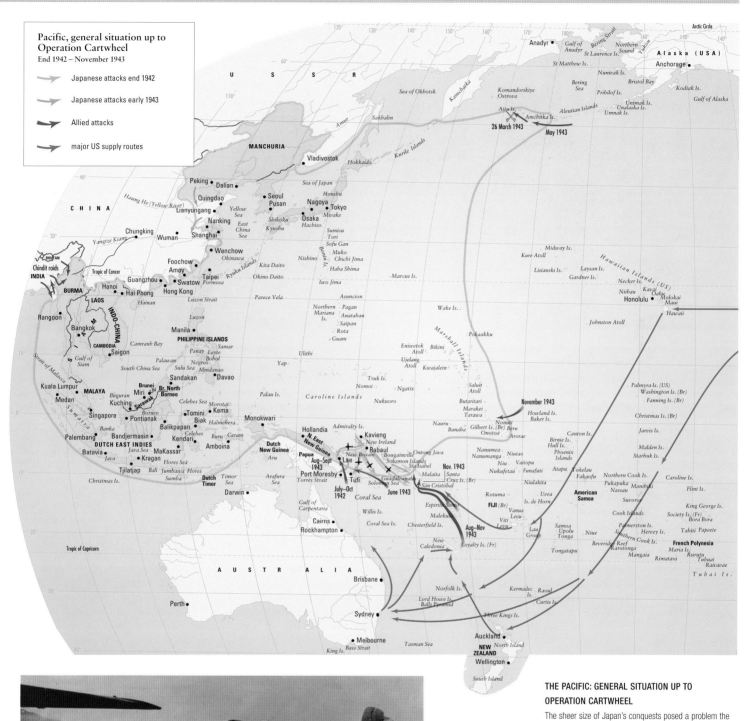

**Pacific, general situation up to Operation Cartwheel**
End 1942 – November 1943

↘ Japanese attacks end 1942

↘ Japanese attacks early 1943

➤ Allied attacks

→ major US supply routes

## THE PACIFIC: GENERAL SITUATION UP TO OPERATION CARTWHEEL

The sheer size of Japan's conquests posed a problem the Imperial forces were never able to overcome. From August 1942 until January 1943 the Japanese navy committed significant forces to the battle for the Solomons, but the main body of the fleet remained anchored at Truk. By late 1943 the balance of power had swung so far in favour of the Americans that Yamamoto's powerful battleships were no longer the decisive weapon their designers imagined them to be. In November 1943 the US assault on Tarawa was successful despite heavy losses. The Japanese fleet failed to intervene.

**LEFT:** B-25 Mitchells of the 5th US Army Air Force pass above US landing craft during the attack on Cape Gloucester, New Britain, December 1943. Some B-25s were later armed with up to 18 heavy machine guns and used for anti-shipping strikes in the Pacific.

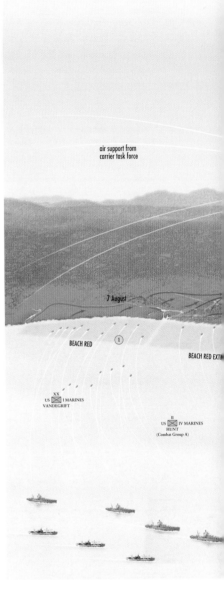

air support from
carrier task force

7 August

BEACH RED ①

BEACH RED EXT

US ☒ I MARINES
VANDEGRIFT

US ☒ IV MARINES
HUNT
(Combat Group A)

**ABOVE:** The Japanese garrison on Tarawa fought to the last man in some of the most savage fighting of the war. This hideous battle revealed just how costly the Pacific war would be despite all the US advantages in naval and aerial firepower.

February 1943, when the Japanese had punched themselves out. Not only had they met men of equal determination, but also they were short of supplies and riddled with tropical illnesses. At length the Japanese commander withdrew his remaining troops to another island, Bougainville. The cost to the Imperial Army was heavy. Over 20,000 men had been lost, almost half from disease and hunger, while the Americans, in spite of desperate struggles, suffered only about 1,000 dead.

On 18 April 1943 Japan suffered another severe loss, although in the form of the life of only one man. The officer in question was Admiral Yamamoto, the architect of the devastating strike at Pearl Harbor which

had given his nation such a flying start in the war. One part of the Pacific struggle in which the Americans held a distinct advantage was in code-breaking. By gathering and deciphering Japanese orders, the Americans learned that Yamamoto would be flown to Bougainville. US fighters were despatched to intercept the flight, the admiral's aircraft was shot down and Yamamoto was killed. The death of such a leader was a great blow, especially to the Japanese Navy.

The Americans made remarkable progress with the means available and their offensives gained momentum from the summer of 1943. Under MacArthur's leadership on land, and Admiral Halsey's control at sea, a gen-

**RIGHT:** Japanese bombers skim the sea as they fly through defensive fire from the US transports off Guadalcanal. This campaign marked the turn of the tide in the Pacific War as the Japanese failed to hold the island despite major reinforcements of both men and warships.

eral push northwards and westwards began. Both commanders cannily followed a policy of bypassing powerful centres of Japanese resistance and moving on to the next target. This 'leap-frogging' brought good results. The bases bypassed were then left to shrivel in isolation and were gradually squeezed by air and naval assault. This was comparable to the German Panzer approach in dealing with centres of stubborn resistance on land. In this way, advances continued through New Guinea and the region of the Solomon Islands, all aimed towards the Philippines. MacArthur particularly wanted to return there in triumph, to territory which had once been part of

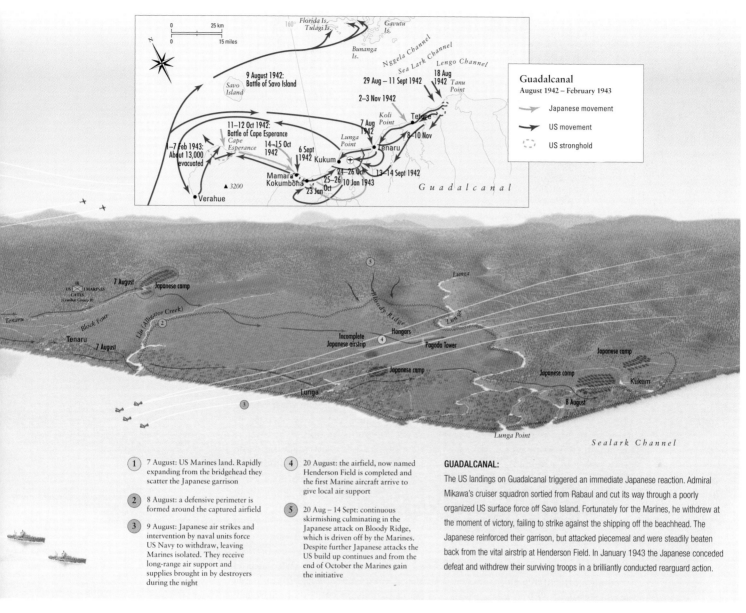

**Guadalcanal**
**August 1942 – February 1943**

→ Japanese movement

→ US movement

⌐ US stronghold

**GUADALCANAL:**

The US landings on Guadalcanal triggered an immediate Japanese reaction. Admiral Mikawa's cruiser squadron sortied from Rabaul and cut its way through a poorly organized US surface force off Savo Island. Fortunately for the Marines, he withdrew at the moment of victory, failing to strike against the shipping off the beachhead. The Japanese reinforced their garrison, but attacked piecemeal and were steadily beaten back from the vital airstrip at Henderson Field. In January 1943 the Japanese conceded defeat and withdrew their surviving troops in a brilliantly conducted rearguard action.

① 7 August: US Marines land. Rapidly expanding from the bridgehead they scatter the Japanese garrison

② 8 August: a defensive perimeter is formed around the captured airfield

③ 9 August: Japanese air strikes and intervention by naval units force US Navy to withdraw, leaving Marines isolated. They receive long-range air support and supplies brought in by destroyers during the night

④ 20 August: the airfield, now named Henderson Field is completed and the first Marine aircraft arrive to give local air support

⑤ 20 Aug – 14 Sept: continuous skirmishing culminating in the Japanese attack on Bloody Ridge, which is driven off by the Marines. Despite further Japanese attacks on the US build up continues and from the end of October the Marines gain the initiative

America's Pacific empire and which he had been forced to leave.

Plans were also laid for another, and different, advance towards Japan. This was the route directly across the central Pacific, traversing groups of islands in turn – the Gilberts, the Marshalls, the Carolines, then the Marianas. Before the war, American strategists had chosen the route in what they code-named 'Orange Plans'. It was the shortest and most direct way to their target. The advance would hop forward from island to island.

Attacks on the Gilbert Islands started in November 1943. The US Fifth Fleet, under Admiral Spruance, was now very powerful, with twelve battle-

ships, nineteen carriers and scores of support vessels. By then the Japanese Navy was becoming overwhelmed by the pace, numbers and strength of the American naval effort and could do little to respond. However, once soldiers and Marines were landed on small islands, close fighting was bitter and costly. For example, the island of Tarawa was defended by 4,000 Japanese troops. Despite heavy bombardments from both air and sea, they were well dug in and protected by artillery. When American Marines landed, supported by tanks, they suffered 3,300 casualties before taking the island. At the end, only seventeen wounded Japanese soldiers remained

alive. The nickname 'Bloody Tarawa' summarised the cost of victory. Here was a warning to the Americans of the difficulties lying ahead when the enemy fought so fanatically and suicidally.

Both American campaigns moved forward like a pair of pincers. By July 1944 MacArthur's forces, in which Australian divisions played a prominent part, had advanced through New Guinea and nearby islands, preparing for an assault on the Philippines. Further north, Admiral Nimitz's campaign was ahead of schedule. The Marshall Islands were taken. The main Japanese base and stronghold at Truk in the Carolines was devastated by attack from carrier-borne aircraft. Then

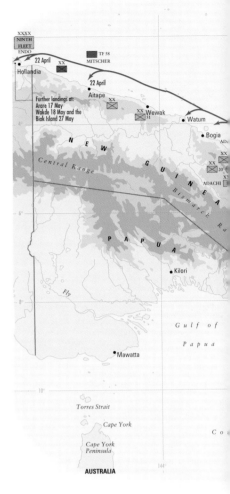

**LEFT:** US Amtracks advance on to the beach during the liberation of the Marshal islands. The beach area has been blasted into a veritable moonscape by repeated bombardments from sea and air. With the naval war dominated by aircraft, battleships were widely used to pulverize Japanese coastal defences before a landing.

**ABOVE:** US landing craft unload supplies to the beachhead on Iwo Jima in the shadow of Mount Suribachi. The 36-day battle for this island cost the US Marines 26,000 casualties: half the landing force. The 22,000-strong Japanese garrison fought to the death.

in June 1944 came the American offensive against the Marianas. The US task force had an ominous strength. The armada included fifteen carriers, holding 900 aircraft. Protecting these, and supporting landing forces with heavy bombardments, were seven battleships. A further 120 smaller warships were in the fleet, as well as troopships carrying 127,000 men.

The Americans went ashore on the island of Saipan on 15 June 1944. Four days later a gigantic air battle developed which proved disastrous for the Japanese. Later the Americans named

it 'The Great Marianas Turkey Shoot'. All Japanese attempts to hit the US fleet were thwarted, for the loss of 480 aircraft over two days, in exchange for about 30 machines. The Americans held two particular advantages in the air struggle. One was their improved radar guidance for aircraft and the second was a new proximity fuse employed by anti-aircraft guns. Both were lethal in their effects. In addition, three Japanese aircraft carriers –one of them *Shokaku*, a participant in the Pearl Harbor raid – were sunk by US submarines and bombers. The Battle of the Philippine Sea was further proof not only of the superiority in power of the US Navy but also of its excellent tactics. Combined operations were being honed to a fine art.

Later in the month, and throughout August, the islands of Tinian and Guam were taken. On the latter, small pockets of resistance continued until the end of the war. Symptomatic of the Japanese samurai spirit, yet foreign to the Western mind, was that as late as the 1970s a Japanese soldier who had never capitulated was discovered on Guam. It is important to remember the effect on Allied strategy and tactics, towards the close of the Pacific War, of the fanaticism and death-wish displayed by the followers of the Emperor, servicemen and civilians alike.

When the Marianas were safely in

American hands a giant step towards victory had been taken. Airfields were rapidly constructed by skilled engineers, using up-to-date equipment and the latest technological 'know-how'. The bulldozer proved itself to be one of the war's most important vehicles. Then the new giant B-29 Superfortresses, capable of reaching the Japanese homeland, could be flown operationally. Furthermore, the US Pacific Fleet now had a springboard from which to escort an invasion of the Philippines.

Based in the Philippines were ten Japanese infantry and one armoured division, under the overall command of General Yamashita, 'The Tiger', who had conquered Malaya and Singapore. For the attack on Leyte, MacArthur deployed two attack forces, carrying 200,000 men of the American Sixth Army, and a massive fleet. Over 500 vessels included 40 carriers and battleships. As the landings started on Leyte, from 20 October 1944, the Japanese

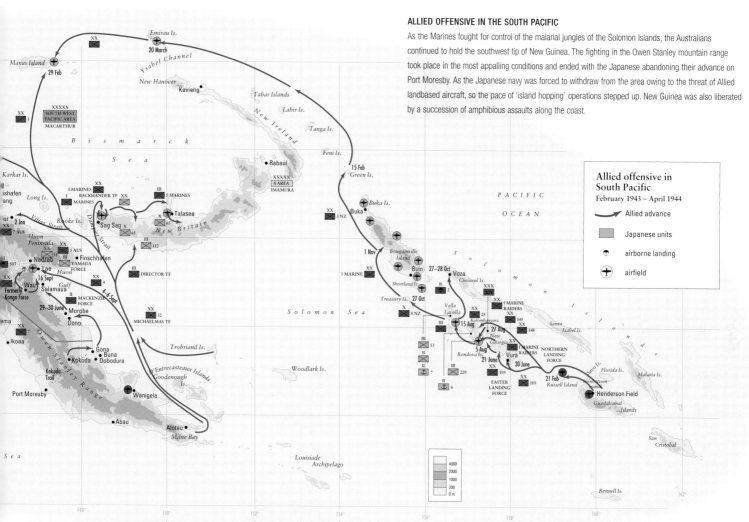

**ALLIED OFFENSIVE IN THE SOUTH PACIFIC**

As the Marines fought for control of the malarial jungles of the Solomon Islands, the Australians continued to hold the southwest tip of New Guinea. The fighting in the Owen Stanley mountain range took place in the most appalling conditions and ended with the Japanese abandoning their advance on Port Moresby. As the Japanese navy was forced to withdraw from the area owing to the threat of Allied landbased aircraft, so the pace of 'island hopping' operations stepped up. New Guinea was also liberated by a succession of amphibious assaults along the coast.

**Allied offensive in South Pacific**
February 1943 – April 1944

↗ Allied advance
▢ Japanese units
⊕ airborne landing
✛ airfield

had about 11,000 men there, a total which was reinforced to 65,000 by the end of the year. The majority remained on Luzon.

The threat to the whole Japanese position in the Far East was so ominous that the Imperial Navy was forced to intervene. What followed was the Battle of Leyte Gulf, the greatest naval battle ever, involving 282 warships. Over a period of four or five days, each side manoeuvred frantically, pursuing and being pursued as contact was made and then broken. The Japanese aimed to hit the invasion transports. The Americans tried to sink enemy warships. Often there was muddle, and both sides missed some golden opportunities. In desperation, during air attacks, some Japanese pilots deliberately crashed their planes into American vessels of the Third Fleet – the beginning of *kamikaze* ('Divine Wind') tactics. But the roll-call at the close of battle was disastrous for

Japan. The Imperial Navy had lost four carriers, three battleships, nine cruisers and ten destroyers. One of the battleships was *Musashi*, with 18in guns the world's biggest. Even such a giant could not withstand the effects of hits from nineteen torpedoes and seventeen bombs. The US Navy had lost three carriers and three destroyers.

The land fighting on Leyte lasted from 20 October until the end of the year. Gradually the Japanese poured in more troops until 65,000 were on the island. The Americans, nonetheless, had three times as many men there. Once again, the desperate defenders were slowly overwhelmed by the strength of well-equipped and well-supported numbers. American success was reflected in the number of casualties. By the end of December 1944 the Japanese had suffered 70,000, while the US total was 15,500. Only Luzon remained in Japanese hands.

As the year closed, the outlook for

the Imperial forces was bleak. The strength of the Japanese Army stood at only some 50 divisions, whose commitments stretched from the East Asian mainland to the hundreds of Pacific islands. The US air forces had almost 18,000 aircraft available for action in the Far East, while Japanese air strength was reduced to 4,600. US naval successes, especially from the remarkable submarine campaign, had sunk half of Japan's merchant fleet, together with two out of every three tankers. Supplies of oil from the Dutch East Indies had virtually dried up – an irony when it is remembered that their acquisition had been a prime motive driving the Imperial Navy into the war. The defensive perimeter of the homeland had shrunk, with Allied forces closing in. Within three years the explosion of success following Pearl Harbor had turned into a firestorm of retribution blowing directly back at the Japanese people.

# The Last Islands: Luzon, Iwo Jima and Okinawa

The opening gambit in the final stages of Japan's downfall began with the invasion of Luzon in the Philippines. In early 1945 about 250,000 Imperial troops were on the island, under Yamashita's command. American landings started on 9 January and the Japanese fell back slowly in front of their advance. At the beginning of February the US pressure had reached Manila, the capital, and a desperate struggle followed. Some 16,000 Japanese troops fought for every street and house until, by 4 March, the city was a total ruin, as devastated as any place throughout the whole war. Although the Americans occupied most of Luzon, groups of Japanese, finally totalling almost 50,000 soldiers, fought on until the end of hostilities. By then, 200,000 Japanese had died in the Philippines campaign, while the Americans had suffered 40,000 casualties.

For the US Navy, two other points were prime targets as stepping stones towards Japan. The first was Iwo Jima, an island of volcanic ash measuring about eight square miles and lying half-way between Saipan and Tokyo. Iwo Jima's importance lay in its position, and already two airfields had been built there, only three hours' flying time from the Japanese capital. On 19 February three Marine divisions were put ashore and immediate-

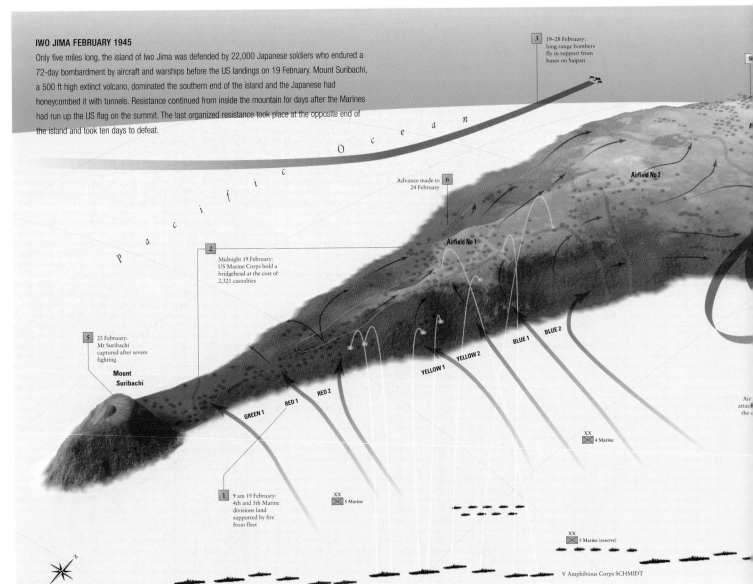

**IWO JIMA FEBRUARY 1945**

Only five miles long, the island of Iwo Jima was defended by 22,000 Japanese soldiers who endured a 72-day bombardment by aircraft and warships before the US landings on 19 February. Mount Suribachi, a 500 ft high extinct volcano, dominated the southern end of the island and the Japanese had honeycombed it with tunnels. Resistance continued from inside the mountain for days after the Marines had run up the US flag on the summit. The last organized resistance took place at the opposite end of the island and took ten days to defeat.

Pacific Ocean

3 — 19–28 February: long range bombers fly in support from bases on Saipan

8

Airfield No 2

6 — Advance made to 24 February

Airfield No 1

2 — Midnight 19 February: US Marine Corps hold a bridgehead at the cost of 2,321 casualties

BLUE 1   BLUE 2

YELLOW 1   YELLOW 2

5 — 23 February: Mt Suribachi captured after severe fighting

**Mount Suribachi**

RED 1   RED 2

GREEN 1

Air attack the

XX 4 Marine

1 — 9 am 19 February: 4th and 5th Marine divisions land supported by fire from fleet

XX 5 Marine

XX 5 Marine (reserve)

V Amphibious Corps SCHMIDT

ly came under the lash of 25,000 well-prepared defenders. On the first day alone, the Marines suffered 2,500 casualties, especially on the beaches. In spite of taking a battering from naval gunfire and aerial bombing, the Japanese fought stubbornly. Over the following five weeks American casualties rose to 25,000, more than 6,000 of whom were killed as, with grenades and flame-throwers, they tackled strongpoints in caves and trenches. The island was not finally taken until 6 March. Of the original Japanese garrison, only 200 were left alive. At the end of March, three airfields were ready to receive American bombers, but the island had been obtained at a terrible cost.

The other target for US forces was

ABOVE: Rockets shower forth from an American LCI (Landing Craft Infantry) as the first wave steams for the beach at Okinawa. This time the Japanese did not defend the beach as heavily as usual, holding back their main forces to fight inland.

the larger island of Okinawa, roughly 70 miles by 8 miles in extent. Both sides appreciated its strategic importance. Okinawa lay only 350 miles from Kyushu in southern Japan and the same distance from both Formosa and the Chinese coast. Bombers flying from airfields there could be escorted by fighters and would threaten all three areas. Therefore the Japanese Imperial General Staff poured in 100,000 troops of the 32nd Army for its defence. Some of the local population of 500,000 were also drafted in to the Japanese Army. Two thousand aircraft,

flying from Formosa and from southern Japan, were made available, many prepared for *kamikaze* raids on the invaders. Learning from previous experience, Japanese generals decided not to defend heavily bombarded beach areas, but to fight defensively inland.

The Americans understood the awesome task which lay ahead. An invasion force of almost 300,000 men was prepared, of whom 170,000 were combat troops. They were carried in, and supported by, a fleet of 1,400 ships, including two battleships and four carriers from the Royal Navy known as

Task Force 57. The first landings were made on 1 April 1945, when 60,000 Americans went ashore, meeting little resistance. Here was a venture reminiscent of 'Overlord' in Europe.

The battles on land, hard and costly, lasted until 17 June. From well-prepared and well-concealed defensive positions Japanese troops fought savagely. Americans made slow but grindingly sure progress against fortifications in such places as Kazaku Ridge, the Sugar Loaf and Conical Hills, all won at a heavy price. By the close of this intense passage of war, the balance

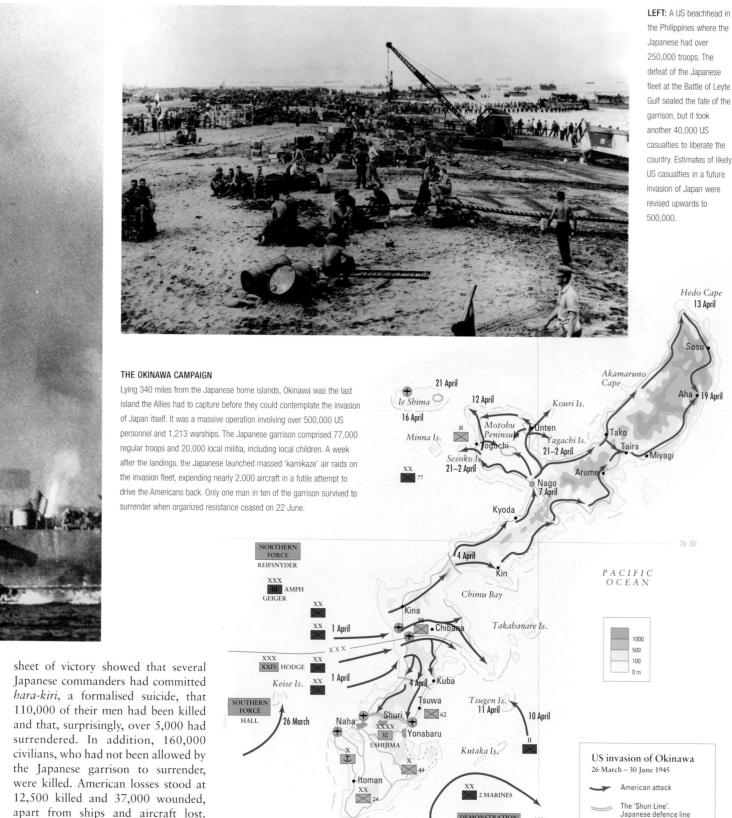

## THE OKINAWA CAMPAIGN

Lying 340 miles from the Japanese home islands, Okinawa was the last island the Allies had to capture before they could contemplate the invasion of Japan itself. It was a massive operation involving over 500,000 US personnel and 1,213 warships. The Japanese garrison comprised 77,000 regular troops and 20,000 local militia, including local children. A week after the landings, the Japanese launched massed 'kamikaze' air raids on the invasion fleet, expending nearly 2,000 aircraft in a futile attempt to drive the Americans back. Only one man in ten of the garrison survived to surrender when organized resistance ceased on 22 June.

sheet of victory showed that several Japanese commanders had committed *hara-kiri*, a formalised suicide, that 110,000 of their men had been killed and that, surprisingly, over 5,000 had surrendered. In addition, 160,000 civilians, who had not been allowed by the Japanese garrison to surrender, were killed. American losses stood at 12,500 killed and 37,000 wounded, apart from ships and aircraft lost. During the struggle for Okinawa, *kamikaze* attacks reached a new intensity – an ominous warning for future operations.

**US invasion of Okinawa**
26 March – 30 June 1945

→ American attack

The 'Shuri Line'. Japanese defence line

# The End in Burma

The story of the Burma Campaign during the first half of 1945 is one of the Imperial Army being slowly ground to defeat. Japanese soldiers fought with their customary tenacity. Their leaders often showed skill in operations, but, with dwindling supplies and increasing illness from tropical diseases, they were usually on the back foot. They were outnumbered and outgunned. Opposite them, the Fourteenth Army, led by General Slim, one of the war's outstanding commanders, drove forward. New forces were available to him, including troops from India and from East and West Africa, who fought magnificently. Success bred improved morale, and the old spectre of Japanese supremacy in fighting was laid to rest. At that stage Chinese forces also advanced into northern Burma. They had suf-

fered badly in 1944 when the Japanese had launched a successful offensive against them, which at one time posed a great threat to the Nationalists' ability to stay in the war. Now, nevertheless, they were helping to push the enemy back.

Slim's forces crossed the river Irawaddy in February, in what was the broadest river crossing anywhere during the Second World War. Two army corps were carried over water up to 4,500yds in width. Then, using tanks, they captured the important Japanese base at Meiktila. Mandalay also was taken after close fighting, and two Japanese armies, the Fifteenth and the Thirty-Third, were cut off. By April their position was hopeless. The Allied advance then speeded up, aiming to reach Rangoon before the monsoon broke. A combined amphibious and

airborne operation was mounted, and Burma's capital fell on 3 May. That, however, was not the end. About 16,000 desperate Japanese troops were left, mainly in the swamps of the Sittang valley. From June until the end of the war the Fourteenth Army fought tough actions to prevent their escape to Malaya or Siam, and to eliminate them.

The Burma Campaign, which had started with disaster, ended in triumph and the greatest defeat ever suffered by the Japanese Army. Altogether, 190,000 Japanese troops had been killed, an enormous contribution to the overall success of the Allies. Yet many of the Fourteenth Army believed then, and still maintain, that their achievement was not sufficiently recognised. Being so far from home, they were 'The Forgotten Army'.

BELOW: Japan built only small numbers of very inferior tanks so Allied forces were able to employ vehicles that were obsolete by European standards right to the end of the war. Here two M3 Grant tanks in service with the British support an infantry attack in Burma during late 1944.

# Bombing Japan

The largest aircraft of the Second World War was the Boeing B-29 Superfortress. It was also one of the most remarkably effective. Originally, it was designed as a 'hemisphere defensive weapon', to bomb Germany directly from the United States had the Nazis conquered the United Kingdom. The four-engine Superfortress had a wing span of 141ft, carried a crew of ten, was protected by eleven machine guns and could fly at speeds in excess of 320mph, holding about eight tons of bombs – a formidable weapon! This was the aircraft which was to play a crucial role in the last stages of the war, putting into practice the theory of the bomber employed as a decisive weapon, administering the 'knock-out' blow. Its arrival proved the superiority of American industrial production and enabled civilian workers, men and women, from Boeing factories in Wichita and Atlanta to play a prominent part in overthrowing the enemy thousands of miles away.

The first Superfortress was delivered in July 1943 and some, based in India and China, raided Japan from June 1944. Near the end of the year over 100 B-29s attacked Tokyo. However, these high-altitude raids caused little damage, attempting, as in Europe, precision bombing of targets far below. In fact, they prompted the Japanese to move some of their declining industrial production to other areas of the country.

A change came early in 1945 when General Curtis LeMay was appointed to lead XXI Bomber Command. Well experienced in the tactics of American and British bombers over Germany, he decided to change the employment of his Superfortresses. They would attack not only economic targets, but also urban areas, aiming to erode civilian morale. For cities and large towns, where there were so many wooden buildings, most aircraft would carry incendiary bombs, guaranteed to start massive fires. Moreover, most raids would be made at night from low level.

Subsequently, the great fire raids began. During this campaign the Americans dropped over 150,000 tons of bombs on Japan. Almost 100,000 tons consisted of fire bombs. Bombing speeded up from January 1945 and by the next month low-level

raids had increased. On 25 February, during a raid on Tokyo, 450 tons of incendiaries destroyed 28,000 buildings. On 9 March the capital was further hit by 200 Superfortresses, which met hardly any opposition. They dropped 1,700 tons of incendiaries, many of a later and more effective design than those used over Germany. Some sixteen square miles of the city, including a quarter of a million buildings, were destroyed, and up to 80,000 people died.

Other cities were hit. Nagoya, Kobe and Osaka were added to the calling-list, with Yokohama to follow. In each case incendiaries caused massive fires, bringing firestorms and the destruction of thousands of industrial and domestic buildings. 'The man who rides a tiger,' says a Japanese proverb, 'finds it difficult to dismount.' War was coming home to ordinary people with a vengeance. Great swathes of blackened destruction could be seen across city after city, and by the end of June three-fifths of Japan's 60 largest cities and towns had been devastated.

LEFT: Japan had made little preparation for civil defence before the war, assuming her forces would be doing all the attacking and other people would be the victims. The remorseless US bombing raids of early 1945 pounded Japanese war production to a standstill.

BELOW: B-29s in the Marianas from which the first devastating bombing raids were launched on Japan. Some of the incendiary raids in early 1945 inflicted more casualties than the atomic bomb missions of August yet still the Japanese leadership refused to sue for peace.

# Submarines

The final defeat of Japan owed
much to another weapon of war.
For some time after Pearl Harbor, surface vessels of the US Pacific Fleet were
not able to match the warships of the
Imperial Navy. Nonetheless, American
submarines operated widely and successfully against Japanese naval and
merchant vessels. By the end of the
war submarines had sunk about 5 million tons of Japanese shipping,
accounting for two-thirds of their merchant ship tonnage. In addition, they
were responsible for one-third of the
Japanese naval vessels lost. Altogether
this amounted to 1,178 ships each of
more than 500 tons – an impressive
success. To these totals must be added
those ships accounted for by the Royal
Navy, especially in the later stages of
the conflict. The Japanese merchant
fleet, which had over 6 million tons
afloat in December 1941, was down to
less than 2 million tons by April 1945.

BELOW: Church service in
the crowded torpedo room
of USS Bullhead during the
submarine's first patrol,
early 1945. By this time
US submarines had all but
eliminated the Japanese
merchant fleet.

LEFT: USS Drum sinks
another Japanese
merchant ship in early
1945. The Japanese paid
dearly for their failure to
develop anti-submarine
forces like those of the
British and Americans.

RIGHT: HMS Tally-Ho sank
the Japanese cruiser
Kuma off Penang in 1944:
she enters harbour flying
the skull and crossbones
flag traditionally raised by
British submariners after a
successful mission.

**ABOVE:** USS *Sea Dog* seen off Guam in May 1945. The US submarines effectively strangled Japan by cutting her off from supplies of oil and strategically vital materials like nickel, rubber and copper.

# Economic Decline

The economic decline in Japan's strength through the early months of 1945 was dramatic. In December 1941 there had been an oil stock of 43 million barrels; in April 1945 the total, imported and refined, was less than 4.5 million barrels. In all war materials, imports and home production were nowhere near equal to the needs of the armed services or civilians. Nickel, lead, rubber, bauxite, copper and iron ore were all in short supply, with sea trade strangled. Comparative figures for the Allies showed the chasm of industrial muscle between the two sides. For example, during 1944 Japanese production and import of coal totalled 53 million tons; in the same period British mines alone produced 184 million tons and the American mines 610 million tons.

This economic squeeze led to food shortages for the blitzed and suffering civilians. Not only was production down, but also in some areas transport was badly affected by bombing, thus limiting the movement of supplies. By the summer of 1945 shortages of food were so bad that a meeting of ministers searched for alternatives. On 2 August the *Nippon Times* reported a plan to collect acorns, 'in abundance everywhere in Japan, and turn them into food'. The paper added that 'the entire people will be called upon to give their aid'. Matters were getting desperate. 'Due to the nationwide shortage of food and the imminent invasion of the homeland,' announced a senior officer at Osaka, 'it will be necessary to kill all the infirm old people, the very young and the sick. We cannot allow Japan to perish because of them.'

# Kamikazes

RIGHT: *Bunker Hill*, seen here from the *Bataan*, was struck by two suicide aircraft off Okinawa on 11 May 1945. The fire and explosions killed 400 American sailors.

RIGHT: The USS *St. Lo* was the first major victim of *kamikaze* attack, hit by a suicide pilot off Samar in October 1944. She sank after a series of explosions when a Japanese aircraft crashed into her forward lift. The Japanese believed the expenditure of nearly 100 pilots on suicide missions was an effective tactic since their aircraft could no longer make conventional attacks with any hope of success.

Against the story of economic ruin lies the impact of the *kamikazes*. This was a practice of war which served to demonstrate the great gulf in outlook, beliefs and customs between the Allied and the Japanese mind in principles of fighting. To understand the reasons why so many airmen were prepared to carry out *kamikaze* raids, the background to what had happened to the Imperial Air Force by late 1944 must be borne in mind.

The Air Force had opened the war with aircraft which served their purpose well and were superior to Allied machines at the time. The Zero was a superb fighter, able to outmanoeuvre and out-shoot the slower and older types operated by the Americans and British. Japanese dive-bombers, torpedo-bombers and medium bombers were all very effective in the early stages. However, the Allies soon improved the construction and performance of their aircraft, constantly developing new types and modifications, while the Japanese made slow progress in design and engineering. They also suffered increasingly from lack of raw materials, fuel and improvements to aero-engines. In short, Allied engineering capability soon exceeded anything that the Japanese could offer. To this consideration must be added the loss of skilled aircrew, whose expertise was irreplaceable, while the Allies appeared to have an endless supply of new airmen and machines.

The gulf grew from mid-1944 and some pilots then were prepared to make suicide attacks, first termed *jibaku* and later known as *kamikaze*. Their lives and outlook were founded on obedience to the Emperor and their nation. For them, such an act served a double purpose, both being effective and also setting an example of nobility in death. They had seen some of their number carry out these sacrificial gestures by deliberately aiming their stricken planes at US Navy ships. 'We must give our lives to the Emperor and country,' one stated, adding that 'This is our inborn feeling.' Allied airmen appreciated that they themselves might have to die for their country, but would not willingly and eagerly choose suicide in a similar fashion. On that score, Eastern and Western outlooks were poles apart.

A strong advocate of *kamikaze* tactics was Admiral Onishi, commander of the First Air Fleet. On 19 October 1944 he formed a Special Attack Corps during the Philippines Campaign. Realising the weaknesses of his air effort when confronted by the numbers being deployed by the Americans, he suggested that the flight decks of US carriers offered fine targets. The only method promising success, in his view, was suicide missions flown by Zeros carrying 250kg bombs. He told his men that the nation was in great danger and requested their sacrifice 'You are already gods,' he said, 'without earthly desires.'

The first major success for a *kamikaze* pilot occurred on 25 October when, at 10.50 a.m. off Samar in the Philippines, the escort carrier *St Lo* was hit and sunk. The pilot crashed his aircraft on the forward lift, aiming for the vessel's magazines. For the Japanese the action raised morale and soon other airmen were prepared to follow suit. Off the Philippines, Japanese pilots launched 94 suicide attacks. Of these, four resulted in direct hits which sank ships, a further 30 struck and damaged vessels, while fifteen others missed the ships narrowly though damaged them. The value of these

attacks is shown by a comparison: only eleven bomb hits were registered from over 300 conventional raids. The *kamikaze*s were ten times more effective in gaining results.

The success of the *kamikaze*s caused Japanese leaders to expand the force. Even greenhorn pilots could be trained to fly the mission with a one-way ticket. Often the aircraft operated in groups of five. While a few dropped foil to defeat the ships' radars, others came in at varying heights. Some preferred to dive on to targets, while other pilots skimmed the waves to reach them. The tactics were at first unnerving to Allied sailors who were unused to this type of

warfare, but gradually the power of anti-aircraft fire, combined with that of intercepting fighters, hit the *kamikaze*s hard. They had more success against US than against British carriers. The latter, although carrying fewer aircraft, had armoured flight decks which usually withstood the crash and explosion. At Okinawa, however, US vessels suffered badly and 5,000 sailors died in these attacks. The carriers *Enterprise*, *Hancock* and *Bunker Hill* were all struck, the last-named suffering 400 crew killed. Nonetheless, for the Japanese these missions were a wasting asset: each time they lost an aircraft and a precious pilot.

*Kamikaze* sorties reached their height during April 1945, when 162 were flown. With an increasing shortage of fuel, aeroplanes and men, the numbers then reduced. Nevertheless, the Japanese planned for a huge onslaught to be made if the Allies tried to invade the homeland. Then every aircraft would become a *kamikaze* machine, so, increasingly, pressure was brought on pilots to volunteer. Any who returned from missions faced a terrible stigma and imprisonment. Commanders estimated that by the time the Americans invaded the islands of Japan, they would have 5,000 *kamikaze*s to meet them.

**ABOVE:** A Japanese pilot crashes his aircraft in the USS *Enterprise* (CV 6) despite the hail of defensive fire put up by the carrier's gunners. With obsolete aircraft and dwindling fuel reserves, the *kamikaze* missions combined cynical calculation with the death wish characteristic of the Imperial forces in the Second World War.

# The Position in April 1945

Much has been made since 1945 of the use of two atomic bombs at the end of hostilities, with the often-implied suggestion that the Japanese were innocent victims of US aggression. Before dealing with the last rites of the Second World War, therefore, it is worthwhile examining the positions and motives of the chief players in the Far East. For all of them, within a period of less than four years, the world had been turned upside down.

In April 1945 the British were involved against Japan in two main areas. Their campaign in Burma was coming to a close, with the Japanese Arrny in the process of being thoroughly defeated. Elsewhere, the Royal Navy's Pacific Fleet was in action, serving alongside the US Fleet in making increasingly close attacks on Japan itself. With the possibility of forthcoming invasions of those islands, British servicemen were being prepared for the final offensives. As the war in Europe was coming to a close, the intention was for the British effort in the Far East to be stepped up.

The United States was by far the most powerful nation in that part of the world. Economic strength had produced armed services which were thrashing the Japanese on land, at sea and in the air. Japan had never fully appreciated the effect that the sudden, unannounced attack on Pearl Harbor had left on the people of the United States. Such treachery, in the opinion of US citizens, should and would bring retribution. There would have to be nothing less than unconditional surrender. The worry for the Americans, however, was the expected cost in lives. The desperation of Japanese defence, with *kamikaze* attacks and a willingness to die readily for the nation, concentrated the minds of US service leaders.

Japanese civilians as well as soldiers, sailors and airmen would fight to the death. Seaborne landings on the mainland, under the cover of an overwhelming aerial umbrella, were perfectly feasible, but what would be the payment in Allied blood? Iwo Jima and Okinawa had given a foretaste. Suggested figures varied. Some thought that there could be a million casualties; others offered that as the number of dead alone. Consequently, although American leaders wanted to settle their own score with the Japanese without help, there was recognition that if the Russians entered the final stages of the war the redoubtable Red Army would be of great assistance. In the meantime, the Japanese would be subjected increasingly to the medicine of aerial bombing.

Inside Japan two divergent points of view emerged. One was held by many civilians and moderate elements in the government. Some of them had known from 1943 that defeat was on the way. In early 1945 there was talk of trying to make peace, but in the climate of the time such thoughts were considered treasonable: they could lead to a visit from the *Kempetai*, the secret police. As the situation inside Japan worsened, with intensified bombing, the movement for peace strengthened.

The other opinion in Japan, strongly held by the armed forces, was for the fighting to continue. The Japanese had suffered heavy defeats and considerable losses, particularly at Iwo Jima and Okinawa, but did not despair. Their theory of war was based on attack rather than on defence. Their

determination to fight to the death, with no thought of self-preservation, gave them confidence in the outcome of a great, final battle. This would be the crucial struggle, the *hondo kessen*, for the home islands. On 20 April 1945 the Imperial Japanese Army summarised this outlook in a communiqué: 'We shall throw everything conceivable, material and spiritual into the battle and annihilate the enemy landing force by fierce and bold offensive attacks.' The message added that 'every soldier should fight to the last, believing in final victory'.

This outlook explains the fact that when cities were being heavily bombed, especially in May and June, with thousands of civilians killed, Japanese military policy was to leave fighters on the ground. They were being kept back for the great final battle. A heartless decision?

At the Potsdam Conference on 25 July 1945 the Japanese were warned that, unless they surrendered, there would be 'prompt and utter destruction'. Yet their leaders, with service commanders exercising a tight control, still refused the unconditional surrender demanded. They announced that the threat would be ignored: 'We will press forward resolutely to carry the war to a successful conclusion.' They were still hoping for a negotiated peace on favourable terms, but were clutching at straws.

These were the underlying factors causing the Americans to step up the bombing campaign against a nation which stubbornly refused to accept reality. By late July, faced by such intransigence, the US Army Air Forces were prepared to employ a new weapon as part of their bombing offensive.

**ABOVE:** These Kawasaki Ki.45 bombers were found by the British after the liberation of Singapore. Given the Allied reporting name 'Nick' they were used in some of the first suicide missions, off New Guinea in May 1944.

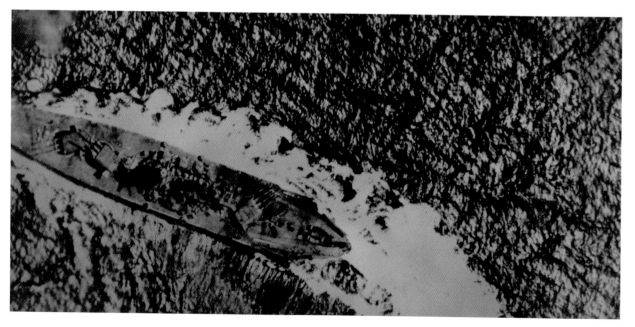

**LEFT:** One of the Japanese navy's two super-battleships under attack by US aircraft during the Battle of Leyte Gulf. Japan had begun the war in expectation of a decisive encounter between fleets of battleships. Even after the domination of aircraft carriers seemed assured, the Japanese retained their powerful battle squadrons intact until the landings in the Philippines finally tempted them to risk all.

# The End

**ABOVE:** The USS *Indiana* bombards Japan itself, July 1945, the first time the home islands had been brought under gunfire since the 19th century. By this time Japan had no options left, but the Emperor and his government persisted in prolonging the suffering of their own people rather than admit they were beaten.

After 1939, the power and size of high-explosive bombs grew until cities and towns world-wide were laid waste, with thousands of their inhabitants killed or injured. By 1945 the RAF were dropping the two largest bombs known as the 'Tallboy', at 5.4 tons, and the 'Grand Slam' or 'Earthquake' bomb, at almost 10 tons.

The search for an even more devastating bomb had continued for some years. Instead of using conventional high explosives, a different form of power was sought, one which could be fitted into a normal sized bomb casing yet had enormously greater destructive effect. Several countries urged their scientists to explore this field, experimenting to split the atom. The prize would be to produce an atomic bomb as the ultimate weapon. During the war German scientists made progress in this field, although at the end they fell well short of the objective. Japanese scientists from April 1940 also attempted to create an atomic bomb. Three years later they had made advances and believed that such a weapon could be constructed. Although they were not able to produce the necessary chain reaction, their work continued. Little imagina-

tion is needed to appreciate what use either Hitler or the Japanese High Command would have made of their labours had the scientists succeeded.

The greatest advances were made by the Allies. In 1939 Albert Einstein had warned President Roosevelt that the Germans were aiming to produce atomic weapons, and soon US scientists were making their own experiments. The potential of an atomic bomb was pointed out to the National Academy of Scientists two years later. 'A fission bomb of superlative destructive power,' they were told, 'will result from bringing quickly together a sufficient mass of Uranium 235.'

From 1942 they were joined by British and Canadian scientists who had been following similar work. The 'Manhattan Project' was started in the United States. By 1943 various aiming points for these bombs were discussed, in the belief at the time that they would produce an explosion equivalent to about 1,000 tons of TNT and thus could be used on the battlefield. At length, early in 1945 the Americans were ready to test a bomb which, significantly, turned out to be far more powerful. A report on 25 April called it 'the most terrible weapon ever

known in human history, one bomb of which could destroy a whole city'.

The first test was held in the New Mexico desert in mid-July, two months after Germany's defeat. Observers saw a light brighter than the midday sun. Gold, purple, violet, grey and blue colours were given off: 'It lighted every peak, crevasse and ridge.' The atom had been split. As we have seen, news of the successful test was sent rapidly to President Truman at the Potsdam Conference. He and his advisers now had to reach a decision on the next step. On Truman's desk stood the message, 'The buck stops here.' The importance of the decision should be viewed through the eyes of the time, not from the safe fortress of historical hindsight. There were a few Allied commanders who believed that the use of the bomb was either unnecessary or immoral. Others suggested that the Japanese might be shown a test explosion, to impress them with the weapon's potential. But in 1945, overall, there was little general doubt. Heavy bombing of Japan had desolated cities and the nation was suffering severely, but it had not surrendered. *Kamikaze*s had shown what could, and probably would, happen to invading forces. Scores of thousands of Allied prisoners languished under brutality in Japanese camps. Most American military commanders and scientists believed that the Japanese would give up only if they received a final, stunning shock, with no prior warning. Every extra day that hostilities lasted brought further deaths, especially to Allied servicemen. War is no party.

On 24 July General Carl Spaatz, leading the US Army Strategic Air Forces, was instructed that the first special bomb should be dropped 'after about 3 August 1945 on one of the targets: Hiroshima, Kokura, Niigata and Nagasaki'. On 6 August the B-29 Superfortress *Enola Gay* left the island of Tinian, 1,400 miles from Japan, escorted by two observation aircraft. At 8.15 a.m., from an altitude of 31,000ft, an atomic bomb, 'Little Boy', was released over Hiroshima. About 43 seconds later the bomb exploded at a height of 2,000ft. Wide swathes of the city were destroyed and almost 80,000 people killed in a terrifying blast equal to 20,000 tons of TNT. The

devastation was followed by the under-estimated dangers of radiation. The desired shock to Japan had been delivered, but, even so, some military leaders there still wanted to fight on.

The Japanese were now confronted with a new enemy as Stalin kept his promise to enter the Far East conflict. On 8 August the Russians declared war and shortly attacked the Imperial Army in Manchuria where, with great superiority in tanks and aircraft, their experienced troops made rapid advances. Within a few days the Japanese Kwantung Army was being brought to its knees. The importance of Soviet intervention is debatable. There is no doubt that Stalin had an eye for the main chance and hoped to make gains in the Far East from taking part. The Americans by then neither needed nor welcomed Russia's move. At home, Japanese leaders were affected far more by American pressure than by anything the Red Army was achieving.

This was reinforced on 9 August when a second atomic bomb was dropped, this time on Nagasaki. Probably 25,000 people died, and heavy damage was caused. Despite the powerful elements among the Japanese leadership who wished to fight to the death, the nation's most respected leader was the Emperor, Hirohito, whose god-like position in Imperial society was virtually incomprehensible to Western minds. In theory he played no active role in creating government policy, but he could now see the writing on the wall. While his politicians and service leaders played for time, arguing and hoping for favourable terms, he made his decision. The nation was at the end of its tether. On 14 August he told his ministers that surrender was the only option. They would have 'to endure the unendurable and suffer the insufferable'. No one in Japan would act against the Emperor's will, so that was that.

Next day the Emperor broadcast to his people, the first time they had ever heard his voice. If they continued to fight, he said, events would 'result in an ultimate collapse and obliteration of the Japanese nation'. For them, his decision was final. At last the war was at an end and on 15 August the Allies world-wide celebrated 'VJ-Day'. The Japanese had sown the wind at Pearl Harbor; they reaped a whirlwind in their own homeland 44 months later.

American forces did not rush in to occupy Japan, which now lay at their mercy. The final scenes were not enacted until 2 September 1945. On that day General MacArthur, surrounded by other Allied officers, was on board the American battleship *Missouri* in Tokyo Bay. For some Japanese there were historic shades of the arrival of Admiral Perry's fleet in 1853! All watched as representatives of the Japanese government put their signatures to an 'instrument of surrender'. The Second World War, which had started on the German-Polish border six years and one day earlier, was now at an end. The killing had officially stopped.

**ABOVE:** As US troops prepared to assault Japan, they were still in action from time to time on Guam, where organized resistance had ceased twelve months earlier. Many Japanese troops retreated into the jungle and emerged to conduct guerrilla raids and sniping attacks until after the war. The last survivor of the garrison did not give himself up for another 30 years.

# Appendices

## Appendix 1. Two Unhealed Wounds

In a sense, the Second World War has never ended. Much of the present form and direction of events at the end of the twentieth century has been shaped by the hurricane which engulfed the world some sixty years ago. In a number of continents, the legacies of the titanic struggle live on, with wounds unhealed.

For example, in the chain reaction of history, at least some of the Middle East's unsolved, and seemingly insoluble, problems can be traced back to the actions of some Germans in the 1940s. To their children's question, 'What did you do in the war, Daddy?' they would have to answer, 'I killed Jews.' The scale of their murders was so great that after 1945 thousands of Jewish survivors went to Palestine, their Promised Land, to escape from the memory of the Holocaust. From that came the establishment of the State of Israel and bitter controversy with Palestinians who had made that country their own homeland – and half a century of bitterness and bloodshed has followed between Jews and Arabs.

What was the Holocaust? This was a racial slaughter unmatched in history. Here was an attempt by the Nazis to remove Jews from Germany, then to exterminate them. The arithmetic was simple in its awfulness. Between 1939 and 1945 about one-third of the world's Jews were done to death. Of the 11–12 million Jews living in Europe at the start of the Second World War, half were dead six years later. They were not casualties of battlefield campaigns, or of concentrated aerial bombing, but were victims of the overall Nazi aim, set out specifically in Hitler's *Mein Kampf*, then in his Last Testament, to have a *Judenrein* (Jew-free) Germany.

The number six million is virtually incomprehensible to the average person's mind. It might be imagined more readily by thinking of a full crowd at Wembley Stadium all being killed, removed, then replaced by a similar crowd, then another, then another . . . That operation would have to be repeated 80 times to equal the number of dead in the Holocaust.

The campaign had started in Germany soon after the Nazis had attained power in 1933. By 1939 about 800,000 Jews had left the Reich, followed by a further 50,000 over the next two years. Most had to pay ransoms or bribe officials in order to be allowed to go. Half of those left never saw the end of the war. After the demolition of Poland and invasion of Russia, the pace of killing intensified.

At the Wannsee Conference in January 1942, a more concentrated and planned organisation was established for the 'Final Solution'. An effective, cost-cutting system was introduced and followed methodically wherever German feet trod in conquest. Consequently, the virus of anti-Semitism stretched all over Occupied Europe, from the Baltic states to Hungary, from Holland to France and from Norway to Yugoslavia. Jews were hunted down relentlessly, then deported.

In Germany itself, concentration, or labour, camps for both Jews and other 'undesirables', such as gypsies and Jehovah's Witnesses, worked thousands to death. They died in such places as Belsen, Dachau, Ravensbrück and Buchenwald. To the east, extermination camps were built to 'process' Jews at, for example, Auschwitz, Maidenek, Sobibor and Treblinka. By the end of 1942 most Jews in Eastern Europe had been shot, gassed or burned. Their belongings, from furniture to wrist-watches and gold teeth to hair, were taken to improve the German economy and help the Nazi war effort. Today, some survivors can forgive, but others cannot; none will forget.

Were the guilty adequately punished? At the Nuremberg Trials, held from late 1945 until early the following year, the chief surviving Nazis were indicted and tried on charges of committing major war crimes. Thousands of others at a lower level, however – industrialists, local officials, soldiers, guards – escaped the net. Of the 200,000 Nazis who played an active part in the 'Final Solution', fewer than 40,000 were tried and convicted. For most, the consequence of their guilty acts has been a resounding silence as they have glided into old age, buttressed comfortably by the post-war German economic miracle.

Since the war, questions have been raised over the reactions of the Allies to what the Germans were doing to the Jews. There are generally two schools of thought. Some ask why the United States and Great Britain in particular did not protest more loudly at the time. Why did they not push harder to rescue the doomed, or make their escape possible? Why, for example, were the railway lines running into Auschwitz not bombed? On the other side, there is the argument that, at first, Allied governments could not imagine that racial slaughter was being carried out on such a scale. Then, when it was, the Allies knew that the only realistic solution for them was to crush Germany by destruction and occupation. Pleas and threats were of no avail against the tight hold exerted on his nation by Hitler; and conquering Germany would be a long, slow exercise which was already taking every effort the Allies could exert. The debate continues.

In the Far East, another aspect of the cruelty of war still lingers and is felt by thousands of older Asians who were affected. It is also recollected strongly by thousands of former Allied servicemen and civilians who were, in their own words, 'guests of the Emperor of Japan' during the war years. For some, their experiences as prisoners-of-war were so terrible that even at the end of the twentieth century they can offer no pardon to their Japanese captors.

With Japan's image of itself as Asia's leading power, combined with a feeling of racial superiority over nearby nations such as China and Korea, there was no surprise when the Japanese made use of their neighbours. Up to 2 million Chinese were taken for forced labour to the islands of Japan, in addition to 43,000 Koreans. Up to 200,000 women, four out of five of whom were Koreans, were used as 'comfort women' by Japanese troops. About 250,000 Asians, including Malayans, Thais and Burmese, were used in the building of the Burma–Siam railway. The sufferings of these people were often horrific, with a high death rate; among the survivors, injuries or mental scars remain. Their hurt has been the manner in which the Japanese have, since the war, largely ignored what happened, with no attempt at any kind of restitution.

To comprehend the Japanese attitude towards Allied prisoners-of-war, it is necessary to look again at their view of *bushido*, the practice of the samurai. They believed in death before surrender and felt scorn for those Allied servicemen who gave in, at all ranks. A ship's captain would be despised for not going down with his vessel. A private soldier would be treated with contempt for not committing suicide. It was noticeable that, in the Burma Campaign, while the British killed 150,000 troops, only 1,700 Japanese were taken prisoner. Japanese warships carried no lifebelts, as sailors were expected to triumph – or die. Decorations were awarded only posthumously. Consequently, on the matter of treating prisoners, Eastern and Western values found no meeting place.

Underlying that factor were two others. One was that Japanese policy encouraged a dislike of Europeans, who were considered to have no business occupying colonies in the Far East. Asia was for Asians. Secondly, much of the brutality handed out to Allied prisoners-of-war was administered by men of lower rank, not always under the control of officers, who turned a blind eye to what was going on. 'Power tends to corrupt . . . ,' said Lord Acton. Often, with a mixture of inferiority complex and a hatred of foreigners, camp guards were easily able to demonstrate his additional comment, '. . . and absolute power corrupts absolutely'.

The Japanese had never anticipated that so many prisoners would fall into their hands and consequently there were, from the start, logistical failings in looking after them. In total, the Japanese took about 200,000 prisoners, who were then despatched to camps in different parts of their homeland or of captured territories. Their fate often depended arbitrarily on where they finished up. Some, by keeping their heads down and working hard, were able to reach the end of the war. Others suffered terribly. Of 20,000 US servicemen captured in the Philippines, nearly half died before 1945. About 60,000 Commonwealth servicemen were employed on the construction of the Burma–Siam railway and 12,000 died.

Across every camp, stories of brutal, inhumane treatment were told. There was little food: only enough was provided to keep men just alive for labour. Prisoners, considered as disposable economic units, were overworked, having to perform for long hours in appalling conditions. That led to loss of weight, so that some survivors who had entered captivity weighing, say, twelve stone, were half that weight when freed. Great shortages of medical supplies led to illnesses being untreated and, in a relentless circle, could bring death. Malaria was a great killer. Thousands suffered from dysentery, which took many lives.

Violence could come at any time, often for no obvious reason. Perhaps a man smiled at the wrong moment, or was suspected of whispering, or did not bow low enough to a guard. These tyrants could be at their worst after drink, or in reacting to some imagined or unintended slight, wanting to assert their authority over the helpless. Beatings with fists, or kickings, were commonplace. Sticks were often used. Prisoners were forced to stand for hours in blazing sunshine, or were locked in confined spaces. Some serious offences resulted in beheading with samurai swords. When protests were made officially, they were often rejected. 'Don't talk to me of International Law,' retorted one Japanese officer when the Geneva Convention was mentioned. 'There is no such thing.' At the outbreak of war, the Japanese government had made no reference to international law, nor to Geneva Conventions.

Since 1945 the war in the Far East has resulted in the collapse of the old empires of France, Holland and Britain. The rise of Communist China and the spreading of the Cold War to Asia has left the United States as the sole Western power in that area. Japan has been able to develop economically, largely under the protective umbrella of her former chief enemy. But the memory of the violence committed against them has never left many of the former prisoners. They recollect that, at the end of the war, 2,040 Japanese were convicted of war crimes and 428 received the death penalty. They also remember how many escaped justice.

## Appendix 2. Casualties

The Second World War altered the balance of power among the major states which had taken part. At the end, there were only two Great Powers – the United States and the USSR. Each had armed forces of overwhelming potential and actual strength. By dint of conquest, although at heavy cost, the Russians had imposed both their presence and their political will across Europe in the east. Their chief enemy, Germany, lay at their feet. In the Far East, their potential enemy, Japan, had been taken out of the war by Allied, especially American, efforts. The US finished the war with the world's most powerful economy which, alone, could outstrip all others combined. In Europe, the United States had played a crucial part in overthrowing Nazism and now the nations of Western Europe looked to the Americans for protection, support and material help after the devastation of war. In the Pacific area, the Japanese were overwhelmed and threats to the American position there removed.

Great Britain was no longer a Great Power in the same league. The costs of war had been immense, and much of the nation's wealth and assets had gone into paying for them. Yet she could proudly claim to have been 'first in, last out' – and had never surrendered. The British relied heavily both during, and immediately after, the war on American material help as an age of austerity began. The old Empire was about to emerge as a new Commonwealth.

What of the loss of people – the greatest price any nation makes in conflict? The heaviest payment there was made by the USSR. Estimates of the losses vary considerably, but possibly 7 million service personnel and 7 million civilians were killed. The figures may have been higher. Poland lost 6 million dead, half of whom were Jews. By the end of the war, 200,000 French servicemen and 400,000 civilians had died. From the United Kingdom, 60,000 civilians had been killed by bombing, and 245,000 servicemen in action. To those should be added 100,000 dead from the Commonwealth and Empire, who came nobly to help what was still regarded as the 'mother country'. German losses were exceptionally heavy, with more than 4 million servicemen killed in action, together with about 600,000 civilians. The Italians had 330,000 dead, half of whom were civilians. The United States lost almost 300,000 servicemen, roughly halved between the European and Far Eastern theatres of war. By 1945, 1¼ million men of the Japanese armed services had been killed, and almost 700,000 civilians.

Most of the dead servicemen from all nations were young, generally aged between 17 and 35. For all of them, whatever their nation, there is an appropriate inscription which is carved on the war memorial in a small English country village: 'We were young. We have died. Remember us.'

# Index

## A

A4 rocket, 191
A6M2 Zero-Sen fighters *see* Zero fighters
Aandalsnes, 48
Abbeville, 53
ABDA (American, British, Dutch and Australian Command), 120
Abyssinia, 10, 16, 27, 131, 132
*Admiral Graf Spee*, 44
Africa and the Mediterranean, 131–53
*Afrika Korps*, 137, 138, 139, 141, 142, 143, 144, 145, 148, 151
Air Raid Precautions (ARP), 75, 77
air war: early stages, 45; Battle of Britain, 64–71; Night Blitz, 72–7; bombing of Germany, 182–9, 218–21; German retaliation, 190–91; dropping of atomic bombs, 250–51; *see also Luftwaffe*; Royal Air Force; United States Air Force/Army Air Force
*Akagi*, 129
Alam Halfa, 143
Albania, 27, 84
Aleutian Islands, 128
Alexander, Sir Harold, 143, 144, 164, 214
Alexandria, 60, 112, 130, 132, 139, 141, 150, 153
All-India Congress Committee, 230
*Altmark*, 44, 46
Algeria, 130, 146, 148
Amiens, 53, 178
Anderson shelters, 75
*Anschluss*, 16
Antwerp, 179, 180
'Anvil', Operation, 170
Anzio, 170
Appenine mountains, 169–70
Ardennes, the, 41, 51, 52, 180, 204
*Armée d'Afrique*, 148
*Armée de l'Air*, 32
Arnhem, 180
Arnim, Dietloff von, 149
ARP (Air Raid Precautions), 75, 77
asdic, 195, 196
Assam, 231
*Athenia*, 44
Athens, 84
Atlantic, Battle of the, 44, 76, 78–81, 103, 112, 155, 192–9
Atlantic Wall, 174–5
atomic bombs, 225, 248, 250–51
Attlee, Clement, 225
Auchinleck, Claude, 140–41, 142, 143
Augsburg, 206
Auschwitz, 209
Australia, 31, 34, 35, 112, 115, 118, 120, 124, 126, 138, 232
Austria, 12, 16, 27, 34, 84, 205, 209
Austro-Hungarian Empire, 14
'Avalanche', Operation, 167–8

## B

B-17 Flying Fortress bombers, 118, 184, 216, 218
B-24 Liberator bombers, 184, 196, 216, 218
B-25 bombers, 125
B-29 Superfortress bombers, 236, 243, 250
Bader, Douglas, 69
Badoglio, Marshal, 166
'Baedeker Raids', 190
Bagehot, Walter, 26
'Bagration', Operation, 159, 178
Baldwin, Stanley, 75
Balkans, 84–7, 136, 160
'Barbarossa', Operation, 88–103, 158, 159
Bardia, 135
Bataan peninsula, 118
'Battleaxe', Operation, 139
Bay offensive, 199
Beaufighter, 74
Beaverbrook, Lord, 68
Beda Fomm, 135, 136
BEF *see* British Expeditionary Force
Belfast, 76
Belgium, 13, 14, 20, 22, 39, 41, 50, 51, 52, 54, 56, 191, 214
Belgrade, 84, 160
Belsen, 206
Benghazi, 135, 137, 142, 145

Berlin: bombing of, 184, 185–6, 218–19, 220; end of European war in, 210–13; Battle of, 211, 212; surrender in, 213; brief mentions, 21, 22, 62, 154, 160, 162, 206
'Betty' medium bombers, 113
Bf 109 aircraft, 35, 68, 142
*Bismarck*, 79–80, 192
Bismarck Archipelago, 232
Bizerta, 149
Blenheim bombers, 45
Blitz *see* Night Blitz
*Blitzkrieg*, 58, 82, 92
'Blue', Operation, 98
Blumentritt, Günther, 175
Bock, Fedor von, 93
Bologna, 214
Bomber Command: strength at outbreak of war, 34; and early stages of air war, 45; actions against shipping, 65; bombing of Germany, 77, 103, 182–9, 190, 192, 218, 219–20; casualties, 221
bombing, 182–91, 218–21, 243, 249, 250 *see also* atomic bombs; Britain, Battle of; Night Blitz
Borneo, 108
Bose, Chandra, 231
Bougainville, 234
Boulogne, 53, 56, 179
Bradley, Omar, 204
Brauchitsch, Walther von, 98
Braun, Eva, 212, 213
Bremen, 184
'Brevity', Operation, 139
Brewster aircraft, 113
Britain: and events leading up to war, 16–17, 20–21; ultimatum to Germany, 19, 21; colonies, 31; armed forces at beginning of war, 32, 34; and supply of materials, 35; and early stages of war, 40–41, 42, 44, 45; and Norwegian campaign, 46, 48; Churchill becomes Prime Minister of, 49; and Western campaign, 50, 51, 52, 53–4; evacuation of troops from Dunkirk, 56–7; and fall of France, 58, 59–60; stands alone against Germany, 62–81; and Balkan campaign, 86, 87; and Russian campaign, 103, 154; and idea of Second Front, 103, 146, 162; American help for, 104–5; and Far East, 108, 112, 113, 114, 116, 122, 124, 226, 229, 230, 231, 248; and Africa, 130–45; and Operation 'Torch', 146, 147, 148; and Malta, 150, 152, 153; increasing threat to Germany, 155; and Casablanca Conference, 162; and Italian campaign, 166; and Operation 'Overlord', 172, 174; and D-Day and after, 176, 177, 178, 180; bombing by, 182–9; German retaliation on, 190–91; and U-boat campaign, 192, 194, 195, 198; and Yalta Conference, 200, 201, 202; and attack on Germany, 204, 205, 206; and Tito, 217; and end of war in Europe, 222; general election in, 224–5; and Potsdam Conference, 225; and atomic bomb, 250; brief mentions, 13, 14, 18, 22, 23, 24, 27, 28, 29, 30, 36, 38, 39, 61, 83, 91, 106; *see also* Britain, Battle of
Britain, Battle of, 64–71, 81, 104, 182
British Army, 32, 53, 56, 122, 206, 230
British Expeditionary Force (BEF), 41, 53–4, 56, 57, 62
Bucharest, 159
Budapest, 160, 209
Buffalo aircraft, 113, 122
Bulgaria, 84, 159–60, 201–2
Bulge, Battle of the, 180–81
Bullock, A., 62, 82
*Bunker Hill*, 247
Burma: campaign, 122–3, 229, 230–31, 242, 248; brief mentions, 31, 109, 113, 115, 124, 226
Burma Road, 106, 107, 115, 122, 229, 230
Bzura, Battle of, 36

## C

Calais, 53, 56, 179
Canada, 34, 69, 184
Caroline Islands, 235
Casablanca Conference, 162
Catalina flying boats, 196
'Catapult', Operation, 60
Caucasus, 82, 98–100, 102, 155
'Cauldron, The', 180
Ceylon, 31, 122
Chamberlain, Neville, 17, 18, 21, 45, 48–9
Char B series tanks, 32
Cherbourg, 174, 177

Cheshire, Leonard, 220
Chiang Kai-shek, 229
China: conflict with Japan, 10, 29, 30, 106, 107, 108, 121, 226, 228–9, 242; Allied help for, 107, 229; and Burmese campaign, 122, 242; situation in, 228–9; brief mentions, 31, 113, 115, 124, 125, 243
Chindits, 231
Chulkov, V.I., 100
Churchill, Winston: and Hitler, 41, 62; and Finland, 42, 46; and Norwegian campaign, 46, 48; becomes Prime Minister, 49; and Western campaign, 53; and Dunkirk, 57; and Roosevelt, 58; resolute opposition to Germany, 59; and Night Blitz, 73; and loss of HMS *Hood*, 79; and Burma, 122; and East Africa, 132; and North Africa, 134, 135, 136, 139, 140–41, 142, 143, 144, 145; works with other Allied leaders, 146, 172; and Second Front, 146–7, 149, 162, 172; at Casablanca Conference, 162; and Italy, 166; and bombing of Germany, 182, 185, 219; and sea trade, 192; at Yalta Conference, 200, 201, 202, 203; and Russian offensive, 208; and 'iron curtain', 217; and end of war in Europe, 222; loses election, 225; and China, 229; brief mentions, 8, 40, 61, 71
'Citadel', Operation, 156
Clark, Mark, 168, 214
Clausewitz, Karl von, 8
Clydeside, 76
Coastal Command, 80, 196, 198
'Cobra', Operation, 177
Cold War, 217, 222
Cologne, 183, 184, 205
'Compass', Operation, 134–5
Compiègne, 58
Condor bombers, 78, 80, 192
Condor Legion, 16, 35
convoys, 139, 194, 195, 197–8
Coral Sea, Battle of the, 126–7
Corregidor, 118
Corsica, 61
Coventry, 76
Coward, Noël, 71
CR.42 fighters, 131
Crete, 86–7, 138, 152
Crimea, the, 98, 159, 203
Cripps, Sir Stafford, 230
Croatia, 89
'Crocodile' flame thrower, 205
'Crusader', Operation, 140–42
Crusader tanks, 139
Cyrenaica, 130, 136, 137, 138, 139, 141, 142
Czechoslovakia: German territory given to, 13; and German aggression, 16–17, 18; and Munich, 16–17, 22, 25; armaments industry, 35, 96; and Yalta Conference, 201–2; Allies in, 205, 206, 208

## D

Dakar, 148
Daladier, Edouard, 22, 42
'Dambuster's Raid', 185
Danzig, 12, 13, 18, 21, 36, 208
Darwin, 126
Dauntless dive-bombers, 129
D-Day and after, 176–81 *see also* 'Overlord', Operation
Delhi, 230, 231
Denmark, 13, 46, 48, 104, 206
Denmark Strait, 79
depth charges, 192, 195–6
Desert Air Force, 142, 145
Devastator torpedo bombers, 129
Divina, River, 92
Do 17 bombers, 73
Dönitz, Karl, 78–9, 192, 194, 196, 197, 198, 213
Doolittle, James H., 125, 128
Douhet, Giulio, 72, 77
Dover, 56
Dowding, Sir Hugh, 64, 65, 66
'Dragoon', Operation, 178
Dresden, 219–20
'Drumroll', Operation, 196
Dulles, Allen, 216
Dunkirk, 48, 53, 56–7, 62, 104, 147, 179
Dutch East Indies, 30, 31, 109, 112, 113, 115, 120–21, 124, 126, 226, 232, 237
Dyle Plan, 51
'Dynamo', Operation, 56

# Index

## E

'Eagle' offensive, 65, 68
'Earthquake' bombs, 250
East Africa, 130, 131, 132–3, 138
Eastern Front (Russian), 10, 71, 82–3, 88–103, 154–61, 154–61, 178, 208–9
Eden, Anthony, 200
Egypt, 131, 132, 134, 135, 139, 143, 145, 162
Einstein, Albert, 250
Eire, 194
Eisenhower, Dwight D., 164, 172, 174, 176, 204, 206, 213
El Agheila, 142
El Alamein, 103, 143, 145, 151, 155
Elbe, River, 205, 206
*Enola Gay*, 250
*Enterprise*, 247
Eritrea, 27, 131, 132
Essen, 184
Estonia, 19, 83, 92, 159, 160
Europe, war in, 36–103, 154–225; causes of, 12–27, 32–5
evacuation, 40

## F

Falaise Gap, 177–8
Far East, war in, 104–29, 226–51
Fighter Command, 34, 62, 64, 65, 66, 68, 69, 70, 71, 72
Finland, 10, 42–3, 46, 82, 89, 92, 158–9, 160
First World War, 8, 12, 13, 14, 15, 20, 22, 23, 26, 30, 32, 35, 50, 74, 75, 98, 106, 222
Fisher, Lord, 8
'Flying Tigers', 107
Foch, Marshal, 8, 23
France: and events leading up to war, 16, 21, 22–3; declares war, 22; colonies, 31; armed forces at beginning of war, 32; and supply of materials, 35; and early stages of war, 39, 41, 42; and Western campaign, 50, 51, 52–3, 54–5; BEF evacuated from 56–7; fall of, 58–60; and Japan, 106, 107; relationship with Britain, 147–8; and Casablanca Conference, 162, 163; and Allied invasion, 170, 172–5, 176–9, 186–7, 214; U-boats based in, 193; and Yalta Conference, 201; brief mentions, 10, 13, 14, 17, 18, 19, 20, 24, 28, 29, 30, 34–5, 36, 38, 45, 46, 61, 78, 104, 159, 222
Franco, Francisco, 16
Free French, 60, 138, 145, 147, 148
Freeman, Sir Wilfrid, 68
'Funnies', 176
Fw 190 aircraft, 149

## G

'Gap, The', 196
Gaulle, Charles de, 58, 60, 147, 148, 178
'Gee' navigation system, 183
Gehlen, R., 159
'General Winter', 96
Germany: pre-war situation, 12–17; and other nations before the war, 16–17, 18–19, 20–21, 22, 23, 24, 25, 26, 27, 28, 29, 31; aggressive intentions towards Poland, 18–19; invasion of Poland, 10, 12, 19, 36; and outbreak of war, 10, 21, 22; armed forces at beginning of war, 34–5; successes of, 36–61; Britain alone against, 62–81; Russian front, 82–103; American response to outbreak of war with, 104; signs Tripartite Pact, 106–7; declares war on USA, 111; and North Africa, 136–7, 138, 139, 142–3, 145, 146, 147, 148–9; and Malta, 150–51, 152; and Unconditional Surrender declaration, 162–3; and Allied invasion of Sicily, 164, 165; and fighting in Italy, 166, 167, 168, 170; and Operation 'Overlord', 172, 174–5; and D-Day and after, 176, 178, 179, 180–81; bombing of, 182–9, 218–21; retaliation to bombing, 190–91; U-boats, 192–9; discussed at Yalta, 201; final stages of war against, 204–23; brief mentions, 8, 30, 32, 112, 224, 225, 250
*Gestapo*, 71, 223
Gibraltar, 61, 112, 130, 132, 146, 150, 153, 162
Gilbert Islands, 235
Gladiators, 131
Goebbels, Josef, 169, 184, 190, 205
'Gold' beach, 176
'Gomorrah', Operation, 185

Göring, Hermann, 56, 62, 65, 66, 72, 75, 89, 102, 213
Gort, Lord, 41, 53, 56, 57
Gothic Line, 170
Gran Sasso, 166, 168
'Grand Slam' bomb, 250
Grant tanks, 142, 144
'Grapeshot', Operation, 214
Graziani, Rodolfo, 130, 134, 135
'Great Asia Association', 31
'Greater East Asia Co-Prosperity Sphere', 31, 116, 122, 226
'Great Marianas Turkey Shoot', 236
Great Slump/Depression, 15, 17, 20, 28
Greece, 84, 86, 136, 138, 160, 202
Guadalcanal, 232, 234
Guam, 236
Guderian, Heinz, 36, 52, 53, 55, 56, 58, 94, 96, 209
Guingand, Sir Francis de, 164
Gustav Line, 170

## H

H2S, 183, 218
Halder, Franz, 71, 83, 98
Halfaya Pass, 139
Halifax, Lord, 20, 21, 62
Halifax bombers, 183
Halsey, William, 234
Hamburg, 205, 206, 223; Battle of, 185
Hampden bombers, 34, 182
*Hancock*, 247
*Hara-kiri*, 241
Harris, Sir Arthur, 182–3, 185, 186, 188, 192, 219, 220
He 111 bombers, 35, 73
He 115 seaplanes, 45
'Hedgehog', 196
Heligoland, 221
Helsinki, 42
Henderson Field, 232
Hess, Rudolf, 12
Himmler, Heinrich, 95, 160, 213
Hirohito, Emperor, 10, 30, 251
Hiroshima, 250–51
*Hiryu*, 129
Hitler, Adolf: before outbreak of, war, 15, 16, 17, 21, 22, 25, 31; and Poland, 12, 18, 19, 36, 38; economic motives, 35; plans in late 1939, 39; and Churchill, 41; and *Altmark* incident, 44, 46; Directive about war in air, 45; and Norwegian campaign, 46, 48; and Western campaign, 50, 52, 53; orders halt short of Dunkirk, 53, 56; and fall of France, 58; and French fleet, 59; and Italy, 61; and Britain, 62, 65, 66, 78; and Russia, 42, 82, 83, 88, 89, 92–3, 94, 95, 96, 98, 100, 101, 102, 107, 155–6, 158; and Balkans, 84, 86; declares war on USA, 97, 111; becomes Supreme Commander of Armed Forces, 98; and North Africa, 136, 143, 145; orders army into Unoccupied Zone of France, 148; and manpower problems, 160; and fighting in Italy, 166; and rescue of Mussolini, 168, 169; and Allied invasion of France, 174, 176, 179; plot against, 178; launches new offensive, 180; refuses to capitulate, 181; and bombing raids, 190; and A4 rocket, 191; and Roosevelt's death, 205; during last stages of war, 208–9; death, 212–13; and air power, 218; brief mentions, 32, 34, 55, 60, 71, 76, 91, 104, 105, 146, 149, 162, 170, 172, 188, 216, 222
Hitler Youth, 16
Holland, 30, 39, 50, 52, 106, 107, 112, 120, 206, 221
Home Army (Poland), 160
Home Guard (Local Defence Volunteers), 62
Homma, General, 118
Hong Kong, 31, 113, 114
*Hood*, HMS, 79, 80
*Hornet*, 125
Horton, Sir Max, 198
Hudson aircraft, 113
Hull, 76
'Hump, The', 229
Hungary, 17, 38, 84, 89, 159, 160, 201–2, 209
Hurricanes, 34, 68, 73, 74, 131, 139, 151
'Husky', Operation, 162, 164–5

## I

Iida, Shojiro, 122
Imperial Army *see* Japanese Army
Imperial Navy *see* Japanese Navy

Imphal, 230, 231
India, 31, 34, 82, 115, 122, 140, 229, 230, 231, 243
Indo-China, 31, 106, 107, 114, 116, 120
Iraq, 138, 148
Italy: and Abyssinia, 10, 16, 27, 132; before the war, 26–7; and Rome-Berlin Axis Pact, 27; and 'Pact of Steel', 17, 27; enters war, 58, 61; invades Greece, 84, 136; signs Tripartite Pact, 106–7; declares war on USA, 111; and Africa, 130, 131, 132, 134, 135, 136, 137, 142, 143, 145, 149; Allied campaign in, 155, 162–71, 172; end of war in, 214–17; brief mentions, 8, 23, 41, 150, 152, 153, 159, 178
Iwo Jima, 238–9, 248

## J

Japan: neutrality at outbreak of war in Europe, 28; conflict with China, 10, 29, 30, 106, 107, 108, 121, 226, 228–9, 242; situation at outbreak of war in Europe, 30–31; expansionism, 30–31; and Russia, 30, 31, 107, 108, 202, 248, 251; reasons for attack on Pearl Harbor, 106–7; plans and executes attack on Pearl Harbor, 97, 108–11; superior forces of, 112, 113; at war, 114–29, 226–51; and Casablanca Conference, 162; bombing of, 243; economic decline, 245; atomic bombs dropped on, 250–51; surrender, 10, 251; brief mentions, 8, 13, 23, 71, 103, 142, 147, 222, 225
Japanese Army (Imperial Army), 30, 108, 116, 118, 120, 228, 230, 232, 234, 236–7, 240, 242, 248, 249, 251
Japanese Navy (Imperial Navy), 30, 107, 108, 109–10, 113, 118, 120, 121, 124, 127, 128, 129, 226, 234, 235, 237, 244
Java, 108
Java Sea, Battle of, 121
Jews, 15, 29, 95, 96, 166, 213, 223
Jodl, Alfred, 63
Jössingfjord, 44
Ju 87 dive-bombers (Stukas), 35, 36, 55, 73, 84, 92
Ju 88 aircraft, 73, 184, 189
Julich, 223
'Juno' beach, 176

## K

*Kaga*, 129
*kamikaze*, 237, 240, 241, 246–7, 248, 250
Kasserine Pass, 149
'Kate' torpedo-bomber, 113
Katyn, 38; Forest, 223
Keitel, Wilhelm, 39
Kenya, 131, 132
Kerch peninsula, 98
Kesselring, Albert, 164, 165, 166, 167, 168, 170
Kharkov, 94, 98, 155, 158
Kiev, 88–9, 94, 158
Kohima, 231
Koniev, Ivan, 210, 212
Korea, 30
*Kriegsmarine*/German Navy, 35, 46, 48, 59, 63, 78, 79, 192, 195, 198 *see also* U-boats
Kursk, 155, 156; Battle of, 156–8

## L

Lancaster bombers, 183, 186, 218, 220
Latvia, 19, 83, 90, 92, 159, 160
League of Nations, 10, 12, 13, 15, 22–3, 27, 28, 31, 201
Lebanon, 148
Leeb, Wilhelm von, 92
Leigh Light, 196
LeMay, General Curtis, 243
Lend-Lease, 104
Lenin, V.I., 14, 24
Leningrad, 42, 88, 89, 90, 92, 93, 94, 95, 98, 155, 158
*Lexington*, 127
Leyte, 237–8
Leyte Gulf, Battle of, 237
Liberty ships, 198
Libya, 27, 131, 134, 137
Liddell Hart, Basil, 34
Lithuania, 19, 83, 90, 92, 159, 160
Lloyd George, David, 12, 20
Local Defence Volunteers (Home Guard), 62
London: evacuation from, 40; French resistance in, 60; bombing raids on, 65, 72, 75, 77; VI flying bombs fall in, 190; V2 rockets land in, 191; Polish ministers

exiled in, 202, 225; and end of European war, 222
Londonderry, Lord, 20
Longmore, Sir Arthur, 131
Low Countries, 41, 45, 50, 58, 175, 176
Lübeck, 190, 206
*Luftwaffe*: re-formed, 15–16; and Spanish Civil War, 16; strength at beginning of war, 35, 55; and Polish campaign, 36; and early stages of air war, 45; and invasion of Holland, 52; and German plans against Britain, 62, 63; and Battle of Britain, 64–71; and Night Blitz, 72–7, 183; and Battle of the Atlantic, 78, 79, 80; and Crete, 86, 87; and Russian campaign, 92, 95, 100, 102, 156; and North Africa, 149; air raids on Malta, 150–51; and loss of air superiority, 175, 186–7; 'Baedeker Raids', 190; and last stages of war, 218, 220; brief mentions, 10, 32, 34, 46, 48, 56, 57, 88, 91, 176, 184, 208
Lüneburg Heath, 206
Luzon, 118, 237, 238

## M

MacArthur, Douglas, 118, 126, 232, 234–5, 236, 251
McCreery, Sir Richard, 214
Maginot Line, 22, 34, 39, 50, 55, 58
Malaya, 31, 108, 109, 113, 114, 116–17, 122, 124, 226
Malta, 112, 132, 146, 150–53, 164, 200
Manchester bombers, 183
Mandalay, 242
'Manhattan Project', 250
Manila, 118, 238
Manchuria, 10, 30, 31, 107, 108, 202, 228, 251
Manstein, Erich von, 50, 155
Manteuffel, Hasso von, 181
Mao Tse-tung, 229
Mareth Line, 149
Mariana Islands, 235, 236
'Marita', Operation, 84
'Market Garden', Operation, 180
Marshall, George C., 147, 163
Marshall Islands, 235
Matilda tanks, 139
'May Week, The', 76
Me 110 fighters, 35
Mediterranean, 27, 59, 61, 86, 113, 162, 164; Africa and, 131–53
Meiktila, 242
*Mein Kampf* (Hitler), 13, 15
Merchant Navy, 41, 194, 198
Messe, Giovanni, 149
Messina, 165, 167
Midway, Battle of, 103, 128–9, 226
Milch, General, 62
Minsk, 93–4
*Missouri*, USS, 10, 251
Model, Walther, 179
Montgomery, Bernard: comments on Gort's achievement, 57; in North Africa, 143, 144, 145; and invasion of Sicily, 164, 165; in Italy, 166, 167, 168; and D-Day and after, 176, 177, 178, 179, 180; and attack on Germany, 204–5, 206, 213, 214
Morocco, 146, 148
Moscow, 88, 89, 90, 93, 94, 95, 96, 97, 98
Mosquito light bombers, 183
Mountbatten, Lord Louis, 230
MS.406 fighters, 32
'Mulberry', 174
Munich Crisis, 16–17, 18, 21, 25, 27, 29, 42, 75
Mussolini, Benito: before the war, 16, 17, 26, 27; joins war, 58, 61; and invasion of Greece, 84; declares war on USA, 111; and African campaign, 130, 131, 132, 134; overthrown, 166, 167; rescued, 168–9; death, 216; brief mentions, 146, 155, 165, 214
Mustang fighters, 184, 187, 218, 220
*Musashi*, 237
Mutaguchi, Renya, 230–31

## N

Nagasaki, 251
Nagumo, Chuichi, 129
Namsos, 48
Nanking, 30
Naples, 168
Narvik, 46, 48
Nehring, Walther, 56
New Deal, 28

New Guinea, 115, 126, 129, 232, 234, 235
New Zealand, 31, 34, 35, 112, 115
Nice, 61
Night Blitz, 64, 72–7, 80, 81, 104, 182, 183, 185, 190
Nimitz, Chester W., 126, 128, 232, 235
Normandy landings *see* D-Day; 'Overlord', Operation
North Africa: campaigns, 130–31, 134–45, 155; Operation 'Torch', 146–9; importance of Malta to, 150, 151–2, 153; brief mentions, 58, 61, 82, 103
Norway, 42, 44, 46–9, 55, 104, 193
Noyelles, 53
Nuremberg, 186

## O

'Oboe', 183
Observer Corps, 74
O'Connor, Sir Richard, 134, 135, 136, 137
Okinawa, 240–41, 247, 248
'Omaha' beach, 176
Onishi, Admiral, 246
Oran, 59–60, 147
'Orange Plans', 235
Orel, 158
Ostrov, 92
Ottoman Empire, 14
'Overlord', Operation, 170, 172–5, 176, 186, 214

## P

P.11C fighters, 32
P.37 bombers, 32
P-40 aircraft, 113
P-51 Mustang fighters *see* Mustang fighters
Pacific: maps of general situation, 105, 233; attack on Pearl Harbor, 97, 108–11; war in, 112–21, 124–30, 226–7, 232–41
'Pact of Steel', 17, 27
Palermo, 165
Paris, 58, 178
Park, Keith, 66
Patton, George S., 164, 165, 178, 205
Paulus, Friedrich, 100, 102
Pearl Harbor: as American base, 31, 112; planning and execution of attack on, 97, 108–11; Americans enter war after attack on, 10, 99, 111; Americans want revenge for, 125, 147, 248; brief mentions, 128, 142, 226, 229, 234, 237, 251
Peenemünde, 190, 191
Percival, A.E., 116
Pétain, Henri, 58, 60, 148
Petacci, Clara, 216
Philippines: as colony of USA, 31; American forces based in, 108, 113; and Japanese plans, 109, 114, 115; Japanese attack on, 118–19; Americans advance towards, 234–5; American attack on, 236–7, 238; *kamikaze* attacks near, 246–7; brief mentions, 120, 124, 226, 232
Philippine Sea, Battle of the, 236
'Phoney War', 40–41, 44, 45, 50, 55
Plate, River, 44
Plymouth, 59, 76
Poland: and Versailles Treaty, 12, 13; territorial demands, 17; pre-war situation, 18–19; and Russia, 19, 25; invasion of, 10, 12, 19, 21, 22; armed forces at outbreak of war, 32; German campaign in, 36–8; revolt against Germans, 160; Russians in, 160, 208, 209; and Yalta Conference, 201–2; and Potsdam Conference, 225; brief mentions, 27, 28, 31, 34, 39, 55, 84, 104, 159
Portal, Sir Charles, 219, 220
Port Moresby, 126, 127, 232
Potsdam Conference, 225, 249, 250
Prague, 18, 206
*Prince of Wales*, 114
'Punishment', Operation, 84

## Q

Quebec Conference, 230

## R

Rabaul, 232
radar, 66, 70, 74
Raeder, Erich, 35, 62, 79
RAF *see* Royal Air Force

Ramsay, Sir Bertram, 56
Rangoon, 122, 231, 242
rationing, 41, 76
Red Army: in Finland, 42; and Russian campaign (1941–2), 82, 83, 89, 90, 91, 92, 93, 94, 95, 97, 102, 103; and Russian front (1943–4), 154, 155, 156, 158, 159, 160; strength, 208; offensive against Germany, 208, 209; and taking of Berlin, 210, 212, 213; brief mentions, 107, 146, 172, 200, 202, 206
Reggio, 166, 167
*Regia Aeronautica*, 131
Remagen, 205
*Repulse*, 114
Reynaud, Paul, 62
Rheims, 206
Rhine, River, 204, 205
Rhineland, 13, 16, 20, 22
Ribbentrop, Joachim von, 18, 19
Ritchie, Sir Neil, 142–3
Rokossovsky, K.K., 210, 212
Rome, 61, 166, 167, 170
Rome-Berlin Axis pact, 27
Rommel, Erwin: in Western campaign, 52; in North Africa, 136–7, 138, 139, 140, 141, 142–3, 144, 145, 146, 148, 149; and Malta, 151–2, 153; in Italy, 166; and preparation for Allied invasion of France, 175; brief mentions, 176, 179
Roosevelt, Franklin D.: and the Depression, 28; and disarmament, 28; and American response to war in Europe, 29, 58, 104; freezes Japanese assets, 107; and Pearl Harbor, 110–11; and MacArthur's departure from Philippines, 118; and North African campaign, 143; works with other Allied leaders, 146, 172; and 'Germany first' policy, 147; and Casablanca Conference, 162; and Italy, 166; and Yalta Conference, 200, 201, 202, 203; and Russia, 202, 203; death, 205, 225; and atomic bomb, 250
Rostock, 190
Rostov, 94
Royal Air Force (RAF): and British rearmament, 20; strength, 34; and early stages of air war, 45; and Norwegian campaign, 48; and Western campaign, 53; and Dunkirk evacuation, 57; weaker than *Luftwaffe*, 62; German plans to remove power of, 63; and Battle of Britain, 64–71; and Night Blitz, 74, 77; Crete as base for, 86; and Burma campaign, 122; and East Africa, 132; and Malta, 150, 15l; attacks on Germany, 155, 182–9, 218–19; large bombs dropped by, 250; *see also* Bomber Command; Fighter Command
Royal Canadian Navy, 194, 198
Royal Navy: and British rearmament, 20; strength at outbreak of war, 32, 34; takes BEF to France, 41; and early stages of war at sea, 45; and air attacks during Phoney War, 45; and Norwegian campaign, 48; and Dunkirk evacuation, 56–7; and French fleet, 59, 60; in Mediterranean, 61, 130, 153; strength after collapse of France, 62; and early stages of Battle of the Atlantic, 79, 80; and Balkan campaign, 86, 87; and war in Far East, 112, 114, 240, 244, 248; protection of convoys by, 194; losses, 198; brief mentions, 46, 182
*Royal Oak*, 44
Ruhr, the, 22, 39, 45, 184, 205; Battle of, 183
Rumania, 38, 82, 83, 84, 86, 89, 159, 201–2
Rundstedt, Karl von, 36, 94, 175, 176
Russia/Soviet Union: Revolution, 14, 24; relations with Germany before the war, 18–19, 24–5, 31; and Poland, 18, 19, 25, 36, 38; situation between the wars, 24–5; and Japan, 30, 31, 107, 108, 202, 248, 251; invasion of Finland, 42–3; campaign (1941–2), 10, 71, 82–3, 88–103; front (1943–4), 154–61, 178; and discussions among Allies, 146; and Yalta Conference, 200, 201–2, 203, 219; and final stages of war against Germany, 208–9, 210, 212, 213; supports Tito, 217; uneasiness about, 222–3, 225; and Potsdam Conference, 225; and atomic bomb, 225; brief mentions, 35, 41, 80, 172, 189, 206
Russo-Finnish war, 42–3, 46, 104

## S

'Saar', Operation, 39
Saar Basin, 13, 15
*St Lo*, 246
Saipan, 236
Salerno, 167–8
Salzburg, 206

# Index

Sarawak, 31
Savoy, 61
Scapa Flow, 13, 44
Schlieffen Plan, 39
Schweinfurt, 184
'Sealion', Operation, 63, 65, 78, 83
Second Front, 103, 146, 147, 149, 158, 159, 162, 163, 172, 186
Sedan, 51, 52, 54
Senegal, 148
Sevastopol, 98
Shanghai, 106
Sherman tanks, 143, 144, 176
*Shokaku*, 236
Siam/Thailand, 31, 116, 122
*Sichelschnitt*, 50
Sicily, 149, 150, 153, 155, 162, 163, 164–5, 166, 167
Sidi Barrani, 134
Siegfried Line, 34, 39
Singapore, 108, 109, 114, 116, 122
Sittang valley, 242
Skorzeny, Otto, 168–9
Slim, William, 122, 231, 242
SM.79 bombers, 131
Smolensk, 93, 94, 158
Sollum, 134
Solomon Islands, 126, 129, 232, 234
Somaliland: British, 132; Italian, 132
*Soryu*, 129
South Africa, 34
South East Asia Command (SEAC), 230
Spaatz, Carl A., 221, 250
Spanish Civil War, 10, 16, 27, 35, 68, 69–70
Speer, Albert, 183, 186, 189, 212
Sperrle, Hugo, 73
Spitfires, 34, 66, 68, 73, 74
Spruance, Admiral, 235
SS, 95, 101, 160, 223
Stalin, Josef: and internal affairs, 14, 24; and Poland, 18–19, 25, 38, 225; agreement with Hitler, 18–19, 24, 25; dictatorship, 24, 91, 154; and Baltic states, 83; and leadership of Red Army, 90; and Russian campaign (1941–2), 91, 96 100; and Russian front (1943–4), 154, 156, 159, 160; works with other Allied leaders, 146, 172; at Yalta Conference, 200, 201–2, 202–3; and Russian offensive, 208; and taking of Berlin, 210, 212, 213; attitude to Germany at end of war, 222–3; at Potsdam Conference, 225; and Far East conflict, 251
Stalingrad, 98, 100–103, 154, 155, 156, 158
Stilwell, Joseph, 122, 229
Stirling bombers, 183
Stuka dive bombers (Ju 87), 35, 36, 55, 73, 84, 92
submarines, 244 *see also* U-boats
Suda Bay, 86
Sudan, 131, 132
Sudetenland, 16
Suez, 61, 132, 148
Sumatra, 108
Sweden, 41, 42, 44, 46, 82
'Sword' beach, 176
Syria, 138, 148

## T

T-34 tanks, 158
'Tallboy' bomb, 250
Tarawa, 235
Taylor, A.J.P., 8
Teheran Conference, 200
Terraine, John, 165, 205
Thailand/Siam, 31, 116, 122

'Thousand Bomber Raid', 183
Thunderbolts, 187, 220
Tientsin, 106
'Tiger' convoy, 139
Timoshenko, Semyon, 98
Tinian, 236, 250
Tito, Marshal, 160, 217
Tobruk, 135, 137, 138, 139, 141, 142, 143
Tojo, Hideki, 146
Tokyo, 107, 125, 128, 243
Tokyo Bay, 10, 30, 251
Tomahawks, 122
'Torch', Operation, 145, 146–9, 151
torpedoes, 192, 193, 198
Toulon, 148
Trenchard, Sir Hugh, 45
'Trident' Conference, 162, 163
Trieste, 216, 217
Tripartite Pact, 97, 106–7, 111
Triple Alliance, 26
Triple Entente, 24, 25, 26
Tripoli, 136, 145, 146
Tripolitania, 130, 135, 150
Truk, 235
Truman, Harry S., 217, 225, 250
Truscott, Lucien K., 214
Tunis, 149
Tunisia, 61, 130, 148, 149, 155, 166
'Typhoon', Operation, 94

## U

U-boats, 35, 41, 44, 78, 79, 80, 192–9; Type VII, 193; U-30, 44; U-47, 44
Udet, Ernst, 62
Ukraine, 35, 82, 90, 94
'Ultra', 70, 142, 145, 195
Uman, 94
Unconditional Surrender declaration, 162
United Nations, 201
United States: at outbreak of war in Europe, 28–9; policy of non-intervention in Europe, 28, 29, 58, 104; bases in Far East, 31, 108; Germany declares war on, 97, 111; and Russian campaign, 103, 154; increases spending on armed forces, 104; helps Britain, 104–5; actions against Japan, 106, 107; and Japan's expansionist plans, 108, 109, 115; attacked at Pearl Harbor, 10, 97, 110–11; armed forces at start of war with Japan, 112; and war in Far East (1941–2), 118, 124–9; and North African campaign, 142, 143; and Operation 'Torch', 146, 147, 148; and Italian campaign, 162, 166; and Operation 'Overlord', 172, 174; and D-Day and after, 176, 177, 178, 180, 181; bombing by, 182, 183, 184, 187, 221; U-boat attacks on, 196; and Yalta Conference, 200–203; and attack on Germany, 204, 205, 206; and Tito, 217; and Russian threat, 223; and Potsdam Conference, 225; and last stages of war in Far East, 226–7, 232–41, 243, 246, 247, 248, 249, 250–51; brief mentions, 13, 15, 23, 30, 71, 79, 83, 91, 222
United States Air Force/Army Air Force (USAF/USAAF), 155, 182, 183, 184, 185, 186, 218–19, 220–21, 250–51
United States Navy, 112, 126, 194, 226, 232, 235, 236, 238; Pacific Fleet, 97, 109, 110, 112, 124, 128, 227, 232, 236, 244; submarines, 244
'Utah' beach, 176

## V

V1 flying bombs, 190, 191, 218
V2 rocket, 191, 218

'Val' dive-bomber, 113
Valletta, 153
Vargos, President, 222
Venice, 216
Verdun, 178
Verona, 214, 216
Versailles Treaty, 8, 12, 13, 14, 15, 16, 19, 22, 28, 30, 222
Vichy, 58, 106, 147, 148
Vienna, 209
Volgoda, 98

## W

Wadi Zem Zem, 145
Waffen SS, 16
Wainwright, J.M., 118
Walker, F.J., 198
Wall Street Crash, 28
War Guilt Clause, 13
Warlimont, General, 136
Warsaw, 36, 38; Uprising, 160
Washington conference, 111
Wavell, Archibald, 130, 132, 134, 136, 138–9, 139–40, 230
*Wehrmacht*/German Army: at beginning of war, 34, 35; in Polish campaign, 36; and leadership, 58; and German plans against Britain, 63; and Russian campaign, 88, 89, 92–3, 93–4, 95, 96, 97, 98, 100, 102–3, 154, 156, 158, 178; and Allied invasion of France, 176, 179, 186; casualties, 178; and final stages of war, 204, 206, 208; brief mentions, 86, 104, 143, 146, 182
Weidling, Helmuth, 213
Weimar Republic, 14–15
Wellington bombers, 34, 45, 182
Wells, H.G., 71
'Western Air Plans', 45
Western campaign, 50–55, 104
Western Desert, 130 *see also* North Africa: campaigns
Western Desert Force, 134
Western Front: inactivity on, 39; campaign *see* Western campaign
West Indies, 31, 34
Weygand, Maxime, 58
Whitley bombers, 34, 182
Wilson, Woodrow, 28
Wingate, Orde, 231
'wolf packs', 194, 195
Wolff, Karl, 216
Woolf, Virginia, 71

## Y

Yalta Conference, 200–203, 219
Yamamoto, Isoroku, 109–10, 128, 234
*Yamato*, 128
Yamashita, Tomayuki, 116, 236, 238
*Yorktown*, 129
'Y' service, 153
Yugoslavia, 84, 159, 160, 217

## Z

Zeppelins, 74
Zero fighters, 113, 129, 246
Zhukov, Georgi, 97, 98, 156, 210, 212, 213